Simply English

Simon Heffer was born in 1960. He read English at Cambridge and took a PhD in modern history at that university. His previous books include: *Moral Desperado: A Life of Thomas Carlyle*, *Like the Roman: The Life of Enoch Powell*, *Nor Shall My Sword: The Reinvention of England*, *Strictly English*, *A Short History of Power* and *High Minds: The Victorians and the Birth of Modern Britain*. In a career of nearly thirty years in Fleet Street he has written for and held senior positions on the *Daily Mail*, *The Daily Telegraph* and the *Spectator*.

ALSO BY SIMON HEFFER

Moral Desperado: A Life of Thomas Carlyle

Power and Place: The Political Consequences of King Edward VII

Like the Roman: The Life of Enoch Powell

Nor Shall My Sword: The Reinvention of England

Vaughan Williams

A Short History of Power

Strictly English: The correct way to write … and why it matters

High Minds: The Victorians and the Birth of Modern Britain

Simply English

An A to Z of Avoidable Errors

Simon Heffer

WINDMILL BOOKS

1 3 5 7 9 10 8 6 4 2

Windmill Books
20 Vauxhall Bridge Road
London SW1V 2SA

Windmill Books is part of the Penguin Random House group of companies whose addresses can be found at global.penguinrandomhouse.com.

Copyright © Simon Heffer 2014

Simon Heffer has asserted his right to be identified as the author of this Work in accordance with the Copyright, Designs and Patents Act 1988.

First published by Random House Books in 2014
First published in paperback by Windmill Books in 2015

www.windmill-books.co.uk

A CIP catalogue record for this book
is available from the British Library.

ISBN 9780099558460

Typeset in Bembo MT by Palimpsest Book Production Limited,
Falkirk, Stirlingshire
Printed and bound by CPI Group (UK) Ltd, Croydon, CR0 4YY

Penguin Random House is committed to a sustainable future for our business, our readers and our planet. This book is made from Forest Stewardship Council® certified paper.

To Martin Edmunds

Quantam meruit

Contents

Introduction

In 2009 Nigel Wilcockson of Random House asked me to write a book on correct grammar and the use of English, and why they matter. He had been alerted to some emails circulating on the Internet that I had written to colleagues at the *Daily Telegraph*, for which I then worked as Associate Editor, drawing attention to mistakes they had made in their copy, to the annoyance of the paper's readers. The result, *Strictly English*, appeared the following year. It dealt thematically with the main issues in written and spoken English, and its aim was to improve the writing style of anyone who read it closely and carefully.

This book is a much expanded variant of that work. In an A to Z format, it seeks to act as a dictionary-style reference book for those with specific questions about the use of English. *Simply English* does not supersede *Strictly English*: it complements it. Although there is some common material, *Simply English* itemises what *Strictly English*, in an extended essay, explains at length – and more. One should illuminate the other. Perhaps someone wishes to know the difference between *perpetrate* and *perpetuate*; or how to use *anticipate* correctly; or how to avoid misusing *prevaricate*; or when to deploy an adverb; or how to write to a bishop; or what a subjunctive is and when to unleash one; or what an accusative is. The answers to these, and many other questions, will be found in this book, and can be easily located under their respective entries in the alphabetical format. A word or phrase printed in small CAPITAL LETTERS in an individual entry signifies that that word or phrase has its own entry.

However, the book is not simply *Strictly English* placed in alphabetical order. This is because in the four years between writing the two books I and Mr Wilcockson noticed many new solecisms and catachreses whether in print or in speech. Also, many people who had read *Strictly English* were kind enough to write to me – some in great detail – about their own irritations with the abuse of English, and alerted me to horrors of which I had hitherto been unaware, or insufficiently aware. I am very grateful to them. As a consequence, this A to Z is a more extensive, heavily revised alphabetical version of *Strictly English*. I am far from sure that every act of violence done to the English language is recorded in the pages that follow; but the most frequent and the most likely are, as are the means of avoiding them, and many more than were recorded in the original work.

Since *Strictly English* was published it has spawned other such books, whose relative merits it is hardly my place to judge. This, like the considerable sales of *Strictly English* in both hard and soft covers, indicated some interesting points about those who speak English. First, a very large number of people feel they were taught the language inadequately, and that after decades of speaking and writing it would like to have a more precise idea of what they are doing, and whether they are doing it correctly. Second, as I suggested in *Strictly English*, many people feel that for better or worse we live in a society where we may be judged not by how we sound when we speak – accents are irrelevant – but by how well we put a sentence together grammatically, and how careful our choice of words is. Third, they feel that acquiring such a skill is useful not just for them, but for those still passing through a schools system that does not always place a premium upon the teaching of correct English in, shall we say, the way that the French school system puts one upon the teaching of correct French. (I had a French teacher who was a native speaker, and who rebuked me severely for not deploying a subjunctive when the context demanded it, as any child in a French school would be expected to do.) Fourth, to judge from the number of books on English usage now in print, the public also finds the subject of what words really mean and how grammar should be used rather fascinating – which it is – or people at least want to take a second opinion on the matter.

When *Strictly English* was reviewed the responses fell into two camps. Professional writers, who from a tradesman's point of view saw exactly what I sought to achieve, noticed the book with flattering respect. However, when academics in linguistics departments of certain universities reviewed it there was outrage. Nowhere in Britain operates closed shops in the way that academia does, and some of these people were manifestly upset that a mere professional writer should enter this field. In addition to the impenetrable and often specious scholarly papers some academics publish on their subject, they moonlight as writers of supposedly popular works in which they patronise the public about aspects of the English language; I suspect they have been deeply annoyed by the rash of rather more practical books on the subject that started with *Strictly English* and was followed by a small torrent of other such works by people they would regard as amateurs. They were, to judge from some of the reviews, especially upset that the book took a prescriptive view, because they appear to have deep political views on this matter. For many of them – and I paraphrase only slightly – I was interfering with the right of self-expression by individuals that is part of the organic growth and change of our language. I am afraid I violently disagreed with them on several counts, and I still do.

It is all very well to tell a young person that he or she can be creative with the English language, while academic linguists sit back and revel in the patois that results. However, if that young person applies for a job, or writes a personal statement when seeking a place in higher education (other, perhaps, than in a linguistics department), he or she may well suffer consequences from being partly illiterate, whether because of poor spelling, poor grammar or a misunderstanding of what a simple monosyllable such as *flaunt* actually means. Or, attending an interview, that young person may be disadvantaged by inarticulacy, or by mangling sentences or misusing words in front of someone who lacks those faults. This will be true especially in commercial contexts, for no one wishes his business to be represented to the public by people who struggle with their first language. From the comfort of a nicely endowed chair at a university it is easy to engage in the theoretical exercise of rubbishing attempts to keep English straight. It is small comfort to the victims of that ideology, some of whom will find themselves employed in callings beneath their potential as a consequence of the propagation of such idiotic ideas. At literary festivals, when I spoke about *Strictly English,* many who bought the book told me they were buying it for children or grandchildren, and I entirely understood why.

We can leave the politically motivated theorists in their ghetto, however, though it is important to know about them, and about how their motives do not coincide with a British strain of self-improvement that dates back to Samuel Smiles and beyond, and which the great grammarians of a century ago – notably the Fowler brothers – identified in their own landmark works. For the avoidance of doubt I must specify my own creeds. I am well aware that words have in some cases changed their meanings steadily over the centuries, and that change and progress necessitate the introduction of new words into the language. However, since the *Oxford English Dictionary* (whose first edition was completed in 1928) effectively codified the language, I am bemused that we should be asked to tolerate someone saying 'he has flaunted all the rules' when but for a moment of ignorance they could just as easily say 'he has flouted all the rules'. If a ready-made, perfectly accessible word did not exist, matters would be different: but it does exist. Similarly, I am aware that grammar has changed over the centuries, not least to avoid ambiguities or enforce greater precision in expression. I am not, however, clear why we should endorse usages such as 'he gave it to my husband and I' or 'you was right'. If you feel such things *are* acceptable, this book is probably not for you.

I am particularly grateful to those readers of *Strictly English* who took the trouble to write to me, some of whose points are found within. Miss Margot Corper was especially helpful. I must also thank Nigel Wilcockson, for applying his keen editorial eye to my manuscript; my agent Georgina Capel; and my wife Diana, for her constant support.

Simon Heffer
Great Leighs
17 November 2013

Bibliography

The following works were especially useful to me in compiling this book and are frequently cited in it:

The Oxford English Dictionary (2nd edition)
The King's English, by H. W. and F. G. Fowler (Oxford, 1906)
A Dictionary of Modern English Usage, by H. W. Fowler (OUP, 1926)
Advanced English Syntax, by C. T. Onions (1904, revised by B. D. H. Miller, Routledge and Kegan Paul, 1971)
Politics and the English Language, by George Orwell (Penguin, 2004)
Usage and Abusage, by Eric Partridge (revised edition, Penguin, 1973)
The Complete Plain Words, by Sir Ernest Gowers (revised by Sir Bruce Fraser, Pelican, 1973)

Author's Note

As in *Strictly English*, to avoid prolixity and tedium only the male gender is used in examples. As always used to be the case, the male should be taken to include the female whenever suitable.

A

A and **an** The indefinite articles, the most common words in the English language. *An* is used before almost all words beginning with a vowel, and before those beginning with a silent *h*. Therefore we say 'a dog' but 'an armadillo'. The only exception comes with certain words beginning with *u*, when the first syllable is pronounced 'you': so we say 'an understanding' but 'a unicorn' or 'a unique thought'. The use of articles before words beginning with *h* is usually straightforward – 'an hour', 'an honourable exception' but 'a house' and 'a hammer'. Many people say, and write, 'an historian' or 'an historic moment' – in my view incorrectly – but it is not usual to hear 'an history of the world', because of the different way in which that noun is stressed. It is correct to write 'a historian' and 'a historic moment', just as it is to write 'a history'. It used to be common among the educated classes to refer to 'an hotel', with the *h* silent in the French manner: but of late this has come to be considered an affectation, as 'hotel' is a properly anglicised word. Unlike indefinite articles in various European languages, ours do not change according to the gender of the noun, because in English nouns have no gender. The indefinite article can also have a rhetorical usage, as in the phrase 'so notorious a crime will never be forgotten', or 'what kind of a man does such a thing?' It is used in such cases for emphasis, but is rare in formal writing.

Abbreviation An abbreviation may either be the initial letters of a set of words, or a shortening of one specific word. BBC, QED and RSPCA are abbreviations, but so are 'quote' (for 'quotation'), 'mac' (for 'macintosh') and 'pub' (for 'public house'). These days, it looks typographically ugly to put full points in between the letters of an abbreviation, as was the fashion a century ago. Some frequent usages seem routinely to have full points, notably *i.e.* and *e.g.*, but in written English it would be better to write in full 'that is' or 'for example'. See also ACRONYM.

Ablative This was one of the cases in classical languages (the others being the nominative, vocative, accusative, genitive, dative and, in Latin, the locative) and was used with the prepositions *by*, *with* or *from*. In English the only recognised case other than the nominative is the accusative, for the object of an action, and with 'WHOM' being ignored by many writers, that might not last long.

Ablative absolute This was a construction in Latin of a noun and participle in the ablative case that schoolboys were taught to translate as 'which dog having been kicked' or 'which book having been read', a stylistic abomination in English.

Able Only sentient beings are *able*. To say that 'this key may be able to open the door' is wrong. A man may be able to open the door using the key, or the key may unlock the door.

-able/-ible Etymology dictates whether an adjective ends in either of these forms, the former tending to derive from medieval French, the latter from Latin. See individual examples such as ADMISSIBLE, and see ADJECTIVES, NEGATING.

Abolish For something to be abolished, it must exist, and its abolition usually entails its permanent absence. One occasionally sees usages such as 'abolish weight gain by following our diet', which is absurd, as the weight gain does not yet exist.

Aborigine and **Aboriginal** It used to be the case that *aborigine* was a noun used to describe the indigenous people of Australia and *aboriginal* was the adjective. In the age of political correctness it is now not so simple. 'Aborigine' is regarded as an anachronism, and the phrase that was widely used to replace it – 'indigenous people' – is now regarded as having been 'imposed' on the aboriginal people as a 'scientific' term that dehumanised those it described. In fact, the preferred phrase among politically correct Australians is 'Aboriginal and Torres Strait Islander people', which is by most objective standards ludicrous. Tasmania, which is a law unto itself, still uses the term 'aborigine' and even 'blacks'. In practice, only an extremist will take offence at the usage 'aboriginal', which can be used in polite conversations and writing to describe the first Australians, though pedants may feel happier with 'aboriginal person'.

Abridgement should be spelt thus with two *e*'s. See ACKNOWLEDGEMENT and JUDGEMENT.

Absentee This is a correct usage to describe one who is not present, even though the rule is that nouns ending in *-ee* ought to describe someone to whom something happens (an employee is someone who is given employment; a refugee is someone who is given refuge). The logic of *absentee* is that it describes someone whom circumstances force to be absent. Many other nouns ending in *-ee* would be better off ending in *-er*: an escapee is really an escaper.

Absolutely This adverb has a legitimate usage, as in 'Louis XIV ruled absolutely', or 'I am absolutely [i.e. completely and utterly] opposed to capital punishment'. However, it is also frequently used pointlessly to express agreement, which is a cliché: 'Do you like Beethoven?' 'Absolutely!' 'Yes' does the job just as well.

Absolutes This is a group of adjectives that do not admit of degree but describe an absolute state, such as *dead*, or *alive*: a person is either one or the other. One point about these adjectives is that they do not have COMPARATIVES or SUPERLATIVES, because if they did the superlatives or comparatives would be illogical. When two people are *dead,* one cannot be 'more dead' than the other, and if three are dead one cannot be 'the deadest'. One of the most common misuses in this respect is *fuller*. If something is *full*, something else cannot be 'more full' than it. Similarly, if there are three full things, one cannot be 'the fullest'. The same principle applies to *empty*. Other words that convey absolute meanings include *wet*, *dry*, *black*, *round*, *square*, *whole*, *unique*, *safe*, *chief*, *final* and *absolute* itself. No word ending in *-less* can have a comparative or superlative, for reasons of logic. If someone is *harmless*, another cannot be 'more harmless', for the limits of innocuousness have already been reached by the first person and cannot, therefore, be exceeded. For particular problems with negating certain absolutes, see **ALWAYS**, **EVERYWHERE**, **NONE** and **NEVER**.

Abstract language This describes things that cannot be experienced by use of the five senses. These are sometimes by nature vague, and some writers or speakers deploy abstract language to create distance by obscuring clarity. If a firm is about to go broke it is better to say so than to resort to an abstract usage such as 'the position is serious' or 'the situation is difficult'. Not all abstract nouns cloud meaning but some, like the two just cited, are made for obfuscation. Unless one is a politician making a speech in which the concealment of embarrassing facts is essential, clarity should always be the prime consideration in use of language.

One cannot always do entirely without abstract nouns: but the fewer abstracts, the better. Another such is 'these things are reminders of . . .' when one could without impairing the sense write 'these remind us'; 'things' is also all too often a word with no point to it. Nouns (notably, again, abstract ones) in verbose constructions also sometimes take the place of simple adjectives. The writer who says 'there is too little justice in the world' would better say 'the world is too unjust'.

Sir Ernest Gowers, in *Plain Words*, was also strict about abstract nouns such as *position* and *situation* being used to remove clarity from statements, and he was right to be so. A desire for euphemism seems to trigger both usages. To describe someone who is seriously ill, say so, not that 'the situation is serious'.

If a company is broke, say so, not that 'its position is serious'. In each example, the abstract nouns create distance; they are used to divorce the reality from the entity. No serious writer, unless briefed to deceive, should seek to do that. These terms are used sometimes where there is no attempt at euphemism. 'I am writing to enquire about your situation' can be paraphrased as 'What are you doing?' just as 'Could you inform me as to your position on this matter?' is 'What do you think about it?'

Otto Jespersen, writing in his *Philosophy of Grammar*, demonstrated for other reasons the difference between the sentences 'I doubt the doctor's cleverness' and 'I doubt that the doctor is clever'. One can see immediately that the former is euphemistic, the second more direct to the point of being insulting. While being rude is not always going to be the intention of a writer, avoiding the abstract wherever possible will always lead to the writer's communicating his meaning more directly.

Abuse and **misuse** *Abuse* tends to be intentional wheareas *misuse* is unintentional or accidental. A politician accused of abuse of his position has behaved with deliberate impropriety. Someone accused of misuse of a vacuum cleaner has, out of stupidity, used it to clear up a fluid spillage rather than simply to sweep a dry carpet. Drug abuse is the taking of a substance that may have a prescribed purpose, such as cocaine for pain relief, and to take it deliberately for stimulatory or mind-altering purposes. Drug misuse is to take a cold remedy in the hope it will ease your arthritis.

Abuse, terms of These range from the gentle and almost affectionate to the deeply offensive, and in the way that many words change their meanings according to social considerations over the course of decades or centuries, so especially do these. There were few worse slights in Elizabethan England than to call a man 'naughty', a term now used only for mischievous children. POLITICAL CORRECTNESS has had a profound influence on the use of such words, though they have never had a place in formal writing except in reported speech. Terms of racial abuse that were deemed merely vulgar a few decades ago could well now lead to one who utters them being brought before a court of law for inciting hatred. Similarly, terms that were routinely used in the mid-twentieth century to describe forms of disability – *cripple*, *spastic* and *mongol*, for example – are now regarded as cruel and have acquired widely accepted euphemisms. This happened not least because of the use of the medical terms as terms of abuse for those who were not thus afflicted. Certain words, such as *imbecile* or *cretin*, would never now be used to describe those with the medical conditions that were once described using these terms. However, they remain current in describing able people who behave stupidly. If one must use a term of abuse, it is always worth remembering that preceding it with an adjective is usually either tautological, or overkill: such as with 'stupid idiot'.

Academic writing All tribes develop their own jargon, and members speak or write to each other in that argot as a mark of their shared exclusivity. A notable example of this is how some academics write in learned journals where they publish the results of their research. Some, especially those in scientific or pseudo-scientific disciplines, can be nearly incomprehensible to outsiders. This is not because the outsiders are necessarily stupid, it is because the academics feel they have to write in a certain stilted, formulaic way or forfeit being taken seriously by their peers. Undergraduates often imitate aspects of this style in order to gain credibility with those who mark their essays. Such language should not be allowed to seep out into normal communications. If you find yourself 'positing' anything other than in a learned journal, it is best to stop immediately. A random example of near-incomprehensible (to a layman) academic writing can be found in Carol Bacchi's 2012 paper 'Why Study Problemizations? Making Politics Visible', which includes this paragraph:

> As an alternative, governmentality studies detail the heterogeneous strategic relations that go into the making of specific 'states', opening up spaces for intervention and movement. For example, the poststructuralist scholar, Rowse (2009), describes

> nation-states as methods for assembling power relations. Such a reconceptualization provides an opening to problematize 'sovereignty in world politics as well as in research practice itself' (de Goede, 2006: p. 5). This recommended shift from static entities to strategic relations promises to open up a whole new field for comparative politics.

Academics, writing to or addressing It is correct to address professional teachers as 'Professor' if they hold a chair or are emeritus/emerita, or as 'Dr' if they have a doctorate and wish to be so addressed. Certain other people working in non-academic posts but in, for example, research institutes or some other form of learned work and who hold doctorates may also wish to be known by their doctoral title as an indication of their qualification to undertake such work. If either a professor or doctor holds another honour conferring a title, then their academic title precedes it: so one would write 'Professor Lord Smith', 'Professor Sir John Smith', or 'Dr Sir John Smith'.

Accept and **except** If one *accepts* something one takes or receives something offered willingly (*OED*); or one agrees to a proposal, of marriage or of some other significant nature; or one reconciles oneself to the assumption of a particular role by a third party; or to learn to tolerate an uncomfortable or disagreeable set of circumstances. So it is correct to say 'he accepted the gift', 'she accepted his offer to join the board', 'Smith became accepted as the leading advocate of the reform', and 'in time, the public came to accept the austerity measures'. *Except* has a number of related meanings, according to the *OED*, but none of them entitles it to be confused with *accept*, though the *OED* records such confusion as first having occurred in the fourteenth century. *Except* means to exclude (and to make a point of saying you have excluded) someone or something from something else, as in 'John was excepted from being received by the Queen'. Its usage signifying 'to object to something' is archaic other than in the usage 'he took exception to her remarks'.

Access is a noun and not a verb. 'Can I access your website?' is a solecism: either say 'Can I gain access?' or 'Can I see?' If the access is literal rather than metaphorical, use *enter*: not 'Can I access the premises?' but 'Can I enter the premises?'

Accrue This means to accumulate over a period of time, and it is most often seen in a financial context, such as 'interest accrued on the investments over the years'. It is an intransitive verb, sometimes wrongly used as a transitive in sentences such as 'the account will accrue interest'. It is better to say 'the account will earn interest'.

Accurate is an incomparable adjective, or an ABSOLUTE.

Accusative case This is the case in classical and certain modern languages which a pronoun or noun adopts when it is the object of a verb: for example, the noun 'bone' in the phrase 'the dog ate the bone'. In English, nouns do not decline, but pronouns do, and give evidence of the accusative case as distinct from the nominative. The inflected accusative pronouns in English are *me*, *him*, *her*, *us* and *them*. *You* does not inflect. In the phrases 'Give the book to me', 'the child found him', 'John saw her', 'show it to us' and 'Mary missed them' the pronouns are all accusatives (the nominatives would be *I*, *he*, *she*, *we* and *they* respectively). There is also the accusative relative pronoun WHOM – 'the teacher to whom I spoke' or 'the woman whom I shall marry' – that has largely fallen into disuse, but which remains a mark of educated and formal speech. Accusative pronouns are essential after a PREPOSITION – one would never write or say 'give it to I' or 'it came from they' unless one were completely illiterate or speaking in dialect in a work of fiction. Nor is the widespread disregard of *whom* to be applauded. That so many people now would write or say 'the prime minister is a politician who I despise' can hardly be represented as evidence of progress. Some people would be tempted to write 'I was afraid of she who must be obeyed', believing 'she who must be obeyed' cannot be altered. But it can, and it must be. The preposition *of* must take the accusative, and so it has to be 'I was afraid of her who must be obeyed.'

A common mistake with prepositions occurs when there are two objects: some speakers or writers remember to put the first in the accusative, but then ignore the second. Few would consider it acceptable to say 'she gave it to I', yet some find little difficulty in saying 'she gave it to my husband and I'. Perhaps the Queen is to blame for the popularity of that solecism, despite Her Majesty's own faultless grammar and her usage of 'my husband and I' only when they are the subject of the sentence. One often hears or reads 'between you and I' which must be 'between you and me'.

Another frequently missing accusative occurs after *than*. Even quite educated people write or say 'she is older than I' or 'you are a better man than I' or 'I have lived here longer than he'. It should be 'me' in the first two and 'him' in the last. We should take as our authority for this the peerless grammarian C. T. Onions, who wrote in his *Modern English Syntax* that 'than, when introducing a contracted comparative clause has (at least from early Modern English times) been treated as a preposition and has been followed by an accusative.' To reinforce Onions's point, one would never write 'a woman than who I was much taller', but 'than whom'. It is, of course, correct to write or say 'she is older than I am', and so on: but if the verb *to be* is absent, the pronoun must be accusative. As Onions says, there is half a millennium of precedent for such a thing, and any other usage – such as 'older than I' – is, in his view, 'pedantic'. He also justified the use of the accusative after *as* or *so* if the verb *to be* was absent: 'she is not as [or 'so'] tall as I am' is fine, but it should be 'she is not as [or 'so'] tall as me'. An accusative is also needed after *such as* – it should be 'a fool such as me', not 'a fool such as I'. The more demotic use 'a fool like me' at least has a correct accusative, though the idiom is slang.

The verb *to be*, as in Latin, should never take the accusative in formal writing, though it frequently does in demotic speech. 'It's me' or 'I'm her' are accepted usages. It may sound impossibly precious and pompous to say 'it is I' or 'I am she', but it is correct, and should still be used in formal writing or speech.

The direct object of a verb must always be in the accusative. A sentence such as 'I was appalled to find only one woman, and she a foreigner, who understood English grammar' is wrong: it must be 'and her a foreigner', for that clause remains an object of 'find'.

Achingly It is tempting to ignore entirely what Eric Partridge called 'vogue words', on the grounds that they are usually meaningless and, as such, soon become exhausted and pass out of fashion. *Achingly* is a typical example: by the time you read this there will be, and indeed will have been, others. Early in the twenty-first century it was considered, for a short time, witty and expressive to describe something as 'achingly modern' or 'achingly chic'. Happily, boredom soon set in, and the moment passed. However, it is useful as an example of how unthinking use of a novelty term becomes tedious and marks the speaker or writer out as being thoughtless about the use of English.

Acknowledgement should be spelt thus, with two *e*'s. See also ABRIDGEMENT and JUDGEMENT.

Acquiesce does not mean to approve. It means to agree to do something with some reluctance. 'Several ministers acquiesced in the Prime Minister's plans to legalise same-sex marriage' means that they supported him in order to preserve their careers, not because they agreed with the policy.

Acronym An acronym is an abbreviation that constitutes a pronounceable word, such as Aids (acquired immune deficiency syndrome), Ofsted (the Office of Standards in Education, Children's Services and Skills) and Unicef (United Nations Children's Fund). So BBC, QED and RSPCA are not acronyms but ABBREVIATIONS. It is usual to have an initial capital letter for acronyms, but to write or print the rest of the word in lower case, though some military acronyms break this rule, such as SHAPE (Supreme Headquarters Allied Powers Europe) and UNPROFOR (United Nations Protection Force). For a good directory of acronyms, look on the Internet at www.acronymslist.com.

Active voice Verbs have two voices, the *active* and the *passive*. The *active* is the more straightforward and direct: 'The boy waved his bat in the air.' The *passive* voice does not change the sense, but alters the emphasis: 'The bat was waved in the air by the boy.' Use the active wherever possible, for the passive establishes a remoteness between the actor and the action. For that reason it is much beloved of politicians.

Actor Correctly, this word is used in the theatrical sense to describe a male of the species who performs in a drama. It is now widely used to describe a player of either gender. However, the Oscar ceremony, which takes place in Hollywood and therefore near the epicentre of POLITICAL CORRECTNESS, still makes awards to the best actress and the best supporting actress. The gender-specific term is inevitably more precise.

Actually has in large part become a CLICHÉ and, like most clichés, almost meaningless. There is little difference in effect between saying or writing 'I hadn't actually seen it' and saying 'I hadn't seen it'. Like many meaningless words, it has become a form of punctuation, something the mind tells the tongue or the pen to do automatically without engaging the normal processes of thought. Some people seem to be unable to resist starting most sentences with it – 'actually, I'm going to have a bath', or 'actually, let's have dinner'. It is just about permissible as a form of subtle contradiction, in speech – 'You were out with that woman again!' 'Actually, I was taking my grandmother to church.' However, such examples will rarely occur in formal writing. 'In fact', which is also a cliché now, may just be preferable if one has set up a thesis in writing but wishes to offer a contradiction to it. 'However' is usually the least tiresome way of doing this, as in: 'She claimed we were late. However, her watch was fast.' On the grounds that in good writing one should always cut out a word that is unnecessary, *actually* can often be dispensed with. Its bastard and even more verbose cousin, the fatuous phrase 'in actual fact', is something for which there is absolutely no excuse. See also FILLERS.

Address, forms of See under the individual headings ACADEMICS, ARMED FORCES, BARONESSES, BARONETS, BISHOPS, CLERGY, COUNTESSES, DR, DUKES AND DUCHESSES, EARLS, ESQUIRE, HONOURABLE, JUDICIARY, KNIGHTS, LETTERS, MILITARY TITLES, PEERS AND THEIR FAMILIES, QUEEN'S COUNSEL, REVEREND, ROYALTY.

Address, to This has acquired something of a vogue usage in recent years. It used to mean to write a destination for a letter on its envelope, to speak at a public meeting or to talk formally to another individual. It is now used to describe someone turning his or attention to almost anything, as in 'he addressed the problem', 'she addressed the question of what to wear' and 'he addressed his pork pie'. The joke soon wears thin, as it does with all such vogue usages.

Adequate The dictionary defines two nuanced usages. One is to mean 'fully satisfying what is required', the other, a more modern development, means 'satisfactory, but worthy of no stronger praise or recommendation'. In either usage no comparative or superlative makes sense, so avoid 'very adequate' or 'most adequate', unless trying to be archly humorous. 'Adequate enough' is a tautology.

Adjectives An adjective is a word that describes a NOUN. A man can be *big, small, tall, short, thin, fat, old, young* and so on – they are all adjectives. In addition to simple descriptive words such as these, adjectives may be manufactured out of verbs, as in 'the living dead', 'a standing rebuke' or 'a running sore'. Indicating possession is also adjectival, as in 'the school's playing fields', though in some such cases a noun can often be used as an adjective without the possessive – 'the school playing field', for example. In other contexts, the first of two consecutive nouns can often have the force of an adjective: such as 'a fruit basket', 'a dinner jacket', 'a tractor driver' or 'running shoes'. Use of a noun and preposition may also be adjectival – 'the road to London' is 'the London road', and when one is awaiting 'the train from Edinburgh', one is awaiting 'the Edinburgh train'. Whole phrases can be adjectival, as in 'he had a came-over-with-the-Conqueror cast of mind'.

Adjectives should be used sparingly. Prose that is over-adjectival may be humorous or ironic: if it is neither, then it is often over-written. Adjectives clutter up prose and frequently detract from what is being said because they may harm clarity. They are popular with the tabloid press because they add a note of sensationalism to a story. They also suggest insufficient thought in the choice or deployment of the noun they are describing. Also, not all adjectives are equal. They fall into two classes: those that describe matters of fact and those that describe matters of perception or opinion. The former are far more necessary than the latter, and therefore less offensive and more excusable. Adjectives may be a statement of the obvious – 'the *old* man', 'the *deep* river', 'the *cold* day'. However, when they are expressions of opinion it is their subjectivity that makes them dangerous. 'The *stupid* child' may be nothing of the sort. Nor may 'the *plain* woman' (beauty being in the eye of the beholder), or 'the *sincere* man'. Adjectives may often be avoided either because they are incipiently inaccurate, or because they add nothing to the meaning of the phrase, or because one chooses a noun with sufficient care to render them tautological or in some other way unnecessary. They do however exist, and far more in some sorts of writing than in others. It is well to be alert to their potency, their power to deceive, and to their dangers. Not the least of those dangers is that so many of them fail to inform the reader but instead distract him.

When adjectives are used to express opinions they should be carefully chosen to convey an exact degree of view. Otherwise, the user risks lapsing into hyperbole. If someone is *dull*, that is a perfectly good adjective with which to describe his condition. *Boring* would be an acceptable alternative. *Tiresome* is slightly stronger, because it suggests that the tedium of the person is becoming an irritant. *Stupid*, *thick*, *revolting* or *shocking* simply take the description into hyperbole.

At the risk of stating the obvious, if you are going to use an adjective, be sure to choose one that conveys exactly your meaning. Speakers or writers will exaggerate for effect, but it is not particularly helpful if one is striving for credibility. In normal prose it may be helpful to confine oneself to adjectives that are objective, and avoid those that are subjective. Also there is no point describing an idiot as 'a *stupid* idiot', or a hero as 'a *courageous* hero', because if the noun is being used accurately the adjective conveys no extra information. 'An *established* convention' or 'an *earlier* precedent' are similarly tautological, because a convention must be established and a precedent must have come earlier. Also, it is redundant to describe someone as 'a *convicted* criminal', because no one (under English law at least) is a criminal unless his criminality has been proved in a court of law by his being convicted of a crime. It is a mark of good style to choose a noun that is sufficiently expressive (and, of course, accurate) to convey the exact meaning required without the need for an adjective. Keep to a minimum even adjectives that convey important factual information, to avoid clutter. And think carefully before using one that does not.

Also, some adjectives do not mean what popular (and incorrect) usage has led us to think they mean. See FULSOME and RARE AND SCARCE for examples.

Adjectives are the staple of the tabloid newspaper, where they give colour and allow easy reader engagement with news stories that for reasons of space must be short, and must convey the maximum information in the minimum space. Readers of such prose too easily acquire two habits. One is the promiscuous use of the adjective; the other is the use of emotive compound construction in which the adjective, often the past participle of a verb, is further larded with an adverb, as in '*heavily* veiled', '*devastatingly* beautiful', '*brutally* beaten' and so on. Such phrases are more damaging to good style than ordinary adjectives because so many of them now have the force of clichés.

Adjectives, as nouns Two examples of adjectives that have become nouns are *homosexual* and *classic*. The late Auberon Waugh took exception to the former, arguing that the noun should be 'homosexualist'. The adjectival usage as a noun is now so entrenched that to write 'a homosexual man' (or, for that matter, 'a lesbian woman' instead of *a lesbian*, or 'a heterosexual person' for *a heterosexual*) would start to smack of pedantry. On the subject of groups, several other words used to refer to them have become nouns – *blacks*, *whites*, *ethnics*, *gays*, *straights*, and so on. The last three have the status of slang, however. The English language is littered with adjectives that have become nouns, and whose usage raises no eyebrows – such as *essential*, *extra*, *regular*, *short* and *official*.

Adjectives, comparison of The comparative of an adjective is used when there are only two items being compared; the superlative may only be used when there are three or more. So one says or writes: 'he is the bigger of the two' or 'she is the prettier'. 'Of all of them, he was the biggest' is the usage when there are three or more. It is correct to say 'he was bigger than any of them', because 'any' is singular and therefore the comparison is implicitly between two people from a larger group. It would be perhaps more felicitous to write 'he was the biggest of all of them'. A common mistake is to describe someone as 'the eldest child', or 'the youngest', when there are only two children. Most superlatives end in *-est*, most comparisons in *-er*. It is, however, unidiomatic or archaic to end some adjectives like this: one would write or say 'the most wanted' rather than 'the wantedest'. Most of what H.W. Fowler calls the adjectives with 'English' endings (*-ed* and *-ing*) take 'most' or 'more' when superlatives or comparatives are required. For adjectives that do not (or should not) admit of comparatives or superlatives, see ABSOLUTES.

Adjectives, confused with adverbs It is an increasingly common solecism to hear an adjective deployed in the place of an adverb (never the other way round). One hears such things as 'I bought it cheaper at Tesco' whereas one should say 'I bought it more cheaply'. A Jamie Oliver recipe book bears the motto 'shop smart, cook clever, pay less'. 'Smart' is allowable because 'smartly' would mean promptly or quickly; but it should be 'cook cleverly'. An adjective describes a noun, not a verb.

Adjectives, from verbs Through ELLIPSIS some past participles of verbs commonly serve as nouns. We may say 'the unwashed', 'the departed', 'the dispossessed' and so on, without needing to add the noun 'people' to the phrase. As well as *-ed* adjectives, the *-ing* ones come from verbs too: 'a *riding* hat', 'a *singing* canary', 'a *jumping* bean', and so on. In Latin such adjectives are known as GERUNDIVES, which grammarians insist do not exist in English. However, a phrase such as 'the detective found a smoking gun' would seem to have something suspiciously like a gerundive in it.

Adjectives, -ical endings See -IC/-ICAL.

Adjectives, negating Fowler set a useful rule for this. He suggested that when an adjective ended in the obviously English *-ed* or *-ing*, it should be negated by the English prefix *un-*; but if the word ended with the Latin-derived *-ible*, *-able* or *-ate*, then the Latin prefix *in-* should be used. Hence, 'undigested' but 'indigestible'. There are obviously exceptions: we would never write 'inremarkable', 'irregenerate', 'unconvenienced', 'inforgettable' or 'infeasible', but generally the rule holds. There is a distinction between IRRESPONSIBLE and 'unresponsible'.

Admissable and **admissible** Both spellings have a long history. Neither appears to be incorrect and the dictionary sanctions both. My own preference, idiomatically, is for the latter, following the principle of *permissible.*

Adopted and **adoptive** The first adjective describes someone who or something that has been adopted by someone else – 'an adopted child', 'my adopted son', 'her adopted country', 'his adopted name'. The second describes something or someone acquired by the act of adoption, as in 'his adoptive father'. 'His adopted home' would be a new residence someone has chosen for himself; 'his adoptive home' would be a residence acquired by the circumstance of his having been adopted.

Adultery is strictly 'voluntary sexual intercourse between a married person and another who is not his or her spouse' (*OED*). Technically speaking, when both parties are married (but not to each other) the act constitutes double adultery. Where both parties are unmarried they can merely participate in *fornication*. The tabloid press routinely use the terms 'cheat on' or 'betray' to describe the moral effect of the adulterer/ fornicator on a third party who is either his or her spouse or long-term sexual partner, which although clichéd sidestep the confusion. (Such terms must, however, be avoided in formal writing.) The dictionary says 'adultery' has been misused to describe 'illicit' sexual relations since 1405, but in this age of legal precision it is well to use the right term, depending upon the nature of the activity. Adultery is no longer used to describe the practice of debasing foodstuffs or drink, which is *adulteration* – 'the wine tasted awful because it had been adulterated'.

Adverbial clause This is a part of a sentence that illuminates the main verb, such as 'I was early *because there was no traffic*' and 'he used to drink in that pub *when he worked in London*'. These clauses are introduced by a subordinating conjunction such as *because*, *when*, *where*, *that* and so on.

Adverbs These words describe or qualify verbs in the way that adjectives describe or qualify nouns. Most, but not all, adverbs end in *-ly*, such as *softly*, *gently*, *rudely*, *impetuously*, *greatly*, and so on. However, so do various adjectives (*lovely*, *ugly*, *lowly*, *comely*, *costly*, *shapely* and so on). This may be a source of confusion. Adverbs such as 'lovelily' sound exceedingly odd, though that did not prevent the great grammarian Eric Partridge from justifying its use. Rather than say or write 'he lived *lowlily*' it would be more idiomatic to use the construction 'he lived *in a lowly manner*', or 'lived *humbly*'. Or, instead of writing 'she played the violin *lovelily*', one could always say 'her violin playing *was lovely*'. Or, one could find a synonym: instead of 'lovelily' she might just as easily have played 'beautifully'. While on the subject of clumsy words, although adjectives ending in *-ly* compare by becoming 'lowlier', 'costlier', 'shapelier' and so on, adverbs do not. An economy would not shrink 'steeplier' than another, it would shrink 'more steeply', just as someone would 'recover more strongly' than someone else, or behave 'more charmingly' – never 'stronglier' or 'charminglier'. The same rule applies to 'leisurely'.

Although they may be overused and may clutter up prose in just the way that adjectives do in the hands of a poor stylist, adverbs can also, like the class of objective adjectives, add precision or detail to a verb if chosen and used carefully. However, one of the more disturbing trends in contemporary English, even among educated people, is for the adverb to fall into disuse and be replaced, out of ignorance or sloppiness, by an adjective – 'he ran down the road *so quick* he fell over' should be '*so quickly* he fell over'. It is an inflexible rule that should you wish to describe or qualify a verb, you must use an adverb. A newspaper in November 2009 published the phrase 'the economy shrank steeper than expected', which was simply barbaric, and suggested that even some professional writers and sub-editors have failed to grasp the distinction between adjectives and adverbs, and that the act of shrinking should have occurred 'more steeply'.

Some adjectives are mistakenly used as adverbs more readily than others: one often hears 'they played too loud' whereas one probably does not hear 'she wept so plaintive'. The more common the adjective, the more likely it is to be enlisted as an adverb: and, as a result, some have passed into idiomatic usage – such as 'buy cheap and sell dear', 'sleep sound' and 'dig deep'. Further confusion is sown when some adverbs look like adjectives. *Hard* has been an adverb for a thousand years (and *hardly* means something quite different). *Big* has been one for about 500, though its most popular application in this part of speech – 'think big' – has been current for more than a century. However, few sophisticated writers or stylists would ever use it as an adverb. Sir Kingsley Amis, who wrote a book on correct usage, was angry that others did not recognise *single-handed* as an adverb. Among those he was presumably angry with was the *Oxford English Dictionary*, which contradicted him on the matter. The correct adverbial use is *single-handedly*.

Adverbs may also qualify adjectives, as in phrases such as 'charmingly pretty', 'graphically stupid', 'deeply shy', 'heavily veiled' and so on. This can easily be overdone and good stylists should observe even greater restraint in doing so than in the use of adjectives. As pointed out in the entry on **ADJECTIVES**, one of the great risks with applying an adverb to an adjective is that it forms a cliché – as in phrases such as 'dangerously ill' or 'supremely confident' – and therefore they risk boring the reader, or suggesting an insufficiency of thought in composition. They also risk being tautological: anyone who writes the phrase 'badly damaged' needs to ask himself how something can be 'well damaged'. If it is desired to convey an idea of a high order of damage, then say 'seriously' or 'gravely', or use some similar adverb that is more logical in the context. The right choice of verb removes the need for an adverb: there is no need to say that someone 'raced quickly', 'gorged greedily' or 'dishonestly stole'.

Even when an adverb is not strictly tautological, it may be unnecessary because it describes something that most people would intuit from the adjective – such as in the phrase 'a fully functioning car'. 'Functioning' suggests the car works properly; it should be modified only if parts of the car do not work, with an adverb such as 'partly'. Also, an adverb may constitute an exaggeration. Before you write a phrase such as 'he failed badly', ask yourself whether he did not simply 'fail'. Even a poor soul who is 'brutally murdered' may just have been murdered with a single shot or blow. Save the qualifier for something even more appalling. Certain adverbs, such as *somewhat* and *rather*, do little other than modify adjectives, though often these are adjectives formed by use of the past participle of a verb, as in 'somewhat depressed' or 'rather damaged'. The use of these words in strict adverbial application to verbs is now rather rare, and found usually only in formal writing, as in 'he somewhat doubted it' and 'he rather hoped she would come'.

Some adverbs are in disguise, for they do not appear to be what they are. There are many of them: any word that qualifies a verb in a grammatically correct way is an adverb. Here are some examples: 'they *also* serve', 'I'm coming *now*', 'she has *just* left', 'we're *almost* there', 'he *always* eats there', 'you will go *far*', 'she *even* wept', 'time *never* drags', 'it went *well*', 'do you come here *often*?' and, most ubiquitously, 'they have *not* seen me'.

Nor are adverbs confined to being a single word: they may just as easily be phrases. 'He walks *by night*' is one such example, as is 'I have suffered *more than I can tell you*' and even 'she sleeps *with a gun under her pillow*'. Adverbs can also take on lives of their own, irrespective of any nearby verb. The most egregious example of this is **HOPEFULLY**. Some other adverbs have become used as fillers or verbal punctuation, to introduce sentences – though this is more common in speech – and is to be deplored in formal writing. For example: 'Incidentally, I saw John today', and 'naturally, I have grapefruit for breakfast'. In some cases, usually when referring to an idea expressed in the preceding sentence, it may be legitimate: 'He felt ill. Similarly, I had begun to run a fever' is an example of a correct usage. And, of course, the opening adverb may be attached to a verb but positioned at the start of the sentence for effect: 'Abruptly, he broke off the conversation and walked away.' See also **FILLERS**.

In some such usages the opening adverb suggests an **ELLIPSIS**. When we see the phrase 'interestingly, I saw Smith today', what are we to make of 'interestingly'? The act of his seeing Smith may perhaps have been interesting, but that is not what we should imagine the speaker meant. What we are to understand – and this is where the statement is elliptical – is something along the lines of 'it may be a matter of interest to you, or to both of us, that I saw Smith today'. It is hardly appalling in speech to use such a construction. In formal writing, however, one might consider saying 'by the way' or 'it may be a matter of interest that I saw Smith today'. Other such adverbial sentence-starters (*arguably*, *actually*, *theoretically*, *obviously* and so on) should be considered candidates for rephrasing, perhaps not least because, as clichés, they suggest a lack of originality or thought on the part of the writer.

Adverbs, forming with -ly/-ally or -ward/-wards There has been some debate about which adverbs should end in *-ly* and which in *-ally*. Several grammars present the rule that adjectives ending in *-al* naturally become adverbs ending in *-ally*, while all the rest take the ending *-ly*. This is not always so, however. Only the first part of the rule is right, and the form for other adjectives remains a question of idiom. Adjectives ending in *-ic*, for example, take *-ally*, with the exception of *publicly*. So one writes *dramatically*, *sporadically*, *emphatically*, and so on. One does not write *tragicly*, *idioticly* or *roboticly*. If in doubt, consult a dictionary. There is a distinction between the adjectival and adverbial usages of words ending in *-ward* or *-wards*. The former is the adjectival usage and the latter the adverbial. So write 'I fell backwards' or 'he moved forwards' or 'she came towards me', but say 'a forward position', 'a backward child' or 'an untoward remark'.

Adverbs, negating When negating certain adverbs, bear in mind that for reasons of logic they may not mean what one thinks they mean. 'He always ate there' is not negated by 'he did not always eat there': it is negated by 'he never ate there'. See also IN-/ UN-.

Adverbs, numerical It used to be considered necessary, if writing a list that ran 'first . . . second . . . third . . .' to write 'firstly . . . secondly . . . thirdly'. This is wrong and there is no logic to it. One should write: 'First, he went to the bar. Second, he ordered a drink. Third, he drank it.' It should be clear that the words *first*, *second* and *third* do not adhere to and do not qualify the verbs and are therefore not adverbs. They are really adjectives with elliptical nouns ('his first action . . . his second action . . .' and so on). However, if one were telling a story about a separate sequence of events, and using a verb common to separate actions, then one would use the numbers adverbially: 'He went firstly to the bar, secondly to the table and thirdly to the car park.'

Adverbs, positioning of This is a complex matter, for the positioning of an adverb will often affect the whole meaning that is being conveyed. The adverb usually follows the direct object: 'she drove the car *fast*', 'he hit the ball *hard*', 'they painted the room *well*'. Those adverbs, not ending in *-ly*, do not function idiomatically anywhere else in the sentence; *-ly* adverbs just about do. One could write 'she carefully drove the car' as well as 'she drove the car carefully '; or 'he gracefully hit the ball' or 'they cheerfully painted the room'. What one cannot do with any sort of adverb in such sentences is put it between verb and object, as in 'they painted cheerfully the room', as it defies idiom and sounds like nonsense. The rule continues to apply where there are indirect objects: 'she drove the car fast to the town' is more idiomatic than 'she drove the car to the town fast'. So too is 'he hit the ball hard to the offside' rather than 'he hit the ball to the offside hard'. Some usages with indirect objects require *-ly* adverbs to come early in the sentence: 'they willingly gave money to the boy' (or 'they willingly gave the boy money') is preferable to putting the adverb anywhere else, unless there were some doubt about how willingly they gave it and the adverb needs to be emphasised: in which case 'they gave the boy money willingly' is correct.

If it is so vexing to split an infinitive (and it is – see SPLIT INFINITIVE), how can one separate a pronoun or noun from a verb with an adverb? It is a legitimate question. I should sooner write 'he went boldly' than 'he boldly went' for the same reasons that I should write 'to go boldly' rather than 'to boldly go': the sense of 'boldly' seems to my ear and to my senses to be reinforced by its being directly attached to 'he'. Usage can become more complicated when indirect objects come into play, such as in 'he walked slowly to the station'; and more so still when auxiliary verbs are introduced, as in 'he had walked slowly to the station'. With INTRANSITIVE VERBS, lacking a direct object, there is more flexibility; one can write 'he grieved deeply' or 'he deeply grieved' – with most usages it is a matter of taste and idiom and a question perhaps best considered under the heading of STYLE. Another option is to write 'boldly, he went', but that seems to become self-consciously poetic. If one puts an adverb too far from the verb, confusion may result. 'She went to the office with her new dress on happily' appears to mean that the garment was being worn with great contentment, which is unfortunate if the meaning to be conveyed is that her going to the office was happy, irrespective of what she was wearing.

The problem is magnified when there is a phrase with more than one verb. 'He had tried quickly to run down the road' suggests that the attempt was launched with haste; whereas if it was his running that was supposed to be quick, the order has to be 'he had tried to run quickly down the road'. With most uses of auxiliaries the adverb must be placed between auxiliary and main verb for the avoidance of ambiguity. 'We shall definitely take John to France with us this summer' has a clarity not achieved by 'we shall take John to France with us this summer definitely' and is stylistically superior to 'we definitely shall take John'. The last of those forms would be used only in response to an assertion that they would not be taking John. An adverb such as *almost* has such a wide application that it must be anchored to the word it modifies: 'she almost reached the top of the hill' means something quite different from 'she reached almost the top of the hill'. The first example suggests she wanted to reach the top, but failed. The second suggests she had not finished her journey.

The presence of an auxiliary – such as *have*, *had*, *must*, *do* or *did* – can be complicating. 'He had almost finished when the bell rang' is quite different from 'he had finished almost when the bell rang'. 'They must nearly have been killed' is subtly different from 'they must have been nearly killed': the first suggests that an intervention of fate prevented death, such as a lorry's having swerved and missed completely a car in which they were travelling; the second suggests that an accident took place, and injuries were sustained, but they did not quite prove fatal. When it comes to positioning adverbs one must take care to put them where the desired meaning is achieved. In sentences with auxiliaries, that will normally be before the main verb. The idea that one should no more split an auxiliary from its verb than split an infinitive would require one to write the rather overblown 'never had I seen such a sight' rather than the more natural 'I had never seen such a sight'.

Also, the writer must bear in mind what he is seeking to achieve. It may be that in certain contexts to write 'she had particularly wanted a diamond necklace' would be inadequately emphatic; and that the sense the writer wishes to convey would be better represented by 'particularly, she had wanted a diamond necklace'. This would make sense had this sentence been preceded by one or several that listed this woman's desires. The only rule in this matter is comprehensibility.

Care in positioning the adverb is especially important when using compound tenses. To insert the adverb gladly into the phrase 'I should have had him shot' requires a little thought. It most naturally and logically goes after the auxiliary *should*, but an argument may be made for it to go after *have*. 'I should have had him shot gladly' would suggest the firing squad were happy in their work. Sometimes, the idiom dictates a different positioning, especially if the adverb is the main point of the statement. In a sentence such as 'this is not to be entered into lightly or frivolously', the desired emphasis puts the adverbs at the end. It is the same with other statements that are by way of a warning or an injunction, such as 'I will not tell you again' or 'please treat your children kindly'. The shorter the sentence, and the less scope for ambiguity, the easier it is to displace the adverb to the end, as in 'we went to work happily'. With a construction such as 'we used to visit my grandmother weekly', the idiom again puts the adverb at the end, since one senses that the point of the statement is to describe how regularly Grandmother was visited. If a statement of one's feelings about visiting Grandmother were to be the main point, the idiom dictates 'we used happily to visit my grandmother weekly'.

The adverb *always* precedes the verbal construction in most cases, as idiom also dictates: 'we always used to visit my grandmother' or, to take other examples, 'it always rains on Sunday', 'you always say that to me' or 'I bet you always do that'. Putting *always* at the end of a sentence makes something of a point of it – 'he said he would love me always' – and its effect should be noted. *Never* conventionally takes the same position, though there is not, outside poetry, an emphatic use of it at the end of a statement. *Sometimes* is more like *always* in that respect, in that a statement such as 'we come here sometimes' creates no difficulties, though it has a force hardly different from 'we sometimes come here'.

Putting adverbs almost as a balance between clauses is also liable to create ambiguities. For example: 'The dresses made by Dior lately have been worn by some of the world's most famous women.' Were the dresses made lately, or worn lately? Probably both, but it was equally probably not the intention of the writer to say so. It should have been either 'the dresses made lately by Dior' or 'have lately been worn by'.

If there are two verbs close together in a sentence the adverb must be allocated specifically to one. 'The minister was said months ago to have signed the letter' does not make it clear whether he signed the letter months ago and this rumour is only now being broadcast, or whether it was being said months ago that he had done so. It must be either 'The minister was months ago said to have signed the letter' or 'The minister was said to have signed the letter months ago', according to the meaning desired. It serves to prove the point that a misplacement of an adverb or adverbial phrase can cause ambiguity and, therefore, incomprehension.

One of the most important questions of word order arises when the word *only* comes into play. *Only* should be positioned as closely as possible to the word it qualifies, otherwise it will qualify a word the writer does not intend it to. 'She only went to the house to see her friend' means that seeing her friend was the sole purpose of her visit. 'She went only to the house to see her friend' means that she went nowhere other than the house to see the friend. 'She went to the house only to see her friend' means that when at the house she engaged in no activity other than seeing her friend. 'She went to the house to see only her friend' means that she went there to see her friend and nobody else. 'She went to the house to see her only friend' means that the unfortunate woman has but one friend. This is a relatively straightforward example; in sentences with longer clauses or a multiplicity of clauses the positioning of *only* is fraught with even more dangers.

Adverbs, used pointlessly Because of the influence of slang or vulgar usage, some adverbs (as with some **PREPOSITIONS**) attach themselves pointlessly to certain verbs, whose meaning is quite complete without them. Examples are: park *up*, revert *back*, watch *out*, test *out*, lose *out*, dry *out*, go *up* until, freeze *up*, free *up*, duck *down*, close *down* and shake *down*. It may also be the case that, just as certain adjectives are redundant because they simply amplify what is already apparent from the noun (as in 'stupid idiot'), so too are some adverbs redundant or tautological because they echo what is in the verb. There is no need to write that 'he stopped completely', 'he raged angrily' or 'he yelled loudly', for reasons that should be obvious in each case. There are particular problems with **FULLY**, for which reason see the entry on that word.

Adverse and **averse** *Adverse* is an adjective meaning 'antagonistic' or 'hostile'. It is not to be confused with *averse*, an adjective that signifies a disinclination towards something or an opposition to it. Thus we say 'they were hampered by *adverse* weather conditions' but 'she was *averse* to going out without a coat on in case she caught cold'.

Advertisements Although in most civilised countries there are strict rules about advertisements being 'legal, decent, honest and truthful', they are still prime examples of how language may be manipulated to achieve an illusory effect. Only politicians come close, and for similar reasons. Any retailer conducting a 'special offer' is merely concealing the fact that he has goods he cannot sell at the price he was originally asking for them. A performer of any description who is described as 'brilliant' usually isn't. Advertisements are prime hunting grounds for those who wish to spot adjectives of exaggeration, and they serve as a constant reminder to writers of the dangers they court in using adjectives in their own writing. Nouns, too, may be misused. 'Fact' in these contexts often means 'assertion', for example. And any description by the advertiser of the qualities of his product will often depend on there being a definition that the advertiser and customer can share of the adjectives used – which may not always be the case. Almost any adjective contained in advertisements by estate agents, used-car salesmen or political parties should be treated as specious. Be aware, too, that the style in which advertisements are written is not something the careful stylist or fine writer should ever seek to imitate. See also **POLITICAL LANGUAGE**.

Advocate It is becoming common in American English to read that somebody who is the spokesman for a particular pressure group 'advocates on its behalf'. *Advocate* is a transitive verb and it requires an object, so the spokesman must advocate ideas, policies or suggestions.

Affect and **effect** *Affect* is a verb with several distinct meanings, and it should not be confused with the verb *effect* – or with the noun. A man who *affects* a bow tie likes to wear one, but the verb suggests there is an element of ostentation, show or dandyism about his doing so. Someone who *affects* deep grief at the death of another is being insincere. One who *affects* an American accent is engaging in a pretence. But the most common meaning of the verb is 'to have an effect on someone or something', and it may be from that this confusion with its cousin arises. If one *effects* something, one executes it or makes it happen – 'he effected the takeover by buying the last tranche of shares'. As a noun, *effect* means 'the state or fact of being operative or in force', as in 'the law comes into effect at once'. It also means the result or outcome of an action – 'the effect of the closure was that he lost his job'. In certain idioms, it can also signify meaning – 'he told her to get lost, or words to that effect'. Also – and this is a variation of its usage to mean a result or consequence – it can describe the impression given by something visual or aural – 'the fan vaulting gave an ethereal effect to the church' or 'Vaughan Williams often creates a pastoral effect in his music'. The plural noun can also signify possessions – 'she had no personal effects when she was found'. The nominal usages of *effect* – 'he had a startling effect on everyone who met him', or 'the policy was put into effect from last Monday' – are far more common than the nominal use of *affect*, which today is current only in the terminology of psychiatry and psychology – 'a feeling or subjective experience accompanying a thought or action or occurring in response to a stimulus' (*OED*). The dictionary cites all other usages as being obsolete.

Affinity literally refers to a family relationship. Used metaphorically, one must speak of an affinity *with* someone or something else, as in 'she felt a strong affinity with her friend'. There may also be an affinity between two people or things – 'there is a strong affinity between her views and those of her husband'. An affinity *to* something is an Americanism.

Afterward used as an adverb is an Americanism: 'The Army often told no one . . . about its raids – not even afterward.' (*New Yorker*, 2 July 2012.) See also -WARD AND -WARDS.

Again This adverb is occasionally used tautologically, usually with verbs beginning with *re-* which itself often indicates repetition. It is pleonastic in phrases such as 'resume again', 'repeat again' and 'replenish again', even if the action is to resume, repeat or replenish for a second time or more.

Agenda was originally a plural collective noun but is now always singular.

Aggravate If one *aggravates* something, one makes it worse: 'I have aggravated my bad back today by carrying things upstairs.' The verb does not mean to annoy or to irritate, which has become its demotic usage in phrases such as 'he really aggravated me' or 'he gave me a lot of aggravation'. The dictionary now lists these slang usages, first detected in the late nineteenth century: and, being slang, they should not be used in formal speech or writing. A further corruption is the noun 'aggro', dated to the London underworld in the 1950s. This unpleasant word also leads people to believe that *aggravate* can mean to offer aggression or intimidation towards someone. It cannot.

Agony and its derivatives such as 'agonising' should be used only in a context that suggests extreme physical or mental suffering. It is hackneyed and an example of overuse to talk about 'the agony of Spurs losing to Manchester United' or 'the agonising decision about which chocolate to eat'. It is correct to say that 'the death of his children caused him agonising grief'.

Agreement Singular nouns require singular verbs, and plural nouns plural verbs. One exception is the word *number*, which always takes a plural – 'a number were leaving in the morning', and so on – except in the context of 'the number five was drawn from the hat'.

-aholic endings As with NEOLOGISMS ending in *-athon* and *-gate* these are an attempt at wit that is now past its best. The coinage of 'workaholic', which borrowed from the addictive attributes of 'alcoholic' and which the dictionary notes having started in America in 1968, then led to 'chocoholic' or 'chocaholic' (America, 1972), 'shopaholic' (America, 1984), 'sexaholic' (not yet in the dictionary) and even 'exercisaholic', among other ludicrous neologisms. The rule is simple: if you spot a new coinage of any other sort, regard the joke as already over, and move on.

Airplane is an Americanism for *aeroplane*.

Akimbo can apply only to arms, signifying hands on hips and elbows pointing outwards. Knees may point awkwardly, but they are not akimbo.

-al endings See entries on COMIC AND COMICAL, ECONOMIC AND ECONOMICAL, HISTORIC AND HISTORICAL, IRONIC AND IRONICAL and MAGIC AND MAGICAL.

Albeit Avoid this word in usages where *though* is more natural, as in 'he was a fast, albeit careful, driver'. It is best used to indicate a meaning such as 'even though', as in 'he was late, albeit he had left on time' – but even that begins to sound archaic.

Alibi, which in Latin means 'elsewhere', has become synonymous with the noun *excuse*. It is not: it means a plea of having been elsewhere at the time a crime was committed. It is a rare case of an adverb having become a noun: originally one would have sought to prove oneself *alibi*. The diluted use of the noun, and indeed its development into a verb, is another thing for which we have to thank the Americans.

All is a pronoun – 'there was plenty for all', for example. See also EACH and EVERY, with which *all* should not be confused.

All right should be written thus: the usage *alright* is ubiquitous in America, though educated Americans avoid it as fervently as we should. *All right* remains all right.

All Saints' Day Note the apostrophe, since the Saints are plural.

All Souls' Day Note the apostrophe, since the Souls are plural. However, the Oxford college is *All Souls*.

Allege This is a word frequently used in journalism in order to avoid a contempt of court through infringing the *sub judice* rule – saying a crime is *alleged* avoids imputing guilt or innocence to the accused. *Allege* must be used with care. A person may be alleged to have murdered another, but he is arrested on suspicion of murder, not for an alleged murder. There may well be no dispute that the death was the result of a murder: what is in doubt until a verdict is reached is who was responsible.

Alliteration This is the use of successive (but not inevitably consecutive) words beginning with the same sound, and unless it is used poetically or with conscious humour it can detract from the sense of what is being written. That was why various famous characters from children's comics had alliterative names – Desperate Dan, Dirty Dick, Minnie the Minx and Biffo the Bear. The use of it in supposedly straightforward prose – 'Be gone, you bustling, bumbling barbarian!' – creates the impression that the writer is trying to be funny, and alliteration is acceptable for a certain sort of humour. Tongue twisters are often alliterative – 'Peter Piper picked a peck of pickled pepper', for example – but the device is not always meant humorously: as in Shakespeare's 'sessions of sweet silent thought'. It is best avoided in everyday prose.

Allude and **elude** If one *alludes* to something one hints at it or suggests it, or makes an oblique reference to it – 'he alluded to the fact that she did not have an unblemished record'. It should not be confused with *elude*, the main definition of which in the *OED* is 'to escape [someone or something] by dexterity or stratagem': 'He eluded his captors.' It also means 'to evade compliance with or fulfilment of (a law, order, demand, request, obligation, etc.)' – 'I managed to elude the requirement' – though this is now rare. It is still frequently used metaphorically to describe incomprehension: 'What she sees in him continues to elude me.'

Allusion is the noun from ALLUDE. It used to mean wordplay or a pun. Now, it means an oblique or subtle reference in speech, writing, music or the visual arts to another idea, fact or work – 'there is an allusion in the painting to the Crucifixion', for example. It often comes in the form of disguised quotation. When someone says, on going to bed, that he is going 'off to the land of Nod', he is alluding to the Bible – whether he knows it or not. It should not be confused with ELUSION, the now almost obsolete noun from the verb *elude*, or ILLUSION, which mainly means 'something that deceives or deludes by producing a false impression'.

Allusions, use of If one is alluding to books, events or people in one's writing, one risks confining understanding of one's meaning to those who have read the same books, experienced the same events or know the same people. Sometimes allusion is valuable and illuminating, but it may have to be explained. A balance must be struck, for if an allusion requires such explanation that it outweighs the insight it conveys, then it is not worth alluding. It is rather like explaining a joke, and it stresses the importance of knowing one's readership. If an allusion is just about showing off how clever the writer is, then it can be exceptionally irritating to the reader. If one is confining allusion to quotation, be sure to quote accurately and that the quotation means what you think it means. See also QUOTATIONS.

Almost An adverb that must be placed correctly in a sentence to avoid ambiguity. See ADVERBS, POSITIONING OF.

Also is not a synonym for *and*. 'She had two boys and a girl' not 'she had two boys, also a girl'.

Alternately and **alternatively** To do something *alternately* is to do it by turns with doing something else: 'He sowed the seeds as he walked along, throwing them alternately to his left and then his right.' It must not be confused with *alternatively*, which is to have a choice in how it is done: 'He could throw the seeds first to his right and then to his left or, alternatively, to his left and then to his right.' With the contemporary use of *alternative* to mean radically different from the accepted norm, to do something alternatively may mean to do it in a radically different way, though such a usage has the status of slang.

Alternatives There can only ever be two *alternatives*. If there are – or you think there are – three or more, then they are *options*. In his superlative biography of General de Gaulle, Jonathan Fenby makes this error: 'Algeria would be invited to vote on a choice between three alternatives.' *Alternative* may also be used as an adjective to describe a means of doing something that is radically different from the norm. 'Alternative medicine' is one such usage, and is conventional. 'Alternative comedy' – a phenomenon of the 1980s in which comedians broke with the conventions of their trade – is still a slang usage, as is the description of something or someone as 'a bit alternative'. *Alternative* is also a useful word when avoiding the logical error 'you have two choices'. In fact, you have one CHOICE, and in this case it is of two alternatives.

Although This conjunction introduces *concessive clauses*, as in 'Although he was late, he missed nothing important.' See also THOUGH.

Altogether and **all together** The first word in its most usual form is an adverb meaning totally or wholly: 'He wasn't altogether stupid.' The second is an adjectival phrase indicating something done in unison: 'They ran to the beach all together.'

Alumnus The danger area for users of foreign words is when they are plurals, or when some concession has to be made to gender. This is especially true of Latin words. The word *alumnus* has passed into English – via America, it seems – and is now routinely used to describe graduates of universities. More than one of these are *alumni*; a woman is an *alumna*, and more than one are *alumnae*. See also FOREIGN WORDS AND PHRASES and PLURALS.

Always The adverb *always* usually precedes the verbal construction, as idiom also dictates: 'we always used to eat a cooked breakfast in the morning' or, to take other examples, 'it always rains on Sunday', 'you always say that to me' or 'I bet you always do that'. Putting *always* at the end of a sentence makes something of a point of it – 'she said she would remember the evening always' – and its effect should be noted. 'Not always' does not mean 'never', it means 'sometimes'.

Ambiguity is a quality that writers of fiction or drama specialise in creating, to instil mystery, tension and PARADOX into their work. If a phrase or statement is susceptible of more than one meaning, then it may lead a reader or audience to a conclusion that, when it is exposed as false, creates surprise and interest. If it occurs in works of fact it is almost always unintentional, and the result of a poor choice of words, PUNCTUATION or word order that prevents the intended meaning from being clear. Avoiding ambiguity is one of the great purposes of the COMMA: as in the famous 'eats shoots and leaves' or 'books plays and travels'.

'I considered this to be one of my better pieces of writing, if not one of the most informative.' How often has one read a usage like this, and imagined one has grasped the writer's meaning, only to realise almost at once that one cannot be sure? In such cases the writer seems to mean that it was not only one of his better works, but, also, one of the most informative. Yet the construction he has used argues that it was certainly one of his better pieces of writing, but it was not in fact very informative: which invites consideration of just how good his better pieces are.

What he should have written was 'I considered this to be one of my better pieces of writing, *as well as* one of the most informative.' The construction he did use is, in logic, susceptible of only one meaning: which is to present the second clause as a negative consideration qualifying the first. This is but one example of how the choice of a certain phrase, in this case a familiar trope, can obscure or distort what a writer is trying to say. It is as if, in this context, the pursuit of elegance itself has trapped the writer into saying the opposite of what he meant. Had he avoided this slightly orotund construction, and stuck to plain words and forms, he would have caused no confusion at all. Another variant of this construction is found in a phrase such as 'it was one of his more obscure, if more thoughtful, remarks', in which for perfect clarity the *if* should be replaced by a *though*.

It was reported that 'a Tory MP left his wife for a woman while she was fighting cancer'. Who was fighting cancer? Was it the wife or the mistress? The sentence demonstrates how easy it is when using pronouns to cause confusion. Choose a pronoun only when the noun it refers to is clear. If it is not, repeat a noun or a proper name rather than cause confusion; or use a formula such as 'the former' or 'the latter'. As I noted earlier, adverbs, if positioned wrongly, also have the power to confuse by creating ambiguity. Not only must they be chosen with care, they must also be positioned with care. Ambiguity will always be avoided if the word is not only chosen correctly, but placed in its best and most logical place in the sentence.

It also helps to avoid ambiguity if one keeps sentences simple and avoids a proliferation of clauses. In her generally well-written book *The Thirties: An Intimate History*, Juliet Gardiner, the social historian, perpetrates this: 'The theatre had entered the blood of Terence Rattigan, the son of a diplomat whose career came to a premature end when he made Princess Elizabeth of Romania pregnant, at prep school, and as a member of Oxford University Dramatic Society (OUDS) he had a one-line part in *Romeo and Juliet* with Peggy Ashcroft and John Gielgud.' One hardly knows where to start in understanding what this means. Most obviously, Rattigan had a father who impregnated a princess while he (the father) was still at prep school; or possibly Rattigan himself achieved this remarkable feat. Either or both of them might also have done it again when at Oxford. We had better leave the complicity or otherwise of Dame Peggy and Sir John out of this.

One reason why English grammar has evolved over the centuries is to avoid ambiguity and to make the structure of language as logical as possible. It is also why grammar should be standardised and the standard adhered to. The ideal condition of a language is one that allows communication without ambiguity or confusion.

Ambiguous and **ambivalent** Something that is *ambiguous* is susceptible of two interpretations. Someone who is *ambivalent* about something finds it hard to settle between two opinions on the question.

Amend and **emend** One *amends* a piece of legislation, or makes *amends* after disobliging another. One *emends* a literary text, usually to restore its original meaning that may have been lost in translation or through a printing error, as in 'the emendation suggested to the line of Horace created a much more sensible meaning'.

American English and missing prepositions There are many phrases or constructions in American English that dispense with prepositions that would be regarded as essential in British English. 'John wrote me that Sunday he graduated school' would in British English be rendered as 'John wrote *to* me that *on* Sunday he graduated *from* school'. In British English 'me' and 'school' are not direct objects, but they seem like them in American English. The direct object of the first clause is an ELLIPSIS – 'a letter' is understood – and 'graduated' is an intransitive verb. Other examples of such phrases, which should not be used in British English, are 'protest the decision' and 'appeal the verdict', whereas a Briton would include 'against' in both phrases.

American spelling As detailed above in the article on Americanisms, this sometimes varies from standard British English in the case of individual words. There are some uniform differences. Americans tend to end words in *-ize* rather than *-ise*. They also use single rather than double letters in past participles of verbs that end in *-l*, such as *traveled*, *leveled*, *shoveled* and *reveled*. In addition, they favour, or rather favor, *-or* endings to words that in British English terminate in *-our*: *color*, not *colour*; *flavour*, rather than *flavor*; *humor* instead of *humour*. Where British English has spellings such as *analogue* and *dialogue*, American has *analog* and *dialog*.

American titles The Americans will call a clergyman 'the Reverend Smith' in a way that we would, or should, not (see the entry on REVEREND). It should also be noted that once an American has held a high elected office it is customary to address him by that title after he has ceased to hold the post – so one says 'President Bush' even though he is no longer in the White House, and does the same with people who have been governors, senators, congressmen, ambassadors and so on.

Americanisms These are wrong only when someone who is not American speaks or writes to other anglophones who are not American, outside America. Throughout this A to Z there are listed many individual examples of a spelling or usage that would be wrong in British or other forms of non-American English. See under AIRPLANE; ALL RIGHT; AMERICAN SPELLING; ANALOG; ANY; APPEAL; ATTORNEY; AUTHORED; AUTOMOBILE; BLOND(E); BREAKOUT; BURGLARIZE; CANDY; CARCASE; CENTENNIAL; CHECK; CHOOSY; COMEDIC; COOKIE; COURTROOM AND COURTHOUSE; CO-WORKER; CURB AND KERB; DOVE AND DIVE; DRAPES; ELEVATOR; FAUCET; FILL OUT; FILMIC; FIT AND FITTED; FLASHLIGHT; GAS; GET; GOOD, USED FOR WELL; GOT AND GOTTEN; HOLIDAYS; HOMETOWN; IMPRACTICABLE; IN THE DAY; JEWELRY; KNOCK UP; LAWMAKERS; LINE; MANEUVER; MATH: MEET AND MEET WITH; MOMENTARILY AND PRESENTLY; MOVIES; NAMED FOR; NORMALCY; OBLIGED AND OBLIGATED; OUSTER; OUTAGE; PARKING LOT; PECKER; PICKY; PURSE AND HANDBAG; QUIT; RAILROAD; RAISE AND RISE; REPETITIOUS AND REPETITIVE; REST ROOM; SIDEWALK; SPECIALTY AND SPECIALITY; STAMMER AND STUTTER; STAND, TAKE THE; STANDOUT; TEAR UP; TESTIFY; TRAIN STATION; WEEKEND. This does not pretend to be an exhaustive list (such a list would also include *diaper* (nappy) and *gurney* (wheeled stretcher), among others), but does cover the words most familiar to speakers of British English.

Just looking at a page of American prose, we can soon tell that this is not English quite as we know it. I do not only mean the interesting typefaces that we and the Americans seem not to have in common: I mean their spelling. This is an aspect of American English that we have so far avoided imitating, at least consciously. None of us, I hope, would dream of writing *honor*, *neighbor* or *color*, or *tire* in reference to a car, or have a *favorite* thing, or think that in Britain we had a Ministry of *Defense*, or imagine that there was such a verb as *practicing* or *licencing*. American orthography departed from ours before either of our nations had properly codified spelling: neither of us is 'right', except in the context of our own cultures. As is noted in the entry on **GOT AND GOTTEN**, the Americans have conservatively stuck to many usages that were common in English at the time of the Founding Fathers but that have long been discarded here by all except a few pedants. The survival and, indeed, flourishing of the **SUBJUNCTIVE MOOD** in American English is the most notable example. Certain words that, to our ears, sound archaic have remained common currency in America: **AUTOMOBILE** rather than *car*, for example; *pitcher*, not *jug*.

The ubiquity of American television programmes, American films and American popular music has ensured that the Americans' way of speaking English constantly impinges upon, or at times seeks to usurp, our own. It seems not to matter how much some of us may affect to despise the Americans for their imperial adventures in the Middle East, their resistance to the notion of man-made global warming, or their determination to set the cause of international cuisine back by several decades; we still seem to be unable to avoid being seduced by aspects of their language. This has been increasingly true during an age of **POLITICAL CORRECTNESS**, a concept invented in America, which developed a vocabulary to complement it from which the British continue to help themselves freely. This is notable in the elimination of gender-specific words – see **ACTOR**.

The Americans are also adept at turning one part of speech into another: 'she sources her ingredients from organic farmers' would be an example, the first use of *source* as a verb being traced to America in 1972. Sometimes the use of an established verb in a solecistic way grates on British ears. It is becoming common in American English to read that somebody who is the spokesman for a particular pressure group **ADVOCATES** on its behalf, rather than that he advocates ideas, policies or suggestions on the group's behalf.

Among and **between** have distinct usages. A person, object or abstract is correctly described as being *between* two things, but *among* several or many: 'he stood between the coast road and the sea' as opposed to 'she sat among the lilies'.

Amongst is an archaic form of **among**, but harmless.

Amoral and **immoral** Eric Partridge, writing in 1947 in *Usage and Abusage*, described his interpretation of the shades of meaning of *unmoral*, *amoral*, *non-moral* and *immoral*. He argues that the first three are synonymous, whereas only the fourth has a distinct meaning ('evil, corrupt, depraved'). *Amoral* he says describes the sense 'not to be judged by a moral criterion; not connected with moral considerations'. Many, and I am among them, will consider that the meaning of this word has subtly altered over the last six or seven decades, to describe a person who has no morals. It is often used not of the evil, corrupt or depraved (though those to whom it is applied may be all those) so much as of those who themselves choose not to be judged by moral criteria. In Partridge's idea, it was another who made the judgements. *Amoral* is today often used of people who, for example, spurn conventional sexual morality, or who will try any ploy short (usually) of downright criminality to advance their careers or prosperity. The dictionary sticks close to Partridge's understanding of the term, but the last revision of the definition is 1989, and I suspect the meaning has altered since then. *Immoral* has weakened accordingly, though should still be used to describe someone aware of moral conduct who chooses, often selectively, not to abide by it.

Amount There is an *amount* of one commodity. When there is a multiplicity, there is a *number*. So one writes that 'he lost a large amount of money' but 'a large number of people attended the meeting'. 'A large amount of people' is a solecism, since things of any quantity that can be counted beyond one must be described as a number.

Amplificatio is the term applied to the passage in a classical argument in which factual background is developed.

Anacoluthon (plural *anacolutha*) is the use of two or more inconsistent constructions in the same sentence. Shakespeare used this from time to time as a stylistic device, such as in King Lear's remark that 'I will have such revenges on you both, That all the world shall – I will do such things . . .' Others perpetrate *anacolutha* by accident, through ignorance, creating a sense of grammatical incoherence.

Analog and **analogue** See AMERICAN SPELLING.

Anaphora is the repetition of the same word or phrase in successive clauses: 'We shall fight on the beaches, we shall fight on the landing grounds, we shall fight in the fields and in the streets. . . .' It can seem mannered or clichéd, so should be used with care.

And is a COORDINATING CONJUNCTION, linking two coordinate clauses that would stand just as well as independent sentences: 'I got up and I went to the bathroom.' Sentences that begin with *and* (or *but*) are not wrong but (except in circumstances where they are deployed deliberately for rhetorical effect) unhappy, for they suggest incompleteness, and refer to sentences preceding that have, presumably, been inadequately completed. Sometimes *and* replaces *to* in a sentence where a verb should be followed by an infinitive: 'I shall try and see you tomorrow' instead of 'I shall try to see you tomorrow'. In formal English, the INFINITIVE is preferable to the CONJUNCTION.

Anglo-Saxon words The Fowlers, and forty years after them George Orwell, argued in favour of the (usually short) Anglo-Saxon word rather than the (often longer) Romance or classical one in good writing. Some people feel they have to use a long word where a short one will do. We have all seen writers do this out of a sense of insecurity: they feel that by saying 'masticate' rather than 'chew' they are confirming a superior intellect or status. The odd long word never harmed anyone: but if one uses a string of them, or lards one's prose with them from beginning to end, one becomes tiresome – even if the words are all so well-known that the reader does not need to pause after each one and look it up in a dictionary. If a writer has to send his readers – and they are intelligent readers – to the dictionary more than very occasionally, then he has failed. The journey should be necessary only if the prose is dealing with a specialist subject, and one is reading it specifically with a view to being educated in that subject. If the topic is of everyday interest, there is no excuse for dragging out words that even sophisticates will have to look up, other than that the writer has decided to try to draw attention to himself.

Most plain monosyllables have polysyllables longing to step into their shoes. Poor stylists cannot bear to use verbs such as *walk, try, wash, eat, tell, ask, see, use, start* or *show* when they may (at no extra cost except to their credibility) use *perambulate, essay, ablute, consume, communicate, demand, perceive, utilise, commence* or *demonstrate*. It is useful to have a store of synonyms to avoid repeating words within a few sentences of each other; but if there is no risk of repetition, stick to simple words. Some elaborate usages can also be confusing. If one hears a man say to his wife 'I understand you are ill', is he telling her that he comprehends the nature of her predicament, or is he simply using the long word as a substitute for 'hear'? It is probably the latter, but other instances of the use of the verb may be more deeply ambiguous. Plain words often help plain meaning. Orwell himself described 'the inflated style' – language stuffed with Latin and Greek – as 'a kind of euphemism'.

Annex and **annexe** The former is the verb, the latter the noun: 'Hitler moved in to annex Austria' means he added it to the existing territories of the Third Reich. 'An annexe was built on to the school' means that the institution in question added a new building to its existing property.

Annoy is not a synonym for AGGRAVATE.

Annunciate and **enunciate** *Annunciate* is an antique way of saying 'announce': the dictionary notes no usage of it since 1883. However, it may be confused with *enunciate*, which means to state publicly, proclaim or announce. A mistake was made in a BBC press release of 4 March 2012, which said that members of the Scottish National Party would 'annunciate the case for independence'.

Anorectic and **anorexic** are both adjectives that have become nouns, the latter a century ago. The dictionary gives both words, as adjectives and as nouns relating to persons with an eating disorder, as correct and interchangeable. *Anorexic* is the more common.

Anticipate and **expect** The old joke is that 'to anticipate marriage is not the same as to expect it'. Yet these days one almost always sees *anticipate* used, even by people with expensive educations, as a synonym for *expect*, which it is not. To *anticipate* marriage is to begin to behave before the wedding in the way that one would take for granted after it – and all that that entails. Similarly, if an heir apparent starts to assume the prerogatives of the king while that king still reigns, he is *anticipating* regal authority. Those who say 'I anticipate I shall arrive at 4 p.m.' simply mean 'I expect I shall arrive at 4 p.m.' *Anticipate* in its correct form, signifying doing something before the appointed time, has for 500 years been a precise and useful verb, and it needs to be preserved.

Antisocial See UNSOCIAL AND UNSOCIABLE.

Antithesis is an opposition or contrast of ideas presented in successive clauses or sentences: 'As I became richer, my brother became poorer.' As with other forms of contrast, such as PARADOX and IRONY, antithesis is useful in creating insight and vividness, but should not be overused.

Antonym is a word that is the exact opposite of another: *dead* is the antonym of *alive*; *antonym* is the antonym of SYNONYM.

Anxious and **eager** *Anxious* means 'troubled or uneasy in mind about some uncertain event; being in painful or disturbing suspense; concerned, solicitous'. Do not confuse it with *eager*, an adjective that displays keenness to do something, but without the sense of uncertainty, worry or suspense.

Any In usages such as 'I don't think that helps any' this pronoun is an Americanism. In British English we would say 'I don't think that helps *at all*'. When used as a conventional pronoun, it may be singular or plural: 'Are any of you coming?' or 'Any of these is suitable.' In the latter example, 'one' is an ELLIPSIS after 'any'. *Any* cannot be followed by a negative. Instead of writing 'any of you will be unable to take part', write 'none of you will be able to take part'. *Any* may be singular or plural: 'Is any man here equal to the task?' is no more or less correct than 'Are any men here equal to the task?'

Any, compounds of At the time that the Fowlers were seeking to codify English usage a century ago one of the changes in progress was the compounding of words beginning with *any-*. By 1926 H. W. Fowler had decreed that 'anybody, anything, anyhow, anywhere, anywhen, anywhither are already single words', as was the adverb *anywise*. There was, he pointed out, no such word as *anyrate* and we should be compelled to agree with him. Fowler essentially conceded that *anyway* had become one word, except in the sense that one would use it as two words today ('I cannot see any way out of this problem'). A similar rule applies to *anyone*. What, though, are we to make of *anymore*? This word is not listed in the dictionary. It is slang and not suitable for formal writing. 'I do not want any more cabbage' shows the correct usage as two words. The colloquial phrases 'I don't live there anymore' or 'she isn't my friend anymore' would in formal English be 'I no longer live there' or 'she is no longer my friend'. *Now* is also an acceptable alternative – 'I don't live there now'.

Anybody, anyone, anything, anywhere All compounds of *any* are singular nouns and may not be plural. 'Is anyone there?', 'anybody is entitled to help', 'anything is possible' and 'anywhere is better than here'. The same stricture about the use of the negative that applies to *any* also applies to its compounds. Use *nobody, none* (or *no one*), *nothing* or *nowhere* instead.

Anymore and **anyway** are adverbs – 'I don't love him anymore' and 'I wouldn't help her anyway'. The adjectival phrases *any more* and *any way* are distinct from the adverbs: as in 'Do you have any more tea?' and 'Is there any way in which I could help?', and they should not be confused. *Anymore* is colloquial (see ANY, COMPOUNDS OF).

Apophthegm is a pithy saying that embodies an important truth in a few words, and which may often be used to clinch an argument; examples are 'the wages of sin is death', Carlyle's 'speech is silvern: silence is golden' or the same author's 'the history of the world is but the biography of great men'. It is also the rhetorical term given to the 'soundbite' that concludes a classical argument.

Aposiopesis is from the Greek for 'falling silent': it is when something is deliberately left unsaid, either because the speaker is so overcome with emotion, or because he wishes to create an effect by leaving the interpretation or completion of a thought to the reader or listener. It is often represented in writing by the punctuation . . .

Apostrophe has a rhetorical meaning that is unrelated to the use of the term for a punctuation mark. It means an exclamatory remark addressed to some specific person or persons, whether present or not. Ozymandias's 'Look on my works, ye Mighty, and despair!' is apostrophic.

Apostrophe, in punctuation This punctuation mark is one of the most essential indicators of meaning in our grammar. The apostrophe at the end of a noun or proper name and before an *s* signifies possession: 'Mr Smith's cat', 'the woman's room', 'the child's toy'. It is also used in contractions such as *don't, won't, shouldn't* and *can't* to indicate a missing letter or letters. Contractions are usual in speech, in newspaper interviews, in direct quotations and in informal writing. Before using them in a piece of formal writing, bear in mind how they will change the tone of the prose to make it more casual.

The apostrophe is never to be used to signify plurals – the so-called grocer's or greengrocer's apostrophe (as in 'apple's,

50p a pound'). Care is also required in using the apostrophe with nouns that have unconventional plurals. One occasionally sees 'childrens' toys' when the writer intended 'children's toys'. 'Children' is already plural, which is why the apostrophe must precede the *s*. A variant of the grocer's apostrophe is to take a word ending in *s* and make it plural by adding another *s* after an apostrophe – for example, 'a brass, some brass's', or 'Mr Harris, the Harris's' instead of the correct 'some brasses' and 'the Harrises'. (Similarly, one keeps up with the Joneses.) It has become a near-ubiquitous fault of punctuation and perhaps the most common grammatical error in our language. It is a rare day, as one walks or drives around Britain, that one does not encounter this error on a handwritten (or, occasionally, printed) notice somewhere. A variety of this irritating error is the insertion of the apostrophe in possessive pronouns such as *theirs*, *hers* and *yours*. The most frequent offender is *it's*, no doubt because of the existence of the identical, and legitimate, contraction: *it's* when used correctly is the contraction of *it is* or *it has*, and must be used in no other context. One sees this solecism in newspapers, on signs and even on menus – 'lamb in it's own jus'.

Variations of this horror include 'mind you're language' or its equally objectionable converse 'let me know when your here'. Sometimes the contraction *they're* is confused with the possessive *their*, as in 'we went to they're house'.

Plurals require no apostrophe, though I would make one exception for the sake of clarity: which is when one is writing about individual letters of the alphabet. If one is writing about examination grades one has no difficulty with *Bs*, *Cs* or *Ds*; but when writing about *As* one may be thought to be writing about the word *as*. So, for consistency's sake, I would counsel in favour of the usage *A's*, *B's*, *C's* and so on, to avoid ambiguities concerning *as*, *is* and *us*. This sensible convention is common in many newspapers.

Some writers feel that when they are using this shortened form to denote a relationship between people or objects, the more formal *of*, the possessive is also needed: as in 'a friend of Tony's'. This is wrong, for it invites the question 'A friend of Tony's what?' All one needs to write is 'a friend of Tony'. Onions charitably points out that the origins of this are in an ELLIPSIS, signifying that what is imagined is a full phrase like 'a friend from among Tony's friends'. This seems unwarranted now when the possessive form with *of* is correct enough. The error was included in a feature in the august *New Yorker* magazine of 1 October 2012: 'I spent most of an afternoon in Salt Lake City with . . . a friend of Mitt Romney's'. It is no more correct in American English than in British. One correctly says 'I went to the dry-cleaner's', the word *shop* being assumed; or 'I spent the day at Johnnie's', the word *house* being assumed. In a phrase such as 'she was eight months' pregnant' the apostrophe is superfluous, 'eight months' being adjectival. It is correct in the phrase 'it was two years' work', for it means 'the work of two years'.

Apostrophes may sometimes be confused with single QUOTATION MARKS: see the entry on that subject.

Appeal requires a preposition. Americans may *appeal* a verdict, or *appeal* a decision, but in Britain we *appeal against* them.

Apposite and **opposite** If something is *apposite* it is appropriate or suitable – 'his address at the memorial service was entirely apposite'. It should not be confused with *opposite*, which means contrary in position to someone or something else – 'their house was opposite the park'.

Appreciate as a transitive verb means to form an estimate of the worth or quality of something. It does not mean to *understand*, or *recognise*, or *admire*, or even *be aware of*. As an intransitive it means to grow in value or worth, as in 'our investments have appreciated significantly this year'. When someone says 'I appreciate that' in response to a criticism he means 'I understand it' or, more usually, 'I understand you'. As an expression of gratitude – 'I appreciate what you have done for me' – it is acceptable, since it means one is forming an estimate (probably a high one) of the value of the services rendered. However, when someone says 'you will appreciate that we are unable to give any such undertaking' the usage is wrong: he means 'whether you like it or not, we cannot promise that'. One of the many abuses of this otherwise precise verb is in the service of aggressive EUPHEMISM.

Appropriate See POLITICAL CORRECTNESS.

Apse The adjective from this noun, describing a semicircular east end of a church, is *apsidal*.

Arab is the term for the breed of horse. Use *Arabian* for a person or as a geographical or a cultural adjective. *Arabic* is the language.

Arbitrator and **mediator** These two offices have similar but subtly different roles. An *arbitrator* will usually hear both sides of an argument and decide which party is in the right, sometimes making an award to the injured party at the expense of the other. A *mediator* has a simpler task, which is to reconcile two parties.

Archaisms It is always best not to write self-consciously, or to use language that draws attention to itself, for such writing detracts from the sense of what one is saying. Larding prose with words such as *betwixt*, or spellings such as *connexion*, will set lights flashing in the minds of your readers. Some usages are on the way out, such as certain words that end in *-f* taking *-ves* in the plural, and their use now must be a question of judgement by the writer about the state of the idiom. *Loaves*, *knives*, *calves* and *hooves* are quite normal: but there must be a question mark over *handkerchieves* and *wharves*. Some phrases now seem archaic, such as the simple expression 'I would not' for 'I didn't want to', or Rupert Brooke's 'would I were' for 'I wish I were'. Others smell of Edwardian bureaucracy, such as 'whence he came' or 'I had the occasion to'. Some would argue that the use of the SUBJUNCTIVE MOOD is archaic, or the use of WHOM: others, including me, would argue they are wrong, and that the fight continues – not to preserve antiques, but to preserve useful distinctions in our grammar. Usages that to some are archaic are to others simply formal, with a proper place in formal prose: such as the conjunction *whereas*. There is, however, an archaic, or pretentious, ring these days to sentences with inverted word order, such as 'of that there can be no doubt' for 'there can be no doubt of that'.

Area is a word that has, or should have, a specific geographical significance, but which has become a catch-all term to refer to a subject or a topic, or to indicate metaphorical approximation. This leads to imprecision and CLICHÉ. 'This used to be a nice area' illustrates a legitimate usage. 'Teaching English wasn't an area I wished to specialise in' is not. Nor is 'growing roses is an area I know a lot about'. And before saying or writing 'the price was in the area [or, indeed, 'the region'] of £50,000', prefer or consider the simpler 'the price was around £50,000'.

Arguably is one of those adverbs attached to no verb in particular that serves as a FILLER to start a sentence. Sometimes it is utterly unnecessary, as in 'Arguably, we should take the coast road.' If, however, one is expecting a serious argument about which road to take, then it would be better phrased as 'There is an argument for taking the coast road.' The word has become a cliché and should be treated accordingly.

Armed Forces, writing to or addressing Service ranks are self-explanatory and seem to cause trouble only when interfered with by other titles. Officers reaching the rank of lieutenant-general are usually knighted, at which point Major-General John Smith becomes Lieutenant-General Sir John Smith. Some senior generals receive peerages, at which point General Sir John Smith becomes General Lord Smith. The same applies to the two other services – Air Marshal Sir John Smith, Admiral Lord Smith and so on. Chaplains and padres would be styled Major the Reverend John Smith, or Squadron Leader the Reverend John Smith. In civilian life only officers of field rank or above would normally continue to use their military titles – though it is rare these days for anyone below the very highest ranks, who technically never retire, to do so. Field rank begins with majors, though captains holding an adjutant's appointment qualify. Should you be asked to address, or to write to, any civilian as Lieutenant Smith he is certainly an impostor of some sort, and you would be well advised to call the police. When writing about private soldiers in certain regiments, be aware that some of them are not called 'Private' – a Royal Engineer is a Sapper, an artilleryman is a Gunner, and a corporal in the artillery is a Bombardier. For a full list see MILITARY TITLES. When writing to a senior officer, always write 'Dear General Smith' or 'Dear Admiral Jones', not just 'Dear General' or 'Dear Admiral'.

Around and **round** To an extent these two words, when used as prepositions, have become interchangeable. In fact, *around* is more idiomatic in America and *round* in British English: so an American would say 'I drove around the block' whereas a Briton would say 'I walked round the garden'. In both countries writers would use *around* to indicate something approximate – 'she looked around 40 years old' or 'I should arrive around nine o'clock'. There are certain idiomatic uses where *around* is necessary, and conveys a distinction. There is no difference between 'I turned round' and 'I turned around', but 'I looked round' means 'I turned my head to look behind me' whereas 'I looked around' means that I inspected a place, as in 'I looked around the shop' or 'I looked around the village'. The adjective is always *round*.

Articles, definite and **indefinite** See A AND AN and THE.

Artiste, which for much of the twentieth century was used to describe a performer, is now regarded as rather arch. Choose *actor*, *singer*, *dancer*, and so on or, although it is ambiguous given its normal usage now to describe a painter or sculptor, *artist*.

As, used as a conjunction *As* and SO are a morass of potential difficulties. *So* would be regarded by pedants as correct and *as* wrong, in the following examples – 'I am not *so* stupid as that' or 'it isn't *so* bad as all that' – because of the emphasis that *so* correctly places on the adjective. During the twentieth century the colloquial usage of *as* became more frequent: I am not *as* stupid as that'. It cannot now be considered incorrect, but pedants will stick to *so*. *As* is correctly used for straightforward similes, for example 'she thought it was *as* cold as the Arctic'. The distinction between the phrases *as far as* and *so far as* is simple: the former is used in positive expressions and the latter after a negative. Therefore one would write 'the police jurisdiction ran *as far as* the border', but 'his illness had not advanced *so far as* I had feared'.

Care must be taken when using *as* to introduce a clause. It is often a sloppy substitute for a more exact conjunction such as *since*, *because*, *on account of*, *for* or *while*, or even the more formal and archaic *whereas*, whose currency has not died out completely. *As* works in the following example, where it is used to introduce a statement consequent upon the meaning of the main clause: 'she was pleased she had taken her macintosh, as it began to rain'. However, were the sentence to read 'she was pleased she had taken her macintosh, but later was annoyed, as it was stolen from the restaurant', it would be technically ungrammatical. The *as* should refer back to the main clause ('she was pleased she had taken her macintosh') but does not: it refers to the subordinate one ('but later was annoyed'). Were the subordinate one removed it would read 'she was pleased she had taken her macintosh as it was stolen from the restaurant', which would be nonsense. A recasting would avoid this problem, possibly just by removing *as* and replacing it with a colon. It would be better still, though, to be more precise with conjunctions, rather than use *as* ambiguously.

Here are examples of how to increase precision:

'The girl cried as she had hurt herself.' Use *because*.

'The woman slept as the house was burgled.' Use *while*.

'As you are here, let's have a drink.' Use *since*.

'They knew each other as they were related.' Use *on account of their being*, or *because*.

'He sold everything he had to buy the house, as it was what he had always wanted.' Use *for*, replacing the preceding comma with a colon.

As, used as a pronoun *As* can be used as a pronoun when it refers to a verbal idea (or ideas) rather than to a noun: for example, when one writes 'they go to the opera and dine afterwards, as one does', that is correct. *As* is not a relative pronoun and it is not a synonym for *such as*. 'The car as was coming down the hill' is a shocking vulgarism. 'The standard of dress was superb, as was prevalent during the *belle époque*' is an illiteracy: it should be '*such as* was prevalent'. The sentence 'He resented the fact that he had no power to refuse the summons, *as* his colleagues had', is wrong. It is also ambiguous: do his colleagues have the power to refuse, or have they already refused? If the second clause began '*such as* his colleagues had' it would be correct: the *such* can refer only to *power*.

As, used in comparisons When using a well-known simile always retain the opening *as*, which colloquially is often omitted: be sure to write 'that man is as rich as Croesus' rather than 'that man is rich as Croesus'. However, *as* is sometimes used redundantly; a person is not 'equally as entitled to help as another', but just 'equally entitled to help'. See also THAN and LIKE.

As, used pointlessly Some combinations of *as* and other words are simply pointless – 'I have no idea as to why he came' or 'she has not as yet signalled her intentions' – or preposterous – 'could this be done as per the regulations'. *As to*, which in bad writing precedes not only *why* but also *how*, *when*, *which*, *where* and *whether*, is entirely redundant; *yet* does not require *as* to precede it; and *as per* belongs in a late Victorian lexicon of counting-house argot. Some writers also feel the need to place *as* pleonastically in front of certain phrases, exemplified by this extract from a magazine in January 2010: 'In 1947 the Palestinians numbered 1.2 million as compared with 600,000 Jews.' One of the more promiscuous abuses of *as* is as a synonym for *because*: 'I could not come as I was busy elsewhere'. This should be regarded as a colloquialism and not suitable for formal writing. See also AS TO and AS YET.

As a matter of fact is almost inevitably used pointlessly. Remove it from any sentence where you see it written and you will notice the sense does not change.

As if and **as though** See LIKE.

As to Sir Kingsley Amis noted the habit of some people in authority – such as policemen – to insert the redundant words *as to* before almost any question. 'We want to know as to why you were in the vicinity of the bank on the evening in question', 'I simply have no idea as to why he came' and 'perhaps you could tell me as to whether you might be able to tell us your whereabouts last Tuesday night' give a flavour of the problem.

As yet is almost always redundant, except in certain circumstances where an action is expected but has not, yet, happened: however, the fact of its not happening will usually be obvious, bringing further into question the use of this little phrase. 'She has not as yet signalled her intentions' loses nothing without 'as yet'.

Ascent and **assent** *Ascent* is a move upwards; *assent* is agreement.

Assertion See FACT AND ASSERTION.

Assonance This is the repetition of vowel sounds within a phrase – for example, 'sea-green incorruptible' – as opposed to ALLITERATION, which is the repetition of the sounds that begin them. It is rather self-conscious and therefore, like alliteration, unless used for deliberately poetic effect may well detract from the meaning of what is being written.

Assume and **presume** The distinction between *assume* and *presume* seems to have been lost altogether. *Assume* retains its difference in sentences such as 'he assumed a new identity' or 'the boy assumed the position'. Yet few people now sense the difference between 'I *assume* you will be joining us for dinner' and 'I *presume* you will be joining us'. More people instinctively understand the meaning of the noun *presumption*, and its inherent insolence and sense of improper entitlement: 'he had the presumption to address me by my Christian name' makes it clear that the other party should have said 'Mr Smith' rather than 'John'. That he presumed to do otherwise demonstrates the force of the verb. It is, as the dictionary defines it, 'to take upon oneself; to undertake without adequate authority or permission'. A subsequent definition uses an idiom that is popular today: 'to take the liberty'. *Presume* means that one takes it upon oneself to do something or to act in a way that one simply does not have the right to act in. So if one *presumes* another is coming to dinner it means that the host has absolutely no right to expect that person to accept the invitation, perhaps because the two of them are not even acquainted. If John Smith *assumes* someone is dining with him it is because he has issued the invitation to someone with whom he is on friendly terms, but has had no confirmation that the person is coming. It is to take something for granted, without any hint of presumption, because one has a right to take it for granted. *Assume* has other current meanings, as I have indicated above, and which the dictionary specifies – but it is only in this context that it and *presume* are confused.

Assure, ensure and **insure** These three verbs may confuse the unwary. The main meaning of *assure* is 'to give confidence to, to confirm or encourage': 'I assure you that this is so'. It may also mean 'to make (a person) sure or certain' of or about something: 'I assure you he will never be out of my sight'. Though *assure* has been used in the past as a synonym for *ensure*, the dictionary cites no incidence since 1878; and there is no excuse for confusing it with *insure*, except in the phrase *life insurance*, which is sometimes and quite correctly rendered as *life assurance*: one's life is insured, providing assurance in the process.

Ensure means 'to make a thing sure for or to a person; to secure' or 'to make certain the occurrence or arrival of an event or the attainment of a result'. Therefore one would say 'I have ensured we shall have plenty of food for Christmas' or 'getting a good degree should ensure you can find a decent job'.

Assure now has a precise commercial meaning, which is 'to secure the payment of a sum of money in the event of loss of or damage to property . . . or of the death or disablement of a person, in consideration of the payment of a premium and observance of certain conditions' (*OED*). However, we would say 'he insured his car against fire and theft' or he 'insured' his life – even if in the latter case he held a life assurance policy.

Asyndeton is an absence of conjunctions: such as in 'wee, sleekit, cow'rin, tim'rous beastie!'

At least is a phrase that, as with all adverbial phrases, must be placed with care in any sentence in which it is used. The difference between 'he hoped he would at least be invited in', 'he hoped he at least would be invited in' and 'he at least hoped he would be invited in' illustrates the point. In the first sentence there are several possibilities of what might happen, the least of which is that he might be invited in. In the second, he is part of a group of several, and he aspires to being invited in even if the others cannot hope to be. In the third there is an ambiguity; in one meaning, others in the group may have abandoned all hope of being invited in but he, at least or distinct from the others, has that hope. In the other meaning he is at least hoping to be asked in – he could have despaired altogether, but things have not yet reached that pass. See also EVEN.

At the end of the day When somebody introduces a statement with the FILLER 'at the end of the day', is it ever necessary? Would it even be necessary if the statement were being made as the sun was setting, or midnight approaching, let alone if it were just after breakfast? What does its use tell you about the speaker's or writer's thought processes?

At this moment in time is an abomination uttered by people who mean *now*.

-athon endings The vogue for marathon contests of endurance – be it dancing, reading aloud from Shakespeare or sitting in a bath full of baked beans – has led to an epidemic of nouns ending in *-athon* – such as *bikeathon*, *swimathon* and the ubiquitous *telethon*. The conceit has now become a cliché, so think carefully before adding to the pile.

Attendee Someone who attends something is an *attender*, though *attendee* has become the common usage. See also -EE ENDINGS.

Attorney is an American term for *lawyer*. It has only specialised usages in British English, such as *Attorney-General* or *power of attorney*.

Atypical and **untypical** appear to be synonymous. If there is any distinction it is that the former has an entirely earnest usage and the latter often a humorous one; and that the former is usually concrete and the latter abstract. *Untypical* often appears – including in several examples in the dictionary – in the rather arch usage 'it was not untypical'. In Greek, the prefix *a-* negates the adjective it precedes, so to say that 'the engraving was atypical of the period' means it was not typical at all; similarly, 'the writing was atypical of Chaucer' or 'the wine was atypical of the vintage'. However, one would better say that 'the weather was untypical for the time of year', or 'his mood untypical of his personality' or 'the calm was untypical of central London', referring to an abstract.

Aural and oral *Aural* is an adjective of listening; it must not be confused with its HOMOPHONE *oral*, which is an adjective of speaking. In an *aural* test one has to listen; in an *oral* test one has to speak, and the *oral* tradition is when stories are passed down from one generation to the next by those who know them telling them. If someone has a complaint in the ear it is an *aural* infection; in the mouth it is an *oral* one.

Authored The *OED* finds a lone use of *authored* in Chapman's *Homer* (Keats's beloved book) in 1596, after which it becomes obsolete until resurrected in America in the mid-twentieth century. (The dictionary still does not believe it is used over here, but that, I fear, will soon have to change.) We on this side of the Atlantic must decide whether we wish to engage in this American habit of making nouns into verbs, or not. Since there appear to be perfectly good existing verbs for the new ones minted by our American cousins I feel we can continue to resist. There is nothing remotely wrong with *written*.

Authoritative and **authoritarian** These two similar words have dissimilar meanings. An *authoritative* man is one who has 'due or acknowledged authority' and is 'entitled to obedience or acceptance'. The adjective may also be applied to evidence of some description, as in 'the book gives an authoritative account of the war', which suggests the book is based on properly verified research and covers all relevant subjects. One who is *authoritarian*, however, is one 'favourable to the principle of authority as opposed to that of individual freedom': in other words, dictatorial. Therefore we might say that 'Stalin had an authoritarian approach to dissent'. The two adjectives were confused in the Wikipedia entry for Jack Hawkins, the 1950s matinee idol, as it stood on 3 September 2012: 'Hawkins' popularity declined with a series of less successful movies, but his authoritarian presence meant he was always in demand.' What the writer meant was that Hawkins's demeanour and popularity as an actor gave him an *authoritative* presence.

Automobile This is an Americanism for *car*, the Americans having stuck conservatively to a European word from the late nineteenth century that has long since passed out of vogue in British English. See AMERICAN ENGLISH.

Auxiliary verbs These attach themselves to main verbs to provide variations of tense ('he *has* gone' or 'we *shall* overcome'), to describe capability, compulsion or permission ('he *can* swim', 'he *must* swim' or 'he *may* swim'), possibility ('he *might* swim') or the passive voice ('he *was* beaten', 'she *will be* found', 'they *were being* overlooked'). Otto Jespersen, quoted extensively by Eric Partridge, pointed out the peculiar idiomatic senses of the negative with auxiliary verbs, such as *must*, *may* and *do*. He noted that the opposite of telling someone he *must not* do something was that he *may* do something else. This is logical, given that *must* is an absolute term. There is a difference between saying 'you *mustn't* swim when the flags are flying, but you *may* swim when they are not' and 'you *must* swim when they are not'. Jespersen also notes the idiomatic usage of a negated *may* to imply, ironically enough, possibility: 'I may not be the brightest light on the seafront, but I do know that' and so on. See also SHALL AND WILL.

Auxiliary verbs and **adverbs** Placing adverbs becomes more complicated when auxiliaries are present. See ADVERBS, POSITIONING OF.

Avenge and **revenge** One *avenges* a wrong done to another, but takes *revenge* upon another for a wrong done to oneself. So: 'He avenged the terrible injustice done to his father' but 'she took her revenge upon the man who had attacked her'. There is a reflexive verb 'to revenge oneself' upon another, but one cannot avenge oneself.

Averse See ADVERSE AND AVERSE.

Avert and **avoid** *Avert* is not to be confused with *avoid*, which means 'to keep away from' or 'to have nothing to do with'. *Avert* has two current meanings. It is something one does to one's own eyes or gaze, turning them or it from a spectacle; or it means to prevent or ward off, as in 'avert disaster'. Phrases such as 'she averted his eyes' are solecistic, and should read 'she avoided his eyes' or, better, 'his gaze'.

Await, wait and **wait for** Because of the difference between TRANSITIVE and INTRANSITIVE forms there may be confusion with *await*, *wait* and *wait for*. *Wait* is intransitive: 'I waited three days for the letter to come'. *Await* and its synonym *wait* for are transitive: 'I await your reply with interest' or 'let us wait for the dawn'. One never writes 'I awaited in the rain', or 'a terrible fate waited him', or any similar barbarisms.

Awake, **awaken** and **wake up** *Awake* is INTRANSITIVE, *awaken* TRANSITIVE. So: 'I awake from a deep sleep' but 'I awaken him from a deep sleep'. The past participles are distinct and must not be confused: 'I awoke from a deep sleep', but 'I awakened him from a deep sleep'. There is a sense that these forms are becoming archaic, or are at least rather formal. It is more usual to hear and see these days 'I wake up' and 'I woke up', and 'I wake him up' and 'I woke him up'.The form in which *awaken* is still commonly used these days is metaphorical – 'the book awakened his interest in the classics' or 'the sight of you awakens deep feelings in me'. *Awake* is also an adjective – 'the children were awake'.

Awhile is an adverb that means doing something *for* a period of time, usually a short one – 'let's halt awhile!' It must not be confused with the article and noun *a while*, which just means a period of time: as in 'I saw them a while ago' or 'I had to wait a while for him' or 'I had to wait for a while at the bus stop'. It would be illiterate to write 'I saw them awhile ago', and so on.

B

Back in the day See IN THE DAY.

Bacterium is single, *bacteria* are plural.

Bad Although the use of ADJECTIVES for ADVERBS is frequently accidental, the use of 'bad' for 'badly' seems in recent years to have become a deliberate fashion. Many people would now employ demotic usages such as 'it hurts bad' and 'I want it real bad' without any sense that they were wrong. See also GOOD, USED FOR *well*.

Bail out and **bale out** are ripe for confusion. The former is used to describe the act of scooping up water in a container and throwing it overboard to stop a boat from sinking; this, according to the dictionary, derives from the name of the buckets – bails – that were used for the purpose. It is often misspelt *bale out* in this context. *Bail out* is also correctly used to describe the provision of financial assistance. This term became common during the banking crisis of 2008–09, but the dictionary cites a usage as early as 1916. Given that another use of the verb *bail* dates back to 1587, and means 'to be security or pledge for, to secure, guarantee, protect', one could argue that this usage has a pedigree of over 400 years. It is common in the phrase 'stand bail', when a third party puts up a financial surety to guarantee an accused person will return to court for trial. *Bale out* is what RAF types did when their Lancaster bomber had been so badly hit by enemy fire that it would crash. In the case of the departing airman, the verb was spelt thus, according to the dictionary, 'as if the action were that of letting a bundle through a trapdoor'.

Baited See BATED AND BAITED.

Bale out See BAIL OUT above.

Balk and **baulk** The former is a noun meaning a ridge or a stumbling block; it was originally an agricultural term referring to a ridge left unploughed. The word is most commonly used today to describe the area at the ends of a snooker or billiards table, where it is spelt *baulk* (in American *balk*). *Baulk* is also a verb that means to object to doing something, or to show reluctance to do it – 'he baulked at eating a plate of tripe'.

Ballot This word is not synonymous with a vote, as in the CATACHRESIS 'they cast their ballots'. A *ballot* is a plebiscite, a poll or an election.

Barbaric and **barbarous** Once almost synonymous, these two adjectives now serve distinct purposes. *Barbaric*, which simply used to mean uncivilised, is now used to describe savagery or ill-treatment on an extreme scale: therefore we would say that 'Stalin's starvation of the Kulaks was barbaric' or 'the Nazis undertook a barbaric persecution of the Jews'. *Barbarous* has become almost amusing in its applications, and tends to refer to a lack of manners, learning or erudition. 'His decision to wear brown shoes was barbarous', or 'the way she spoke was barbarous', or 'it was barbarous the way he played the piano so badly' give a fair indication of how the word is used today.

Bare and **bear** *Bare* is raw or naked; *bear* is an animal or a verb meaning to carry, literally or metaphorically.

Baronesses, writing to or addressing Life peeresses in the United Kingdom are always baronesses (though that is not compulsory; there is nothing in law to prevent a life peeress, or a life peer for that matter, being given any other rank in the peerage). Unlike lords who are barons but are not referred to as such, baronesses are. So if Mary Smith, after a lifetime of devoted public service, receives a life peerage and becomes Baroness Smith of Brighton, that is how we would refer to her in the first instance in a piece of writing. Subsequently she would be Lady Smith. She is never Lady Mary Smith. She would be addressed in person as 'Lady Smith', but would be 'Baroness Smith' on an envelope and 'Dear Lady Smith' in a letter.

Baronets, writing to or addressing Baronets are not knights, even though they share the same title of *Sir*. Baronets are baronets, and their titles are heritable. Sir John Smith, 4th Bt, on his death may be succeeded by his son Charles, who becomes Sir Charles Smith, 5th Bt. The baronet's wife is Lady Smith, unless she is the daughter of a duke, a marquess or an earl, in which case she may choose to be styled Lady Mary Smith. Baronets and their wives should be addressed as 'Dear Sir John' or 'Dear Lady Smith', the letters ending 'Yours sincerely'. In person, one would say 'Sir John' or 'Lady Smith'.

Basically This word is now hardly ever used in its literal meaning, but is rather used pointlessly as a FILLER, or a form of punctuation, as in remarks such as 'I basically thought he was an idiot' or 'basically, I don't want to go there'. Its literal usage, as a synonym for *fundamentally*, means that if one wrote 'I thought he was basically an idiot' it would be acceptable. However, the *OED* lists the first use of the word as 1903, which suggests the English language survived for a very long time without this particular word. If a writer needs to use it at all, it should be with extreme care.

Bated and **baited** That prime work of modern literature, *Harry Potter and the Prisoner of Azkaban*, includes the phrase 'the whole common room listened with baited breath'. A mousetrap or a fish-hook may be *baited*; but one's breath is *bated*, a contraction of abated, or shortened.

Bathos is anticlimax. 'He came; he saw; he had a cup of tea' is bathetic.

Battle This is an intransitive verb and its correct use requires a preposition. One does not *battle* cancer, one *battles against* it, or possibly *with* it.

Baulk See BALK AND BAULK.

Be The verb *to be* is the fundamental verb. It is INTRANSITIVE and has no object. It describes a subject of a sentence: 'I am tired', 'you are angry', 'he, she or it is lost', and so on. Having no object, it must take a nominative pronoun such as *I*, *you* (singular and plural), *he*, *she*, *we* or *they*, which in speech (and not just demotic speech) it hardly ever does. It is second nature for us to say 'that's her', 'it's him' or 'it's me', and in speaking or writing dialogue it would now sound pompous or unreal to say anything else. However, the correct forms are 'that is she', 'it is he' and 'it is I'. In formal writing, in contexts longer than those simple statements, one should always stick to the correct form. 'It was them who were there at the time' must be 'it was they who were there at the time'; similarly, write 'it was I who sent for you', 'it will be she who will see you' or 'it is they who must be held to account for this', rather than be seduced into any barbarism. See also SUBJUNCTIVE.

Bearing in mind An example of a participle serving as a conjunction, as in 'they should be here by evening, bearing in mind the traffic'. See also CONJUNCTIONS.

Beat and **beaten** A common mistake among poor speakers of English is that 'something can't be beat'. This, too, is sliding into polite speech. The correct participle is *beaten*.

Because See AS for the misuse of that word for *because*. *The reason is because* is a tautology.

Because of See CAUSE.

Begging the question Most people who use this term seem to think it means 'inviting the question'. It does nothing of the sort. H. W. Fowler gives a summary of the problem that cannot be bettered: he defines it as 'the fallacy of founding a conclusion on a basis that as much needs to be proved as the conclusion itself'. So if one were to say 'it is good to smoke because tobacco has health-giving properties', that would *beg the question* about the health-giving properties of tobacco. However, if one were to say in response to an assertion by another that all Frenchmen are philanderers that it 'begged the question about the philandering of Frenchmen' it would in fact do nothing of the sort, since no other conclusion is being based on that questionable statement. If they were to say 'France is a degenerate nation because all Frenchmen are philanderers', it would then beg the question whether all Frenchmen were philanderers, because the statement is merely an assertion and no proof is offered. Instead of the sentence being an assertion supported by a statement of proof, it is merely two linked assertions – the second of which begs the question.

Begin idiomatically requires a verb and not a noun to follow it. 'He began to attend school' is correct. 'He began school' is not.

Being that As in 'being that he was a good man', this is a horribly common prolixity for 'because' or 'since'.

Bellwether, which originally meant the leading sheep of a flock around whose neck a bell was hung, is now used to mean something that indicates a trend: 'she is a bellwether of fashion'. It is spelt thus, and not 'bellweather' or 'bellwhether'. It has nothing to do with weather forecasting.

Beside and **besides** *Beside* is a PREPOSITION that signifies adjacency – 'she sat down beside him'. *Besides* is an adverb with two distinct meanings. The first is 'additionally', as in 'I don't want to have any dinner. Besides, I am very tired'; the second is 'except', as in 'no one besides him remembered the war'.

Best practice is both JARGON and a CLICHÉ, and therefore on its way to becoming meaningless.

Between must refer to a position, literal or abstract, within two other positions – 'he was between his two aunts at the theatre' or 'she was at school between 1970 and 1980'. It is a solecism when used to describe the relations between more than two places, people or things. See also AMONG AND BETWEEN.

Betwixt is an archaism for *between* and looks arch if it is used in what purports to be serious prose.

Biannual and **biennial** *Biannual* describes something happening twice a year: *biennial* describes something that happens every two years. They are easily and frequently mixed up. There can be a similar, but less promiscuous, problem with *triennial*, *quadrennial*, *quinquennial* and even *septennial*.

Bible Note the initial capital letter. Where the term is used figuratively – '*Wisden* is the cricketers' bible' – it does not require a capital letter; nor does the adjective *biblical*.

Big is correctly an adjective, as in 'the big man' or 'a big win'. However, it has been used as an adverb since the sixteenth century, though its most popular application in this part of speech ('think big') has been current for a mere century, and one often hears sports commentators say of a comprehensive victory that someone has 'won big'. Such usages are avoided by sophisticated writers.

Billion Until recently, a *billion* in the United Kingdom meant a million million; but now the international usage, taking its lead from America, is to signify a thousand million.

Bishops See CLERGY, WRITING TO OR ADDRESSING.

Blackguard This term of reprobation is spelt thus but pronounced 'blaggard'. However, in *The Times* of 28 October

2013 there appeared the phrase 'the blaggard who assaulted Anna', which suggests that both the writer and his sub-editor need spelling lessons.

Blanch and **blench** To *blanch* something is to whiten it by removing its colour – it is often done with almonds. Do not confuse it with *blench*, an intransitive verb that means to become pale – 'he blenched at the prospect of the interview'.

Blatant and **flagrant** Something that is *blatant* is glaringly obvious, but it lacks a sense of scandal, notoriety or outrage that would make it *flagrant*. So we would say 'his dislike of his boss became fairly blatant' but 'his affair with his secretary was pretty flagrant'.

Blench See BLANCH AND BLENCH.

Blind See POLITICAL CORRECTNESS.

Blond(e) In British English the French usage is imitated, so a man is *blond* and a woman *blonde*. In American English, *blond* is used for both genders.

Blood sports and **field sports** Those who shoot or hunt practise *field sports*. *Blood sports* is a politically loaded term popularised by opponents of field sports, and often used unwittingly by newspapers that have no editorial objection to them.

Bloodstock and **livestock** *Bloodstock* is a term used to describe thoroughbred horses. It is not to be confused with *livestock*, a term used to describe farm animals.

Boat See SHIP AND BOAT.

Bombay or **Mumbai** See PLACE NAMES.

Bon vivant, bonne vivante and ***bon viveur*** It is one thing to use the correct term *bon vivant* for a man, but it is imperative not to foul up by failing to use *bonne vivante* for a woman who enjoys the finer things in life. *Bon viveur* is a phrase unknown in correct French but persists in bad English. See FOREIGN WORDS AND PHRASES.

Book titles If writing these, italicise them.

Bored One is bored *with* something, not bored *of* it. One may also be bored *by* someone or something, and the effect of using that preposition is to make the act more specific. 'I am bored with him' suggests a chronic problem, 'I am bored by him' suggests something more episodic.

Both See EACH, ALL AND BOTH.

Both . . . and The construction *both . . . and* can obviously be used only with two subjects; and it is important to take care where the *both* is placed. 'He killed both his mother and his wife' makes perfect sense in a way that 'he both killed his mother and his wife' does not – it requires another clause, such as 'and diposed of their bodies', to make grammatical sense. It is also important to ensure that there is a parallelism in the items joined in this construction. If one writes 'both the meat and vegetables were undercooked' it implies something is missing: the absence of the definite article before vegetables suggests that they and the meat are being taken as a single item and something else is about to be added. 'Both the meat and vegetables and the sauce were undercooked' would make logical sense in one respect, though not necessarily in another. 'Both the meat and the vegetables were undercooked, as was the sauce' is grammatically correct.

Bottom line is a cliché and, like all clichés, should be avoided.

Brackets See PARENTHESES.

Brake and **break** *Brake* is a verb meaning to stop by use of a mechanism to do so, or a noun meaning the mechanism itself. *Break* is a verb meaning to split up into pieces, or a noun meaning an interval in some other activity.

Brave is an adjective much overused by the tabloid press, and a lesson in the dilution of the force of adjectives. If a woman is *brave* because of her reaction to the way in which her philandering husband embarrasses her publicly, how are we to describe her if she endures with courage and fortitude a horrible and potentially fatal illness? How can the ordeal of one experience compare with that of the other?

Breach and **breech** *Breach* is the action of breaking, and the verb means to break. It may be used literally – 'the waves breached the sea wall' – or figuratively – 'it was a clear breach of the rules'. The *breech*, however, is the backside, or in the plural – *breeches* – a garment worn over that part of the anatomy: it takes a plural verb. The words should not be confused. However, the *London Review of Books* did confuse the two in its issue of 30 August 2012: 'You do not need to breech the security-enhanced gate to hear gladiatorial chants of combat from the big screen.'

Break See BRAKE AND BREAK.

Breakout is a noun in British English signifying an escape from prison. In American English, and now frequently used in Britain, it is an adjective meaning suddenly popular and successful – 'the group released its breakout single in 1995'. In British English we would say *breakthrough*.

Breath and **breathe** *Breath* is the noun – 'I could hardly draw breath' – and *breathe* the verb – 'I could hardly breathe'.

Breech See BREACH AND BREECH.

Brilliant in its figurative sense, meaning extremely clever or of superlative talent, is a much over-worked adjective. A performer of any description who is described as brilliant, or a commodity or object similarly described, almost certainly isn't. The word should now only be used to describe a bright light: some newspapers apply it to so many columnists, series, special offers or free gifts that it is remarkable that their readers have not been blinded.

Britain and **British Isles** *Britain* is the shorthand description for Great Britain, being England, Scotland and Wales; and is also frequently used for the United Kingdom of Great Britain and Northern Ireland, even though it explicitly excludes those who live in Northern Ireland. A Briton is one who lives in Great Britain. The *British Isles* are a geographical rather than a political term, and it refers to the mainland of Great Britain, the mainland of Ireland, and all the islands around their coasts.

Broadcast, like CAST, has an irregular imperfect: 'The concert was *broadcast* last Thursday', not *broadcasted*.

Broke and **broker** The former is the verb and the latter the noun. One writes that 'he is going to broke the deal between the two parties' or that 'he was the broker between the two parties'. However, one increasingly sees *broker* used as a verb, which is wrong – 'they brokered the deal in the early hours of the morning'. This usage has been found as far back as the seventeenth century but in the age of globalisation has become ubiquitous. Perhaps it is confusion with the past tense of *break* that causes some to imagine a verb *to broke* is wrong. It is not. The past tense of *broke* is *broked*, the present participle *broking*. Thus 'they broked the deal by the end of the session' and 'he had spent his life broking'. Someone who is *broke* has no money.

Brutalise This verb means to make someone brutal, not to treat them brutally. Hence, 'the boy was brutalised by regular beatings' means the beatings turned him into a brute.

Bullock A *bullock* is a castrated bull, not a small one that will one day grow into a bull.

Bureaucratic language is distinguished by its PROLIXITY, convolutedness, pomposity, obscurity, JARGON and often deliberate lack of clarity. It should not serve as a model for ideal prose writing, nor be allowed to infiltrate everyday speech. The language of bureaucracy has a vocabulary that remains floating in the inkwell of a clerk in Edwardian England. Rarely would you hear such gems as 'beyond peradventure', 'whence he came', 'in the event that' or 'had the occasion to'. These and others like them remain the stock phrases of the robotic bureaucrat who cannot bear – or considers himself paid insufficiently – to think about what he is writing and to communicate in plain English. At least certain phrases – 'beyond peradventure', for example – do seem to have died, but others – such as 'in the first instance' (for 'first') and 'in the process of' (for 'while') – remain and, for so long as they do, are a temptation to the verbally weak-minded. Do not use a phrase where a word will do. Also, do not use an archaic phrase unless you wish your readers to laugh at you.

Burglarize is an Americanism for the British English verb *burgle*.

Burgle and **rob** *Burgle* refers to the criminal practice of entering premises in order to steal some of the contents. It is wrong to use the verb *rob* in this context. To engage in robbery is to steal from a person or a vehicle. Bank robberies are usually bank burglaries, but the former phrase has become idiomatic.

Burma or **Myanmar** See PLACE NAMES.

Business letters demand strict formality: when sent on behalf of a company they create a distinct impression of what sort of company it is, and individuals too can do themselves no favours by sending a badly crafted letter to a government agency or a private business with whom they are having dealings. This is especially true if applying for jobs, or making some other request whose likelihood of being granted depends to some extent on the character of the applicant. If such letters begin 'Dear Sir', 'Dear Madam' or 'Dear Sir or Madam' – and in some particularly formal contexts, especially when the recipient is unknown to the writer and the business to be transacted concerns the state, they should – then they must be ended with 'Yours faithfully'. A letter beginning 'Dear Mr Smith', 'Dear Mrs Smith', 'Dear Miss Smith' or 'Dear Ms Smith' should end 'Yours sincerely'.

Sir Ernest Gowers, in *Plain Words*, makes some further points specific to business letter-writing that I must acknowledge here. If you are replying to a query, make sure you understand exactly what you are being asked (this in itself will be a safeguard against verbosity). 'Begin by answering his question' is also good advice, as is 'confine yourself to the facts of the case'. Gowers also warns his readers against formality, but he means what we would probably better term now 'impersonality'; he urges officials in particular to be 'friendly' towards their correspondents. He would not have countenanced any informality in the sense of slang or sloppy grammar, and neither should the rest of us.

But is a coordinating conjunction, linking two clauses that could otherwise just as well stand as separate sentences. The conjunction introduces an element of contrast: 'I had been to Brighton, but John had never visited it.' As with *and*, it is not wrong to begin a sentence with *but*, but it does suggest the previous one has finished at the wrong time. When writing the conjunction *but*, always pause and wonder how the sentence would read if you exchanged it for *and*. *But* should be used only when there is a definite contrast to be introduced, usually after a conditional clause: 'I would have given him some help, but he had been ungrateful in the past.' Yet sometimes one reads it when the simple conjunction *and* would be correct: 'I turned off the light but went to sleep' is manifestly crying out to be changed to 'I turned off the light *and* went to sleep'. However, in certain cases *but* is correct where *and* might be thought to be so: 'I asked her to marry me *but* she said no' is better than 'I asked her to marry me *and* she said no', because simply asking the question does not guarantee a positive answer, and a refusal is not necessarily surprising.

By and large is seldom anything other than padding, and a cliché. Avoid the phrase.

C

Caesarean section is spelt thus. Americans may spell it *Cesarean*, but *Caesarian* is wrong.

Called and **named** There is a distinction between these two verbs that Dickens exemplifies in *Our Mutual Friend*, when Miss Peecher says: 'Speaking correctly, we say, then, that Hexam's sister is called Lizzie: not that she is named so.' The distinction is between the name formally given to a person at birth, and what others might choose to call him or her as a variant of or substitute for it. The former England cricket captain Andrew Flintoff was so *named*, but is widely *called* Freddie.

Callous and **callus** The former is an adjective that describes extremely hard-hearted behaviour, as in 'he had a callous disregard for the suffering of others'. The latter is a piece of hardened skin, as in 'his hands were covered with calluses'. It and the adjective share the same etymology but not the same spelling.

Can and **may** The usages of *may* and *can* are often confused these days, with a consequent loss of precision. *May* is about having permission to do something, or entertaining the possibility of doing it; *can* is about having the ability. If a man asks a woman whether he *can* kiss her the answer will, unless he has some shocking disability that restricts his movements, probably have to be 'yes'; his ability to complete the manoeuvre is not in doubt. Were he to ask, as he more correctly should, whether he *might* kiss her, she can at least express an opinion on the matter. So when one hears someone ask 'Can I sit down?' and we establish that his ability to do so is not in question, it more accurately becomes a matter rather of whether he *may*. *Can* is usually used wrongly for *may*; it is difficult to imagine abuses in the other direction – 'Can you swim?' and 'May you swim?' clearly ask two completely different questions, and 'Might you swim?' asks a third. The first is a query about whether the person interrogated has the ability to swim. The second is whether he has permission to do so. The third is about whether there is a possibility that he could go for a swim – his ability to do so and his freedom to do so being taken for granted.

Candy is an Americanism for *sweets*.

Canvas and **canvass** The former is a noun and describes a piece of material – as in 'the canvas on which he painted was three feet wide' – or a metaphorical platform – 'his work was carried out over a broad canvas'. The latter is a verb, which means to promote a product or a person through advertisement or recommendation, as in 'the candidate canvassed in the town all afternoon'. To *canvass opinion* is a phrase that uses another meaning of the verb, which is to discuss or debate, and from that discussion or debate draw a conclusion, in this case about opinion on a specific question.

Capital and **capitol** *Capital* has any number of meanings. As a noun it may refer to the chief city of a nation, or to an accumulation of money, or in abbreviation to a letter of the alphabet written in the upper case. As an adjective it may refer to money – 'a capital transfer' – or to something that claims someone's head – 'a capital sentence' or 'capital punishment'. Whatever it means, do not confuse it with *capitol*, which is now an American seat of government – either the federal one in Washington DC, or the buildings containing the legislatures of the capitals of individual American states. The original Capitol was the temple of Jupiter Optimus Maximus, on the Capitoline Hill at Rome.

Capital letters and capitalisation An inflexible rule about capital letters is that they begin sentences. Another is that they begin proper names. Beyond that, keep them to a minimum as they clutter up prose. The Victorians used to capitalise most names they could find, almost to the extent of German practice (every German noun begins with a capital letter). We are now moving towards the French practice, in which so few words begin with capital letters that it comes as rather a shock to find one that does. Individual publications and publishers make their own rules about this. It is probably best, if one has to make up one's own mind about it, to have a logical rule and stick to it. Of choice, I would capitalise according to the following scheme.

In the United Kingdom, and writing for a domestic readership, it should be the Queen, the President, the Prime Minister, the Chancellor of the Exchequer. Abroad it should be the Queen of Spain and the President of the United States as heads of state: but the French prime minister, the German finance minister, and so on. This means no disrespect, but simply avoids clutter. Similarly, do not bother to capitalise titles such as the shadow secretary of state, the chief executive of Tesco, the chairman of Lloyd's – unless you happen to be working for any of those institutions and house style dictates it. There is no need to award them to job titles – a managing director is just as important if his job title begins in lower case.

Note also the distinction between 'the Queen' and 'queens throughout history', and between 'the Government' and 'governments around the world'.

For other titles, I would say in the first instance the Earl of Essex and thereafter the Earl, and the Archbishop of Canterbury and thereafter the Archbishop; but it would be an earl, an archbishop, and so on. Capitalise institutions at home and abroad because they are proper names, such as the House of Commons, the Garrick Club, the US Senate or the Melbourne Cricket Club. Geographical features vary in their capitalisation. When using the word 'river' with its name the word is capitalised, as is idiomatic: River Thames, River Seine, River Rhine and so on, and also where the order is inverted: Hudson River, Chao Phraya River. Deserts (the Sahara Desert, the Gobi Desert and so on) follow the same pattern, as do mountain ranges (the

Rocky Mountains), hills (the Blackdown Hills) and forests (the Black Forest). Indeed, it is a good rule to apply it to any geographical feature with a proper name (Camber Sands, Niagara Falls, the Grand Union Canal). Some publishers, however, have a house style that avoids capitalising anything except proper names, so do not be surprised to see variations on this. See also PUNCTUATION.

Carcase is the British English spelling for the corpse of a beast: *carcass* the American.

Carnival Exotic communities put on an event called *carnival* (without a definite article), comprising brightly dressed women swaying to tropical music: 'the carnival' is something genial provincial towns put on, in which a pretty girl sits on the back of a slow-moving lorry, and there may be a coconut shy somewhere on a field at the end of the procession. This is perhaps as good an example as any of how evolving social conditions do not so much change our language, as introduce new distinctions to it.

Case, the Some phrases are redundant, and may often be cut out altogether. This is usually true of the phrase *the case*; or, as I might just have written, 'this is usually the case with the phrase *the case*'. The phrase has become a FILLER and is used at the expense of a more precise word – *true* will often suffice.

Cases Case is the modification of nouns and pronouns to reflect their relation to other words in a sentence, also referred to as DECLENSION. Except for special plurals such as *children, hooves* (and others with singulars ending in *-f*), *feet* and the now rather antique *kine*, English nouns do not inflect in the way that Greek, Latin or German ones do. For example, the German noun *Name* becomes *Namen* in the accusative and dative cases, and *Namens* in the genitive; in all plurals it is *Namen*, and the noun is but one of twelve distinct classes. With the exception of the case used to signify possession, there are no fancy endings for the writer or speaker of English to master so far as nouns are concerned. As mentioned under **PRONOUNS**, certain of them do inflect when they are the direct or indirect object of a verb or after a **PREPOSITION**, and their inflections must be observed in the correct contexts.

English has the equivalents of the Latin cases, but, in the absence of inflections, uses prepositions to activate most of them. The two case distinctions in pronouns are the **ACCUSATIVE**, or the case that one uses in writing or speaking when the pronoun is a direct or indirect object (the words that have inflected are *me*, *him*, *her*, *us*, *them*); and the **GENITIVE**, which signifies possession (*my*, *your* (singular and plural), *his*, *her*, *its*, *one's*, *our*, *their*). In nouns, the nominative case is the straightforward noun – 'a table', say. The vocative is the case of addressing it – 'O table!' (This made generations of schoolboys hoot when learning Latin, a testament to the puerility of much English humour.) The accusative case is for English nouns identical to the nominative – 'a table'. The genitive signifies possession: 'of a table'. Its shortening – 'a table's' – is perhaps not so much an inflection as an appendage. The dative is 'to' or 'for a table' and is also the indirect object – 'I sent the food to a table' or 'she asked the restaurant for a table'. The ablative signifies 'by', 'with' or 'from a table'. Latinists will recall the **ABLATIVE ABSOLUTE**, in which a noun and a participle were put in the ablative case to signify a completed action by certain people, and which was translated by the ugly formula 'which boys having been kicked' or 'which flies having been swatted'. There is no equivalent in English, and modern style hardly permits such a stilted construction in contemporary usage.

We cannot entirely do without a sensibility of case in English, even if English has tried to do without it by losing most of its inflections. Anyone trying to say 'me went to the pub' or 'I told he to stop' will be laughed out of town; there will also be a frisson when a more sophisticated user of the language makes a common slip such as 'this did not come as a shock to John and I'. It is important to make sure that a preposition always takes an accusative: a usage such as 'I was afraid of he who is all-knowing' will simply not do. The direct object of a verb must always be in the accusative too: we can have no truck with 'I was appalled to find only one woman, and she a foreigner, who understood English grammar'. It should be 'and her a foreigner' as the phrase remains the direct object of the verb *find*. Were the verb to be supplied (though that would be pleonastic) and the phrase were to become 'and she was a foreigner', that would be all right. The verb TO BE strictly should take the nominative case – hence the wrongness of the occasionally heard pomposity 'be you whom [or whomever] you may be', because *whom* is an accusative. See also the POSSESSIVE.

Cassandra She was the daughter of Priam, but Apollo, who fell in love with her, gave her the gift of prophecy. However, when she deceived him, he decided that nobody should believe her prophecies, even though they were true. Thus when the term is used to signify a prophet of doom it ignores its true meaning, which is to signify someone whose prophecies or predictions are ignored.

Cast, like BROADCAST, has an irregular imperfect: 'She cast [not casted] aside her cares and went off to work.'

Caster and **castor** The former is someone who casts metal. A *castor* is a small wheel attached to the base of furniture, such as a chair or a table, for ease of its movement, or it is a device that scatters sugar over a pudding. *Castor oil* is a repellent substance given in former times to children complaining of stomach-ache to ensure a rapid evacuation of their bowels.

Catachresis is an improper use of words, notably the application of a term to something to which it does not properly apply; it is well-used to describe the perversion of a metaphor. To describe someone as *prevaricating* when in fact he is *procrastinating* is catachrestic.

Catalog and **catalogue** See AMERICAN SPELLING.

Catalyst A *catalyst* is not a cause; it is a substance that increases the rate of a chemical reaction, so metaphorically it is correctly used when describing an agent that speeds up a rate of change: 'His influence was the catalyst that caused her French studies to make more rapid progress.'

Catholic and **catholic** In everyday speech a *Catholic* is a member of the universal church of the same name, who acknowledges the Pope as his or her spiritual authority. The most common form is *Roman Catholic*; but there are also variants such as *Anglo-Catholic*, someone who worships within the Church of England largely according to the Catholic rite. The adjective *catholic* with a lower-case initial *c* means *universal* or *wide-ranging*, as in 'he was a man of catholic tastes' – which does not mean he took dictation in matters of taste from the Pope, but that his tastes were extensive.

Cause *Due to, owing to* and *because of* are used by many writers as though they were interchangeable. They are not. *Due to* should not open a sentence: and it can be used only when something (*noun a*) is due to something else (*noun b*): as in 'mass starvation was due to crop failure' or 'my lateness was due to the cancellation of the train'. It is wrong in a sentence such as 'the business did not flourish due to a shortage of customers': it should either be 'because of a shortage of customers' or 'the failure of the business was due to a shortage of customers'. This is because in the first example there is no noun to which the result is due: it refers back to the verb, 'flourish'. In the second the noun is present – 'failure'. 'The postponement of the start of Essex's match against Surrey, due to heavy overnight rain' is correct. To say 'due to heavy overnight rain, Essex's match against Surrey has been postponed' is not, as the syntax demands that *due to* qualifies the cricket match and not the postponement. *Owing to* does not have these limitations and may be used to open a sentence. There should be no strict fetish banning the use of *because* at the start of a sentence, so that may be used instead. Nevertheless, *owing to* would be preferred by many, including me.

The idiomatic use of *because* has become far looser in recent decades, to the point where it seems too pedantic to confine it to its correct use as a conjunction. Its correct use is as in 'he left because he found a better job'. Had the first clause been nominal – that is, 'his departure' – then it would more correctly be rendered 'his departure was due to his finding a better job'.

Caused by requires a noun and not a verb: 'His death was caused by gluttony' is correct, 'his death was caused by his continually gorging himself' is less felicitous, and would be better rendered as 'his death was due to his continually gorging himself'.

There is also the somewhat more rarified *for*: 'I did not notice him, for he was in disguise.' This device may be used to introduce an expression that is confined to one of opinion, or to a statement of fact. Virginia Woolf was attached to it, and it makes a prominent appearance early on in *Mrs Dalloway*. The book begins: 'Mrs Dalloway said she would buy the flowers herself. For Lucy had her work cut out for her.' Two of the next four paragraphs open with the same formula: 'For having lived in Westminster . . . one feels . . . a particular hush' and 'For it was the middle of June'. Woolf's usage is largely rhetorical, because except in the first of the three times she engages in it the word *for* is unnecessary. It creates a sense of controlling, almost hectoring delivery of pronouncements that certainly indicates the insecure state of mind of Mrs Dalloway, and for that matter the character of the author herself. It can easily be overdone by the sane and stable. *For* cannot be used like *because* to introduce a sentence that details the consequences of a cause; in the sentence 'because she was late, she missed the film', *because* cannot be replaced by *for*. However, one may just about write 'she missed the film, for she was late'; a sort of sense is conveyed, but it is not idiomatic, and *because* here would be far more satisfactory. A Woolfish 'she missed the film. For she was late' takes us back to the edges of sanity. Today, the idiomatic usage of *for* seems a little arch. It is best confined to prose where, in order to avoid repetition of *because*, it may provide a variation: 'Because Smith had lost the key we had to stand outside. We became very cold, for it was the middle of January.'

The other phrase routinely used to attribute cause is *on account of*; either with a GERUND – 'he had to buy a new tie on account of his other's being ruined' – or suffixed by the phrase *the fact that* – 'he had to buy a new tie on account of the fact that his other one was damaged'. The sheer prolixity of this construction, which has its roots in the worst sort of bureaucratic language, should itself indicate its lack of suitability for crisp, tight prose.

Celibate is used these days to denote someone who abstains from sexual activity. Its strict meaning is one who is resolutely unmarried.

Censer, censor and **censure** A *censer* is an instrument used for spreading incense in the air, notably in religious ceremonies. The verb from it is *cense* – 'the priest censed the air'. A *censor* is an official who prevents the publication or broadcast of material deemed to be offensive or damaging to the institution he represents, usually the state. There is a matching verb – 'he censored her reports before they were printed'. To *censure* is to reprimand, and there is a matching noun – 'it was not the first time he had received a censure'.

Centennial is an Americanism for *centenary*, a 100th anniversary.

Centred around is an illogicality. The phrase must be *centred upon*. The centre is a fixed point, so something has to be centred upon it.

Certain As well as being an adjective, it may serve as a pronoun: 'Most people present supported him, but certain of them threatened to change their minds.'

Chair and **chairman** See POLITICAL CORRECTNESS.

Champagne Only use this noun to describe the effervescent drink that comes from the eponymous region in France. Other fizzy wine is just that. The use of *champagne* as an adjective to convey a sense of celebration or luxury – as in 'champagne moment' or 'champagne socialist' – is frivolous and becoming clichéd.

Chaos is now overused to mean *disorder*, and is a good example of HYPERBOLE. It originally meant the primordial state, out of which the universe was created.

Charge This verb does not mean to *assert* or *proclaim*: to write or say that 'he charged that he had been falsely accused' is wrong. *Charge* means either to load or fill, to ask a price, or formally to accuse someone of a crime and put him on trial for it.

Check Whereas a Briton will ask for the *bill* in a restaurant, an American will ask for the *check*. It is also the American spelling of *cheque*.

Children's It must be emphasised that this is the correct possessive or genitive of the plural of child. One correctly writes 'it is the children's bedtime'. A sentence such as 'he spent years in a childrens' home' is a SOLECISM.

Chivalric and **chivalrous** The dictionary defines the former as meaning 'of or pertaining to chivalry', which seems correct, though it then suggests it is a SYNONYM for the latter, which if so robs the language of a part of its precision. *Chivalrous* today refers to conduct by a man conforming to the knightly ideal of courage, virtue and gallantry. So one would say that 'the history book outlined the *chivalric* customs of the twelfth century', where the adjective describes how knights conducted themselves; but to say 'his behaviour towards his wife was *chivalrous*' would suggest that he opened doors for her, complimented her on her dress and her looks, and turned a blind eye to anything she did that might irritate him were he not in possession of such good manners.

Choice One frequently hears someone say: 'You have two choices.' The Prime Minister, David Cameron, was reported in *The Times* on 30 June 2012 saying just that: 'The problem with an in/out referendum is it actually only gives people those two choices.' The same newspaper wrote on 27 September that 'Nick Clegg put two choices before the Liberal Democrats yesterday'. You do not have two choices: you have *a choice*. A *choice* requires two (or more) options. A man may have two, five or a dozen ties to choose from. He still has only one *choice*, not two, five or twelve.

Choosy is the slang term to be preferred to the popular Americanism *picky* to describe someone who is fastidious or discriminating.

Chord and **cord** *Chord* is a musical term. A *cord* is some sort of string, as in whipcord. Either spelling may be used for the vocal cords and the spinal cord.

Christian name A term used to describe the names given to people of the Christian faith. Now, because of POLITICAL CORRECTNESS, it is widely replaced by *forename* or *given name*.

Chronic like aggravate, has suffered from its popularity as a slang word expressing disapproval or irritation. *Chronic* illnesses – and there the word is used in its correct sense, from the Greek, as lasting a long time – often are dreadful and tiresome, but that does not sanction the transference of this adjective to indicate those states as well.

Church, the In England the *Church* (note the capital letter) signifies the Church of England, the Established Church.

Cite, **sight** and **site** are HOMOPHONES that must not be confused. The verb *cite* mainly means to quote, or bring forward proof, as in 'he cited chapter and verse from the Bible' or 'I can cite evidence that he was somewhere else at the time'. *Sight* is a spectacle or the faculty of vision. *Site* is a place or position.

Classic and **classical** As the late Sir Kingsley Amis pointed out, *classic* is an example of an adjective that became a noun. Far from its original meaning (as an adjective) of indicating something from antiquity, something that is a *classic* is now taken to have qualities of excellence, style and possibly even timelessness. The adjective has also come to mean the same thing. *Classical*, on the other hand, is only an adjective, and in history only refers to ancient times.

Clauses Charles Talbut Onions defined a sentence as an expression containing a SUBJECT and a PREDICATE: the predicate being that part of the sentence that contains what is said about the subject. So in the sentence 'the dog ate the bone', 'the dog' is the subject and 'ate the bone' is the predicate. If that is all a sentence does, it is a simple sentence. If it has more than one subject and predicate, however, then each subdivision of the sentence with its own subject and predicate is a *clause*. The sentence then becomes what Onions calls 'a compound sentence'. 'I had no idea that grammar was so easy to grasp as this' is a complex sentence: it consists of a main clause ('I had no idea') followed by a subordinate clause ('grammar was so easy to grasp as this'), introduced in this example by the conjunction *that*.

Let us examine more closely the various different types of clauses. The main clause will introduce a subject and predicate, and there may then be various types of dependent clause – noun clauses, adjective clauses and adverbial clauses, named according to what function they perform in the sentence. A noun clause is found in '*the last thing I want to do* is to go'. There is an adjective clause in 'the house that we saw *was sold*' and an adverbial one in 'I must eat something *because I am hungry*'. A relative clause will be introduced by a relative pronoun, as in 'she drank the cocktail, *which her friend had ordered for her*' or 'he introduced his wife to the doctor, *whom he had met on holiday*'. Clauses may also be fashioned to create a literary technique, such as paratactic clauses (see PARATAXIS), that stand side by side with each other without any coordinating or subordinating conjunctions, such as Milton's 'I waked, she fled'.

There are several different types of subordinate clause: those that take the role of a noun, an adjective or an adverb. One does not need to understand such technicalities to write English correctly, but these examples of each type may be useful:

> 'It is quite apparent that the boy is a fool.' (Noun clause: provides a subject.)
>
> 'The dog that jumped into the road was run over.' (Adjective clause: describes the dog.)
>
> 'He wrote the book until it was time for dinner.' (Adverbial clause: complements the verb.)

There are further varieties within these groups that only scholars of linguistics or grammarians need concern themselves with: full details are contained in Onions. Many adverbial clauses are of time or place or reason, and so are introduced by *when*, *since*, *until*, *before*, *after* (time), *where*, *wherever* (place) or *because*, *why*, *how* or *whereas* (reason). The point about a subordinate clause is that it cannot stand alone and make sense: it is sometimes called a dependent clause because it depends on another clause to show its full meaning. The one I quoted near the beginning of this section – 'grammar was so easy to grasp as this' – is meaningless on its own. The main clause, 'I had no idea', however, can function on its own.

There are also coordinate clauses. These are clauses that do make sense on their own. They are commonly introduced by a conjunction such as *and*, *but*, *or* and *nor*. If you look at these examples you will see that what comes after the conjunction, or indeed before it, makes sense independently, though those beginning with *nor* require inversion, as indicated in the example below:

> 'I had been to Brighton, but John had never visited it.'
>
> 'She put away the breakfast things and then she went to the village.'

> 'He had nothing to contribute to the discussion, nor did he wish to do so.' (That is: 'And he did not wish to do so.')

> 'Either Mary would walk from the station, or John would collect her by car.'

The main point that most people need to know about clauses is that they require careful examination to ensure that the logic of the sentence is maintained throughout all of them. There is a particular danger with clauses that include participles. To make matters more interesting, subordinate clauses may have further clauses subordinated to them, and subordinate clauses may co-ordinate with each other. The confusion this can cause may help explain why this book expresses a prejudice, now and again, for short sentences. Accurate punctuation is crucial in sentences with several clauses, in order to keep the meaning clear.

It is also important, in sentences with several clauses, that the subjects remain what the writer intended. Examples of this not being the case continue to proliferate. In the report of the Culture, Media and Sport Select Committee on 1 May 2012, it was stated that 'as the head of a journalistic enterprise, we are astonished that James Murdoch did not seek more information . . .' Mr Murdoch was the head of the enterprise and not the committee. In his life of General de Gaulle, Jonathan Fenby claimed that 'as Governor of Algeria, the Americans and Giraud appointed Maurice Peyrouton'. This suggests the Americans and Giraud were the Governor, not Peyrouton. On 21 August 2012 the *Guardian* reported that 'when he died last year, the then French president Nicolas Sarkozy paid tribute to Ruiz . . .' This suggests it was Monsieur Sarkozy who died, and not Ruiz. Reading any of these sentences back carefully for sense should have told the writer that something was astray.

A similar danger is found in clauses with **PARTICIPLES**: for more examples, and how to avoid such errors, see that entry.

In sentences that are composed of many clauses there are important considerations for the **SEQUENCE OF TENSES**: see the entry on that subject.

Clearly has a literal meaning and an ironic meaning: but it can also, like ABSOLUTELY and BASICALLY, be used pointlessly, as a filler or form of punctuation. 'I could see the coast clearly from the prow of the ship' is the literal usage. 'I could see he clearly hadn't been drinking lemonade' is the ironic usage. 'Clearly, we should talk about this' is the pointless usage.

Clergy, writing to or addressing One of the most common mistakes in addressing or mentioning any professional person is when referring to clergymen (or, increasingly these days, clergy-women). The Reverend John Smith or the Reverend Mary Smith is correct. The Reverend Smith is not. His or her Christian name, or rank, is required: so the Reverend Mr Smith, or the Reverend Miss Smith, or the Reverend Dr Smith will also do. The Reverend Smith is the product of that most God-fearing of countries, America, but it is an abomination here. We should no more write 'Reverend Smith' than we should 'Sir Smith'. Most members of the episcopate are doctors of divinity, and it is quite correct to refer to the Archbishop of Canterbury or the Bishop of Bath and Wells in the first instance, but to call them Dr Smith subsequently. Write to 'Dear Archbishop', 'Dear Bishop' or 'Dear Dean', or 'Dear Dr Smith', as you choose. Most parish clergy will be 'Dear Mr Smith' or 'Dear Mrs [or 'Miss'] Smith', unless holding a doctorate. See also REVEREND. On the envelope, write to 'The Most Reverend Dr John Smith' for an archbishop, 'The Right Reverend Dr John Smith' for a bishop, 'The Reverend Dr John Smith' or 'The Reverend John Smith' for a member of the general clergy.

Clichés The use of a *cliché*, a stock and familiar phrase well-worn in speech and prose, displays a paucity of original thought on the part of the speaker or writer. It is easily forgiven in speech: less so in writing, where the writer has supposedly had the time to reflect upon his choice of words. Here are a few obvious ones to make the point: 'a bolt from the blue', 'sick as a parrot', 'quintessentially English', 'blind as a bat', 'spread like wildfire', 'done and dusted', 'a pack of lies' and 'play fast and loose'.

Cliché is also a close cousin of **JARGON**, the stock phrases and formulas used by certain groups of people to talk to each other and to freeze out the public. They are also much beloved of a certain sort of bureaucrat, barely concealing his tedium at having to deal with the people who pay his salary. There are some clichéd phrases including prepositions that have become tired and are verbose. They exemplify the failure of writers to think about the words they are using, and they radiate pomposity: 'in respect of your letter of . . .' or 'with regard to your letter'. The officialese of these should be obvious at once; they have no place in humane communication, and may usually be cut out altogether. **SLANG** and **IDIOM** are heavy with clichés: however amusing in conversation, they should for that reason alone be avoided in serious or formal prose. The popular press has exhausted some words as stock clichés, rendering them nearly meaningless. Little weight is carried now by the metaphorical use of verbs such as 'soar', 'crash', 'launch', 'emerge', 'fuel' and 'clash'. Nouns like 'toff', 'fat cat', 'clampdown' (and its cousin 'crackdown') and 'icon' are just lazy labels for people or for abstract activities; so too are phrases such as 'damning report' and 'shock finding'. See also **METAPHOR**.

Climacteric, climactic and **climatic** A *climacteric* is an event of huge significance, a turning point or a decisive moment: 'The invasion of Normandy was a climacteric in the Second World War', for example. *Climactic* is the adjective from *climax*, as in 'it was a climactic moment in the play'. *Climatic* is the adjective from *climate*, as in 'the climatic conditions were terrible'.

Coarse and **course** *Coarse* is an adjective meaning rude or rough, as in 'he had very coarse manners'. *Course* is a noun used to describe a track or trajectory, as in 'they rode round the course' or 'he was on course to win'.

Coast and **coastal** Both may serve as adjectives. The latter defies the Fowlers' rule that the suffix *-al* should be used only with words of Latin origins (*-alis* is a common adjectival suffix in Latin, so they were holding to logic; the origins of the noun *coast* are in Middle English and medieval French). The distinction between *coast* and *coastal* is that the former is a less specific adjective – 'the *coast* road' could start 50 miles from the coast itself – and the latter conveys the sense of being in the area of the coast – 'a *coastal* path' is likely to be within sight of the sea.

Cockney rhyming slang is a peculiar form of dialect and has passed into mainstream slang too, in some cases. People far from London know what *having a butchers* is (*butcher's hook*: look), or what the *apples and pears* are (stairs). Perhaps more recondite is what someone means when he is having trouble with his *chalfonts* (*Chalfont St Giles*: piles) or when he considers another man to be an *iron* or a *ginger* (*iron hoof*: poof, and *ginger beer*: queer). These are rare examples of double slang, and show how slang often passes straight into the realms of the politically incorrect, or downright rude and offensive.

Collapse A house of cards can collapse, but despite what some modern dictionaries, surrendering on the point, say, one cannot collapse a house of cards. One can make it collapse, or knock it down. *Collapse* is an INTRANSITIVE, not a TRANSITIVE, verb.

Collective nouns See NOUNS OF MULTITUDE.

Collide and **collision** One occasionally reads in newspapers about people who have died or been injured in a car that has *collided* with a tree. This is remarkable, because a *collision* requires both parties to it to be in motion. The Latin verb *collidere* means to strike or clash together, and for those who mind about such things the etymology is strict. So two moving vehicles may collide, as may a car and a cyclist or even a car and a pedestrian, but not a car and a tree. Like so much of our language this is a question of logic based on the etymology; there is no perversity about it. Those who use the word wrongly are careless or ignorant writers.

Colloquialisms These begin as informal language and over time infiltrate the formal tongue. The language does not inevitably suffer as a result. It is a question of IDIOM. A good writer judges what is considered colloquial and what is not, and chooses his words accordingly. A century ago no piece of formal writing would have contained the word 'pub': the writer would have said 'inn' or 'public house'. Now, the word is entirely acceptable in a formal context. The same is true of words such as 'advert' or 'ad' (for advertisement), 'phone' and 'hi-tech'. 'Telly' (for television), 'uni' (for university) and 'loo' (for lavatory) remain in the realms of SLANG. Ruling on the distinction between slang and colloquialism becomes a matter of taste. My criterion is that when something is an abbreviation or an informal adaptation of a word or phrase, it is a colloquialism – hence 'pub' and 'phone'. Slang is at once more vulgar and may in some instances require glossing – such as the description used by some young people of someone with a disposition to violent behaviour being 'well tasty'. Colloquial violations of grammar are never acceptable in formal writing, for grammar is codified in the way that the meaning or usage of words is not. 'It's him' is fine in speech but 'It is him' is wrong in formal writing – it should be 'It is he'.

Colons A *colon* usually expands or elaborates upon what has been contained in the cause preceding it. However, to the Fowlers it was not so simple as that. They specified five correct uses for the colon, and they hold good today.

The first was between two successive clauses that could stand as sentences on their own, such as 'sentence was passed: the prisoner broke down'. It is especially effective with antithetical clauses, that is, successive clauses that express opposing thoughts, as in 'the sun shone: she wept'. The second was for introducing a short quotation, as I have done frequently in this book: 'See the example after mention of Aldous Huxley in the next paragraph.' The third is when introducing a list, as in 'he made a mental note of whom would be invited: Mr Smith, Mr Jones, Mr Brown, Mrs White'. The fourth is when something that becomes expected as a result of a first clause is delivered in a second, as in 'the jury considered its verdict: it found Smith guilty'. The fifth is where the clause after the colon proves or explains the contents of the first, as in 'Smith rifled the drawer: he was determined to find the letter'. In several of these cases the colon is not the only form of punctuation that can be used, but it is often the most elegant and helpful, in the way it breaks up the sense of the sentence distinctly.

I think there is a sixth class, an amalgam of examples one and four. Were the fourth example to read, instead, 'the jury considered its verdict: the judge went and watched tennis on television', it would be an example not quite entertained by the Fowlers. Example one has a direct relation between the two events described, of the prisoner's reaction to the sentence. The judge's going to watch tennis is a parallel event consequent on his having sent the jury out and not himself being required in court until they return, and not on the verdict they eventually reach. A semicolon could be used, but to my mind it would not draw attention to the contrast sufficiently.

There is also another important distinction between a *semicolon* and a *colon*. A colon can be used to separate two clauses the second of which is not an independent sentence in Onions's and the Fowlers' definition of the term. Examples are 'the murderer was revealed: Smith' and 'there was only one thing for it: surrender'. In some writing the colon can be replaced by a dash, as in this example from Aldous Huxley: 'The old shyness, he noticed, as they shook hands in the lobby of the restaurant, was still there – the same embarrassed smile, the same swaying movement of recoil.' It is a question of taste and fashion, and I suspect the fashion has changed in favour of the colon since Huxley wrote in the mid-1930s.

The colon also has a rhetorical use, in slowing down a passage of prose and helping it become declamatory: the same is true of the semicolon, and both were much employed in his finest speeches and most florid writing by Winston Churchill. In one he exhibited the ideal rhetorical use of the colon, by presenting a paratactic conclusion to a sentence: 'Success is not final, failure is not fatal: it is the courage to continue that counts.'

Comedic is an American adjective used pretentiously in British English to mean COMIC.

Comic and **comical** *Comic* – the adjective and not the noun – and *comical* appear to have lost almost all distinction in meaning when one is compared with the other. A *comic* situation has almost no perceptible difference from a *comical* one, other than in the minds of the strict. They will see the former as something intended to be funny, the latter as something in which the intention was anything but – as in 'the minister's speech was so bad it became comical'. For the most part this nuance is now lost, but that should not prevent the scrupulous from continuing to observe it.

Commas A *comma* in its simplest incarnation separates parts of a list: 'She went to the supermarket and bought bread, cheese, wine, fruit and coffee.' More elaborately, it helps define clauses that, if not so defined, could struggle to convey their accurate meaning. They also, as in this sentence and in the one before, separate parenthetical matter from the main thrust of a sentence. A comma may also be used, as in the preceding sentence, to introduce a contrast. The comma's purpose is as a signpost or aid to the reader in his understanding of what is being said, and to eliminate AMBIGUITY: it has an important role in the maintenance of logic, but also in increasing the ease of comprehension central to the notion of good style.

The placement of commas in routine sentences is something many writers find difficult. There are five fundamental rules that solve most problems.

First, commas should be used sparingly and logically. Some writers insert them after every few words, irrespective of the need for them or of the sense this punctuation then conveys. Commas are only required where to spare them would create problems of ambiguity or comprehension. In prose they are not respiratory guides.

Second, where commas are parenthetical, be sure to remember to end the parenthesis, or else the logic of the sentence may become hard to follow. One occasionally reads sentences such as 'they went to the beach, which was crowded so they returned to the hotel'. A comma is required after 'crowded' to separate that statement – an adjectival clause, for it describes the beach to us – from the rest of the sentence by completing the parenthesis. Remember, also, to use the correct relative pronoun when using a parenthesis: it will be *which* rather than *that* for abstracts or inanimate objects. Parentheses are often seen in sentences with adverbial phrases in them, such as in this example: 'she closed the curtains and, with the deftest of movements, got into bed'. One can see the offences to logic and style of omitting the second comma and therefore of failing to complete the parenthesis, just as in adjectival clauses. The same applies to rhetorical parentheses, which often appear in dialogue or in oratory: the parenthesis must be completed. Therefore logic and style require: 'I ask you, members of the jury, to acquit my client', and 'Where, I ask you, is my fountain pen?' The application of logic should be sufficient to avoid making mistakes with any sort of parenthesis, as the removal of the second comma from each of the examples just given will show. Another rhetorical (though unparenthetical) use will normally only be found in dialogue – as in 'I shall kill you, you swine', or 'I shall never leave you, not for a second', where the comma is used to introduce a rhetorical emphasis.

Third, in a list no comma is required before a final conjunction, though the Oxford University Press have always made an exception for this – and it is known as 'the Oxford comma'. It is also common in American writing. When one reads 'his wife was wearing a blue dress, necklace, high-heeled shoes, and a hat' one should see that, whatever Oxonians may believe, the comma after shoes is superfluous. A comma may, however, be used in this position to remove an ambiguity, such as in this example – 'he went to the bar and ordered three pints of beer, a sherry, a whisky, and water' – which indicates that the water was a separate drink from the whisky. Had the drink been mixed, the correct way to cast the sentence would have been 'three pints of beer, a sherry and a whisky and water', though a comma could for the same reasons of clarity be added after 'sherry'. It is also correct to use commas in lists of adjectives – not that one seeks to encourage adjectival writing. 'The room was dark, ugly, smelly, damp and filthy' requires commas in precisely those places. Where only two things or qualities are listed a conjunction and not a comma is needed: as in 'the boy was clean and tidy' or 'he resigned with dignity and good grace, and left the office'. The comma in that last example is required for reasons of good style, clarity and the avoidance of ambiguity; however, another after 'dignity' would be redundant and confusing.

Fourth, a comma should not separate a verb from its subject or object, unless that comma be the first of two forming a parenthesis. When one sees a sentence such as 'the man knows, that his son will get a bad report', or 'everybody thought, the team deserved to lose' we can see the superfluity of the punctuation mark. Were the first sentence to read 'the man knows, whatever his wife may tell him, that his son will get a bad report', that use of the parenthetical commas would be entirely proper.

Fifth, in good style no comma is required before quotation marks, even though some publishers ignore this point. One either has no punctuation at all or the formality of a colon, but not a comma. 'Smith said: "I have no intention of leaving"' is correct. So is 'Smith said "I have no intention of leaving"'. However, 'Smith said, "I have no intention of leaving"' is not. The fundamental point is this: the shorter one's sentences, the harder it is to make mistakes with commas and other forms of punctuation.

The famous example of the difficulty caused by poor punctuation, 'Eats shoots and leaves', is a modern equivalent of Fowler's 'he stopped, laughing' and 'he stopped laughing'. Fowler's two examples mean entirely different things, and the comma demonstrates a PARTICIPLE in the first sentence, while its absence shows a GERUND in the second. Along similar lines is the venerable children's joke 'she cooked, Grandma!' 'Eats shoots and leaves' is an extreme example because each of the verbs could be a noun: the installation of a comma or commas removes any such ambiguity. The same game may be played with 'books plays and travels', and there are numerous other examples.

A comma in the right place may stop serious misunderstandings as well as those that are merely amusing. There are many simple examples of how a comma here or there can change the meaning of a sentence, and of how a supreme stylist will position his punctuation with the greatest care to ensure that the right information is communicated to the reader. Take this sentence: 'She hit the thief who was escaping with her umbrella.' Now look at the various ways of punctuating it. 'She hit the thief, who was escaping with her umbrella' suggests that the thief was escaping with her umbrella, and she hit him. 'She hit the thief, who was escaping, with her umbrella' suggests that as the thief was escaping (without her umbrella) she hit him with it. One could even have: 'She hit the thief who was escaping, with her umbrella.' That last sentence, which is eccentrically punctuated, has the same meaning as the one before it, but it opens up a different array of meanings. It suggests there was more than one thief; that there was one thief among them who was escaping; that she managed to hit that particular thief; and that it was worthy of note that she hit him with her umbrella. So, depending on the information one wants to convey, one punctuates accordingly.

The first, unpunctuated sentence is susceptible of so many different meanings that it is a stylistic abomination. It defeats the first rule of writing, which is that one's meaning should always be clear. It is also true that the final example should, to avoid any doubt, and to eliminate the bizarre punctuation and make its meaning precise, be recast as: 'She hit with her umbrella the thief who was escaping.' For reasons of emphasis that, too, can be punctuated in various ways, but no form of punctuation will alter this clear meaning. It may be punctuated as 'she hit, with her umbrella, the thief who was escaping', in which the writer feels that the important part of the sentence – the part that needs to be emphasised – is the part that refers to the weapon she used. Or it may be punctuated 'she hit with her umbrella the thief, who was escaping', which emphasises not the weapon but the action the thief was taking. Finally, it may be punctuated 'she hit, with her umbrella, the thief, who was escaping', which emphasises both the weapon and the thief's action. It also looks cluttered: the good stylist will want to stress only one part of any sentence.

In the following sentence, published in 2009 in a newspaper, one can see how the simple insertion of a comma will help stave off ambiguity, even if it cannot provide elegance. It was reported that 'the Queen sent a letter of condolence to a pensioner whose dog died after he wrote to Buckingham Palace about the death'. First, to be correct reported speech the auxiliary *had* needs to be inserted after *dog*; but then a comma needs to be inserted after *died*. Otherwise it appears that the dog itself achieved the remarkable feat of writing to the Sovereign about its own demise before it happened, dying shortly thereafter. As remarkable was this sentence about how 'the body of a 45-year-old darts fan was recovered from beneath ice in a frozen lake in Frimley Green, Surrey, where he had been watching the darts world championships'. The unfortunate man had not been watching the darts match under water. A comma would not be enough to save this statement from absurdity. One either changes the word order, or divides the statement into two sentences such as: 'The body of a 45-year-old darts fan was recovered from beneath ice in a frozen lake in Frimley Green, Surrey. He had been watching the darts world championships nearby.'

In a more complex sentence commas must be used to avoid the danger of ambiguity or downright error. In a sentence such as 'the chief executive, invited by the chairman to address the board, having arranged his notes did so', only one meaning is possible given this punctuation. Were the comma to move from after *board* to after *notes* the meaning would change. The chief executive would still be addressing the board, but the invitation would have come from the chairman to do so only once the notes were arranged: and there would be some doubt about who (either the chief executive or the chairman) was arranging the notes. Better still to divide up the sentence: 'The chief executive was invited by the chairman to address the board. Having arranged his notes, he did so.' This is also an instance where the use of the PASSIVE VOICE is excusable, since the *he* in the second sentence clearly refers to the chief executive in the first. Had the active voice been used – 'the chairman invited the chief executive' – the pronoun would seem to refer back to the main subject, which would be wrong.

I would not favour using a comma before a conjunction in a sentence that, without it, holds no danger of ambiguity. Therefore I would regard 'she closed the door, and removed the key' as exhibiting an unnecessary use of the comma by the writer. However, in a sentence such as 'she closed the door, and the window, which was open, blew shut', the comma before *and* is essential if the verb *close* is not to be seen to apply to *window* as well. Dividing the sentence would provide a more elegant and less cluttered solution: 'She closed the door. The window, which was open, blew shut.'

Commence is a pompous way of saying *start*, and an example of why the Anglo-Saxon should be preferred to the Romance.

Commit to An abomination that is moving outside sport and into the rest of life is the idea that a person has to *commit to* something. This always requires the reflexive pronoun and almost never has it: a player commits *himself* to the team.

Community One vogue expression in recent years has been that of the word *community*: we no longer have authors, we have 'the writing community', and presumably also 'the reading community', and so on. This sort of thing is just silly: it represents the cloying desire by people in the public sector or in marketing to seek to develop a jargon to make more human groups of people about whom they are talking, or to whom they are trying to 'reach out'. By lapsing, often unwittingly, into absurdity, they achieve the opposite. Their jargon alienates them from intelligent people, not just by its ludicrousness but also by its capacity to patronise. In non-fiction writing, unless one wishes to be deliberately satirical, sticking to the mainstream is always the best policy.

Comparatives One often hears reference to 'the eldest son' when there are only two sons available; or 'the youngest child' when there are only two children. For a superlative – normally an adjective with the suffix *-est* – to be used there have to be more than two things or people being compared. If there are just two then the comparative – normally ending in *-er* – must be used. Therefore, in the two examples just given it would be 'the elder son' and 'the younger child'. See also ABSOLUTES.

Compared to and **compared with** Although the English verb *compare* is partly formed by the Latin preposition meaning 'with', the dictionary has from its earliest days drawn a distinction between contexts in which one writes *compared with* and those in which one writes *compared to*. If one is using *compare* in the sense of to liken something to something else, then one uses *to*: the most famous example in our literature is 'Shall I compare thee to a summer's day?' If one is simply establishing a comparison – 'I wouldn't compare prosecco with Pol Roger' – one uses *with*.

Complacent and **complaisant** One who is *complacent* is satisfied about life or events, and does not easily see the potential for his complacency to be disturbed. One who is *complaisant* is eager to please or is compliant.

Complement and **compliment** A *complement* is a number of people or objects, or something that adds to them. A *compliment* is what one pays to, for example, an attractive woman or a handsome man; therefore, a charming remark is *complimentary*. Something that augments something else is *complementary*, as in a complementary saucer with a cup. *Complimentary* is also used as a pompous or self-consciously genteel euphemism for 'free of charge' or 'provided at no additional cost', even when it is manifest that the offer is a cynical exercise by which no compliment to the customer is intended, as in 'Would you like some complimentary tea or coffee?'

Complex and **complicated** Something that is *complex* is composed of a number of constituent parts. The human body, for example, is exceptionally complex. Something that is *complicated* tends to have many strands or parts too, but is also difficult to unravel or comprehend: 'The grammar of medieval Welsh was exceptionally complicated.'

Compound nouns These are formations of two nouns with the first taking the place of an adjective: it is arguable whether this disguises the fact that the first noun in the compound has actually become an adjective. See the entry on MURDER for a conspicuous example of how this has happened. Other examples are 'clothes brush', 'dog basket', 'floor polish' and so on. Some compound nouns have unusual plurals: such as 'lords lieutenant', 'commanders-in-chief', 'fathers-in-law', 'courts martial', 'poets laureate' – because in English nouns have plurals but their adjectives do not. Other compound nouns have irregular plurals such as 'passers-by' and 'gins and tonics', according to idiom. See also PLURALS.

Comprise A book may *comprise* fifteen chapters, but is not *comprised of* them. Those who say or write such a thing are confusing it with *composed of*. Another correct way to make the point would be to say that the book 'was constituted of fifteen chapters' or that 'the fifteen chapters constituted the book'.

Conceptualise There are those of us who will always struggle to be persuaded that *conceptualise* is any better a word than *imagine* or *conceive*. Before minting such a word in this way – and the habit of adding *-ise* to an adjective is a popular American one – think carefully about whether a feasible alternative already exists.

Conditionals There are a number of ways to express a *conditional* sense in using verbs. 'I should go', 'I would go', 'I could go', 'I ought to go', 'I may go', 'I might go', 'I should like to go' and 'I would like to go' are the main examples: and they may all introduce a clause beginning with *if*. Eric Partridge observed that 'conditional clauses have always caused trouble to the semi-educated and the demi-reflective; to the illiterate they give no trouble at all.' To avoid being herded into one of those categories, let us take each example above in turn. 'I should get married if I had any money' expresses a simple fact. 'I would get married if I had any money' expresses a determination that, should money arrive, I would be resolved to marry. 'I could get married if I had any money' notes that my ability to marry is dependent on my being able to afford it. 'I ought to get married if I had any money' means that I would feel an obligation upon me to marry if I had the means to do so. 'I may get married if I have any money' denotes that I have the option to marry should I come into funds. 'I might get married if I had any money' denotes a possibility of my marrying if only the money to do so were available. 'I should like to get married if I had any money' and 'I would like to get married if I had any money' are variants of the first two meanings above.

Onions divided conditional clauses into three main sorts.

The first, the *open condition*, covers those sentences 'in which the main clause does not speak of what would be or would have been, and the if-clause implies nothing as to the fact or fulfilment'. These use the indicative mood: Onions's example is 'if you are right, I am wrong'. Other examples are 'if they win the toss, they will bat' or 'if she wears that dress, she will catch cold'; nowhere is it implied that the other person is right, that they will win the toss, or she will wear that dress.

The second, the *rejected condition*, covers 'those in which the main clause speaks of what would be or would have been' and the if-clause implies a negative. His example is 'if wishes were horses, beggars would ride', it being obvious that wishes are not horses. Writers and speakers using this construction may not realise it, but they are using the past subjunctive (*were*); and it is the use of the subjunctive in the if-clause that signals the rejection of the condition. Other examples are 'if you had any sense you wouldn't do that', the clear implication being that you have no sense; or 'were you to let me help you, I should show you another way of doing it', the implication being that you are so stubborn that you probably will not. In these clauses, *would* and *should* are imperfect subjunctives, and they follow the rules for *shall* and *will*.

The third type of conditional sentence has a main clause identical to that of the first type, but has an if-clause that 'marks the action as merely contemplated or in prospect or implies a certain reserve on the part of the speaker'. Onions's first example is 'if this be so, we are all at fault'. Acute readers will note the indicative is used in the main clause and the subjunctive (*be*) in the if-clause; the subjunctive is there to indicate the 'reserve' on the part of the speaker. Another example is 'were she to drive over to see me, I shall show her my garden'. Onions pointed out a century ago that this sort of sentence was largely in rhetorical or formal use, and it has become distinctly less idiomatic since then. The first two types cover most of today's eventualities.

Clauses of the first type operate in the future and past as well as the present. They always remain in the indicative and not the subjunctive mood. Examples are 'if she drove that fast, she was stupid' or 'if he goes to France, he will spend all his money'. (As Onions points out, it has long been idiomatic for the future tense in an if-clause to be replaced by the present tense, as an equivalent to 'if he shall go to France'.) The second sort of clause can also be in the past or future tense, and requires the appropriate subjunctive. For the present tense, we have noted that it requires the past subjunctive: '*Were* she to leave her husband, she would make a terrible mistake.' The past tense requires the pluperfect subjunctive: '*Had* she left her husband, she would have made a terrible mistake.' The past subjunctive is also used for the future, making it indistinguishable from the present and therefore conveying an ambiguity that can only be eliminated by a specific reference to time. For example: '*Were* she to leave her husband in the months to come, she would make a terrible mistake.'

There can be a shift of time between clauses of the second type, and most sophisticated users of English have no difficulty mastering this. 'Had I not drunk so much I should not have so bad a hangover now' is an example: the rule with clauses of this type is to stick to the subjunctive mood. In formal writing always keep to the rules. Conditional clauses do not need to contain *if* to make them conditional: there are many other words or forms that convey an idea of possibility or eventuality. Among them are Fowler's despised *provided* – 'provided he passes the examination, he will get a job'. Here are some others: 'Supposing you won the lottery, what would you spend your winnings on?' 'In the event that he comes, what shall we feed him?' 'In case of fire, break glass.' 'On the condition that you drive carefully, you may borrow my car.' It will be noted that, like *provided*, most of these forms are merely a verbose alternative to *if*. In sentences containing the subjunctive, *if* may also be dispensed with by an inverted word order. Instead of 'if I were to go, it would cause a disturbance', one can say 'were I to go'; instead of 'if I had seen her, I would have told her the truth', one can say 'had I seen her'; and so on.

There are two degrees of conditional sentence. One occasionally reads a sentence such as 'if Smith plays for United next Saturday he will be making his hundredth appearance for the team'. This is fine, for it assumes there is a possibility that Smith could play for United. Sometimes, however, one will wish to make a conjecture about something that simply is not going to happen. If there were absolutely no prospect of Smith's playing for United – because he has broken his leg, or has dropped dead – then one would write 'if Smith played for United next Saturday he would be making his hundredth appearance for the team'. Most idiomatic writers would realise that, having used the first verb correctly in the conditional tense, a *would* would need to follow. The writer could also have started with a subjunctive – 'were Smith to play for United' – which would naturally precede a *would* in the following clause.

Before leaving the matter of conditionals, it is important to note that the vogue for using *may* and *might* as though they were interchangeable is wrong. The distinction can be summed up in the difference between 'the boy *may* still be alive' (but we cannot verify the fact) and 'the boy *might* still be alive' (had he not caught the plane that crashed). In the first sense we simply do not know; either outcome is possible. In the second we know very well he isn't alive, but we are reflecting that had he acted differently he might not have died; *might* is a post-conditional usage. Perhaps a further confusion is that *might* is also the past tense of *may*: so where we would correctly write, in the present tense, 'I hope I may be able to see you in London', in the past it would be 'I hoped I might be able to see you'.

Conference Anyone watching a meeting of trade unionists or Labour activists will have heard the noun *conference* thus stripped of its definite article: 'I put it to conference that . . .' When reporting or describing such occasions, outsiders do best to maintain correct forms and not go native.

Confidant(e) *Confidant* is a useful borrowing from the French to describe a man in whom one confides, but if we wish to use it about a woman then we must call her a *confidante*, as the French would. The Americans do not observe this nicety. See BLOND. Do not confuse with *confident*.

Confirmatio This is a rhetorical term from classical argument and it signifies the clinching evidence of a thesis.

Conjunctions The *OED* says that a conjunction is 'one of the parts of speech; an uninflected word used to connect clauses or sentences, or to coordinate words in the same clause'. Conjunctions come in two categories: they are either *coordinating* or *subordinating*. A coordinating conjunction links two clauses that would stand just as well as independent sentences; a subordinating one introduces a subordinate clause. The coordinating conjunctions are *for*, *and*, *nor*, *but*, *or*, *only* and *yet*: examples of how they coordinate are 'the door was open, for he was already inside', 'I was awake, but I was not dressed', 'they would have arrived sooner, only their car broke down' and the most usual of all such constructions 'the dog was lying by the fire and he stretched out his legs'. Onions also points out that some coordinating conjunctions are preceded at times by coordinating adverbs: *both* may precede *and*, *either* may precede *or*, *neither* may precede *nor*, and *not only* may precede *but* and *also*.

If a writer seeks to make his prose easier to read by shortening his sentences he will often be able to achieve this by cutting them in two. This will be feasible only if the constituent parts are coordinating clauses, and the effect may be achieved by removing the conjunction, as in: 'The dog was lying by the fire. He stretched out his legs.' Orwell's prose is remarkably lacking in conjunctions precisely because his sentences are so short.

The trick is less easily accomplished (and sometimes may not be accomplished at all) in sentences with subordinate clauses, for these include at least one that is not grammatically independent of the others. Subordinating conjunctions introduce either noun clauses or adverbial clauses. An example of the former is where a clause says that something *is*, *was*, *had*, *would* or *will be*: such as in 'she hopes *that he will come*', 'I never dreamt *that she would do that*', 'they wished *that it had stopped raining*' and so on. An adverbial clause is one that illuminates the main verb, as in 'I used to go fishing *when I was a boy*', 'I was late *because the train was delayed*', 'she left her coat *where she could easily find it again*', 'we saved our money *in order that we might have a holiday*'. Onions enumerates several different types of subordinate adverbial clauses. In addition to the types of which I have already given examples there are also conjunctions that introduce comparisons (*as*, *than*, *as if*, *as though*), conditional clauses (*if*, *unless*, *whether*, *so long as* and *that* preceded by *supposing*, *provided*, etc.) and concessive clauses (*though*, *although*, *even if*, *even though*, *notwithstanding that*).

In contemporary usage, some participles have been enlisted as conjunctions; they have become synonyms for words that already serve that purpose. 'He didn't do too badly, considering his age' is one such example; an even more frequent usage is 'the concert is postponed owing to illness'. Partridge lists several of these but in the seventy or so years since he wrote their number has multiplied, to the point where all sorts of participles can serve as conjunctions: 'it was a surprise that he ate anything, seeing he was so ill' or 'they should be here by evening, bearing in mind the traffic'. Sometimes the conjunction *that* is lost in an ellipsis, which is considered now to be acceptable if there is no ambiguity as a result: 'they wished [that] it had stopped raining' causes no confusion whereas 'he believed [that] she didn't' may well.

It is also wise to be sparing with conjunctions. A cluttering of *that*s, for instance, may become tiresome and verbose. 'He drove the car he had hired earlier' makes perfect sense and requires no conjunction after 'car'. 'I knew he saw she understood' needs a conjunction somewhere to break up the staccato verbs and avoid any confusion: best after 'saw'. A phrase such as 'he argued that it was important that politicians should remember that their policies had a widespread effect that was not always obvious' is just shocking and thoughtless. The sentence should be recast, perhaps as follows: 'he argued the importance of politicians' remembering that their policies had a widespread, and not always obvious, effect'. The surviving *that* is important for the avoidance of ambiguity. It is not their policies that the politicians should remember, but the effect they have.

There is no need to avoid beginning sentences with conjunctions, though it may be more felicitous to think of ways to avoid doing so. See AND and BUT. For the distinction between the conjunctions *that* and *which*, see the entry for RELATIVE PRONOUNS. The conjunction *which* should always be preceded by a comma.

Connexion is an archaic spelling of *connection*: and therefore if used today is self-conscious and distracting.

Connive One *connives at*, not *in*, something: the dictionary confirms the etymology as being from the Latin verb *connivere*, to shut one's eyes. To connive at something means to turn a blind eye to it; and, usually, the object at which there is connivance is not a moral, ethical or admirable one: as in 'she connived at her boyfriend's deception of her parents'.

Connote and **denote** Whatever is *connoted* is indicated subsidiary to a main point. Something that is marked out as the main point is *denoted*.

Considering For the use of this participle as a conjunction, see CONJUNCTIONS.

Contemptible and **contemptuous** *Contemptible* is an adjective describing a low or mean person who behaves in a way that excites contempt in others. *Contemptuous* describes the feeling those others have towards the contemptible one. However, it is a word whose main idiomatic usage now appears to describe insolence towards authority, with the undertone that the authority concerned is not worthy of respect.

Continual and **continuous** A *continual* noise is frequent, but with interruptions. A *continuous* noise is one that never stops. They are often confused, as in the newspaper report that said 'the Prime Minister has continuously blurred the line'.

Continuous future is a gradation of the FUTURE TENSE: see the entry on that subject.

Continuous past is a gradation of the IMPERFECT TENSE: see the entry on that subject.

Continuous present is a gradation of the PRESENT TENSE: see the entry on that subject.

Contractions, use of The use of a *contraction* such as *don't, can't, shouldn't, you're* or *they're* in a piece of prose gives it an informal tone: therefore, such devices may be unsuitable in writing that is supposed to convey formality. Also, if you are contracting pronouns and the verb *to be*, be sure to choose the right form, and do not confuse *your* and *you're*, or *their, there* and *they're*. See APOSTROPHES.

Contradict One should take care in using the verb *contradict*. For there to be a contradiction there has to be a statement, for a *contradiction* is a categorical statement in opposition to another. If one person says 'the dog is black' when it is obvious that the beast is white, then to affirm its whiteness is a contradiction; and one may say 'I contradicted his assertion that the dog was black'. However, if what one is taking issue with is not a statement, but a suggestion, or advice, or a conjecture, then one does not strictly contradict it: one rejects it, disputes it, contests it, ignores it, doubts it. And to dismiss a contention with recourse to hard evidence is a *refutation*. See REFUTE, REBUT AND REJECT.

Conviction In the criminal sense, this must be of a statutory offence. So one is said to be *convicted* of murder, burglary, fraud or any other offence specified by law. But one cannot be convicted of paedophilia, which is the name of the perversion and not the crime.

Convince and **persuade** are often used as if interchangeable: they are not. To *convince* someone of something is to make him admit the truth of a contention put to him thanks to the force of one's argument. To *persuade* someone of something means to induce him to believe something. The dictionary says that one can be convinced by persuasion, but that seems to me to undo the force of *convince* and to lose some of the nuance between the two verbs. If one is convinced of something, one's conviction about it is much firmer than if one is merely persuaded of it, which seems to leave room for doubt and possibly even for persuasion back in the other direction. *Convince* carries with it an element of proof: *persuade* an element of faith. Someone can convince me of his age by showing me his birth certificate. He can persuade me of the Christian miracles if I choose to believe him, but he can offer me no proof.

Cookie Since the coming of the Internet, the noun *cookie* has acquired a legitimate usage on both sides of the Atlantic, to signify a method by which operators of websites collect information on those who visit them. In its earlier meaning as a biscuit it is an Americanism, though used widely in Britain.

Coordinate clauses See CLAUSES.

Coordinating conjunctions See CONJUNCTIONS.

Cord See CHORD AND CORD.

Correspond to and **correspond with** The former phrase means to bear a close relation to something, as in 'the description of the man corresponded closely to that of Smith'. The latter phrase means to exchange written communications with someone, as in 'the Duchess and Leigh Fermor corresponded with each other for years'.

Could See CONDITIONALS.

Council and **counsel** A *council* is a deliberative body. *Counsel* as a verb is straightforward – to counsel someone is to offer him advice. As a noun it requires special treatment. *Counsel*, meaning advice, does not take an article – 'he received much counsel'. *Counsel*, meaning a barrister (or a group of barristers) takes no article either: 'counsel for the prosecution refused to cross-examine the witness' or 'he has retained counsel to defend him'. The phrase *counsels of despair*, indicating expressions of pessimism, is usually plural.

Councillor and **counsellor** A *councillor* is a member of a council, of whatever description, with the exception of the Privy Council, of which he is a *Privy Counsellor* (of the Sovereign). A *counsellor* is an adviser or, in a modern sense, one who acts as a mentor.

Countesses, writing to or addressing In the United Kingdom peerage a *countess* is the wife of an earl; in European aristocracies she is the wife of a count. One writes to the wife of the Earl of Essex as 'Dear Lady Essex', and one addresses her in person as 'Lady Essex'. See also EARLS.

Country mile Popular phrases vie with one another for the prize in idiocy. One well out in front is exemplified in the phrase 'he finished ahead of the next horse by a country mile'. No authority that I can find specifies that the mile is any different in length in rural parts from what it is in urban ones. Presumably those who use this ludicrous cliché imagine they are being clever or funny, or possibly both. Their audience knows better.

Couple and **pair** *Couple* is a singular noun that must almost always take a plural verb. So say 'the happy couple were off on their honeymoon' or 'they were a couple of idiots'. The exception is in impersonal phrases such as 'it was a couple of days before the wound started to heal'. To describe two things as a couple rather than a pair suggests a closer degree of association; but it also suggests a lack of similarity. 'A *couple* of dogs' could be two of different breeds that are out hunting together; 'a *pair* of dogs' would denote two of the same breed, colour and size, just as in the world of art a pair of objects are usually identical. *Pair*, like *couple* and indeed *number*, must always take a plural verb. One must say 'a pair of boys were playing in the street' and never 'a pair of gloves is always an acceptable present'. Game birds are referred to in pairs as 'a brace'. *Couple* cannot be used to denote more than two. See NOUNS OF MULTITUDE.

Courtroom and **courthouse** are Americanisms, much loved in Britain because of the popularity of American police and courtroom dramas. In British English we would use *court* for either; or for the latter, more specifically, *magistrates' court*, *Crown Court*, *Court of Appeal* or *Supreme Court*, depending on the nature of the tribunal.

Co-worker is an Americanism for *colleague*.

Credible, **creditable** and **credulous** In the course of one's reading one will find that these all seem to end up in one another's place from time to time. *Credible* is an adjective applied to something or someone who is capable or worthy of being believed. *Creditable* is an adjective that from the early sixteenth to the late eighteenth century meant the same thing. Since then it has been applied to something that brings credit or honour to someone or something – 'it was a creditable performance'. *Credulous* is an adjective applied to someone who was 'born yesterday': it means too ready to believe, or ready to believe despite insufficient evidence: 'He was so credulous he thought the moon was made of green cheese.'

Crescendo A misunderstanding of musical terms leads to the misuse of the term *crescendo*, which is a gradual rising of the dynamic in a passage of music. Therefore nothing can 'reach a crescendo'. It is not a synonym for *climax*. Before using any musical term (*pianissimo*, *fortissimo*, *diminuendo* and so on) in a metaphorical sense, be sure you have verified what it means.

Criterion The plural is *criteria*.

Culminate and **conclude** For something to *culminate* it requires a progression, usually upwards or towards some sort of climax, as in 'the snowdrifts culminated above the roof of the house' or 'the argument culminated in a fight'. To say 'the performance *culminated* with the National Anthem' is wrong; it should be *concluded*.

Curb and **kerb** On both sides of the Atlantic Ocean we *curb* our enthusiasm, but here we step off the *kerb*; in America, and with alarming frequency here, the edge of the pavement – or *sidewalk* – is the *curb*.

Curmudgeon A *curmudgeon* is not a bloody-minded old man. He is a miser and subject to avarice. That may make him difficult, but bloody-mindedness is not what defines him.

Currant and **current** A *currant* is a small fruit; a *current* is the flow of something, such as water or electricity, or an adjective meaning 'of the moment'.

Cusp, as a metaphor taken from astrology, signifies the beginning of something – 'she was on the cusp of adulthood'. In astrology, it means the beginning or entrance of a 'house', when one astrological sign has taken over from another. It is incorrect to use it as meaning an end, as in 'he was on the cusp of finishing'.

Cygnet and **signet** A *cygnet* is an immature swan; a *signet* is a form of seal that is used to close up or authenticate documents.

Cynic and **sceptic** A *cynic* finds fault with everything or everyone, attributes the worst motives to others, and inevitably sees bad where others are inclined to see good. A *sceptic* – in American English, *skeptic* – is by contrast simply doubtful and questioning, rather than freighted with assumptions of others' malevolence.

D

Dashes These are occasionally interchangeable with COLONS. From a stylistic point of view, the *dash* is likely to be more prevalent in dialogue or rhetoric. The *colon* will be more frequent in formal writing. The dash is by its nature dramatic and exclamatory and therefore will be an infrequent visitor to serious prose. For stylistic reasons it is important to use these devices sparingly. They give prose the appearance of being cluttered, they can cause ambiguities and they can distract. Since the writer's aim at all times should be to be understood precisely, these effects are undesirable. When a single dash is used for emphasis it may sometimes be almost an instruction to the reader to find what follows it either shocking, funny or remarkable. This too may be overdone, and suggests a lack of self-confidence on the part of the writer. It can also become bathetic if what follows the dash is something of an anticlimax. Take this sentence from Galsworthy: 'All very well to determine that she would not torture Tony, would keep away from him and spare his senses, but without him – she would be dull and lonely.' The sentence would also be improved if it contained a main verb. Double dashes are often used as a substitute for brackets, as in the following sentence: 'He stood on the platform waiting to be approached – they had never met before and he would not know her by sight – and eventually a woman came up to him.' Dashes may also be used in prose to signify an interruption in the main flow. See also PARENTHESES and PUNCTUATION.

Data is a plural and takes a plural verb: 'the data are revealing'.

Dates When it comes to writing dates one may prefer to write *3 September 1939* rather than *3rd September 1939*, because the abbreviation seems unnecessary. Either form seems to me preferable to the American practice of writing *September 3 1939*, because it seems better to separate the two numbers by the word. In describing a period between two dates, use the following formula: 'from 1939 to 1945' or 'from 4 August to 19 September' rather than put a dash between the two dates. If you must use a dash, omit 'from'.

Dative The *dative* case in languages that inflect is the one that is used for the prepositions *to* or *for*. It is also the indirect object: 'I sent the food *to* a table' or 'she asked the restaurant *for* a table'.

Deaf See POLITICAL CORRECTNESS.

Death, euphemisms for In her essay on upper-class speech, Nancy Mitford attacked *euphemisms*, and especially attacked those for *death*, as betraying lower-class sensibilities in speech. This may have been the case in the 1950s, but today euphemism seems to transcend most class boundaries, thanks to British (and especially English) squeamishness. There are all sorts of euphemisms for this inevitable event. A 'loved one' (a term that seems only to be used posthumously, or when the reaper is heaving into view or into one's consciousness) may 'pass away', or 'pass on', his bereaved family and friends may 'lose' him, he may 'lose his life', or if they are feeling especially Bunyanesque he may even 'pass over to the other side', where he becomes 'deceased' or 'departed'. The last two terms are reminders of how the aspiring, under- educated person passes through a phase in which he feels it is right to imitate the language of bureaucrats, few of whom know how to speak or write English properly. 'Joining the heavenly choir' is simply Monty Python. To Mitford and her class the person just *dies*, and thereafter is *dead*.

Debate The verb requires no preposition. One debates economic policy, and does not debate *about* it. As a noun, however, *debate* may require a preposition – 'today's Commons debate was *on* farming'.

Deceased This is a pompous term for *dead*, often misappropriated as a genteel euphemism (see DEATH, EUPHEMISMS FOR). It really only belongs these days in legal or official language, as in 'the deceased was travelling at 80 mph when the accident occurred'. Do not confuse it with *diseased*, which means ill.

Decimate A word people insist on wrenching from its correct etymology is *decimate*. As every schoolboy used to know this was a punishment meted out to Roman legions, in which every tenth man was killed. Its correct sense in English, therefore, is the reduction of the strength of a body of people by 10 per cent. It does not mean more or less than that, though it is often used to describe the near elimination of a contingent, and has been wrongly used now for over 100 years. The greatest absurdity of all is a statement such as 'the workforce was decimated by 20 per cent', followed closely by 'the town was decimated completely'. It is also used catachrestically for *devastate*: 'Campaigners claim the £34bn project will decimate the countryside', said the *Mail on Sunday* on 26 August 2012.

Declension See CASES.

Definite article See THE.

Defuse and **diffuse** *Defuse* is what one does to a bomb, or when one takes the metaphorical heat out of a tricky situation: 'He managed to defuse the argument by uttering some soothing words.' *Diffuse* as a verb means to spread something out. The adjective *diffuse* means widespread. The former rhymes with *confuse*, the latter with *profuse*.

Delude, delusion and **illusion** To *delude* someone is, according to the *OED*, 'to befool the mind or judgement of [someone], so as to cause what is false to be accepted as true', as in 'he deluded her into thinking that he loved her', or 'the prime minister deluded the public into thinking he was a Conservative'. The noun is *delusion*. There is a distinction between *delusion* and *illusion*: the former is in many senses a more extreme form of the latter, and the element of malicious deceit or fraud usually resulting in a *delusion* (except where it is self-inflicted, as in a 'delusion of grandeur') is often absent from an *illusion*. The *OED* defines *illusion* as 'something that deceives or deludes by producing a false impression; a deceptive or illusive appearance, statement, belief . . . an unreal visual appearance, an apparition, phantom.' It can also mean 'a mental state involving the attribution of reality to what is unreal; a false conception or idea; a deception, delusion, fancy.' Hence, 'I was under no illusions about his honesty', or 'he created the illusion that he knew what he was doing', or 'the conjuror specialised in illusions'. It should not be confused with ALLUSION or the now almost obsolete ELUSION.

Democracy is an especially abused term, used at election times by political parties who will be glad to put it in abeyance for up to the following five years while they engage in elective dictatorship.

Demonstrative pronouns These are the pronouns used when pointing something out, with a distinction between *this here* and *that there*, or in the plural *these here* and *those there*. A common SOLECISM is when one hears someone say in a shop, pointing to an object, 'I want one of them' when he means 'I want one of those'. Demonstratives may also be used metaphorically, in the absence of a physical object, but only logically when referring back to something already expressed, as in sentences such as 'black olives – I can't stand those'. *Them* is a simple accusative, as in 'he gave them the ball'.

Denote See CONNOTE AND DENOTE.

Dependant and **dependent** *Dependant* is a noun. *Dependent* is an adjective. For example: 'His dependants were dependent upon him', 'the child was dependent upon his father' or 'the child was a dependant of his father'.

Deprecate and **depreciate** To *deprecate* something is to seek deliverance from it by prayer. However, the dictionary lists a usage from as long ago as 1897 where it means to express disapproval of something, and this usage is now commonplace and widely accepted. The extension of the meaning of *deprecate* has been compounded by the term *self-deprecating*, when somebody (usually with a degree of cynicism) disparages himself in order to court popularity. Where one is minded to *deprecate* something it may sometimes be more exact to say that one disapproves of it, regrets it, or cannot condone it. To make matters worse *deprecate* is also confused by some with *depreciate*, which is what happens to an asset when it declines in value.

Derisive and **derisory** *Derisive* describes something that projects derision, such as a derisive shout or a derisive article. *Derisory* describes something that should provoke derision, such as a derisory suggestion or a derisory offer.

Despite and **in spite of** are interchangeable.

Detract and **distract** *Detract* is a verb that means to take away from, to diminish or lessen: as in 'the hat she wore detracted from the beauty of her costume'. *Distract* may mean to divert – 'her attention was distracted by the barking dog' – or it may mean to throw someone into a mental condition in which he is at a loss to know what to do – 'the shock of her bereavement distracted her greatly'. The two verbs should not be confused. It would be wrong to say 'the hole in the wall distracted from the appearance of the garden'.

Devastate See DECIMATE and TABLOID PRESS.

Dialog and **dialogue** See AMERICAN SPELLING.

Die and **dice** It never fails to surprise some literate people how many of their peers think that *dice* is a singular. It is a plural. The singular is *die*.

Different from/than/to Something is different *from* something else, not *to* it or, even more abominable, *than* it. The last is a colloquial Americanism, such as Timothy Snyder writes in his book *Bloodlands*: 'A Red Army taking American supplies from the east was an entirely different foe than a Red Army concerned about a Japanese attack from the east.'

Different, **used redundantly** In the phrase 'he slept with three different women', the adjective is pointless. 'He slept with three women' is perfectly adequate to convey the meaning, because the three women in question must inevitably have been different from each other. 'Very different' may be permissible if the three women were very distinct from each other in physical or mental characteristics.

Diffuse See DEFUSE AND DIFFUSE.

Digitise succinctly puts a complex electronic procedure into one word. It demonstrates legitimate language change caused by a new necessity, and how vocabulary must keep expanding to describe new concepts and objects.

Dilemma A *dilemma* can only be between two courses of action. It is from the Greek word meaning 'two propositions'. If somebody cannot decide between several options he may have a *problem*, or even a *quandary*, but he does not have the good fortune of merely having a dilemma. I am not clear why it should be thought that when a dilemma represents being forced to choose between two equally unpalatable options it has horns upon which one can be impaled (though it may have something to do with a charging bull) but at least that cliché serves to remind people that dilemmas, like horns, come in pairs: the unicorn being a mythical beast, and the rhinoceros an exception for this purpose.

Dinosaur To describe someone with outdated attitudes or opinions as a *dinosaur* is now a cliché.

Disabled is an adjective that is now frequently misused. In sentences such as 'the law now demands disabled access to the theatre' it is not the access that is disabled, but the people who need it. One should write 'the law demands access for the disabled to the theatre'.

Disclosed and **revealed** The latter is a tabloid, or sensationalist, inflation of the former. If unexceptional facts (often supplied to a newspaper by a celebrity's public relations adviser) are described as having been *revealed* when, in fact, all they have been is *disclosed*, what verb is to be used for something that is a genuine revelation?

Discomfit and **discomfort** These two verbs and their derivatives, such as *discomforting* and *discomfiting*, have distinct meanings; and the latter is occasionally used in error for the former. *Discomfort* is the older of the two words, and the dictionary defines it in its extant sense as 'to make uncomfortable or uneasy, mentally or physically'. *Discomfit* has only the psychological usage: to say that a man was discomfited by his wife's behaviour means he was embarrassed or put on edge by it. To say he was discomforted by it would mean that it had, somehow, made him physically uncomfortable.

Discreet and **discrete** sound the same, and are spelt almost the same, but mean two completely different things. Until twenty or thirty years ago there were few difficulties with these terms, because the latter was used only in learned journals. It has now become one of those academic terms that non-academics come across in everyday life and use: perhaps this is because of the large number of scientists who feed the appetite for expert commentary on television's twenty-four-hour news channels. *Discreet* means tactful, understated, restrained, lacking in vulgarity or advertisement; *discrete* means separate. *Discreet service* is service carried out without show or ostentation; a *discrete service* is one distinct or separate from something else.

Disgraced This is frequently used to exaggerate a moral condition and is another tabloid inflation. See TABLOID PRESS.

Disingenuous Since *ingenuous* is used to describe a person whom the dictionary describes as 'honourably straightforward, open, frank, candid', *disingenuous* is therefore a disobliging negative of the word.

Disinterested and **uninterested** At least one dictionary (I shall not embarrass its publishers by naming it) has put its hands up and surrendered over the correct usage of *disinterested*: it now says that it can mean *uninterested*. However, insistence on its correct usage is not a point of pedantry; it comes from the desire to retain an important adjective that indicates a not especially subtle distinction. If one is *disinterested* in a question one takes neither side in it. One can see both sides of the argument and is well placed to act impartially as an arbiter in the matter. If one could not care less about the point at issue, one is *uninterested* in it. One might attend a football match in which one supports neither side, or supports a team that is not one of the two playing, and one can be *disinterested* in the outcome. One could go to the match under sufferance, being bored by football itself, and be *uninterested* in it. The *OED* still stigmatises the misuse of *disinterested* as a 'loose use', even though the first person it can find to have been loose with it was John Donne in 1612. Most abusers are from the twentieth century, and it is manifest from the contexts in which they employ the word that they have not realised it has a meaning different from *uninterested*.

Dissatisfied and **unsatisfied** A man who is *dissatisfied* with his dinner thinks it is of poor quality. A man who is *unsatisfied* after eating his dinner has not had enough, and hungers for more.

Dissent and **dissension** *Dissent* as a noun describes a state of contrary opinion: 'There was general dissent in the House from the Minister's view.' *Dissension* is a magnified form of dissent. It describes a more widespread feeling of opposition, and one that could result in violent uprising or rebellion: 'The failure to repeal the Act caused great dissension throughout the country.'

Dissociate and **disassociate** *Dissociate* means to cut oneself off from a group or body of opinion: 'He dissociated himself from the party.' *Disassociate* means to detach or separate, as in: 'I can never disassociate the two ideas from each other.'

Distrust See MISTRUST AND DISTRUST.

Divisio is a rhetorical term to describe the development of a new strand of argument. A writer may be constructing an argument about why it is bad to feed children on huge quantities of chocolate. He may begin by discussing the poor effects on the children's health. The *divisio* comes when he also points out that the money the chocolate costs could be better spent on something else, or saved and used to reduce household expenditure.

Do Some verbs are used as maids-of-all-work in a way that suggests laziness on the part of the writer, or a lack of precision in his thinking, or both. *Do* is an obvious offender, notably in the SLANG construction 'do some ironing', 'do some cooking', 'do some painting', 'do some gardening' when one verb (and a more precise verb at that) – to iron, to cook, to paint, to garden – will serve in place of two. It is common in informal speech, but to be avoided in formal writing. See also SEE.

Donate and **give** One *donates* money or goods with a charitable intention. Where money or goods are given without that intention, they are simply *given*. Hence 'he donated a fortune to the museum' but 'she gave her children £1,000 each'. See also GIFT.

Doolally (deolali), going Idioms are often generational; younger people may not know that *going deolali* (anglicised now, according to the dictionary, as *doolally*) was Indian Army slang for becoming insane, after the name of the town in India whose military hospital housed those of unsound mind until they could be sent back to 'Blighty'; or that someone who is only 'fifteen annas to the rupee' or 'elevenpence ha'penny to the shilling' is in our times 'a couple of sandwiches short of a picnic'. However colourful some idioms are, they are best avoided if most of one's readers will not understand them.

Double negatives Avoid double negatives. They are offences against logic and, if they are an attempt at being funny, they fail. Sometimes they occur by accident: not obvious stinkers such as 'he said he would not never go there', which can only be the product of illiteracy and stupidity, but a phrase such as 'of all the casualties, she was the least unscathed'. *Unscathed* is entirely the wrong word; it needs to be one of its antonyms, *injured* or *hurt*. Statements such as 'it was impossible that she could not succeed' are mind-twisters; it is much better to say 'it was certain she would succeed'. Still further down the literary scale, phrases such as 'not inconsiderable' and 'not inexpensive' are unfunny if they attempt to be humorous, arch if they attempt to be anything else. They have no place in civilised writing, except in the most obvious forms of parody.

Any clause that contains more than one of *no*, *nothing*, *never*, *nowhere*, *none*, *nobody* or *no one* is almost certain to have a logical problem within it and should be examined with great care before being allowed out of captivity. If one is about to use a negative to imply a positive, it is always preferable to pause, reflect and use the positive. Why write 'no one is missing' when one means 'everyone is here'? Or 'nothing is wrong' when one means 'all is right'? Such phrases should only be used in response to a direct question: 'Is anyone missing?' or 'Is anything wrong?' Obvious double negatives are not the problem, for all but the illiterate will spot them; it is those that come in longer sentences, usually including verbs that themselves have a negative import, that cause unexpected difficulties.

Be especially alert to sentences such as 'I cannot doubt that there may not be times when you feel like that', which will confound almost everyone who reads or hears it. It is also a trait of pompous authority figures to use the double negative: we had, in living memory, a prime minister, John Major, who used phrases such as 'not inconsiderably' with a frequency that increased as his credibility sank.

Doubt that and **doubt whether** It is a solecism to use *if* after the verb *doubt*. One either doubts *whether* something is so, or doubts *that* it is so. The use of *whether* suggests an invisible *or not*. This conjunction is used in preference to that where the doubt is reasonable, as in 'I doubt whether the boy is clever enough to pass his examination'. To say 'I doubt that the boy is clever enough' means one is absolutely sure the boy is not clever enough. To put it another way: one would say 'I doubt that there are fairies at the bottom of the garden' rather than 'I doubt whether there are fairies'. Used either after a negative, or rhetorically, the construction must be *doubt that*. 'We cannot doubt that tomorrow is Tuesday.' 'Can you doubt that he is lying?'

Doubtful and **dubious** To say that 'the result is doubtful' means that it is uncertain, or cannot be determined. To say 'the result is dubious' implies that it is fraudulent. People who are *doubtful* are, literally, filled with doubt about certain issues or questions: 'He was doubtful about the likely success of the enterprise.' People who are *dubious* have a character defect that makes them seem untrustworthy or unreliable. A *dubious* statement is one that is questionable. A *doubtful* statement is one expressing doubt.

Dove and **dived** *Dove*, to rhyme with *cove*, is used in American English as the past participle of the verb *dive* – as in 'he dove off the cliff'. It is not used in British English, in which one would say *dived*.

Dr, use of The title *Dr* can bring all sorts of difficulties. Not all medical practitioners are so termed. Members of the Royal College of Surgeons and certain other specialists style themselves *Mr.* In teaching hospitals some of the more senior medical men may be neither *Dr* nor *Mr* but *Professor*. Should their distinction have been marked also by a knighthood, or even a peerage, their title of chivalry or nobility immediately precedes their name: so it would be Dr Sir John Smith, or Professor Lord Smith. A surgeon who was knighted or ennobled would, obviously, stop using the honorific *Mr.* Most people who hold doctorates of philosophy, science, music, letters, laws or divinity would use the title only in a relevant context: when in a university or some similar academic position or, in the case of doctors of divinity, while in the cloth. Composers or conductors with doctorates of music used to style themselves *Dr* (Dr Vaughan Williams, Dr Sargent), but this has fallen out of fashion. Those who hold only honorary doctorates of any description would not usually use the title. In America anyone with a doctorate of almost any description or of any value will style himself *Dr.* This is not necessarily a mark of charlatanry so much as a sign of that society's regard for the benefits of erudition.

Draconian Draco was an Athenian ruler in the seventh century BC and he ran a tight ship, with strict laws and harsh punishments. The adjective *draconian* is used today correctly when it describes something similar, such as 'the draconian penal code in Iran that causes drug dealers to be hanged and children to be flogged'. To describe 'the council's draconian parking regulations' is simply absurd, or at best an example of HYPERBOLE.

Draft and **draught** are frequently confused HOMOPHONES, both as nouns and verbs. The verb *draft* means 'to draw off or out and remove (a party of persons, animals, or things) from a larger body for some special duty or purpose'. It often has a military sense: 'The government drafted half the regiment for service overseas.' It also means to make a rough or preliminary copy of a document: 'He drafted his speech.' Its nouns are thus: 'there was a draft of troops that evening' or 'the second draft of the article was better than the first'. The noun may also be used to describe a number of troops – 'he was part of the draft that left that evening' – or an order to move money – 'he transferred the money by banker's draft'. The verb *draught* is now archaic, though an indication of what it could mean is retained in the compound *draughtsman*. It has specific meanings as a noun: such as the action of drawing or pulling, or the animal used to undertake those tasks. From there it transmutes into an adjective – *draught beer*, a *draught horse*, and so on. One drinks a *draught* of ale, or of water. The board game is *draughts* (in America, checkers), and *draught* is a special nautical term describing 'the depth of water that a vessel draws, or requires to float her' (*OED*). It also means a current, stream or flow, as in 'there's a nasty draught coming from somewhere'. In American English, that would be spelt *draft*.

Drapes is the American term for *curtains*.

Dry To say something is *dry* is usually sufficient to convey the sense that it is not wet, or even just damp. Something that is *dried out* is normally no different from something that is simply dry, unless one wishes to signify that it is completely *desiccated* – that is, it is (or was) a living thing with a dry outer surface that has also become completely dry inside too: in which case it is probably better to say it is *desiccated*. When talking, for example, of clothes, it is enough to say 'she had to dry the washing' and no need to say 'she had to dry out the washing'.

Dubious See DOUBTFUL AND DUBIOUS.

Due to See CAUSE.

Dukes and duchesses, writing to or addressing The Duke of Anywhere is always called by that title, unlike other ranks of the peerage, who may be the Marquess of Anywhere at first citation and subsequently Lord Anywhere. He may be 'the Duke' at second mention. Similarly, the Duchess of Anywhere is at a second mention 'the Duchess'. A non-royal duke can be addressed as 'Dear Duke' in correspondence, his wife as 'Dear Duchess'. In conversation, say 'duke' or 'duchess' unless a member of the ducal household or a public official is formally addressing them, in which case say 'your Grace'.

E

Each, all and **both** In its simplest form, *each* is a pronoun – 'each was spoken to'. It is singular. So one would say 'Mr Smith, Mr Brown and Mr White each has his own house' rather than 'have their own house'. With groups, use *all*. 'The Smiths, the Browns and the Whites all have their own family tree'; but 'each family has its own family tree'. Sometimes there appear to be pronoun problems with the use of *each*, as in 'John and Mary each ate their apples'. That is wrong. The clumsy 'John and Mary each ate his or her apple' would be correct. The problem is avoided by using *both* or, where there are more than two subjects, *all*, as in 'John and Mary both ate their apples' or 'Mary, John and Jane all owned their own houses'.

It is incorrect to write 'they each went to London'. If you must use *each* (and it would be better to write *both* or, if more than two, *all*), write 'each of them went to London'. The same is true with other persons; *you each* should be *each of you*, *we each* should be *each of us*, and so on.

There is also a subtle distinction between the usages of *each* and *both* or *all*. To say 'we each went to see mother' may imply we went separately; 'we both went' or 'we all went' implies we went together.

Each other and **one another** *Each other* has a distinct usage from *one another*. If there are two people, and only two, they talk to *each other*, or to *one another*. If there are three or more people, they talk to *one another*. Similarly, 'John and Mary wrote to each other' is correct but 'John, Mary and Jane wrote to each other' is not. 'John, Mary and Jane wrote to one another' is. The possessives are 'each other's' and 'one another's'.

Eager See ANXIOUS AND EAGER.

Earls, writing to or addressing An earl is the middle rank in the hereditary peerage, below a marquess and above a viscount. His wife is a countess. His daughters are all ladies; his sons honourable, unless the eldest has a courtesy title. When writing about an earl call him the Earl of Anywhere at first mention, subsequently Lord Anywhere. When writing to him, address him as 'Dear Lord Anywhere' and sign 'Yours sincerely'. See also COUNTESSES.

Earmark and **hallmark** An *earmark* is a sign of ownership, originating from agriculture: it used to signify to whom sheep belonged. It is also a verb, though its contemporary use moves it from the original meaning of the noun: 'he earmarked the wood for future use' means that he set it aside for a particular purpose. It must not be confused with *hallmark*, which is a sign stamped on sterling silver. It is 'the official mark or stamp used by statutory Hall-marking authorities in marking the standard of gold and silver articles assayed by them, without which articles of these metals may not legally be sold' (*OED*). The name comes from the stamping of goods in the assay office at Goldsmith's Hall in London. The noun may be used metaphorically as a token of breeding or superiority – 'he bore the hallmark of having been to a public school', or 'his good manners were a hallmark of his character'. It is also a verb – 'it was hallmarked as sterling silver'.

Earn The past tense is not *earnt*, some sort of parallel formation with the verb *learn*, for which the past tense may be *learnt*; it is *earned*.

Easter Saturday The day between Good Friday and Easter Sunday is not *Easter Saturday*. It is *Easter Eve* or *Holy Saturday*. Easter Saturday is the Saturday after Easter Sunday.

Economic and **economical** *Economic* has evolved into an adjective describing financial affairs, usually on a national scale, or pertaining to the management of the political economy. Therefore we have phrases such as 'economic policy', 'economic crisis', 'economic recovery' and 'economic considerations'. *Economical* is an adjective describing the frugal use of resources. If one has an economical meal, an economical holiday or an economical central heating system, one is spending as little money as possible on any of them. In the last twenty years the word has also taken on what was once an original and amusing metaphorical usage, after a senior civil servant, Sir Robert Armstrong, admitted that he had been 'economical with the truth'. He made his point well at the time, and everyone immediately understood what he meant, but the phrase and its adaptations have become hackneyed, and are now best avoided by thoughtful writers.

Edible has usurped the Ango-Saxon *eatable* as the adjective to describe a food that can be ingested.

-ee endings In recent decades there has been a rash of mintages of words (many of them pointless or, where not pointless, illogical) ending in the suffix *-ee*. The prevalent view, indeed, seems to be that anybody who does something is a person ending in *-ee*. Someone who goes to a meeting is an *attendee*; someone who gets out of a jail is an *escapee*. There is little sense to this. Someone who goes to a meeting is an *attender*. Someone who escapes from somewhere is an *escaper*. Subjects of verbs are usually people whose titles end in *-er*, such as *trainer*, *examiner*, *interviewer*, *employer*. In logic, the suffix *-ee* should describe not someone who does something but someone to whom something is done, or for whom something is made to happen, such as *trainee*, *examinee*, *interviewee* and *employee*. A *referee*, for example, is someone to whom some matter is referred. Some usages defy this logic but seem to make perfect sense, such as *absentee* (unless one interprets the word as being not one who is absent, but one who by circumstances is made absent). The point about some new *-ee* nouns that one sees is that they are not necessary; there are words already in the language to do their job.

Effect See AFFECT AND EFFECT.

Effective and **effectual** – and their negatives, *ineffective* and *ineffectual* – have shades of meaning now so close as to be almost identical. The dictionary defines *effective* as meaning 'powerful in effect; producing a notable effect' but then, to complicate the issue, as also meaning *effectual*. Under *effectual* the usage meaning 'powerful in effect' is cited as 'rare': *effectual*'s main meaning seems now to be 'produces its intended effect'. In the negative, *ineffectual* seems to be a shade beyond *ineffective*; someone who is ineffective does not produce the desired effect, but someone who is ineffectual is a failure.

Effete means worn out, weak or degenerate. It does not mean *effeminate*.

Egoism and **egotism** are not interchangeable. *Egoism* is what Americans and psychologists would call 'self-obsession' – the inability to consider any situation or question except in how it relates to oneself. *Egotism* is a different sort of objectionableness, and is about the projection of oneself; this usually manifests itself when somebody else becomes the favourite topic of his own conversation.

Egregious Something *egregious* is outstanding in a bad way: as in 'an egregious error'. It is not, in contemporary usage, outstanding in a way that causes it to be celebrated or renowned.

Either and **either . . . or** Either is a singular noun. It is the positive of *neither*, is one of two, and is often misused. 'Would either of you three get me a drink?' is so obviously wrong as, I hope, to require no further elucidation. 'Would one of you three' or 'would any of you three' would both be correct. However, fewer writers or speakers understand that 'she had rouge on either cheek' is wrong (Fowler calls this construction 'archaic'); it is on *both* cheeks: *either* in such a context means one or the other, not both. 'She had rouge on each cheek' would not be wrong but, since as a rule there are two cheeks on the face, 'both cheeks' is to be preferred. Being one of two, *either* is also singular: 'either of them is well-placed to win the match' is correct. As with *neither*, prefer 'both John and I are happy to help' to 'either John or I am happy to help', since the second usage suggests that the help of only one is needed. *Or* is the inevitable complement to *either*, never *nor* or *and*: 'Either John or Mary would fetch the children from school.' *Either* also has an adverbial use, in negative sentences. 'I don't want to do that either' is the natural response to an invitation to take an alternative course to one already offered. A positive response would be 'I want to do that too'.

Eke out As a nation we seem constitutionally incapable of using the phrase *eke out* correctly. Since the thirteenth century *eke* has meant to increase, lengthen or add to. Therefore, if one *ekes out* something, one extends it, or makes it last longer: so it would be correct to say that 'she eked out her supply of water for five days' or 'I eked out my salary for a month'. Yet one constantly reads about a person 'eking out his existence' to suggest a life of struggle or hardship. It is easy to see why the mistake is made, but a mistake it is. If one is eking out an existence, one is making it last longer: which is not usually what is meant. Inexplicable, however, was a phrase heard in a BBC weather forecast early in 2012: 'Bad weather eking its way south.'

Elder and **older** *Elder* began its life as the comparative of *old*, a role since usurped by *older*. As an adjective, *elder* most frequently now signifies seniority in a relationship. One would say 'my elder son' (of two sons) not 'my older son', the latter usage inviting the question 'Older than whom?' The usage 'elder son' immediately signifies the existence of a younger son. There are certain idiomatic usages, such as 'elder statesman', and the adjective has moved to be a noun in phrases such as 'the elders of the church', to signify senior members of a congregation.

Elevator is an Americanism for the noun *lift*.

Elicit and **illicit** *Elicit* is a verb, meaning to draw forth something, usually a fact or other information: 'From what she said, he elicited the fact that she was lying.' It should not be confused with *illicit*, which the dictionary defines as an adjective describing something 'not authorised or allowed; improper, irregular . . . not sanctioned by law, rule or custom' as in 'he operated an illicit printing press' or 'he traded in illicit alcohol'.

Ellipsis is something unsaid in a sentence, but which all experienced writers or speakers understand is there: such as in the first clause of this sentence, where the elliptical phrase 'that is' is omitted between 'something' and 'unsaid'. Until the late eighteenth century the dash (–) in prose to signify something omitted was known as an ellipsis; and it is the term used to describe the omission of words in a quotation that is signified by a run of full stops, thus . . .

Elusion This noun, meaning a dexterous escape, is now particularly rare, except when used in error for ALLUSION or ILLUSION: see those entries.

Emerge The dictionary defines *emerge* as to come out of a liquid or out of darkness and, either way, to become visible. It is easy to see how the word acquired a figurative meaning from this sense, and it has had it for 300 years; but that figurative meaning has now been debased to the point where the verb covers anything that comes to one's attention. It is now used so ubiquitously that it has come to act as a synonym for *happen*, *derive from*, *come out of* or even just for the verb *to be* ('It's Monday, it emerges'). Often, when one reads that something has *emerged* it is simply that it *is*. A verb once used to evoke the appearance of a sea monster from Stygian waters, or an ogre from pitch darkness, is now used to try to convey a sense of excitement about the occurrence of the most banal of facts. There are many other examples of such exhausted words in our language. See, for instance, ACHINGLY, KEY, LEGENDARY and LITERALLY, and also METAPHORS.

Empathy and **sympathy** *Empathy* is the state of feeling someone else's feelings – be it their pain, their grief or their joy. It is a word that came into use at the beginning of the twentieth century, and reflected the dilution of the concept of *sympathy*, which had originally meant the same thing. By the twentieth century *sympathy* had come to mean fellow feeling or merely accord, or the expression of regret with another's sorrow or misfortune.

Employee See -EE ENDINGS.

Empty is an incomparable adjective: something cannot be *emptier* than another thing that is *empty*.

Emulate If one seeks to *emulate* another, one seeks to match his achievements and, perhaps, surpass them. It does not mean to copy or imitate. So it is correct to say: 'Johnnie sought to emulate his brother's achievement in winning a place at Cambridge.'

Endemic, epidemic and **pandemic** *Endemic* is an adjective meaning prevalent or common – 'crime was endemic in that part of the city'. An *epidemic* is an outbreak of a disease on a large scale in a certain area – 'there was a flu epidemic that winter' – and it is also an adjective – 'the outbreak was of epidemic proportions'. A *pandemic* is an epidemic on a massive scale: 'The Spanish flu pandemic after the Great War killed thousands across the whole of Europe.'

Enormity and **enormousness** In his speech in Chicago in 2008 on the night he won the United States presidential election, Barack Obama spoke of the *enormity* of the task ahead of him. I am unclear whether this is now accepted American usage to describe something that is *enormous*. The word is used in such a fashion here, and appears to be one of those whose wrong usage has been accepted by some dictionaries (though not by the *OED*). An *enormity*, in its first current usage given by the dictionary, is a 'deviation from moral or legal rectitude': though it does concede that, influenced by *enormous*, it can mean 'extreme or monstrous wickedness'. So an *enormity* is something bad, a transgression: it is not simply something big. One should speak not of the *enormity* of the task, but of its *enormousness*: even if one is President of the United States.

Enquiry and **inquiry** The dictionary suggests these terms are, up to a point, interchangeable: as are the related verbs *enquire* and *inquire*. It does, however, specify that an official investigation is an *inquiry*: as in a court of inquiry or a judicial inquiry. An inquiry is really a formal investigation, usually conducted by a judge or senior official into some aspect of government activity or something for which the state has ultimate responsibility. An individual asking the time of a train *enquires*, or makes an *enquiry*. Part of the problem with the interference of the state in our lives, and the apparent ubiquity of its bureaucrats, is that many of us find ourselves using – or misusing – the jargon of officials in our everyday language. We use the word *inquiry* when we mean *question* or *query*.

Ensure See ASSURE, ENSURE AND INSURE.

Enter into One only ever *enters into* an abstract, such as 'he entered into an agreement with his friend', or 'they entered into a protracted dispute with each other'. One simply *enters* a building, without the need for a preposition.

Enunciate This means to proclaim or state publicly; it may also mean to pronounce, in the sense of articulating sounds. See the entry on ANNUNCIATE AND ENUNCIATE for a possible source of confusion.

Envision does not exist, though it is an increasingly popular verb with speakers of American English, who from time to time *envision* certain turns of events. The verb *envisage* does exist, and has been doing the same job for hundreds of years.

Epigram and **epigraph** An *epigram* is a pointed saying, usually witty, and often but not exclusively uttered *in memoriam*.

Milton's 'they shall read this clearly in thy charge: / New presbyter is but old priest writ large' is epigrammatic. Do not confuse with *epigraph*, which is a quotation placed at the opening of a book or document, such as 'Only connect . . .' at the start of E. M. Forster's *Howards End*.

Equal is an incomparable adjective; when Orwell wrote that some were more equal than others, he was using a linguistic abomination to make a fierce point about the hypocrisy of communism. One cannot be *more equal*, or *most equal*. See ABSOLUTES.

Erupt and **irrupt** To *erupt* is to burst or break out. Do not confuse it with *irrupt*, which is to burst or break in, as in 'the house suffered an irruption of floodwater'.

Escapee See -EE ENDINGS.

Especially and **specially** are both adverbs, but the former is the more emphatic. Compare 'you will be in trouble, especially if you do that' with 'he went to the shop specially to buy a bunch of flowers'. *Specially* has the sense of 'for a particular time'.

Esquire, use of Be sure not to use the abbreviation *Esq.* – which is how *esquire* is usually written – with any other title. One occasionally sees the solecism 'Mr John Smith Esq.'; and anyone who is a knight, baronet, peer or clergyman, or holds any rank in the armed forces or any academic distinction that confers the title of doctor or professor, is not by definition an esquire. The abbreviation *Esq.* must precede any letters following the surname: so it is 'John Smith Esq., FRCO', not 'John Smith FRCO, Esq.' It is only used in written English.

Ethnic This word is an adjective and not a noun – a phrase such as 'the area was full of ethnics' is SLANG and not POLITICALLY CORRECT.

Euphemisms In the era when people used to cover their table legs in the interests of propriety, *euphemism* – using mild or evasive language to describe potentially unpleasant realities – perhaps had its uses. But these days, saying 'smallest room' when one means 'lavatory', or 'passing away' when one means 'dying', seems arch, silly, comical and tasteless. It also reduces clarity and suggests a lack of perception in use of language. Euphemism also has a political use. One of the prime targets for Orwell in *Politics and the English Language* is the use of euphemism. To make his point he uses, quite understandably, an extreme example. He says that an English professor defending Russian totalitarianism 'cannot say outright, "I believe in killing off your opponents when you can get good results by doing so."' Instead, Orwell puts into the professor's mouth a sixty-five-word circumlocution that disguises the matter. Politicians and marketing men occasionally use individual words in a downright dishonest way, sometimes in the form of euphemism, sometimes not.

Nancy Mitford stigmatised euphemism as a tool of the lower or less educated classes, painting it as part of the sentimentality shunned by more hard-minded people such as her: like Orwell, she saw its use as tribal, though she singled out a different tribe. Her class made a point, during the rise of the middle class in the period between the end of the Great War and the end of Mrs Thatcher, of mocking the faux-gentility they felt they detected in such people, and the careful avoidance of directness that they discerned to be part of it. DEATH may be the best example, but there are plenty of others. Anything to do with bodily functions, be they digestive, excremental or carnal, was ripe for attention. So too were references to psychological or physical illnesses or handicaps. Whatever the upper classes would say, they would not 'spend a penny' or 'wash their hands', nor would they 'go courting' or have 'a young man'. They would know no one who was 'simple' or 'soft in the head', but they would know people who were mad or were lunatics. The invention of POLITICAL CORRECTNESS, which takes euphemism into a different stratum of paranoid art form, seems a standing rebuke to the likes of Mitford, and to their determination to call a spade a spade. Euphemism is no longer the province of the genteel class.

Today, there are plenty of coy and vulgar euphemisms much beloved by the red-top press: 'toyboy', 'love child', 'love nest', 'cheating' and 'stunner' are what might more directly be called 'gigolo', 'illegitimate child', 'flat', 'committing adultery' and 'mistress'.

Euphuism, not to be confused with EUPHEMISM, is a term used to describe unduly flowery, affected or high-flown writing. Its name comes from the style of John Lyly's *Euphues*, written in 1578–9, and it is not to be imitated these days by anyone who wishes to be treated seriously.

Even needs to be treated with care. The difference between 'even she could not believe it' and 'she could not even believe it' should be obvious. In the first instance the sense is that even one so credulous as she was could not believe it; in the second it means she could not even believe it, let alone accept it or act upon it. See also AT LEAST.

Even if and **even though** These are conjunctions that introduce conditional clauses. See CONDITIONALS.

Every is singular, as are its derivatives *everything*, *everyone*, *everybody* and *everywhere*. Correct usages are 'every boy is good', 'everyone has arrived', 'everything is in order', 'everybody knows she is ill' and 'everywhere is covered with snow'. Instead of writing the correct but wordy 'every man and woman must make up his or her own mind', write 'all men and women must make up their own minds', or even simply 'all must make up their own minds'. See also ALL and EACH AND ALL.

Everyone and **every one** *Everyone* refers to a unanimity of people, as in 'everyone thought the book was excellent'. *Every one* refers back to a multiplicity, as in 'every one of them was different', or 'every one was brightly polished'. There is also the slightly archaic idiomatic usage, as in 'they were against him, every one.'

Everywhere and **nowhere** 'Not everywhere' does not mean 'nowhere'. It means 'somewhere'.

Evidence As a verb, this is an abomination, and an example of the widespread determination to turn any noun into a verb. A club posted a sign on its notice board advising its members to carry their pass as 'it evidences your membership'. In fact, 'it provides evidence of your membership', or proves it.

Evoke and **invoke** To *evoke* is to summon or call up a sentiment or memory, as in 'his writing perfectly evoked England before the war', or 'the music evoked memories of her childhood'. To *invoke* is to seek help either from a supreme being or another powerful person, as in 'she invoked God to help her overcome her tribulations' or 'he invoked the King to spare him any further suffering'.

Ex- Be careful how you use this prefix, which indicates that someone is no longer what the unprefixed name would indicate (ex-wife, ex-employee, ex-soldier, and so on). I received a press release in October 2013 headlined 'Ex-Gay Christian Counsellor hounded out by Psychotherapist Associations'. I was not sure whether the person to whom the story referred was formerly homosexual but still a Christian and a counsellor, formerly a homosexual Christian but still a counsellor, or formerly a homosexual Christian counsellor. It turned out he was none of those combinations, but a man who was formerly homosexual, still a Christian, but no longer a counsellor. If the prefix had to be used then he should have been termed 'Christian Ex-Gay Counsellor. It might have been easier to say 'Christian Formerly Gay Counsellor', but even that is unsatisfactory. It may be one of those phrases that does not easily lend itself to a headline. It does, however, illustrate the dangers of ambiguity when using the prefix with a compound noun.

Exaggeration is a danger inherent in using adjectives: choose them with care, because use of an excessive adjective makes it difficult to describe things that really are so. Care is also required in choosing descriptive nouns. A minor accident is not a *catastrophe*, a heavy fall of rain is not necessarily a *deluge* and a difference of opinion is not always a *row*. Nor is a sportsman who wins one important prize a *titan*. See HYPERBOLE.

Examinee See -EE ENDINGS.

Except See ACCEPT AND EXCEPT.

Exception that proves the rule This phrase does not mean that something in a category that fails to be consistent with other members of that category somehow proves, or verifies, the rule that they are all the same – which would be nonsense. It proves the *existence* of the rule. However, there is another interpetation, relying on the Latin verb *probare* (from which *prove* derives), which also means *test*. The exception, in that interpretation, invites scepticism about the rule.

Exclamation marks Exclamations should be terminated with an *exclamation mark*, though in most intelligent writing such forms will be confined to dialogue. Exclamatory writing in most English prose betrays an excitable nature, something not always easy to reconcile with a desire on the part of the writer to be taken seriously. Sophisticates use the exclamation mark only in moments of jest or parody, and then rarely.

Execute Sir Kingsley Amis, in his lively polemic against bad English, correctly laments the illogicality of using the verb *execute* in the sense of putting a criminal to death. 'By rights,' he observes, 'the sentence, not the criminal, is executed.' This is so: but the dictionary discloses that the abuse of this verb was first noted in 1483, so the battle is probably lost.

Exhaustive and **exhausting** These two adjectives are subtly different. If someone conducts an *exhaustive* inquiry, he leaves no part of the subject in question unexamined. An *exhausting* inquiry is one that tires out all who make it.

Exit One complex misuse of an intransitive verb is found with the verb *exit*. It has long offended the logic of pedants, being the third person singular of the Latin verb *exeo*, to go out. So when people said, as they have done for 400 years, 'they exit' or 'I exited', Latinists would wince because they felt it was not an English verb. However, this became an accepted English usage as an intransitive verb. Then, thanks to America, it became a transitive (or perhaps, in the light of subsequent developments, semi-transitive) verb, the first use of which the dictionary puts at 1976. Since then we have had people exiting buildings, exiting cars, exiting motorways, and so on: an unnecessary abomination, given the reliability of the verbs *leave* or *quit*. Now we have the verb in a fully transitive sense, where the exiting is something somebody does to something else: in January 2010 a newspaper quoted a businessman saying 'we are going to exit our business from the City of London', with *exit* now meaning remove or take away. Perhaps those who use the term would argue that it puts new precision into the language. The businessman was talking not simply about taking his custom elsewhere, but about closing his enterprise in London and reopening it somewhere else. However, why could he not simply have said that he planned to relocate from the City of London?

Exordium This is a term from classical rhetoric, meaning an introduction.

Expect is not a synonym for *anticipate*. See ANTICIPATE AND EXPECT.

Explainable and **explicable** *Explicable* dates from 1556, and *explainable* from 1610. In the battle between them *explicable* has the upper hand, with the citations in the dictionary for the alternative much scarcer, and used, it seems, rather by accident: the second most recent is from 1842, and in a letter from Charles Dickens. Yet one often hears, even in the broadcast media, this term being used, presumably in ignorance by speakers who do not know that *explicable* exists. As Latin dies out in all but the most exclusive schools one may expect such abusage to become more common, as writers and speakers conclude that something to be *explained* must be *explainable*.

Exterminate is not a synonym for *kill* unless the killing referred to is mass slaughter. The Nazis *exterminated* the Jews, and Stalin *exterminated* the ruling class of the part of Poland he occupied, but one kills a few rats or a few people. The fashion for pest controllers to refer to the extermination of their quarry – no doubt to reassure their customers of the thoroughness of their work – is another example of HYPERBOLE.

F

Fact and **assertion** *Fact* is often used when the writer or speaker means *assertion*, a statement that is an expression of opinion unsupported by evidence. *The fact that* is a cliché and has become almost meaningless. In a sentence such as 'the fact that I am here suggests I am interested' the meaning can be conveyed just as well by saying 'that I am here suggests I am interested'.

Faint and **feint** A *faint* is a sudden and temporary loss of consciousness. A *feint* is a dummy attack or blow, as in 'he made a *feint*, as if to hit him'.

Falling pregnant See PREGNANT.

Fantastic is perhaps less prevalent as a cliché than it was in the Swinging Sixties, but a cliché it remains. There is nothing wrong with using it in its exact sense, to describe something that is the stuff of fantasy.

Farther and **further** *Farther*, as an adverb, refers to literal distance; *further*, as an adverb, refers to time or figurative distance and means 'to a greater extent'. So one would write 'he walked several miles farther before resting', and 'she needed to contemplate further before finally making up her mind'. *Further* is also a verb and adjective. As a verb, it means to advance something, as in 'he wished to further his career'. As an adjective it means 'additional', or 'more extended', as in 'further education' or 'there was no further point in arguing'. The distinction between *farther* and *further* is rarely observed now, with *further* being used frequently for literal as well as figurative distance.

Fast *Fast*, meaning quick, is an adjective and not an adverb, so 'run fast' is a solecism, though the dictionary gives a longish history of that particular usage. However, 'stand fast' is all right: the adverb *fast* means to hold firm or stick to one place, and has a long history.

Fatal, **lethal** and **mortal** *Fatal* literally means concerning one's fate or destiny, or relating to fate. It is widely used to describe a course of action that ends in death – 'his bad driving led to a fatal crash' – but does not necessarily have to imply death. A 'fatal prophecy' may just as easily foretell a course of events that are decreed by fate, but do not lead to death. *Lethal* and *mortal* provide no such reassurance. Something that is *lethal* is designed to bring about death, such as a 'lethal weapon' or a 'lethal overdose'. Someone or something that is *mortal* has death as an inevitability – as in 'all men are mortal' and 'they chose to engage in a mortal struggle'.

Fatwa Because we are used to hearing that a *fatwa* has been issued by Muslims to demand the death of an infidel or of one who has offended Islam, we assume it is synonymous with a death sentence. It is not: it is simply a decision taken by a clerical authority within the faith, and can apply to any course of action.

Faucet is an Americanism for the noun *tap*.

Feedback has become a tiresome piece of office jargon to signify an opinion or thoughts expressed in response to a policy or service provided by the institution. When someone says 'I'd appreciate your feedback about the new procedures' what he means is 'I should like to have your opinion'.

Feint See FAINT AND FEINT.

Ferment and **foment** A *ferment* is the process of leavening bread or brewing alcohol using yeast or other means and provides the verb *to ferment*. It is sometimes used metaphorically, as in 'he threw the ideas into the ferment'. The verb *foment*, with which it should not be confused, means to encourage, foster, instigate or help spread, and is often used in the context of revolutions or revolutionary acts.

Fewer and **less** The abuse of the latter for the former has become one of the more egregious mistakes in English usage. Customers launched a rearguard action against the neglect of the valuable word *fewer* a few years ago when a supermarket put up signs over some of its tills that invited customers with '10 items or less' in their baskets to use them. It should have read '10 items or fewer'. One has *less* of a single commodity; *fewer* of a multiple of them. So one has less sugar, less heat, less cheese, less grief, less work, less money; but one has fewer days off, fewer friends, fewer worries, fewer soldiers, fewer cream crackers and fewer pets. It is idiomatic to say or write that 'the marriage lasted less than ten years', since what is being discussed is a singular space of time rather than a multiplicity of years. A similar principle applies with a phrase such as 'the garage was less than ten miles away', describing as it does a singular distance and not a multiplicity of miles.

Fictional and **fictitious** *Fictional* is a word of fairly recent invention – the dictionary gives its first use as 1843. It can be used metaphorically to describe something that is invented, or has no basis in fact, but its strict meaning is creative, referring to a story composed for a novel or drama – 'it was a fictional account of life in the Second World War', for example. *Fictitious* is a far stronger word, meaning invented or feigned, and carries a strong undertone of dishonesty or the intent to deceive.

Field sports SEE BLOOD SPORTS AND FIELD SPORTS.

Fill out is what Americans do to forms. Britons fill them *in*. In British English, *fill out* is an intransitive verbal construction used to describe someone putting on weight – 'he had filled out in his early twenties'.

Fillers These are redundant words or phrases whose use shows a lack of careful thought on behalf of a speaker or writer. Our language, written and spoken, is littered with pointless words that are verbal tics or fillers: words and phrases such as *actually*, *really*, *in fact* or, perhaps most vacuous of all, *in actual fact*. Some people appear incapable of eliminating these in speech; it ought to be far easier to do so in writing. Why say 'he fell asleep on the majority of occasions he went to work' when one can say 'he fell asleep most times he went to work'? Why say (to use a popular horror) 'at this moment in time' when one can say 'now'? Why say 'it is possible to go there' when one can say 'I can go there'? Why say (to use another popular horror) 'when all is said and done' when probably one need say nothing at all? Our speech tends to be full of fillers such as those. They allow us a moment to mark time in our speech and think what we really want to say. They are tiresome in that context, but unpardonable in a considered piece of writing. Concision is the writer's weapon against obscurity, and precision his shield against incomprehension. If a word is unnecessary, do not use it. Clarity of expression reflects clarity of thought, and helps a reader not just to understand, but to take seriously, what the writer is saying to him. See also PLEONASM.

Filmic is an Americanism, used pretentiously by some Britons to mean *cinematic* – 'the novel had obvious filmic potential'.

Fine See SLANG.

Fine-toothed comb This is the correct way of referring to a comb with slender teeth placed very close together. *Fine-tooth comb* is an acceptable variant. *Fine toothcomb* is not.

Firing line and **line of fire** See LINE OF FIRE AND FIRING LINE.

First and **firstly** *First* is an adjective and *firstly* is an adverb: so write 'first, second, third' not 'firstly, secondly, thirdly'. See ADVERBS, NUMERICAL.

First floor In America, this is what the British would term the *ground floor.* Their *second floor* is our *first floor,* and so on.

Fit and **fitted** There seems to be uncertainty in the minds of some writers about whether certain verbs have a distinct past tense at all. *Fit* certainly does, though that does not prevent people from writing 'it fit me perfectly' when they mean 'it fitted me perfectly'. *Fit* as an imperfect is an Americanism. Timothy Snyder, in his excellent book *Bloodlands*, gives a textbook example: 'Rohm also nurtured personal ambitions that ill fit Hitler's plans to rebuild the German military.'

Fit for purpose is now a cliché, so avoid it if you wish to say or write something original and penetrating.

Flagrant See BLATANT AND FLAGRANT.

Flammable See INFLAMMABLE AND FLAMMABLE.

Flashlight is the American word for *torch.*

Flaunt and **flout** are frequently confused, usually with the former being used for the latter, as in 'he was flaunting all the rules of good conduct'. The dictionary does not entirely surrender on this, pointing out under its entry for *flaunt* that it is sometimes used for *flout*: 'erroneous', it says, and it is. To *flaunt* something means to display it ostentatiously or conspicuously; to *flout* something is to disregard it with contempt, the object normally being a law, rule or code.

Flounder and **founder** are often confused. *Flounder* means to stumble, or to fall into a mire. *Founder* has predominantly nautical meanings, in that a ship is deemed to founder when it fills with water and sinks. It has acquired a metaphorical meaning, signifying 'come to grief' or 'be wrecked' – 'he foundered after his wife left him'. Given the similarity of meaning – the image conveyed by both verbs is of failure or fall – it is often hard to tell whether either verb is being used accurately or not. The noun *flounder* is a type of fish.

Following has become a clichéd and therefore tired substitute for the more straightforward *after*. 'He was less mobile following his fall' can be more sensibly rendered as 'he was less mobile after his fall'.

Foment See FERMENT AND FOMENT.

For As a synonym for because, see CAUSE.

For the most part is a pleonastic introductory phrase from the same stable as BY AND LARGE.

Forbear and **forebear** To *forbear* is to endure something. A *forebear* is an ancestor.

Forbidding and **foreboding** 'Durham Cathedral is an ancient and sometimes foreboding place', a magazine journalist wrote in February 2013. I presume the writer meant that this always grand and sometimes gloomy edifice was *forbidding*. One must doubt that the building has the ability to feel pessimism or dread about the future, which is what *foreboding* means.

Forego and **forgo** *Forego* means to go before or to precede. It is routinely confused with *forgo*, which means to forsake or refrain from – 'he chose to forgo breakfast that morning'.

Foreign words and phrases Read any book in English for long enough (especially if it was written more than about fifty years ago) and you will come across a foreign phrase. Because of the leanings – or 'penchants', if you prefer – of our education system many of the foreign phrases we use in English are from Latin or French, for decades the two most popular languages taught in our schools once Greek fell into decline. We anglicise words because we have no shorthand word or phrase in English to describe the same idea, or because the original phrase became so well known through its frequent use that it supplanted any existing English equivalent. We say that 'the hearing was held in camera' because it is easier and shorter than saying 'the hearing was held without any outsiders being permitted to be present'. However, some words or phrases are not idiomatically considered English and we regard them as foreign, italicise them when we write them, and use them either to show off, be amusing or to express to another person familiar with that language a nuance that might not be present in the simple English. Someone who chooses to say '*post hoc, non propter hoc*' could say 'after it, not on account of it', but is showing a familiarity with Latin rhetoric and indeed logic by using the former.

Greek supplies many of our words, or parts of our words, but they have long since been transliterated and anglicised and only a scholar would know their origins. Most of the Latin that is now around has itself been anglicised – 'in camera', 'sine die', 'et cetera' – and there is only the odd phrase that retains a meaning so distinct as to be used in its original form without yet having become English – such as when we speak of an *ex cathedra* pronouncement, or something being not *de jure* but *de facto*. Engaging in activities *pro bono* could yet go either way, but I would still italicise it. 'Hoi polloi' is a rare survival of raw Greek, to describe the masses. Should you use it, remember two things: first, that 'hoi' is the definite article, so you don't need another one – 'the hoi polloi' is wrong. Second, it is plural, so hoi polloi *do* something, not *does* something.

If you are writing a French phrase, use accents where they are required: there is no point in trying to burnish your image by dropping a wry *chacun à son goût* in a frightfully *décontracté* way if you omit the grave accent and the circumflex. German, from which the odd phrase has been known to turn up, also has the occasional accent: and nouns all begin with a capital letter unless they have been anglicised. It is probably the case that 'schadenfreude' is now English enough not to require either the initial capital or italicisation. This is not yet true of *Weltanschauung*, or other terms beloved of those who talk about philosophy. There is nothing especially wrong with using foreign phrases, provided they have no exact English equivalent. The Fowlers deplored the attempt to translate phrases such as *demi-monde* and *esprit d'escalier* literally as 'half-world' and 'spirit of the staircase' when those translations ignored the idiomatic sense of the French and seemed, as a consequence, absurd. The first phrase refers to high-class prostitutes or kept women; the second to that ability to think of a devastatingly witty rejoinder only after the event. As one can see from the translations of the idioms, the French phrases really are superior and deserve to penetrate English usage. There are many other French phrases, or words, that have no equivalent in English and for which a case may thus be made. One is always, however, up against the fact that so few anglophones speak French in any degree today, let alone in one that allows them command of idiom.

Some authors drop French in to show off the fact that, after a fashion, they speak it. The show-offs are the ones who use phrases or words that do have perfectly acceptable English equivalents: there is no need to write that a steak was served *à point* when, by expending fewer words and letters, one can write that it was served rare. However, no English phrase that does not require several more words can quite convey the meaning of the Italian style of cooking pasta *al dente*. In some cases the use of another tongue is pointless, and merely rubs the reader's nose in the fact that he doesn't understand it. When we can say that the law takes no account of trifles, why say *de minimis non curat lex*?

Always italicise foreign words and phrases that have not passed into common English usage (and, if they are German nouns, give them an initial capital letter): so write *mauvais quart d'heure* but 'panache', or *Drang nach Osten* but 'angst' or 'blitzkrieg'. For years, maybe decades, a foreign word is italicised when we write it as a sign that it is still a stranger to our language; then one day it will be quietly accepted as naturalised, and the italicisation will end. However, if you are going to use foreign phrases, for heaven's sake use them correctly. There will always be somebody reading what you have written who will speak the language better than you do, or understand it better, and you risk humiliation if you are careless or go off piste (and 'piste', like many other foreign words, is one that is now anglicised). Those who write *nom de plume* or *bon viveur* show themselves at once to be charlatans: a Frenchman would write *nom de guerre* or *bon vivant*. The first of those terms is merely a flashy way of saying 'pseudonym', or the perfectly harmless 'pen-name': the second is something that English cannot quite match. See also GOURMAND AND GOURMET, CONFIDANT(E) and BLOND(E).

The danger area for users of foreign words is when they are plurals – as discussed in the case of hoi polloi, above – or when some concession has to be made to gender. This is especially true of Latin words. The word 'alumnus' has passed into English – via America, it seems – and is now routinely used to describe graduates of universities. More than one of these are 'alumni'; a woman is an 'alumna', and more than one are 'alumnae'. 'Larvae', 'data', 'media' and 'genitalia' are all plural, though this does not prevent some writers (especially in the journalistic trade) from using them with singular verbs. It remains the convention in British English that if one is using a noun anglicised from the French one still respects its gender. Therefore, as with 'confidant' above, a noun like 'savant' would become 'savante' if referring to a woman.

It is perhaps easier to make a fool of oneself in writing English prose by using a foreign phrase than by any other means. I recall reading some years ago in a newspaper the work of a writer who, deciding to show off, had inverted *rus in urbe* as *urbe in rus*, which because of the mangling of cases had former Latin masters and many of their pupils writing in their legions to the newspaper concerned. If in doubt, leave it out. There is usually an English substitute the use of which will not betray a lack of grounding in foreign tongues.

In terms of foreign works of art, whether literary or musical, the convention is usually that they are rendered in the original unless an element of translation is involved, in which case they take the translated title. Thus Wagner's opera *Götterdämmerung* is so called when sung in German, but is *Twilight of the Gods* when in English; and *Die Meistersinger von Nürnberg* becomes *The Mastersingers of Nuremburg*; Fellini's *Otto e Mezzo* is *Eight and a Half* when shown with English subtitles; and Proust's *À la recherche du temps perdu* becomes *In Search of Lost Time* when translated. There are idiomatic exceptions: no one translates *Cosi fan tutte* or *La Dolce Vita*, and musical works that have no words may remain in the original, again according to idiom, as in *Le Tombeau de Couperin* or *Eine Kleine Nachtmusik*; but the translation rule holds in most cases.

Forensic has the meaning of 'pertaining to the courts of law', according to the dictionary: its etymology is traced back to the word *forum*. Even with its permissive attitude towards the misuse of words, the dictionary does not yet sanction its use to mean *detailed*, *rigorously examined* or *scrutinised*. One often hears that someone has made 'a forensic speech' or has undertaken 'a forensic examination' of something, or done 'forensic research'. In each case the adjective is abused, unless any of these activities is related to a court of law. The error no doubt stems from a misunderstanding of the term *forensic science*. Forensic science is highly detailed, because of the requirements of evidence needed to convict a criminal. That does not mean that everything else in life that is highly detailed or closely examined is *forensic*.

Forever and **for ever** In American English these two terms mean eternally, persistently or continually. They are interchangeable, though there is a preference for the single-word variety. In British English opinion has changed over the centuries: the two-word phrase is taken to mean continually or incessantly, whereas the one word is taken to mean eternally. However, the dictionary cites examples that suggest an interchangeability going back to the seventeenth century.

Forgo See FOREGO AND FORGO.

Formally and **formerly** There is no excuse, except the gravest lapse in concentration, for confusing the homophones *formerly* and *formally*. The first refers to a past state; the second to a style of formality. So, 'one was formerly a student', but 'one is formally reprimanded for a misdemeanour' or 'formally dressed'.

Former may only be used to describe the first of two things. If there are more than two, then one says 'the first'. One may also say 'the first and second' of two things.

Formulae or **formulas** It is a matter of taste whether one uses the Latin or English plural; the word is well anglicised, but the Latin is not incorrect. I prefer the English plural, given that the word is so long anglicised.

Fornication See ADULTERY.

Forward and **foreword** The former is an adjective or adverb signifying a position in front, as in 'the forward movement' or 'they ran forward'. A *foreword* is a preface to a book.

Forward planning is a tautology. It is impossible to plan for something that occurred in the past.

Founder See FLOUNDER AND FOUNDER.

Fowlers' five rules, the These are the five rules for good writing set out by the brothers Fowler in *The King's English* in 1906, and they still hold good today: 'Prefer the familiar word to the far-fetched. Prefer the concrete word to the abstract. Prefer the single word to the circumlocution. Prefer the short word to the long. Prefer the Saxon word to the Romance.' See RULES OF GOOD WRITING.

Fraction Educated writers will use the phrase 'a fraction of the cost went towards overheads' without thinking of its logic. What such writers inevitably mean is 'a small fraction', which although still vague is a perfectly acceptable statement. They forget that nine-tenths is also a fraction, and so to use the noun without qualifying it with an adjective is almost meaningless.

Free To describe something obtainable that carries no cost as being *free* is to use another vulgarism. It is better to say that the item is *free of charge*.

French as an adjective is always capitalised. This is obviously so in the case of 'the French people' or 'the French language' but is equally so when one writes of 'French windows', 'French kisses' or 'French letters'.

French words and phrases See FOREIGN WORDS AND PHRASES.

Front and **front up** Vulgar usage invents and abuses its own verbs, such as taking the adjective or noun *front* and creating the verbal phrase *front up* or simply *front*. We hear this as in 'he fronted up the bid for the Olympics' or 'she fronts her own band'. We also hear that people 'front up a television show'. In the first example the vulgarism could be avoided by the verb *lead* or *direct*; in the second by *lead* again; in the third by the verb *present*.

Fulfil is the correct spelling in British English. In America, it is *fulfill*.

Full is an incomparable adjective or ABSOLUTE, and therefore the words *fuller* and *fullest* make little logical sense. If something is full, nothing can be 'fuller' than it is, and if three things are full, none of them can be 'the fullest'.

Full stops A sentence ends with a *full stop*, also sometimes known as a *period*, particularly in American English. Typographic fashion now dictates that, to avoid clutter, full stops are not used after the individual letters of abbreviations. However, what works well when rendering 'MCC', 'RAC' or 'UNESCO' may be less satisfactory when rendered 'eg' or 'ie', which many still prefer to have as 'e.g.' or 'i.e.' See also PUNCTUATION.

Fuller, fullest See FULL.

Fully is an adverb that must be used with care: when deployed with certain verbs it is meaningless, because the verbs themselves are absolute, and therefore *fully* is inevitably tautological. Verbs such as *abandon*, *convince*, *cede*, *close* and *stop* are but five examples: there are countless others.

Fulsome We have all read the phrase about someone making a *fulsome* apology. Those who write it usually believe that the adjective means *full* or *plentiful*. It has not meant that since the early sixteenth century, and after 500 years of obsoleteness we may legitimately consider that use redundant. It has since the seventeenth century meant something that is overdone or grotesquely flattering or obsequious, and therefore insincere. It was probably unnecessary to have this change of meaning at the time – *fulsome* served a useful purpose in its old sense and there are plenty of other adjectives to describe its new one – but such surrenders were common in the age before formal lexicography. Since the codification of the language such surrenders still happen, but they are unnecessary when perfectly good words exist to describe whatever a word is being manipulated to describe.

Funny One of the problems of SLANG or COLLOQUIALISM is that it often removes the freedom from ambiguity that correct language has. Take Mrs Thatcher's memorable phrase during her political assassination that 'it's a funny old world'. Her audience knew that the adjective *funny* meant odd or peculiar, and that she was using it satirically. In good writing, use *funny* to mean something that makes one laugh. If you mean *odd*, *peculiar*, *strange* or *weird*, say so.

Further See FARTHER AND FURTHER.

Future perfect tense This tense describes a completed action in the future, as in 'by the end of next month I shall have taken my exams' or 'you will have finished that book by the weekend'.

Future tense This describes a simple act in the future, as in 'I shall go to town tomorrow' and 'she will start school in September'. See SHALL AND WILL for the important distinction between these two auxiliary verbs used to build the future tense. There is also a *continuous future tense*, to describe an activity that lasts more than an instant and that will be happening in the future, as in 'I shall be reading a book this evening' and 'you will be arriving home just as I leave for school'.

G

Gage and **gauge** A *gage* is an item left to secure a loan; it may also be an abbreviation for *greengage*. A *gauge* is an instrument for measuring quantities.

Gamble and **gambol** To *gamble* is to wager, either with money or metaphorically with something else at stake. To *gambol* is to leap, but is now used in a wider sense of meaning to *frolic*.

Gang English slang has the habit of taking a word that is accurate in certain contexts and making it inaccurate in others. Eric Partridge offers a good example of this with the word *gang*. It is correct to use it of workmen or criminals; to use it about 'a set, a clique, a fortuitous assemblage of idle or harmless persons is to fall into slang'.

Gaol See JAIL AND GAOL.

Gas in British English is a form of energy, or something given off by certain other substances. It has two other usages in American English that need to be noted: as a synonym for petrol, a usage not current in Britain, and as a euphemism for flatulence, which occasionally is heard these days north-east of Land's End.

-gate endings See VOGUE WORDS.

Gauge See GAGE AND GAUGE.

Gay is a popular slang term for *homosexual*, both as an adjective and as a noun, and has become so popular that it has almost forced the word's original meaning of *happy* or *carefree* out of use. Pedants who stick to the old sense are to be applauded. See HOMOSEXUAL.

Genitive case The *genitive* signifies possession – 'of a table', for example. Its shortening – 'a table's' – is perhaps not so much an inflection as an appendage. Nouns in English do not inflect in the way that, for example, those in Latin or German do.

Geographical names See PLACE NAMES.

German words Some of these have passed into English, for example 'blitz', and such nouns do not need an initial capital letter or to be italicised (all German nouns are capitalised in that language). The twentieth-century tradition of rendering umlauts – which lengthen a vowel – by inserting an *e* instead is now out of fashion. Use the umlaut: so write 'Führer', not 'Fuehrer'. See also FOREIGN WORDS AND PHRASES.

Gerundives The *gerundive* is deemed by grammarians not to exist in English, though it is prevalent in Latin, the language from which most grammarians took their template. In Latin it is a *verbal adjective*, identical to the GERUND but used to qualify a noun rather than being a noun itself, and formed only from transitive verbs: 'the detective found a *smoking* gun' and 'the girl wanted a *crying* doll' use what seem to be gerundives. We had better just call them *adjectives*.

Gerunds Certain participles can also serve as nouns. These are known as *gerunds*. For example, 'they saw her drinking' uses the participle *drinking* as an adjective, to describe *her*; but 'her drinking is becoming a problem' uses *drinking* as a noun, and therefore it is a gerund. The past participle can also serve as a gerund: '*His having watched* it showed him how boring it was' for example. So too can the passive past participle, such as in '*her having been forgotten* presented a problem'. Once you have decided to deploy a gerund you need also the possessive pronoun, and the possessive of any noun. One would say 'I deplored *his having been left out*' or 'she remembered *John's coming* last Christmas'.

If there are risks of ambiguity, or clumsiness of construction, do not forget that there are other ways of conveying the same sense: 'they saw her drink' avoids the participle (though it creates an ambiguity, since 'her drink' could be the drink belonging to her), just as 'the amount she drinks is becoming a problem' avoids the gerund. With the past participle, turning the sentence around obviates a gerund: 'it presented a problem that she had been forgotten' or, given the preference for the active voice over the passive, 'it presented a problem that they had forgotten her'.

Accomplished use of the gerund suggests the speaker or writer is sophisticated because it also suggests a grasp of English grammar usually associated with those who have been taught it formally, *or* (sometimes *and*) the grammar of foreign languages. It is not a usage that comes easily to the uneducated. The Fowlers talked of the 'fused participle' to indicate the use of a participle that was not a gerund but remained correct. An example they gave was as follows. They used the sentence 'I dislike my best friend violating my privacy' which they pointed out could also be rendered 'I dislike my best friend's violating my privacy'. In the second instance the gerund was used correctly. In the first, what they termed the fused participle effectively became the compound noun 'the violation-by-a-friend'. Like some other explanations they advance, this seems a needless complication. All one needs to note is that the usage without the possessive is clumsy, though much validated by repetition in the last 100 years or so. The usage with the possessive is correct.

Where the gerund follows a verb there may sometimes be doubt in the writer's mind about whether to use the possessive. This needs to be removed. It may seem instinctive to write 'I regret him leaving his wife', since transitive verbs seem to cry out for a direct object. However, the correct form is 'I regret his leaving his wife'. In the same way, one would say 'we have no hope of its being sunny tomorrow', not 'it being sunny'. There is also a tendency to feel that the possessive may be dispensed with where a proper name is used, such as in the sentence 'no one took account of Mr Smith having the right to vote': yet there is nothing wrong with its being 'Mr Smith's having the right to vote'; indeed, many would argue that such a usage was entirely correct and desirable.

With abstract nouns the correct use of the gerund seems even more important, as in 'the committee believed the decision's being taken would bring an end to the matter'. To lose the possessive would leave a sense of incompleteness, not to say ambiguity or lack of clarity. Like many sentences in which participles or words that appear to be participles occur, confusion can be avoided by making them short and structuring them properly.

There can be a potential problem when the noun that must take the possessive is long and complicated, and possibly multiple, as in the sentence 'he deplored the foreign ministers of the allied countries' having spoken so bluntly'. When a problem such as this arises it is not the fault of the gerund, but the fault of the writer's having cast his sentence so badly. There is nothing wrong with 'he deplored the blunt speaking by the foreign ministers of the allied countries'.

Fowler defines a usage called the 'converted participle' where a participle, by idiom, stands alone. His first example is: 'Talking of test matches, who won the last?' The subject of the second clause deliberately has no relation to the participle in the first. This he relates to the gerund, saying it is a shortened version of the archaic *a-talking*. In the last century the idiom has taken root and no longer seems worthy of comment. The participle does not need a noun because it is, as a gerund, a noun in itself; that is why it is not wrong to adopt this usage. For the distinction between constructions that should use the gerund and those that should use the infinitive, see INFINITIVES.

Get Under the influence of films, television shows and pop records we have started to adopt certain American phrases in popular or demotic usage even though we have perfectly good

English ones already. In restaurants one may hear people in the early stages of Americanisation asking if they may *get* a beer, a glass of wine or a plate of spaghetti when they really mean may they *have* one. In our usage, asking a waiter whether we may *get* a fillet steak implies that we are seeking permission to go into the kitchen and fetch it ourselves.

The misuse, or more often thoughtless use, of the verb *get* long precedes the transatlantic influence, however. In *Usage and Abusage*, Eric Partridge quotes a passage in which the word is used in these different senses: to mount ('I got on horseback'), to receive ('I got your letter'), to reach a destination ('I got to Canterbury'), to take a form of transport ('I got a chaise'), to change condition ('I got wet'), to catch a disease ('I have got such a cold'), to rid oneself of something ('I shall not be able to get rid of [it]'), as an auxiliary for the passive voice ('I got shaved'), to learn something ('I got into the secret'), to obtain or procure something ('getting a Memorial before the board'), to return ('I got back'), to fetch something ('I got my supper'), to travel physically ('I got to bed'), to travel metaphysically ('I got to sleep'), to rise ('I got up'), as an auxiliary for a reflexive verb ('I got myself drest [sic]'), to exit ('I got out'), to enter ('I got into'), and to possess ('I have got nothing for you'). He could also have described certain other usages such as to be compelled to do something ('I've got to go') or simply to feel obliged ('I've got to help'), to be struck ('he got me in the ribs'), to recover ('she got over it'), to realise the truth ('get real') or to realise a sum of money ('they got £500,000 for the house'). I do not doubt there are many more, such as the slang 'I got you' to mean 'I understood you'.

It is desirable generally to use the short word rather than the long: but *get* and its relations are an example of obscuring meaning and repelling the interest of the reader by over-simplification – a charitable term for Partridge's 'slovenliness'. A lazy writer or speaker will use the word in these many contexts rather than make the effort to be precise. Other words, more definite, more evocative, more accurate and often not much longer, may be substituted. Many of them are, like *get* or *got*, but one syllable. 'I hired a chaise', 'I reached Canterbury',

'I caught a cold' or 'I must go' are far better English. Sometimes, the *get* is superfluous: as in 'I dressed' rather than 'I got myself drest'. The verb *to be* works perfectly well in expressions of the passive – 'I was shaved' for 'I got shaved'. It is especially egregious to say *have got*, when the simple *have* will do. See also GOT AND GOTTEN.

Going forward This is a ludicrous example of management speak, as used in such phrases as 'going forward, we hope to have new structures in place' or 'we shall attend to these problems going forward' (the second of these examples is also a TAUTOLOGY). In the first example, where some less clichéd synonym might be useful, what is wrong with *in future*?

Good, used dishonestly Public and private corporations sometimes engage in manipulation of language. How often has one travelled on the London Underground and been told by a smug announcer that a *good* service is operating? He means a *scheduled* or a *normal* service, or something approaching it; unwittingly, he is using the adjective of value to draw an oblique comparison with the normal bad service, which does not live up to the promise of the schedule. There is a fine line between EUPHEMISM and downright misrepresentation. See also POLITICAL LANGUAGE.

Good, used for *well* Few Americanisms have registered more strongly in British English in recent years than the vogue for answering the polite question 'How do you do?' or 'How are you?' with the rejoinder 'I'm good.' To many Anglo-Saxon ears this still sounds like a profession of one's moral condition rather than an observation about one's physical well-being. Such things are silly in speech; they should be avoided in writing of any degree of formality, or in any communication where one does not wish to be thought semi-literate. People are far more forgiving of an alien IDIOM in speech than when they see it in writing, simply because there is more time to reflect on what one is committing to paper before one does so. Those Britons who attain a decent level of bilingualism may show it off when they get to Manhattan or Palm Beach, but it is best not to try it at home.

Gorilla and **guerrilla** A *gorilla* is a large simian. A *guerrilla* is an irregular soldier.

Got and **gotten** These distinct spellings are what happens when societies with a common language live so separately from each other and have long-standing, independent cultures. It is why some verb forms are different in America from how they are in Britain (see DOVE AND DIVED and FIT AND FITTED, for example). The Americans say *gotten* where we say *got* not out of perversity, but because at the time of the Pilgrim Fathers we all said it. America has stuck conservatively to this form, as it has with the SUBJUNCTIVE mood, and we have not.

Gourmand and **gourmet** The latter has passed into English as one who is a connoisseur (ditto) of food; yet some think it is interchangeable with *gourmand*, which has not entered our language, and means someone who is greedy.

Graffiti This is a plural frequently used as a singular. One scrawl on a wall is a *graffito*. For similar abuses, see PLURALS.

Grammar Correct grammar – the use of words in their orthodox relation to other words – is not difficult to master. It is a question of logic, and if regarded as such it will, by all but the most resolutely illogical minds, become second nature in anyone's usage of English. Grammar is designed to keep our language comprehensible and free from AMBIGUITY. Good grammar alone will not be enough to guarantee a good written style: that depends too on the choice of words and the concision and originality with which they are used. However, grammar is the foundation of good style. Its violation or disregard has the same effect on language as amputating limbs from a healthy being. The orthodoxy of its use has been established not only by logic, but by custom, practice and precedent. In educated and formal usage there is agreement about what that orthodoxy is. Users of English depart from it only if they wish to display a lack of conformity, which in formal contexts may cause those with whom they communicate to make assumptions about their intelligence and grasp of the language. Those who have studied a foreign language tend to have a reasonable knowledge of grammar, though they are unlikely to have learned very much about it when acquiring their mother tongue.

Grammar is the science of using the components of language correctly. It is about ensuring that nouns and verbs agree; that verbs take the correct prepositions and govern the right pronouns; that adjectives and adverbs are used appropriately; that tenses and participles are accurate; that clauses have the right subject and do not go off on an unplanned course of their own; and how in some instances the choice of the wrong word can lead to grammatical error. Above all, grammar is the means by which language remains logical, comprehensible and clear. If we learn to spot that offences against grammar are in fact offences against logic and clarity, we will come close to winning this particular battle in the war against bad English.

Great is a word that has legitimate usages (though in this age of HYPERBOLE, its currency has been debased); but it does not mean much. If one wishes to express that much thought has been given to a subject, say so: do not say that *great* thought has been given to it. This implies (albeit ungrammatically) that a profound philosophical mind has been at work on the matter, which may not be the case. In SLANG parlance, almost anything that merits approbation or esteem is *great*, and that alone should be reason enough to avoid the word.

Great Britain See BRITAIN AND BRITISH ISLES.

Grisly and **grizzly** The adjective *grisly* means something that causes one to feel frightened, terrified or repelled, as in 'it was a grisly tale of murder' or 'the details of his death were grisly'. *Grizzly* has two meanings. The first is to describe something or someone with grey hair or a grey complexion, and has the variant *grizzled* – 'he was a grizzled old man in his eighties', for example. It may also refer to someone, usually but not inevitably a child, who habitually cries or whines (*grizzles*): 'Little Johnnie was often grizzly.'

Groups, and **verbs** In describing one of a *group* that has a common characteristic, any verb must refer to several and not to the individual item. So one would write 'he was one of those men who *refuse* to be beaten' rather than 'he was one of those men who *refuses* to be beaten', as the relative clause describes the group and not the individual. The same would apply to 'it was another of those things that *make* you mad' rather than '*makes* you mad'.

Grow The verb *grow*, which is both transitive and intransitive, has in recent years acquired a separate form of transitive use that is peculiar and wrong. People can grow potatoes or trees or plants, but can they grow a business? They cannot. They can, and may, *make it grow*. Growing a plant or a vegetable describes the act of enabling nature to take its course, but a business must be made to grow by human wit, enterprise and endeavour.

Guerrilla See GORILLA AND GUERRILLA.

Gun A *gun* is a weapon; but it is also the word used to refer to men or women who participate in game shooting. 'The gun on my left shot a very high partridge.'

H

Hallmark See EARMARK AND HALLMARK.

Halve One can *halve* the price of something, or *halve* a grapefruit; but a price cannot *halve*. It has to *be halved*.

Halves There can only be two of these, except at Eton College, where the word is synonymous with *term*, and there are three in a year. This dates from when the school year was divided into two long *halves* instead of three terms.

Handicapped people See POLITICAL CORRECTNESS.

Hangar and **hanger** A *hangar* is a covered shed or shelter, originally for carriages but now usually for aircraft. A *hanger* is something upon which something else is hung – 'her coat was on a hanger in the wardrobe'. It is also a special term in forestry, signifying a wood on the side of a steep hill or bank.

Hanged and **hung** Men are *hanged*. Pictures and pheasants are *hung*. A remark such as 'he was hung from the yardarm' is slang.

Hanging participle see PARTICIPLES.

Hard, though looking like an adjective, has also been an adverb for a thousand years, as in 'she hit him hard' or 'I worked hard for weeks'. *Hardly*, which is also an adverb, was used until the nineteenth century to mean *harshly* or *painfully* or *with hardship*. It now means *scarcely*, *barely* or *only just*, as in 'we had hardly arrived when the show started' or 'I hardly know how to answer your question'.

Haver To *haver* is not to be indecisive; it is to waffle.

Having is the most dangerous and frequently misused participle, as in sentences such as: 'Having arrived on holiday, the hotel was disgusting.' It is not the hotel that has arrived on holiday, but the traveller. For a deeper discussion of this problem, see PARTICIPLES.

He and **him** The former is the NOMINATIVE, the latter the ACCUSATIVE. Demotic usage has it that one would say (but not correctly write) 'It's him' when the correct form is 'it is he'. See also PERSONAL PRONOUNS.

Head and **head up** It is perfectly good, if rather journalistic, English, to write that 'the minister now heads a cabinet committee'. Were one to write that he 'heads up' the committee, that would be vulgar, the adverb being unnecessary.

Head of government and **head of state** A *head of government* is not always the same as a *head of state*; in France and America, for example, it is, because the president holds both posts; but in Britain the head of state is the Monarch, the head of government the Prime Minister. For that reason one does not write 'Mr Cameron's government' but 'Her Majesty's government'.

Heave See STRONG VERBS.

Her See SHE AND HER.

Hero This is a frequent example of tabloid hyperbole. If a man who scores a goal is a *hero*, what term do we reserve to describe one who wins the Victoria Cross? Choose descriptive nouns with care.

Heroin and **heroine** *Heroin* is an illegal, mind-altering substance. *Heroine* is a noun used to describe a female who has displayed exemplary courage, or who is the chief female character in a story or drama. For the *Independent* to describe Holly Golightly as the 'heroin' of *Breakfast at Tiffany's*, as it did on 2 April 2013, was unfortunate.

Hid and **hidden** One sees occasionally usages such as 'he had hid in the forest' or 'it was hid in the bookcase'. In both cases – the past participle and the passive – the correct usage is *hidden*. *Hid* is the imperfect of *hide* – 'she hid in the cupboard'.

Hieroglyph This is the noun used to describe the characters that formed the means of written communication in ancient Egypt. The adjective is *hieroglyphic*, which is frequently used in error for the noun.

Historic and **historical** A *historic* event is one that will take its place in history; a *historical* one already has. If something is *historical* it is of the past; if something is *historic* it stands out, or will stand out, as a landmark in history. The dictionary notes the use of *historical* as a SYNONYM for *historic* as an affectation of the Victorians, with no use cited since the nineteenth century. Therefore, we may accept that the idiomatic usages of these two words are settled, and as detailed above.

Hoard and **horde** These two homophones have very different meanings. A *hoard* is an accumulation or a collection that is hidden away, though the word is also used figuratively, as in 'he had a sizeable hoard of information'. A *horde* was the term used to describe Asiatic nomads, usually Tartars, who went from place to place fighting and pillaging. It is now used to describe a large gathering of people, especially if there is an unruly, wild or violent element to them, as in 'hordes of hooligans fought their way through the streets'.

Hoi polloi It is plural, so takes a plural verb, and as 'hoi' is a transliteration of the Greek word meaning *the*, it does not require the English definite article. See FOREIGN WORDS.

Holidays In American English, this has become the phrase used to describe the period over Christmas and New Year, fashioned to avoid giving offence to those who might be mortified at living in a culture in which Christianity is occasionally practised. Its use to describe that period in Britain is to be deplored, not least for its inexactitude. There is nothing wrong with 'the Christmas holidays'. Otherwise, what in British English are called *holidays* are in America *vacations*, though that term has long been used here to describe a university holiday.

Hometown is an Americanism: in British English the more usual form would be *home town*.

Homogeneous and **homogenous** are often confused. *Homogeneous* means alike or similar, and is the opposite of *heterogeneous*, which means different, so one would say 'the customs of the two peoples are homogeneous but their languages are heterogeneous'. It also means something that is of a uniform character throughout. *Homogenous* means genetically related, and having a common ancestor.

Homonyms A *homonym* is a word that is spelt and pronounced in the same way as another word, but has an entirely different meaning, such as *rose* (the flower) and *rose* (the past participle of the verb *to rise*).

Homophones A *homophone* is a word that sounds the same as another word but, unlike a homonym, is spelt differently and means something different, such as *cord* (a piece of string) and *chord* (three or more notes in music played simultaneously).

Homosexual This is an adjective that has become used as a noun. One can describe 'a *homosexual* man', 'a *homosexual* encounter', 'a *homosexual* inclination', but 'a *homosexual*' is as wrong as saying 'a handsome', 'an ugly' or 'a tall'. The late journalist Auberon Waugh used to make much of this, and frequently used the somewhat bizarre, but not incorrect, term *homosexualist*. The dictionary cites the first usage of that term as 1931, but cites the first misuse of the adjective as 1912, only twenty years after the first adjectival use. Pedants would always write 'a homosexual man' or, for that matter, 'a lesbian woman' or 'a heterosexual man [or woman or couple]'. Some homosexual men and women are happy to refer to themselves as *queers*. Others should use that term with caution for fear of causing offence. See **GAY**.

Honourable, use of A son or daughter of a baron, baroness or a viscount in the United Kingdom peerage, or the son of an earl without a courtesy title, is entitled to style him or herself as 'the honourable'. This is shortened to 'Hon.' These days it is used only as a form of written address, on an envelope, in the Court Circular or on the visiting cards of those keen to emphasise their status. Envelopes are the only places where the honorific 'the Honourable' should be used for the son of an earl (if he is not the elder son with a courtesy title) and the children of viscounts and barons, as in 'the Hon. John Smith' or 'the Hon. Mary Smith'.

Hopefully One adverb in particular, *hopefully*, has been extracted from its correct usage and is used (following American influence) as a self-functioning statement of faith before a clause to whose verb it is unconnected: as in 'hopefully, Mary will be given a better report next term'. Needless to say, it is not the giving that will be done hopefully, even though it is the only verb around with which this lonely adverb might associate itself. What the writer meant was 'it is to be hoped', 'I hope' or 'one hopes' that Mary will be given a better report. This tiresome usage is now so ubiquitous that those who object to it are sometimes dismissed as pedants. It remains wrong, and only a barbarous writer with a low estimation of his readers would try to pass it off as respectable prose. *Hopefully*, correctly used, is an adverb that means 'full of hope', as in 'it is better to travel hopefully than to arrive', and 'she awaited hopefully the delivery of the letter'.

Horde See HOARD AND HORDE.

Hove There is no such verb, contrary to increasingly popular belief. See STRONG VERBS.

However, like WHATEVER and WHOEVER, may take a subjunctive in relative clauses expressing doubt or uncertainty: 'However it *be* depicted, what he did was still wrong.' There is nothing wrong with beginning a sentence with *however*, as in: 'However, it was soon apparent that the rain had stopped'.

Humerus and **humorous** The former is a bone in the arm, known as the funny bone because of its homophone, the adjective *humorous*.

Humour is a great asset in most writing. It needs to be fresh, used in a suitable context and, preferably, should be effortlessly amusing. If a writer cannot meet these conditions, then he should avoid trying to be humorous.

Hung See HANGED AND HUNG.

Hyper-/hypo- These two similar prefixes for English words come from the Greek and are a source of confusion. *Hyper* means over and *hypo* means under. Someone who dies of *hypothermia* has perished from the cold; of *hyperthermia*, from the heat. *Hypertension* and *hypotension* are two other terms often confused. Some writers, used only to hearing such words, have produced such terms as *hypomarket* and *hypoventilation* when they mean quite the opposite. Looking up unfamiliar words in the dictionary before committing them to print is always a good idea.

Hyperbaton is a phrase in which the normal order of words is inverted, for the sake of emphasis, as in this example from

Keats: 'Much have I travelled in the realms of gold / And many goodly states and kingdoms seen . . .'

Hyperbole is an exaggerated statement, designed for effect and not to be taken literally: 'I shall kill that boy when I find him.' It may also be present in writing when a poor choice of adjective or descriptive noun inflates what should accurately be said. See GREAT for an example of a promiscuously misused adjective now deployed to mean anything that is simply agreeable.

Hyphens and **hyphenation** In the nineteenth and early twentieth centuries these proliferated in English writing, joining words that custom and practice have since completely fused, such as 'road-sweeper' or 'girl-friend'. They would also join words that have defiantly remained separate, but which we now see no point in hyphenating, such as 'ballet-dancer' or 'shooting-brake'. They also used to appear in street names, so one would read in Victorian fiction about people living in 'Belgrave-square' or 'Curzon-street' (note the lower cases of the ordinary nouns). Hyphens cause clutter. We do not use them in any of these instances today and our language is none the worse for it. We do still use them in certain restricted senses, notably to link compound words as adjectives – as in 'she was a rosy-cheeked girl' – and this is largely for the avoidance of ambiguity.

For example: it is quite correct to write that a girl with long hair is 'a long-haired girl', or that a house with a flat roof is a 'flat-roofed house'. 'A long haired girl' and a 'flat roofed house' could well be interpreted as being very different in nature and in appearance from their hyphenated alternatives. The rule should be generally observed to avoid any misunderstandings. Certain (although now very few) nouns are hyphenated: one example is when we choose to describe a person according to age. We should write 'the nineteen year-old appeared in court'. However, were we to make his age adjectival by giving him an extra noun, we should need an extra hyphen, thus: 'the nineteen-year-old youth appeared in court'. All words in a compound adjective need to be hyphenated, as in 'the dark-greenish-blue stamp', or 'a *fin-de-siècle* moment'. The exception is where a proper name becomes the adjective: one would not hyphenate 'a Great Eastern Railway train', or a 'Corpus Christi College tie'. There are also other, idiomatic, exceptions such as 'a happily married man'.

Hypo- See HYPER-/HYPO-

I

I and **me** *I* is the first person nominative, *me* the accusative. In formal writing one would write 'it is I'. In speech, only a self-conscious pedant would do so now: otherwise one would use the demotic and unexceptionable 'it's me'. However, it should not be used in formal writing. There is often a problem when the personal pronoun is combined in a sentence with another name. One too frequently hears such solecisms as 'my father gave Tom and I some money' which should of course have been 'Tom and me', and accusative pronouns coming after the verb. *Me* is used when the first person is the object of a sentence – 'he gave it to me' or 'it seemed absurd for me to do that'.

I before *e* except after *c* This is a spelling mnemonic designed to make it easy for children to remember that in words such as *chief*, *niece*, *piece*, *relieve*, *believe*, *field*, *yield* and *thief* the two vowels appear in that order; whereas in verbs such as *receive*, *deceive*, *perceive* and *conceive* the *c* immediately before the two vowels dictates that the *e* precedes the *i*. It also holds true in nouns such as *ceiling* and nouns derived from the verbs such as *receipt, deceit* and *conceit*. However, the rule does not apply where the *c* makes an *sh* sound rather than an *s* – as in *sufficient*, *coefficient*, *deficient* and their derivatives, such as *deficiency*. There are also a number of nouns where *ei* does not make the *ee* sound and that do not follow the rule – *weight*, *freight*, *beige*, *protein*, *height*, *leisure*, *neither*, *seize* and so on.

-ic/-ical endings For the distinctions between COMIC AND COMICAL, ECONOMIC AND ECONOMICAL, HISTORIC

AND HISTORICAL, IRONIC AND IRONICAL, and MAGIC AND MAGICAL see the entries under those headings. Knowing when one says or writes *comical* rather than *comic*, *historical* rather than *historic*, and so on relies on understanding important distinctions between the two related words. Adjectives ending in *-ic*, when they become adverbs, take *-ally* (with the exception of *publicly*); no one would write *tragicly*, *dramaticly*, *idioticly* or *roboticly*. *Tragical* and *psychical* have become antique usages, now replaced by *tragic* and *psychic*. The Fowlers argued that no noun of Anglo-Saxon origins should be made into an adjective ending in *-al*, though they conceded exceptions in *coastal* and *racial*. If in doubt, remember it costs nothing to consult a dictionary.

Icon and **iconic** This noun and adjective are grotesquely overused, especially in journalism, to describe almost anyone or anything of even remote celebrity. An *icon* is a representation, used in the Eastern Orthodox church, of an important Christian figure. In modern technological language it has come to be used to describe an item on a computer screen that if clicked takes the user into a new application, and that is a perfectly legitimate usage. As a shorthand for a person or object of supposed significance it is a cliché and to be avoided.

Idioms and **idiomatic usage** The dictionary defines an *idiom* as 'the form of speech peculiar or proper to a people or country'. It is, literally, the way we speak our language. The differences between American English and the way English is spoken in the British Isles highlight two different idioms of the same language. That is what the word means in its broadest sense.

Yet there is a more specific sense, given as a subsidiary meaning in the dictionary as 'a form of expression, grammatical construction, phrase, etc., peculiar to a language'. Those who have learned a foreign tongue will know that these special phrases, or idioms, have to be learned separately, not least because if translated literally they fail to convey their exact meaning. For example, the French phrase *le petit coin* literally means 'the little corner'. This takes us only part of the way to its idiomatic meaning, the *lavatory*. A Frenchman, similarly, translating into his own language an English idiom such as 'getting his leg over' or 'kicking the bucket' would perhaps struggle to realise that the first meant sexual intercourse (usually with an overtone of illicitness) and the second meant dying. Idioms may be peculiar to a section of society and not easily understood by those not of that milieu, even if they technically speak the same language: 'not safe in taxis' was a phrase once peculiar to the world of debutantes but which eventually spread, perhaps as the taxi-taking classes expanded, to describe to anyone a man who could not be relied upon to keep his hands to himself when alone with a woman. Idioms can also be generational: see DOOLALLY (DEOLALI), GOING.

Idiomatic language is common in speech and in dialogue in novels and dramas. It should have little place, except for overtly comic effect, in the writing of serious non-fiction. As one can gather from 'kicking the bucket' and 'getting his leg over' many (but by no means all) idioms are slang (and therefore not all slang is idiomatic) and all except the rare, newly minted ones are clichés. Since good style tries to avoid both vices, idioms are best reserved for the most informal speech or intimate communications, unless one is writing fiction. Like the use of any cliché, their use tends to suggest a paucity of thought by the writer.

In writing dialogue it is idiomatic to use the standard contractions of certain phrases such as *it's*, *can't*, *won't* and so on. It is a matter of taste and judgement about whether to use these in formal writing. Just one use of a contraction in, for example, a newspaper article can change its entire tone of voice from the formal to the casual. It is up to the writer to decide what effect he is seeking to achieve. In formal writing generally there should be no use of contractions. If suddenly one is used the writer should be conscious of the impact it will have on the reader, for whom it will come in the nature of a gear change.

Idiom is also a term used to describe the state of the language: it refers to what is accepted by convention rather than by strict grammatical rules. For example, the use of conjunctions in certain contexts has become a question of idiom, with the elimination of 'that' from sentences such as 'I hope that I shall see you'. See CONJUNCTIONS. See also CLICHÉ and SLANG.

Idle and **idol** The former is an adjective meaning lazy; the latter a noun meaning something or someone to be worshipped, once of religious significance, but now more likely to apply to a celebrity.

If and **provided** In their book *The King's English*, the Fowlers railed against *provided*. 'Provided is a small district in the kingdom of if,' they wrote, in one of those entertaining observations that show the considerable charm of their supposedly pedantic book. 'It can never be wrong to write *if* instead of *provided*; to write *provided* instead of *if* will generally be wrong, but now and then an improvement in precision.' A contemporary example shows the eternal truth of this rule. 'You won't be caught for speeding provided you don't break the speed limit' loses nothing by having *provided* removed and replaced by *if*. Sometimes, however, as even the Fowlers conceded, *provided* is necessary, not least to avoid giving the wrong impression. I would reframe their rule as follows: where *provided* describes a straightforward option or condition (as it normally will), replace it with *if*; yet on the rare occasions that it describes an indispensable or essential condition, retain it. So '*provided it is nice* this afternoon, we shall go for a swim' becomes 'if it is nice'; but 'I told him that I would look after him *provided he resolved* to mend his ways' is preferable to 'if he resolved' since the use of *provided* establishes that his mending his ways is not a casual option, but an important and indispensable condition of his being looked after.

If and **whether** Do not use *if* in a sentence to introduce any idea for which there is an alternative – 'I don't know if I'll go' must be 'I don't know whether I'll go', the test being whether the phrase *or not* may logically be appended to the statement. There is a subtle difference, which is worth noting, between two phrases such as 'do let me know *whether* you can come' and 'do let me know *if* you can come'. In the former, the questioner is seeking to establish whether or not the person he is inviting is able to come. In the second, the answer has already been given that the person invited probably cannot come, but that may change: so the questioner is asking the potential guest to let him know if he can come – in other words, if the situation changes. It is also a solecism to use *if* after the verb *doubt*. See DOUBT THAT AND DOUBT WHETHER. A correct usage of *if* describes an eventuality, as in 'if Paul does that again I'll hit him'.

If-clauses See CONDITIONALS.

Ill and **sick** If people are *ill* they are laid up; if they are *sick* they are vomiting.

Illicit See ELICIT AND ILLICIT.

Illusion See DELUDE, DELUSION AND ILLUSION.

Imaginary and **imaginative** *Imaginary* is an adjective applied to something that is a work of the imagination. *Imaginative* is an adjective applied to the quality of creative thought. They must not be confused.

Immanent and **imminent** The former means inherent or contained within, as in the phrase 'God is immanent in everything'. The latter means in the immediate future, as in 'his arrival was imminent'.

Immolate Because of Brunnhilde's decision to jump into the flames in what is known as 'the immolation scene' at the end of Wagner's *Götterdämmerung*, it is widely believed that the verb *immolate* means burn. It does not. It means to sacrifice a life. It is an equal immolation to jump, in the spirit of sacrifice, off a cliff.

Immoral means evil, corrupt or depraved. It is not an adjective that can have a comparative or superlative because of its

ABSOLUTE nature. When someone says 'he is the most immoral man I have ever met' they are using the language wrongly, because one is either immoral or one isn't; and if one is, there are no degrees of the condition. Better to say 'he is the most depraved man'. See also AMORAL AND IMMORAL.

Immune The *OED* suggests that one is *immune to* a disease, but *immune from* an obligation, burden or penalty. The most frequent contemporary usage is medical, in which one is 'immune to measles'.

Immured and **enclosed** For someone or something to be *immured* he or it must be walled in, as was the practice at one time with certain unfortunate nuns and monks. To be confined anywhere else is not to be immured, but *enclosed* – usages such as someone being 'immured in a coffin' are plain wrong – though it is a verb that does admit of certain metaphorical usages, such as 'she was immured by her work'.

Impact is another example of a noun being turned into a verb. On 25 July 2012 the *Guardian* reported that 'iPhone sales were being "impacted by rumours" of new products'. The newspaper itself was quoting an authority on the subject, and the positioning of 'impacted' within quotation marks suggests that the *Guardian* did not endorse the usage. It occurs frequently, as in 'my husband's death impacted seriously on the family'. It would be correct to write 'my husband's death had a serious impact on the family'.

Imperative mood The *imperative* is a truncated form of expression used when giving orders – 'sit', 'stay' and various other commands used to dogs are all imperative, as are human instructions such as 'come in', 'go away' and 'give me that'. It is peculiar to speech and not found in formal writing except in accounts of dialogue and certain types of written text, such as cookery books and instruction manuals.

Imperfect is the name given to the simple past tense in English – 'I went', 'he came', 'you saw', 'they ran', 'we stayed' are all imperfect verbs. The tense refers to an action in the past that is completed. There is also in English a continuous past distinct from the imperfect – 'I was walking', 'I was reading' and so on – and a past tense using the auxiliary *used* to indicate something that happened habitually – 'I used to walk to school every day' and 'I used to read a newspaper'. Strong verbs, such as *go*, *come*, *see* and *run*, have special formations in the imperfect, other examples being *drank*, *ate*, *stole*, *broke* and so on. They are normally of Germanic derivation, where some (but not all) verbs take this form. Weak verbs add *-ed* to the present tense to put them in the imperfect, such as *wounded*, *asked*, *walked*, *bolted*, *crashed* and so on. See also PERFECT TENSE.

Imply and **infer** To *imply* is to create an impression of a certain state of affairs without directly saying so. It is often confused with *infer* (it is seldom the other way round). You may say that someone you know is a blackguard and a scoundrel. From that I may *infer* that you do not like him. You are certainly *implying* that you don't. Yet time and again one reads that someone is *inferring* that someone is a scoundrel when in fact he is *implying* it. To *infer* is to draw an impression from something one hears or reads. The entirely uneducated have no trouble with these words because they rarely use them. It is only once people have learned of their existence that they seem to have problems with them.

Impracticable, impractical and **unpractical** These three ways of negating what appears to be broadly the same adjective need to be distinguished from each other. *Impracticable*, meaning practically impossible – 'his plans were completely impracticable' – has a venerable pedigree dating back to the seventeenth century. *Impractical* developed in the nineteenth century as a MALAPROPISM for *impracticable* and has now supplanted it, not least with help from America. Purists will stick to the original usage, or to *unpractical*, which dates back to the seventeenth century. See also PRACTICABLE AND PRACTICAL.

In actual fact and its shorter sibling **in fact** are FILLERS, and can usually be removed from any sentence containing them without any harm being done.

In depth has become a CLICHÉ.

In spite of and **despite** are interchangeable.

In the circumstances is correct and *under the circumstances* is not, for reasons of logic: the etymology of the word tells us that *circumstances* are things that *stand around* us, so we are in them, not under them.

In the day is the American way of saying 'the other day' or 'a little while ago'. BACK IN THE DAY is their way of saying 'a long time ago'. It is now frequently heard in British English, where it is an affectation and is taking on the status of a cliché.

In the event that is a verbose way of saying *if*.

In to and **into** *Into* is a valuable preposition, indicating the passage to a state of being in somewhere. There is a distinction, and not always a subtle one, between it and *in to*. One says 'I went into the room', 'I got into trouble' and 'I walked into the wood' but 'I walked in to a lamp-post'. The choice to be made in selecting what sort of preposition to use is based on a simple criterion: does the action described result in the subject's ending up within the object? If it does, then use *into*. If it does not, use *in to*.

in-/un- On the question of how to make a word (usually an adjective, sometimes an adverb) negative, H. W. Fowler sets an etymological rule: 'It may be safely laid down that when adjectives ending in the obviously English *-ed* or *-ing* are to be negatived, the English *un-* is better than the Latin *in-*; *indigestible*, but *undigested*; *indiscriminate*, but *undiscriminating*.' There are inevitable exceptions: one would never say or write *irregenerate*, but rather *unregenerate*; though the dictionary finds four attempts at the former since 1657, by writers adhering to Fowlerite principles, the last of them in 1892. Nor would we countenance *inforgettable* or *unconvenienced*. However, generally the rule holds good. Sometimes the prefix can make a profound difference in meaning: see the example of IRRESPONSIBLE AND UNRESPONSIBLE. Fowler's rule about 'Latin' and 'English' holds generally good with adverbs, with idiomatic exceptions. The former are adverbs made from adjectives that have Latinate endings such as *-ate* and *-ible*, the latter from those with Anglo-Saxon endings such as *-ed* and *-ing*. So one would write 'he marked it indelibly', 'he chose indiscriminately' but 'she lost undeservedly' and 'he grinned unprepossessingly'.

Inappropriate See APPROPRIATE.

Incidentally is most frequently used as a filler, introducing a sentence, and can often be removed without causing harm, as in: 'Incidentally, I saw your mother in the shop.'

Incomparable adjectives are those such as 'very correct', which are ABSOLUTES by nature and therefore not susceptible of being COMPARATIVES or SUPERLATIVES: something is either correct or it is not, and there cannot in logic be degrees of correctness.

Indefinite article See A AND AN.

Indicative mood Verbs have three moods, the *indicative*, the IMPERATIVE and the SUBJUNCTIVE. (Some also decree that the INFINITIVE is a mood, but, as the dictionary does, I see it as just being the form of the verb that simply describes its notion – *to walk*, *to run*, *to stand*, *to sit* and so on.) The indicative mood is the most common of the three and is used for the most straightforward statements of positive description or intent: 'I went to school', 'I go to school' and 'I shall go to school' are examples of the imperfect, present and future indicative tenses of the verb *to go*. In much modern writing and in demotic speech the indicative has also moved on to the ground once occupied by the SUBJUNCTIVE mood, which was used to describe nuances of intent or desire, and degrees of certainty and uncertainty. Whereas one used to say or write 'I so wish I were married to him', it is now more usually 'I so wish I was married to him'. This is to be regretted, as the demise of the subjunctive removes some of the subtlety from the English language.

Ineffective and **ineffectual** See the entry for EFFECTIVE AND EFFECTUAL for a discussion of the distinction between these terms.

Infer See IMPLY AND INFER.

Infinitives This is the basic state of any verb – *to eat, to sleep, to read* and *to walk* are all infinitives. The Fowlers expended much ink and energy on when, in certain constructions, to use a GERUND, and when to use an *infinitive*. Is it – to use their examples – 'a duty to make' (infinitive) or 'the duty of making' (gerund)? Or is it 'aiming to be' or 'aiming at being'? A century later, the idiomatic usages in each case appear to be better established. The Fowlers tried to point the way, arguing that after a noun the usage is usually of the gerund, after a verb it is usually an infinitive. This is sometimes true, but not inevitably. It may sound, and indeed be, as correct to say 'he relished the chance to play against Smith' as it would be to say 'he relished the chance of playing against Smith', but good style prefers the latter because of its seeming to flow more easily. By contrast, 'she was aiming at buying the dress before the weekend' is clumsy and unnatural compared with 'she aimed to buy the dress', partly because of the repetition of the participle ending *-ing* in the first example, partly because it sounds more long-winded. Yet most of us today would say 'I had a duty to look after him' rather than the more pompous-sounding 'I had the duty of looking after him'. Perhaps a subtle difference has grown up between the two usages. The former gives the impression of a moral obligation, the latter, with its definite article, of one ordained by some rule or statute. The Fowlers concede that if a noun takes an indefinite article it probably requires a gerund, but with a definite article it needs the infinitive. This is still true today, and one can discern a natural distinction between 'he wanted a chance of playing against Smith' and 'he wanted the chance to play against Smith'. Both are correct.

Many verbs of intention or desire naturally take an infinitive – *hope to*, *long to*, *wish to* – and no one would seek to make a construction using the gerund instead, not least because no precedent exists. It does with aim – 'she aimed at being in London by 6 p.m.' – which is unusual. Over the last century the gerund does appear to have retreated in the face of the infinitive in all other contexts. If one used a construction today such as 'she had the ability' it would be the ability *to do* something, not *of doing* something. It is much more likely, though, that a writer would simply say 'she could'. Indeed, deciding to be less verbose may eliminate many difficulties with this construction. Does one write 'he had the intention of seeing her' or 'he had the intention to see her'? Again, good style demands the former, but 'he intended to see her' is shorter, says the same thing, and avoids any doubt. There are inevitably exceptions. Where once we would have said 'I did not think to do that', the idiomatic usage has become 'I did not think of doing that'.

There are verbs for which a following infinitive is mandatory, though this is often concealed by sloppy usage of the conjunction *and*. 'I will try and do better', 'she was going to go and see him' and 'will you come and see me' should all have the conjunction replaced by *to* in formal English. The infinitive may be in the passive voice as well as in the active – the passive infinitive is, for example, the construction 'to be found'. It may, in both voices, have other tenses: the perfect is 'to have found', the perfect passive is 'to have been found', the future is 'to be about to find' and the future passive is 'to be about to be found', and there are other permutations. The perfect infinitive is often misused. One sometimes reads 'he would have wanted to have been there', which is wrong. The correct usage is 'he would have wanted to be there': the sense of the past is conveyed by the finite verb and it is illogical to repeat it in the infinitive. Similarly, one would say 'to be there would have been delightful', not 'to have been there would have been delightful'. Note also the logical difference between 'I should have liked to see her' and 'I should like to have seen her'. The first implies that the opportunity of his seeing her may still be current; the second that the opportunity is in the past. The perfect infinitive should be used only when attached to a finite verb in a past tense, as in 'to have seen her meant more to him than anything' or 'to have lived in those times would have been glorious'. Usually, though, where one may have the instinct to use a perfect infinitive, one ought correctly to use the present. One of the rare legitimate usages is to refer to a completed action after a verb of perception: 'he appears to have broken his leg' or 'she seems to have been lucky'. See also SPLIT INFINITIVE.

Inflammable and **flammable** The dictionary says these adjectives are interchangeable, both meaning something that is easily set on fire. *Inflammable* also has a wide metaphorical usage, however, as in 'his temper was highly inflammable'.

Informed about and **informed by** Care should be taken with the verb *informed*. If one is told some news, one is *informed about* or *informed of* a fact or facts. However, if one decides to go on holiday to the South of France because one has learned that the weather is hot there, or the food is good, one takes a decision *informed by* such knowledge.

-ing For guidance on the correct usage of words ending in *-ing*, see GERUNDS and PARTICIPLES.

Ingenious and **ingenuous** *Ingenious* is an adjective applied to something clever in its invention or construction. *Ingenuous* is an adjective applied to a person who (as the dictionary has it) is 'honourably straightforward; open, frank, candid'. *Disingenuous* is therefore a rather disobliging negative of the word.

Inquiry See ENQUIRY AND INQUIRY.

Institutions Capitalise institutions at home and abroad, because they are proper names: the Bank of England, the Federal Reserve or the European Central Bank, for example. Consider idiomatic usage before deciding whether an institution is singular or plural. Whatever you choose, consistency is essential. If you start off by writing that 'the BBC has [rather than 'have'] said today that it is changing its schedules', do not put the BBC into the plural later on.

Insure See ASSURE, ENSURE AND INSURE.

Interested One is *interested in* a subject, not *interested by* it.

Interface This voguish noun means the place where two systems or forces meet, as in 'the interface between our staff and our customers'. There is nothing wrong with speaking of 'the relationship between our staff and our customers'. The noun *interface* now has the status of JARGON. The verb – 'our staff and customers interfaced' – is an atrocity.

Interject is not a synonym for *interrupt*, as misused in a sentence such as 'the backbencher interjected during the minister's statement to point out an error of fact'. To *interject* is to insert something into a conversation and is a transitive verb requiring an object, as in 'he interjected an observation about the weather during the discussion'.

Interment and **internment** *Interment* is a burial, usually of human remains. *Internment* is detention without trial.

Interviewee See -EE ENDINGS.

Into See IN TO AND INTO. *Into* does exist, but by association with it people have made the preposition *onto*. This, however, does not exist. See ON TO AND ONTO.

Intransitive verbs do not require an object: 'I laughed', 'you reflected', 'he slept', 'she walked', 'it smelt', 'we tried', 'they hoped'. Some verbs may be intransitive or TRANSITIVE: they can function with or without an object. Examples are 'I sang', 'I sang a song'; 'you ran', 'you ran a race'; 'he drove', 'he drove the car'; and so on. There is confusion over whether some verbs have a transitive form. See, for example, COLLAPSE and GROW. For a graphic misuse of an intransitive, see EXIT.

Introductory phrases, redundant words Beware the pleonastic introductory phrase. How often does one read 'it is obvious that', 'by and large', 'for the most part', 'as a matter of fact', or some other piece of padding before a phrase such as 'the economy is not getting any better', when the sentence could just as easily start with that phrase itself?

Invoke See EVOKE AND INVOKE.

Involve and **involvement** *Involve* literally means to wrap something up in something, or to entangle it. It has a legitimate (but limited) metaphorical usage, but this is now used so widely that it has been rendered meaningless. Why say 'two vehicles were involved in an accident' when one can say they 'had an accident'? Why say 'would you like to be involved in planning our fête this year?' when you can say 'would you like to help?' The noun *involvement* is used with equal lack of precision. There is no need to write that 'Smith's involvement in the crime was disputed' when one should say that his part was disputed. Lazy writers use both the verb and noun to describe various forms of participation by people or objects in enterprises, activities, events or other specific contexts. If tempted to use either, think of a more precise synonym – which is likely to turn out not to be a synonym at all, but simply the right word.

Ireland and **Eire** *Ireland* is the name in English of the large island to the west of Great Britain. *Eire* is the Gaelic name for it, also used to designate that part of the island that is the Republic of Ireland.

Ironic and **ironical** A statement that is *ironic* contains irony. One that is *ironical* is 'of the nature of irony'. The distinction is a fine one; the former statement will be more blatant in its irony, the latter less so.

Irony and **sarcasm** *Irony* uses words to mean something opposite to what they appear to express. If a child does something stupid and is told what a clever boy he is, that is *irony*: its relations with *ridicule* and *sarcasm* are often, but not inevitably, close. It is (among other things) ironic if a man wins a case of champagne in a raffle when he has just become teetotal. It is sarcasm to tell someone who has just failed his exams that he will undoubtedly have a brilliant career.

Irregular verbs These usually present difficulties in the past tenses – the IMPERFECT, PERFECT and PLUPERFECT. See STRONG VERBS for some of the most obvious examples, and also SING, SANG AND SUNG; SPRING, SPRANG AND SPRUNG; and STRIVE. There are some irregularities with apparently weak verbs too – those that form a past tense simply by adding the suffix *-ed* to the present tense. There seems to be uncertainty in the minds of some writers about whether certain verbs have a distinct past tense at all. *Fit* certainly does, though that does not prevent some people from writing 'it *fit* me perfectly' when they mean 'it *fitted* me perfectly'. Does one write 'I *quit* my job' or 'I *quitted*'? In British English one writes the latter, though a battle has been raging on that question for many years and is not won yet: the former usage is an Americanism. What about CAST AND BROADCAST? They are both irregular and do not add *-ed* in the past: so we have 'he *cast* his bread upon the water' and 'the concert was *broadcast* last Friday'. Nor is *cast iron* known as *casted iron*, for this very good reason. Partridge disputes the point about *broadcast* and cites the dictionary in support. He was doubtless right in the 1940s; but the latest revision of the dictionary says the form *broadcasted* is now 'rare', and our knowledge of IDIOM tells us that is correct. One sees occasionally usages such as 'he had *hid* in the forest' or 'it was *hid* in the bookcase'. In both cases – the past participle and the passive – the correct usage is *hidden. Hid* is the imperfect of *hide* – 'she *hid* in the cupboard'.

Other irregular past participles from strong verbs include *mown, sawn, dreamt, spilt, leapt, slept, swept, kept, wept, rent, sent, bent, spent, sewn, sown, shown, spelt, smelt* and *spoilt. Spoilt* is a special case: see the entry for that word. American English has the odd strong past participle that we do not share, such as *dove* from *dive* and *gotten* from *get*: these must be avoided in British English. Some grammarians have decreed a distinction between certain of these irregular words when they are used as adjectives and when they are used as past participles or preterites (the technical term for the imperfect tense of verbs). It has been argued that there is a *well-mown* lawn, but that the lawn is *well-mowed*; and that one *spilled* the milk but cries over *spilt* milk. If this was ever the case it certainly is not now. All the words in the list above, and many others like them, serve perfectly well as the imperfect tense of their verbs.

Irresponsible and **unresponsible** One who is *irresponsible* is incapable of taking responsibility. One who is *unresponsible* has no responsibility, usually for a certain matter or action, but it is more idiomatic to say 'not responsible'.

Irritate is not a synonym for AGGRAVATE.

Irrupt See ERUPT AND IRRUPT.

Is where and **is when** Usages such as 'abseiling is where [or 'is when'] you come down the side of a cliff on a rope' are clumsy and vulgar. Say or write either 'abseiling is the practice of coming down the side of a cliff on a rope' or 'the practice of coming down the side of a cliff on a rope is known as abseiling'.

-ise/-ize endings American English had a strong influence in the last century in minting verbs by taking nouns and adding the suffix *-ise* (or, as the Americans spell it, *-ize*) to them. This also happened with adjectives. However, there was a long pedigree of both in British English. *Standardise* appears in the late nineteenth century; but *particularise* in the late sixteenth. However, the Americans gave us *monetise* in 1867 (and again, in a subtly different sense, in 1954), *corporatise* in the 1940s and *privatise* in the 1950s; *digitise* was coined in 1953. Some of these words usefully described something in one word that would otherwise have required several. *Privatise* was itself a preferred shorter term for *denationalise* and meant 'sell off state-owned assets to private corporations or individuals'. DIGITISE succinctly puts a complex electronic procedure into one word. Perhaps it is the efficacious way that the *-ise* suffix forms a verb that has made it so popular: but not all such uses may be judged so necessary. Some people will take many more years to become used to *diarise* – to put an engagement in a diary – for example. The spelling differs according to which side of the Atlantic one is on. In America they write 'authorize' but in Britain it is 'authorise'. However, *-ize* is becoming more common in British English, notably in scientific writing.

Islamic and **Islamist** The rise of Muslim fundamentalism in recent years has given us cause to be more precise in our use of the terminology of that faith. An *Islamic* person is a follower of the Prophet Mohammed, and no extreme intent need be imputed to him. An *Islamist*, by contrast, expresses a fanatical devotion to his faith, sometimes to the point of violence, and inevitably adopts a fundamentalist approach.

It is obvious that See INTRODUCTORY PHRASES, REDUNDANT WORDS.

Italics, use of If writing the name of a book, or a ship, italicise it: *The Canterbury Tales* or the RMS *Titanic*. Also italicise films, newspapers, magazines and paintings. It is a matter of taste whether to italicise the names of poems or give them within single quotation marks. My prejudice is to italicise poems known by a specific title and put ones generally known by their first lines in single marks: so *Paradise Lost* or *The Waste Land*, but 'I wandered lonely as a cloud' or 'My love is like a red, red rose'. Also italicise foreign words and phrases that have not passed into common English usage (and, if they are German nouns, give them an initial capital letter): so write *mauvais quart d'heure* but 'panache', or *Weltanschauung* but 'angst' or 'blitzkrieg'. See also FOREIGN WORDS AND PHRASES.

Its and **it's** The most frequent offender in the list of punctuation mistakes is *it's* used for the possessive *its. It's* is the contraction of *it is* or *it has*, and must be used in no other context. 'The dog chewed its bone' is correct, 'the dog chewed it's bone' is an abomination. See also APOSTROPHES.

J

Jail and **gaol** *Jail* is the American spelling of the word for a prison, but has superseded the traditional *gaol*, which is now considered archaic.

Jargon Each sub-tribe in society perpetuates its own jargon, which is always a handicap to widespread communication. *Jargon* is a word that originally meant 'the inarticulate utterance of birds, or a vocal sound resembling it'. It has come metaphorically to be 'applied contemptuously to any mode of speech abounding in unfamiliar terms, or peculiar to a particular set of persons'. One has an insight into this when overhearing the conversation of members of the medical profession or the Bar, or when reading their learned journals; or, at another extreme, when listening to conversation between members of the army or former professional sportsmen who now act as commentators on television. Some jargon, however, in time passes into everyday use thanks to the layman's exposure to it through media such as television and the press.

Sir Ernest Gowers, a senior civil servant and therefore a man exposed regularly to jargon of a peculiar sort, raised objections to elements of it in his book *Plain Words* in 1948: yet his dissatisfaction with words such as *multilateral*, *bilateral* and *unilateral* cannot now hold. It is not just that they are ubiquitous, for that does not make them right: it is that they are in fact clear, and serve a comprehensible function. Equally, just as some words change over time from being abstruse to being common, others change from terms of abuse to badges of honour (as both *Whig* and *Tory* did), and one needs to decide at what stage in their development some words are before one uses them. Writing is all about judgement, and if one wishes to remain formal one will know by experience and often by instinct what vocabulary, or argot, has a place in such writing and what does not. Jargon is also a close cousin of CLICHÉ, and one should be alert to the insidious way in which the jargon of officials seeps into the language of the general public – recent examples include phrases such as 'blue-skies thinking' (or 'blue-skies' anything, for that matter) and 'best practice'.

Jewelry is the American spelling of *jewellery*.

Journalese is a pejorative term, coined at the time of the rise of the cheap or 'yellow' press in Britain in the 1880s, to describe what was thought to be the demotic variant of English in which cheap newspapers addressed their readers. Insofar as it survives today, it is sometimes apparent in what are widely known as the 'red tops'. While direct and clear, it is not a form of prose that should be imitated by anyone outside the genre who aspires to seriousness in writing. See TABLOID PRESS.

Judgement is the correct British spelling: *judgment* an Americanism. The same distinction is true of ACKNOWLEDGEMENT and ABRIDGEMENT.

Judicial language, American British English is becoming increasingly littered with phrases familiar from the televising of American police or legal dramas but that have no legitimate place in idiomatic English – several examples are given under AMERICAN ENGLISH AND AMERICANISMS and individual entries, such as STAND, TAKE THE and ATTORNEY.

Judiciary, writing to or addressing A Justice of the Supreme Court (formed in 2009 to replace the House of Lords as the highest court in the land) is a life peer and is styled Lord Smith. An appeal court judge is usually a knight or a dame. Therefore he or she will be styled Lord Justice Smith or Lady Justice Smith and will be addressed in person as Sir John Smith or Dame Mary Smith. A High Court judge is a knight or a dame. He or she will be styled Mr Justice Smith or Mrs Justice Smith (irrespective of whether she is married). Should there be more than one High Court judge with the name of Smith, the forename will also be used to distinguish them: so there may be Mr Justice John Smith and Mr Justice George Smith (this applies to Lords Justices of Appeal too, who would be known as Lord Justice John Smith, etc.). A judge of the Crown Court is His Honour Judge Smith, or Her Honour Judge Smith. They will not usually be knighted or given a damehood. If they are Queen's Counsel they may use the letters 'QC' after their names: higher judges do not do this. Justices of the Supreme Court and Lords Justices of Appeal are also Privy Counsellors: their title of 'Rt Hon.' would be used only in formal documents or when addressing them on envelopes. Note that the plural of Lord Justice is Lords Justices.

Jurist and **juror** A *jurist* is someone expert in the law, notably in jurisprudence: a *juror* is one who sits on a jury in a court of law or a coroner's court.

K

Karma is a word from Buddhism and Hinduism that means fate or destiny shaped by a person's actions. It is a term beloved of those who indulge in psychobabble, having become a synonym for *atmosphere* or *context* – neither of which it is. Its misuse is seen in phrases such as 'there was bad karma in the office' or 'his life had always had good karma'. Avoid it.

Kerb is the correct spelling in British English for the edge of the pavement. In America it is *curb*.

Ketchup, kitchup, catchup and **catsup** are all terms used for a sauce made out of fruits or vegetables, most famously tomato ketchup, using the juices thereof. *Ketchup* is the correct British English term; *kitchup* is an obsolete variant of it; *catchup* and *catsup* are used in American English.

Key has become an adjective overworked to exhaustion in phrases such as 'he was a key player' or 'this is a key policy'. Think of another adjective, such as *important*, *central* or *essential.*

Kids It can never be acceptable to refer to children as *kids* except in dialogue, or when one is setting out to be deliberately frivolous. This word began as an Americanism and has now been properly anglicised as part of our own SLANG. Like many such demotic usages it does not grate in parts of the tabloid press or in certain advertisements, but its use in anything approaching formal writing is to be abhorred, unless one is discussing the reproductive activities of goats.

Kind of a A phrase such as 'What kind of a husband does that?' has a superfluous article in it. 'What kind of husband does that?' does the job just as well.

Kindly This word is often misused. When we read signs such as 'passengers are kindly asked not to put their feet on the seats', what those making the request really mean is 'passengers are asked to be so kind as not to put their feet on the seats'. As Fowler pointed out, even if the tone of the request was kind, it does not do to boast about having that quality. The same could be said of the phrase 'polite notice' that appears ubiquitously.

Kneel *Knelt* is more usual today as the past participle of *kneel* than *kneeled*.

Knights, writing to or addressing There are many orders of knighthood in Britain – the Garter, the Thistle, St Michael and St George, the Royal Victorian Order, the Order of the British Empire and plain old Knights Bachelor – but what they all have in common is that the title dies with the holder. A knight is addressed in person or referred to by his Christian or forename preceded by 'Sir' – Sir John, Sir Jasper, Sir Galahad and so on. The wife of a knight is Lady Smith, unless she happens to be the daughter of a duke, marquess or earl, in which case she may choose to be Lady Mary Smith. Knights and their wives should be addressed as 'Dear Sir John' or 'Dear Lady Smith', the letters ending 'Yours sincerely'.

Knit The past participle is *knitted*. *Knit* as the past participle – 'we were knit together' - is now archaic.

Knock up is a vulgar Americanism meaning to impregnate. In British English it used to describe a hammering on a door to wake someone or alert them, or to warm up with bat and ball for a game of cricket.

Koran, Qur'an and **Quran** *Koran* has long been the British English transliteration of the Arabic word for Islam's holy book.

However, Muslims (who used until recently to be transliterated as *Moslems*) say their preferred transliteration is *Qur'an*, though they are also content with *Quran*. Some on the more radical edge of Islam say that writers who persist in using *Koran* (and *Moslem*) show their implicit hostility to Islam, though how they arrive at that conclusion and on the basis of what evidence is unclear. This moves us into the choppy waters of **POLITICAL CORRECTNESS**.

L

Last and **latter** Something can only be the *last* of three or more things or people; and can only be the *latter* of two.

Last Post is written thus, without the definite article.

Latin For the dangers of misusing Latin tags, see FOREIGN WORDS AND PHRASES. As noted at FULL STOPS, certain Latin abbreviations, notably e.g. (meaning *for example*), i.e. (*that is*) and q.v. (*which see*) may be more identifiable if one includes full stops after each letter.

Laudable and **laudatory** Someone who is *laudable* deserves praise; something that is *laudatory* conveys it.

Launch Only ships used to be *launched*. Now books, initiatives, plans, schemes, even people find this verb being applied to them. There is nothing wrong with such metaphorical usages if the writer using them is convinced that he is doing so for the first time; or, if he knows very well he is not, if he believes that their staleness will not repel his readers or cause them to misinterpret what he is telling them; or if he does not mind being branded as a lazy or second-rate writer. See METAPHOR.

Lawmakers This is an Americanism and is perfectly legitimate when used there, but not in British English. The British would say *legislators*, or *parliamentarians*. The word's passage into British English is one of the effects of American police and courtroom dramas on television.

Lay and **lie** *Lay* is a TRANSITIVE verb. *Lie* is an INTRANSITIVE one. So we would write 'lay your coat over there' but 'the dog can lie there until we leave'. A man *lies*, he *lay*, he *has lain* in bed; but he *lays* a hedge or a table, he *laid* it and he *has laid* it. The two participles are *lying* ('I was lying in bed when the postman called') and *laying* ('my wife was laying the table when I walked in'). Confusion often comes with the similarity between the imperfect of the intransitive verb ('I lay in bed last night', and so on through all the persons) and all but the third person singular of the present tense of the transitive one ('I lay the table before dinner', 'you lay', 'we lay', 'they lay'). If one is clear what action is being described – the difference being between a person (or animal) lying down and laying something else down – there should be no confusion. If you read or hear someone say 'he lied', it means the person concerned had not told the truth.

Lead and **led** *Lead* (to rhyme with *fed*) is a form of metal. It is not the past participle of the verb *to lead*, which is *led*. The *Guardian* confused the two words on 15 May 2012, when it wrote of the newly elected French president: 'Hollande, who lead the party for 11 years . . .'

Leading question A *leading question* is not necessarily a prominent one nor a difficult one, but one that contains a strong indication of the answer desired in the way it is framed.

Leak and **leek** The former is literally an escape of liquid from a supposedly secure container, or, metaphorically, the disclosure, improperly, of supposedly secure information. The latter is a vegetable.

Learned and **learnt** As past participles, the British generally prefer *learnt* but the Americans insist on *learned*. The same rule applies to *earned* and *earnt*, *spelled* and *spelt*, *burned* and *burnt*, *dreamed* and *dreamt* and *smelled* and *smelt*. As an adjective, used to describe someone as *well-educated* or *well-read*, the word must be *learned*, pronounced with two syllables, as in 'my learned friend' or 'he was greatly learned in the classics'.

Learnings is a new jargon word for *lessons* in corporate-speak: 'What are your learnings from this course?' rather than 'What [lessons] have you learned from this course?' It is utterly unnecessary and to be avoided.

Least, lesser and **lessor** For there to be the *least* of any number there have to be three items or more. To be the *lesser*, something has to be the *lesser* of two. Do not confuse *lesser* with *lessor*, the name given to someone who rents out a property on a lease.

Legendary has become a grotesquely overused adjective, being applied to people who have had moderate success or fame in the recent past at soccer, acting or as popular entertainers of some description, as in 'the legendary Roy Orbison'. A *legend* was originally an account of the life of a saint, but it has since the early seventeenth century been used to describe a tale of antiquity, handed down often through the narrative tradition, for which the historical evidence is either scant or non-existent. The late Mr Orbison is of recent provenance and that he existed is beyond question. It is best to confine the term to people who are genuinely the stuff of legend over many generations, such as St George, Robin Hood, King Arthur or the Erl King.

Leisurely is an adjective – 'he took a leisurely stroll' – not an adverb. One does something 'in a leisurely way'.

Lend and **loan** In British English *lend* is a verb – 'he lent me some money' – and *loan* a noun, meaning the thing, money or goods that is or are lent – 'I was unable to pay off my outstanding loans from the bank'. *Loan* was however frequently used as a verb in the Middle Ages, but after the seventeenth century was largely confined to American usage. It is now considered an Americanism and although the usage 'he loaned me his car' has crept back into British English in recent years, it is unnecessary given the ready availability of the perfectly serviceable verb *lend*.

Less See FEWER AND LESS.

Lesser See LEAST, LESSER AND LESSOR.

Lest is a rare surviving subjunctive. It remains a very useful but underused word: 'he refused to drink any whisky lest he have to drive' or 'I took an umbrella with me lest it rain' are examples. *Lest* never takes a subjunctive auxiliary such as *should*, *would* or *might*, the use of the pure subjunctive making an auxiliary unnecessary.

Lethal See FATAL, LETHAL AND MORTAL.

Letters, writing Should you find in a second-hand bookshop an etiquette guide from the period before 1939 you will find in it elaborate instructions on how to write a letter to a person of rank. Obsequiousness both in the form of address and in the valediction was the fundamental rule. Letters to the Sovereign were supposed to begin 'May it please Your Majesty' and to end with the confirmation that the writer remained 'Your Majesty's most humble and obedient servant', something unlikely to be true and even less likely to be proved true. As one went further down the social scale the degree of deference decreased, but not too markedly. Letters to peers below the rank of duke and to bishops would begin 'My Lord'. At the very bottom of the scale, a letter to an untitled man (other than a tradesman, who would be 'Dear Mr Smith' or 'Dear Smith') with whom one was unacquainted would begin 'Dear Sir', to a woman 'Dear Madam'. The envelope for the former would be addressed to 'John Smith Esq.' (irrespective of whether Mr Smith met the criteria for the appellation *Esquire*); the envelope addressed to a married woman at her home (as opposed to her business) address would say 'Mrs John Smith'. A few people cling to these vestiges of formality today, and they are not wrong to do so. For most people, however, this is an age of greater informality, with deference in decline, and a woman no longer identified principally by the name of her husband; and the way we write letters often reflects that. If writing to someone as 'Dear Sir' or 'Dear Madam', finish with 'Yours faithfully': in all other instances, use 'Yours sincerely'.

A separate etiquette appears to have established itself in the matter of emails. Because of the instant nature of communication they are often very informal, which may be well between people who are intimate friends or even more than that. In any email between people who know each other less well or not at all the forms of letter-writing should be followed – 'Dear Mr Smith' to start and 'Yours sincerely' to finish. This book does not pretend to be a guide to manners, but in most cases when one is saying thank you for something – a gift, or a decent lunch – it is probably best to write a letter. And, except in extreme circumstances, important matters such as noting the birth of a child, a wedding or offering condolences upon a bereavement should be done by the traditional method and not electronically.

For details of how to write to people of rank or high office, see under **ARMED FORCES, BARONESSES, BARONETS, BISHOPS, CLERGY, COUNTESSES, DR, DUKES AND DUCHESSES, EARLS, JUDICIARY, KNIGHTS, MILITARY TITLES, PEERS AND THEIR FAMILIES, QUEEN'S COUNSEL, REVEREND AND ROYALTY, VISCOUNTS AND VISCOUNTESSES**; also **ESQUIRE** and **HONOURABLE**. Envelopes are the only places where the honorific 'the Honourable' (abbreviated to Hon.) should be used for the son of an earl (if he is not the elder son with a courtesy title) and the children of viscounts and barons, as in 'the Hon. John Smith' or 'the Hon. Mary Smith'. As the late Hugh Massingberd, the distinguished genealogist, used to put it, the title *Hon.* was something about which 'only the postman knows'.

Libel and **slander** *Libel* is the written defamation by one person of another. *Slander* is defamation by the spoken word. However, broadcast defamation is considered *libel* because there is usually an accurately transcribed record of it. Court proceedings and those of parliament are privileged and therefore, if reported verbatim, exempt from libel.

Licence and **license** *Licence* is the noun; *license* is the verb in British English (and, in America, both the noun and the verb).

Lie See LAY AND LIE.

Light and **lit** The verb *to light* now takes as its past participle the word *lit*, though until the mid-twentieth century in formal speech one would have said or have written *lighted*, as in 'she lighted her cigarette' or 'the man lighted the fire'. This usage survives in a different meaning of the verb *to light*, which means to come across or upon something – 'they lighted upon the thief in the kitchen'. Metaphorical light is subtly different. It remains a matter of taste whether one says or writes 'she lit up the room when she entered' or 'she lighted up the room'. We now say 'she lit a cigarette' or 'he lit the fire', but she holds 'a lighted cigarette' or walks past 'a lighted candle' or 'a lighted lamp'.

Like is a word often misused for *as*. It has other misuses too. It is the filler of choice for current youth, which is its most abominable usage, in statements such as 'he was, like, coming down the road'. Its abuses far pre-date the early twenty-first century, however. *Like* is best regarded as a verb that expresses affection for something – 'we like the Smiths' – or a means of making a direct comparison – 'he looked like his father'. It has turned into an adverb under American influence, and has the meaning 'in the manner of', which ought to be resisted in formal writing. 'You cook it like my mother used to' should be 'you cook it as my mother used to'. 'A strumpet like her' should be 'a strumpet such as her' (it will be noted that, following Onions's precept, I am using the accusative case after *such as*). Another vulgarism is *like that*, as in 'Why does she talk like that?' instead of 'Why does she talk in that way?' Similarly, do not write 'she looked like she had been kicked in the teeth' or 'it sounded like it was all over'; write 'she looked as if' or 'it sounded as though'. That last pair of examples also illustrates the distinction between *as if* and *as though*. *As if* is used in metaphorical or abstract contexts, *as though* in literal ones. The woman has not actually been kicked in the teeth; she is reacting as if she had; but the event is real and it sounds as though it has ended. Clauses with *as if* or *as though* also take a subjunctive: 'it was as if she were up in the clouds' or 'I felt as though I were drowning'.

Limp and **limpid** *Limp*, as an adjective, means to lack stiffness or firmness: it is commonly used figuratively – 'his character was pretty limp' – as well as literally – 'the lettuce was limp'. *Limpid* means clear. It should not be confused with *limpet*, a sea-creature.

Line is the American word for the British English *queue*, which is both a noun and a verb. Americans do not queue: they *stand in line*.

Line of fire and **firing line** The former is the place where shots rain down after they have been fired. It is far more dangerous than *the firing line*, whence the shots come, and the two should not be – but often are – confused. The *Guardian* made this error in a sub-headline on 11 October 2012 when, writing of a possible attack on the perks of civil servants, it announced: 'Flexible work, childcare and holidays in firing line.'

Literal and **littoral** The former means exact; the latter a coastline.

Literally is one of the more abused words in our tongue. Should you find yourself about to write it, pause and consider whether it is really necessary; it almost never is. One hears people say 'he literally jumped out of his skin', when we all know full well he did nothing of the sort: *literally* in this sense, according to the dictionary, means 'with exact fidelity of representation'. One cannot say 'he literally died' unless he is dead, and died as a result of the event being described; but people do say it when 'he' still lives and breathes. To make matters worse, circumstances in which one could use the adverb accurately would almost always render its use tautological. If one has fallen down the stairs, nothing is added to the statement 'I fell down the stairs' by extending it to 'I literally fell down the stairs'. So avoid this usually pointless, and often silly, word.

Litotes is a device by which a quality is expressed by negating its opposite, and which creates a sense of understatement: 'It was not a pretty sight.' See also MEIOSIS.

Livestock See BLOODSTOCK AND LIVESTOCK.

Livid The literal meaning of this adjective (as opposed to the metaphorical, which means *angry*) does not mean intensely coloured, for example 'the curtains were a livid orange'. It refers to the black and blue discolouring caused by a bruise, and is correctly used in a phrase such as 'his wounds were livid'.

Loath and **loathe** To be *loath* to do something is a perfectly acceptable way of expressing reluctance. It does not require an *e* on the end of the adjective; that belongs only on the end of *loathe*, a verb that means to dislike extremely.

-log/-logue See AMERICAN SPELLING.

Long words are never to be preferred to short ones: there is no reason why one should write *communicate* when one could write *talk* or *write*; and no reason why one would write *purchase* when one could write *buy*. See RULES OF GOOD WRITING.

Lords and ladies For details of how to address members of the aristocracy, see the entries for individual ranks in the peerage: **BARONESSES, BARONETS, COUNTESSES, DUKES AND DUCHESSES, EARLS, KNIGHTS, PEERS AND THEIR FAMILIES, VISCOUNTS AND VISCOUNTESSES**; see also **CLERGY, HONOURABLE, JUDICIARY, MILITARY RANKS.**

Lose It is quite enough to *lose*. One does not need to *lose out*, and nor does the superfluous adverb add anything to the idea of failure. Instead of saying 'he lost out in the race', say 'he lost the race'.

Lovely has its own adverb. Eric Partridge, the distinguished grammarian and expert on slang whose *Usage and Abusage* is one of the more important books ever written on English, wrote in 1947 that 'lovelily is good English and it means beautifully'. One can only assume that he was trying to give this strange word the kiss of life, but was too late. It is better now to stick to the alternative form that he gives, which is that one does something 'in a lovely manner' – or possibly even just *beautifully*.

Lowlily The word is in the dictionary but, as mentioned in the section on adverbs, it is clumsy. The sentiment it conveys is perhaps better expressed as 'in a lowly manner'. It may well be that it is also, on the rare occasions that it is used, used wrongly. *Lowly* means humble; if *lowlily* were being used to describe something that was low in any other sense (such as a voice, a ceiling or a mode of behaviour) then it would be a **SOLECISM**.

Luminous, which means radiating light, or light itself, should not be confused with **NUMINOUS**, which means divine or sublime.

Luxuriant and **luxurious** If something is *luxuriant* there is plenty of it. A woman may have luxuriant hair. If it is *luxurious* it is of high and sumptuous quality. One can avoid wrong usage by contemplating the absurdity of it. Should the woman have *luxurious* hair one could infer it was a wig, made to a high specification and bought at a high price, the adjective having no bearing on its quantity. A *luxuriant* fabric would be abundant, the adjective having no bearing on its quality.

M

Magic and **magical** A *magic* moment is when something illusory or supernatural appears to have happened. A *magical* moment is when it is quite obvious that something illusory or supernatural has not happened, but the ambience of the occasion could cause one to think that it might. The adjective in *-ic* is literal; the one in *-ical* metaphorical, suggesting that something has the properties or likeness of magic. The dictionary defines *magical* as 'of or relating to magic' in the first definition, but a second one, almost as old and now more idiomatic, is 'resembling magic in action or effect; enchanting'. See also –IC/ -ICAL ENDINGS.

Magna Carta is written thus, without the definite article.

Magnate and **magnet** A *magnate* is a person of power, influence, status and, usually, wealth, as in 'he established himself as one of the country's leading business magnates'. A *magnet* is a piece of metal that attracts other metals, or, used metaphorically, a person or institution that attracts other people, as in 'she was a real man-magnet'.

Major This has become an all-purpose adjective to describe something large or significant. Therefore, like all such adjectives, it is often used lazily and without sufficient thought. Sometimes it is not needed at all; at others, it would be better to replace it with something more specific. So we have a 'major disaster' to signify one entailing a great loss of life or damage to property; a 'major composer' is one whose works appear frequently in the repertoire; a 'major problem' is one that is not easily or straightforwardly solved; a 'major discovery' is one of great significance. As can be seen, it is always a better idea to choose a more precise adjective, to give more force to the expression; and in each of the above cases to allow the noun to stand alone and to follow by giving evidence of the stature of the person or thing mentioned. So rather than say Wagner was a 'major composer', say he was a composer who wrote ten world-famous operas; and explain the scale of a disaster by saying it cost hundreds or thousands of lives and millions of pounds' worth of damage. Avoiding *major* forces a writer to be specific in his detail.

Majority and **minority** As NOUNS OF MULTITUDE these words may legitimately be used with a plural verb, as in 'a majority of people vote no'. However, the nouns may only be used correctly when applied to something that is a multitude – that is, something of which there is more than one: so to write or utter a phrase such as 'I do that the majority of the time' is simply wrong. Time is one commodity; *majority* may often be a synonym for *most*, but it cannot be so in this context, or others like it. One may write 'I ate the majority of the sweets', because sweets are numerous, but not 'I ate the majority of the soup', because soup is singular. Weather forecasters have the habit of using phrases such as 'cloud will cover the majority of the country' when they mean 'most of the country'. They should not be imitated. See also FEWER AND LESS.

Malapropism Mrs Malaprop is a character in Richard Brinsley Sheridan's play *The Rivals*, noted for choosing the wrong word when speaking, as in 'I have since laid Sir Anthony's preposition before her' and 'my affluence over my niece is very small'. When someone talks of another 'flaunting the rules', rather than *flouting* them, he is committing a *malapropism*.

Man The *OED* defines *man* as 'a human being, irrespective of sex or age', adding a note that 'Man was considered until the 20th century to include women by implication, though referring primarily to males. It is now frequently understood to exclude women, and is therefore avoided by many people.' It is hard to see how use of this term to mean humankind could cause offence to anyone who was not actively looking for it. See POLITICAL CORRECTNESS.

Management-speak This, or its synonym *corporate-speak*, is that particular jargon used by executives who are sticking to a script within a company that uses the terminology popular in business schools or on management training courses. Thus we have words and phrases such as *scoping (out)*, *prioritise*, *going forward*, *tasked*, *pre-awareness*, *synergy*, *thinking outside the box*, *pushing the envelope*, *ownership of a task* and other abominations that should not intrude into polite speech or formal writing, and when used in the narrow context of business are evidence of an introverted tribalism that causes one to fear for the thought processes of those who propagate its language.

Maneuver is the American spelling of *manoeuvre*.

Maniacal and **manic** *Maniacal* means acting like a maniac, in other words appearing deranged or unhinged. *Manic* means *of*, *relating to*, *characterised by*, *resembling* or *affected by mania*. That is its literal sense. It now means hyperactive, frenetic or excessively enthusiastic, in a colloquial usage. The former is stronger, and carries darker tones, than the latter. See also –IC/-ICAL.

Marquesses A *marquessate* (sometimes written *marquisate* and even *margesite*) is the second highest rank in the United Kingdom peerage, a marquess being below a duke but above an earl. If writing about a marquess refer to him as the Marquess of Anywhere at first reference, then Lord Anywhere. His wife is the Marchioness of Anywhere, subsequently Lady Anywhere. His heir may have a courtesy title, usually an earldom or viscountcy; younger sons will be known as Lord John Smith (using the family surname). All daughters will be Lady Anne Smith, and so on. Write to a marquess as 'Dear Lord Anywhere', and sign off 'Yours sincerely'. Address the envelope to 'The Marquess of Anywhere'. Address him in person as 'Lord Anywhere'.

Marriage and **wedding** are not interchangeable terms. *Marriage* is an institution; a *wedding* is a ceremony in which each of the principals commits to their *marriage*.

Masterful and **masterly** It is strange that *masterful* and *masterly* cause terrible problems. Perhaps this is because some people think *masterly* is an adverb; it is not. Both words are adjectives meaning subtly different things. A masterful man is someone who, as Shelley put it, has 'wrinkled lip, and sneer of cold command': he has qualities of dominance. *Masterly* describes an exceptional ability in something, such as a masterly command of the English tongue, a masterly cover-drive or a masterly way of baking a lemon meringue pie. If one behaves domineeringly, one behaves masterfully. If one does something exceptionally well, one does it in a masterly fashion. The last citation the dictionary has for *masterly* as an adverb is 1887, and it was not common before then.

Math is an Americanism. In British English, if we seek to abbreviate *mathematics*, we maintain the plural of the original word and shorten it to *maths*.

May See CAN AND MAY.

May and **might** As explained in the entry on CONDITIONALS *may* and *might* are not interchangeable.

Me See I AND ME.

Meantime is one word and a more popular usage in America than in Britain, where one would say 'meanwhile'.

Media is a plural noun, so one writes that 'the media are hounding me', not 'the media is hounding me'. See also FOREIGN WORDS AND PHRASES.

Meet and **meet with** A newly popular British usage, borrowed from America, is *meet with*. The preposition is unnecessary, but we can see why the Americans use it. They do so for the creditable reason of avoiding what they consider to be an **AMBIGUITY**. If you say 'I met him last week' in American English you imply that you met someone for the first time. If you say you 'met with him' you imply that you knew him already – you had met him before – and this was but the latest of a series of encounters. To the educated ear on the British side of the Atlantic, *met with* sounds wrong. We simply *meet* each other. We may qualify the phrase, if there is a danger of a misunderstanding, with a detail such as its having been for the first time, or that it happened last week as opposed to earlier or later. In British usage, if someone says 'I met the policeman last Thursday' the listener or reader instinctively knows what happened, without the help of a preposition.

Meiosis is understatement, or the representation of something as less than it really is. It is sometimes confused with litotes, which simply creates the sense of understatement by negation. 'Shakespeare was a competent playwright' is *meiotic*.

Memoir and **memoirs** A *memoir* is a biographical work that one writes of another, usually of someone known personally. *Memoirs* are autobiographical. So: 'Lord Rosebery wrote a memoir of Lord Randolph Churchill' but 'Tony Blair has written his memoirs'.

Metal and **mettle** The former is a hard compound such as iron or steel; the latter is a synonym for *character* or *spirit*.

Metaphors and metaphorical usage *Metaphor* is the means by which a word or phrase that in literal terms means something specific is applied to a thing, person or concept to which it does not literally relate. 'We are faced by a sea of troubles' is metaphorical. We may lapse into metaphor without realising it in our everyday speech. It is, essentially, usually an extended simile – which the dictionary defines as 'a comparison of one thing with another, especially as an ornament in poetry or rhetoric'. 'My love is like a red, red rose' is, like any sentence in which two things or people are compared using *like*, a simile. Shakespeare's sonnet that begins 'Shall I compare thee to a summer's day' begins with a simile but turns into an *extended metaphor*.

Metaphor has its place in the writing of non-fiction, journalism and even letters. The device is perhaps used most effectively, and frequently, by writers of fiction. Writers or speakers using metaphor require great mental agility. They must conceive, first, the idea that they wish to communicate, but then find a non-literal means of doing so. However, if the metaphor is to be successful it has to be original and logical. There is nothing wrong with using such figures of speech that fulfil this requirement.

Indeed, as the Fowlers wrote in 1906, metaphor is the inevitable development of a language that contains only a primitive vocabulary to start with, but must find more sophisticated means of describing more profound concepts. They also pointed out how many words commonly used in English to describe everyday things began as metaphors: the example they give is the verb *explain*, which originally meant 'to lay out flat'. I am not concerned with such etymological history here, fascinating though it be: my purpose is to discuss metaphors that are not so established, and which are used self-consciously rather than unconsciously. As such, I am dealing with metaphors that we mint, or think that we mint, ourselves rather than those that only the etymologist would recognise as having begun their lives as metaphors, but are now part of our everyday vocabulary. The Fowlers discriminated between 'living' and 'dead' metaphors in this way, the living ones being the fresh, obvious and active ones that we use consciously. Perhaps we need to be alert to a third division, which I would term 'decaying', being those that are neither very recent nor original but do not have centuries of bottle-age on them either. We have all heard phrases for the first time that seem illuminating because of their freshness, but which after a year or two of heavy usage cease to light up anything except the lack of originality of the person using them.

Users of metaphor must beware of two dangers in particular.

One is CLICHÉ. The other is the MIXED METAPHOR, in which the metaphor becomes illogical (see below). A *clichéd metaphor* is one that is decaying. It takes on the status of an old joke. It will usually be a phrase, not a word, that once meant something concrete but has, through the acceptance of the validity of the metaphor, come to mean something abstract. An example of a clichéd metaphor would be: 'Several ministers have resigned: the rats are leaving the sinking ship.' We all know that phrase. We know it so well that it is almost meaningless, not least because through its familiarity it fails to convey the drama of the event. If the writer seeks to convey a startling insight by its use, he fails because we have an automatic rather than a fresh response to a form of words that seems to have been generated automatically, and is far from fresh itself. That is why I would presume to call it 'decaying': it may never die, though.

As for *mixed metaphor*: in the entry on ADVERBS, there is quoted a solecism about how an economy 'shrank steeper'. Aside from the illiteracy of this usage, there should also be a consideration about its logic. If something is shrinking, can it do so steeply? It almost certainly cannot, and therefore it is a mixed metaphor. It can shrink rapidly, or even dramatically, but not steeply. We can understand why the writer was tempted into this usage. The graphs that show economic decline may, in times of sudden and precipitate downturn, look like a steep slope going downwards. But the writer is not talking about a graph: he is matching the economy to a physical entity, and describing it as shrinking in size. When dealing in metaphors, logic must always be the prime consideration. Keep all metaphors simple. The minute they become complicated, the writer loses his reader.

But as well as being logical, metaphor must always be fresh if it is to be effective. New metaphors or similes are coined daily, despite what we consider to be the lack of originality of thought encouraged by our education system. The problem with new metaphors or similes is that they quickly become old. They tend to be overworked by those in search of a quick thrill, or who wish to propagate a sense of sensationalism. The principal culprits, therefore, are to be found in the mass media.

Words that had a literal use were, one day, seized upon by a writer and given a metaphorical one. See **LAUNCH** and **TRANSPIRE** for examples.

As ever in writing, logic remains important and the writer should not offend against it. Metaphorical nouns should always be allied with appropriate verbs. For example, one might write that 'I have a mountain of work to do', suggesting a pile of documents requiring attention. But one would not write 'I have a mountain of holes to dig'. There will have to be similar restrictions of the use of certain verbs as applied to any nouns with similar properties: if your metaphor has a concrete use, be guided by it when you decide to use it in the **ABSTRACT.**

There are many examples of words whose literal meaning has been complemented or supplanted by another, and whose branching out in this way has long since delighted us enough. A cursory perusal of a tabloid newspaper will quickly turn up plenty of them. *Searing* used to be a process applied to meat, wounds and flesh in general. Now anyone written about in the newspapers who has had an even remotely unpleasant experience can usually be relied upon to have found it *searing* too. There are many more of these colourful, but tired, usages (see, for example, **PLUNGE** and **SOAR**). Should you ever find yourself about to write anything metaphorical that you have picked up from elsewhere, don't.

Some words seem incapable of being uttered in contemporary English without a clichéd label being attached to them. One rarely hears of wit being anything other than 'razor sharp'. People or traits are seldom described as English (unless for reasons of identification) without being 'quintessentially' so. *Quintessentially* is a metaphor, *quintessence* being a term from classical and medieval philosophy: 'a fifth essence existing in addition to the four elements, supposed to be the substance of which the celestial bodies were composed and to be latent in all things'. Even if one is not aware of the derivation of *quintessentially*, and therefore that it is a metaphor, one must be aware from the frequency of its use that it is a **CLICHÉ**, and there might be a better way of describing exceptional Englishness.

The best fiction writers use metaphor sparingly, so that when is is used it has an effect. Graham Greene, in *Brighton Rock*, wrote of the villain Pinkie encountering a group of blind people:

> The Boy met the leader and pushed him out of the way, swearing at him softly, and the whole band hearing their leader move shifted uneasily a foot into the roadway and stood there stranded till the Boy was safely by, like barques becalmed on a huge and landless Atlantic. Then they edged back feeling for the landfall of the pavement.

By choosing that particular metaphor Greene is able to convey a sense of dangerous, perhaps even lethal, isolation: the elemental terror offered by the sea evokes the physical terror offered by Pinkie. However, because Greene's metaphors are as rare as islands in that ocean, they impress the reader and are packed with meaning. Also, he sets up the metaphor with a **SIMILE** ('like barques becalmed') and then extends a metaphor out of it. Extensive use of metaphor in fiction or poetry is outmoded today.

Look at the language of Churchill's great speeches from 1940, particularly these phrases from his 'finest hour' speech after the fall of France, to see metaphor used in its most powerful sense:

> Hitler knows that he will have to break us in this island or lose the war. If we can stand up to him, all Europe may be free and the life of the world may move forward into broad, sunlit uplands. But if we fail, then the whole world, including the United States, including all that we have known and cared for, will sink into the abyss of a new dark age made more sinister, and perhaps more protracted, by the lights of perverted science.

He sustains the metaphor over two sentences. The first thought is light; the second darkness. At the end of a speech that had been mainly about matters of fact – and miserable fact at that – and a review of the terrible plight that Britain, alone, now faced, the use of a sonorous metaphor such as this was, and remains on the page seventy years later, exceptionally potent.

Metonym is a word used as a symbol for an idea, institution or concept: 'Whitehall' is a *metonym* for the apparatus of government in Britain; 'Fleet Street' a *metonym* for the press; 'Carey Street' for bankruptcy.

Might See MAY AND MIGHT and CONDITIONALS.

Military titles Service ranks are self-explanatory and seem to cause trouble only when interfered with by other titles. Officers reaching the rank of lieutenant-general are usually knighted, at which point Major-General John Smith becomes Lieutenant-General Sir John Smith. Some senior generals receive peerages, at which point General Sir John Smith becomes General Lord Smith. The same applies to the two other services – Air Marshal Sir John Smith, Admiral Lord Smith and so on. Chaplains and padres would be styled Major the Reverend John Smith, or Squadron Leader the Reverend John Smith. In civilian life only officers of field rank or above would normally continue to use their military titles – though it is rare these days for anyone below the very highest ranks, who technically never retire, to do so. Field rank begins with majors, though captains holding an adjutant's appointment qualify. Write to 'Dear General', 'Dear Admiral', or 'Dear Air Marshal' and sign yourself 'Yours sincerely'. Address officers in person by their ranks – 'Good morning, Admiral', and so on.

There is some complication with the rank of private soldiers, for not all of these are known as 'Private', and the nomenclature varies from regiment to regiment. The following regiments in the British Army term their private soldiers thus: Army Air Corps, 'Airtrooper'; Duke of Lancaster's Regiment, 'Kingsman'; Foot Guards, 'Guardsman'; Fusiliers, 'Fusilier'; Household Cavalry (and Royal Armoured Corps, Honourable Artillery Company and Special Air Service), 'Trooper'; Rifle Regiments, 'Rifleman'; Royal Artillery, 'Gunner'; Royal Corps of Signals, 'Signaller'; Royal Electrical and Mechanical Engineers,

'Craftsman'; Royal Engineers, 'Sapper'; Royal Irish Regiment (and Royal Irish Rangers), 'Ranger'. Musicians in military bands are known as 'Musician', though a 'Trumpeter' in the Household Cavalry, a 'Bugler' in the Rifles, a 'Drummer' in the infantry or a 'Piper' in Scottish or Irish regiments is known by that particular name.

Militate and **mitigate** Some writers and speakers tend to confuse *militate* and *mitigate*, although their meanings are so distinct from each other that the dictionary has not followed the example of PREVARICATE and PROCRASTINATE and suggested that because they sound similar they may as well, these days, mean the same thing. If one *mitigates* something one lessens or alleviates its effects. A barrister pleading on behalf of his client in court before sentence is passed may ask the judge to award a lesser sentence than he may have considered handing down because the offence is *mitigated by*, for example, a plea of guilty. In turn the judge may *mitigate*, or lessen, the sentence. To *militate* means to strive, originally in the manner of a soldier, and in the last century of heightened political change it has come to mean to campaign for or against an idea or policy. The confusion of these two words is probably not provoked by ignorance of their meanings but by lack of concentration: it is almost a malapropism.

Minority See MAJORITY AND MINORITY.

Misrelated participle See PARTICIPLES.

Mistrust and **distrust** are nearly, but not quite, synonymous. To *mistrust* a man is to regard him with suspicion, and therefore not to trust him. To *distrust* him is to have the complete opposite of trust, the distrust founded upon knowledge, not suspicion.

Mitigate See MILITATE AND MITIGATE.

Mixed metaphor An example of a mixed metaphor (and, indeed, of the clichéd too) would be: 'After the death of his wife Smith was holed below the waterline, and feared that his goose would be cooked.' In one sentence we move from the sea to the farmyard to the kitchen. We have to add confusion to our boredom. People in officialdom, in an attempt to try to interest the general public without necessarily informing them, seem especially prone to the dodgy metaphor. During the bad winter of 2010 a Mr Grommet from the Meteorological Office was reported by the *Daily Telegraph* as having said: 'We are in a situation where some of the advisories did not get picked up and were not presented strongly enough. In these circumstances we need to sit around a table and look at the thresholds to see if they should be made more flexible.' Such a statement is not necessarily comprehensible even to those with a degree in physics. A similar, and more graphic, example, was when a European Union official observed: 'Cameron really will have to navigate his way through Scylla and Charybdis and may well find a brick wall on the other side.' As well as mixing his metaphors – with two classical sea monsters and a wall – he showed himself unaware of the evils of cliché.

Modernise This verb is a prime example of dishonest usage by politicians. It conveys an idea of progress, but all it really means is *change*, which is not necessarily progressive or positive.

Momentarily and **presently** *Momentarily* is an Americanism for the British *presently* (correctly used) or *in a moment*. The adverb *momentarily*, used in English since the seventeenth century, has been deployed to indicate that whatever is being done is being done fleetingly. The Americans, and now we, use it to indicate that it will be done 'in a moment'. This is a loss to British English, since the original usage is valuable – it is clear what 'he paused momentarily before moving on' means. If something is happening *presently*, it will be happening soon. It is not happening now, although that is the American understanding of the word – the British would say, instead, 'at present'.

Mongol This is no longer an acceptable term when used to describe one afflicted by Down's syndrome. It can be a historical term – 'the Mongol hordes' – but a native of Mongolia is a Mongolian.

Morass means a stretch of swampy ground, but is more usually deployed figuratively, and not always logically or successfully. Its first metaphorical use, as a situation from which it is difficult to extricate oneself, dates from 1867, according to the dictionary. Because both the concrete and the ABSTRACT senses are current and familiar, care must be taken: the abstract must obey the logic of the concrete. During the financial crisis of 2008–09 pundits would often describe the problem of overwhelming public debt as having created a *morass*: it seemed a fair use of the term. However, what does one do with a morass? One can deal with it – by devising a plan of how to extricate oneself, if one has lacked the forethought to avoid entering it in the first place. One can, obviously, extricate oneself or, failing that, sink more deeply in. One can drown in it. One can slide in, and one can stagger out. However, one cannot grasp a morass. It seems geologically unlikely that one could clean it up either: if cleaning up is required, then *morass* had better be replaced by *mess*. One probably does not climb out, but is pulled out, or wades out. See METAPHORS.

Morpheme A non-phonetic element of a word, such as its *root*, *prefix*, *suffix* or *inflection*. The term is generally confined these days to technical discussions in linguistics.

Mortal See FATAL, LETHAL AND MORTAL.

Movies is an Americanism for *films* (originally *motion pictures*), but is now frequently used among Britons, especially those with a connection to or interest in the film industry, so has the status of JARGON.

Murder and **mystery** In *Usage and Abusage*, Eric Partridge is strict about the wrongness of the noun *mystery* becoming an adjective, arguing that no self-respecting writer would use the phrase 'mystery murder'. Today we often hear the term 'murder mystery', which is little better, though the noun *murder* has become an adjective in such contexts as 'murder suspect', 'murder inquiry', 'murder squad', 'murder trial' and so on. Just as nouns have become verbs, so we must accept that they can become adjectives too. It is interesting that the *OED* does not seem to accept this, but lists phrases such as 'murder charge' as COMPOUND NOUNS – two nouns used together where one takes the role of an adjective to describe the other. It has a similar set of compounds for *mystery*, such as 'mystery novel'. Perhaps in this way order can be preserved, and words kept in their categories, but the tide seems to be against it.

Muscle and **mussel** The former is a part of the body; the latter a bivalve.

Musical terms These are often used metaphorically and, equally often it seems, wrongly. See CRESCENDO, for example. If using a musical term as a metaphor – *overture*, *finale*, *con brio*, *coda*, *counterpoint*, *falsetto*, *Leitmotif*, *minor key*, *piano* (to mean softly) and *fortissimo* are among those that occur in non-musical contexts – be sure you know precisely what it means. It may have a special spelling (see CHORD AND CORD) and, if an Italian word, a plural drawn from that language (*crescendi*, for example).

Mutual does not mean shared: it means reciprocated. The frequent misuse caused the Fowlers much agony a century ago, but the dictionary has surrendered, perhaps because the most notable offender was Charles Dickens. The Fowlers argued that 'our mutual friend is nonsense . . . it takes two to make a friendship, as to make a quarrel; and therefore all friends are mutual friends, and friends alone means as much as mutual friends'. Dickens would have better called his book *Our Common Friend*, though the dictionary concedes that he and others avoid that adjective because of its ambiguity. A correct use of *mutual*, cited by H. W. Fowler, would be for two people to be mutual (that is, common) well-wishers of each other. Well-wishing does not require reciprocity in the way that friendship does, so the use of the adjective *mutual* in this instance is not tautological. It would, however, be wrong to say that if both people were well-wishers of a third they were necessarily mutual well-wishers: they would be common ones.

My See POSSESSIVE PRONOUNS.

Myriad, which means innumerable and comes from the Greek word meaning ten thousand, is an adjective that requires no preposition. A man may have *myriad* problems, but he does not have a *myriad of* problems.

Myself See REFLEXIVE PRONOUNS.

Mystery See MURDER AND MYSTERY.

N

Named See CALLED AND NAMED.

Named for is an Americanism. In standard British English one says *named after*, as in 'the girl was named Jane after her godmother'.

Names, proper Proper names always take an initial capital letter. Foreign proper names can present complications. If there is doubt about a proper name, the *Oxford English Dictionary* or its *Concise* version often has a ruling, and I tend to follow those. The alternative is to look on Google and see which spelling of a particular word has the greater currency: *Habsburg* (at time of writing) has 4,440,000 entries, *Hapsburg* just 197,000. One may then draw one's own conclusions: mine is that the former is correct. See also PLACE NAMES.

Narratio is a term from rhetoric, and is the passage in a classical argument in which the polemicist provides the initial evidence supporting his contention.

Naturalist and **naturist** should not be confused. A *naturalist*, in the most generally used sense, is one who takes an interest in natural history and in observing the natural world. A *naturist*, although the noun has sometimes been used to signify a *naturalist*, is more usually a nudist.

Naught and **nought** *Naught* means nothing: 'Say not the struggle naught availeth'. *Nought* is a number – 0 – or in American English, zero.

Naughty As an example of how custom, practice and social change alter the meaning of words over time, compare how *naughty* was used 400 years ago with how it is used now. As the dictionary confirms, between the fifteenth and the seventeenth centuries the adjective was used to mean 'morally bad or wicked'. It supplies the proof, from one of Barrow's sermons of 1678, by citing his phrase 'a most vile, flagitious man, as sorry and naughty governor as could be'. Now it is used largely satirically, or to describe the mild offences of a child. Perhaps *naughty* was diluted by overuse, and we are all agreed on what it means today. Words ought to change their meanings when social or technological change dictates, not because people cannot be bothered to use them correctly, and the fashion of their ignorance catches on. In a sense that is a democratic decision, though one that can be validated by authorities such as lexicographers caving in to abuse. Being in the vanguard of change means one risks being misunderstood, or even thought to be ignorant. There remain words (see FLAUNT AND FLOUT, for example) on whose correct usage we should not, for the moment, choose to sign the act of surrender: not for reasons of pedantry, but because important distinctions will be lost to our language if we do.

Nauseated and **nauseous** Something that is *nauseous* – a smell or a taste, for example – has the power of making one who is susceptible feel *nauseated*. It is quite wrong for one who is feeling nauseated to say, as one sometimes hears, 'I am feeling nauseous', because that means he has the power to make others feel nauseated.

Naval and **navel** *Naval* is an adjective describing something pertaining to a navy or navies. *Navel* is the part of the body from which the umbilical cord is cut at birth. Do not confuse them, as the *Financial Times* magazine of 12 January 2013 did, when it wrote of 'naval-gazing'.

Negation and negatives To *negate* any word is, depending upon its sense, to create an idea of its direct opposite. Almost anything can be negated: nouns ('not John'), pronouns ('not him'), adjectives ('unappealing'), adverbs ('inelegantly'), verbs ('not to say'), conjunctions ('not until') and even prepositions ('not among'). This variety of usage means that the creation of ambiguity or downright incomprehensibility is sometimes possible if the negator – such as the word *not* – is placed thoughtlessly in the sentence. The negator must accompany the word it is negating. Where it acts as an adverb (as *not* does) it should come between the subject and the predicate, as in 'John is not coming today'; though there are certain idiomatic exceptions. For example, there is the emphatic negative response to the statements of others ('I should say not!' 'I should think not!' 'I hope not!' and so on), and the use of the negative to introduce a participle ('never having been here in my life' and 'no one having told me that was the rule').

In most statements one must place the negative carefully in order to convey precisely the meaning one wishes. Think of the difference, for example, between 'I am not going to church today' and 'I am going not to church today'. In earlier times these two statements would have been considered synonymous. Now, the second might mean that the person is going somewhere, but not to church – though it is an awkward way of saying so. Understanding the context of a negated statement will also help to overcome **AMBIGUITY**. 'He could not eat breakfast' means something entirely different depending upon whether one has already been told that the subject has a terminal illness, or that he has a terrible hangover, or that there is no food in the house. Always ensure that any negation is consistent. There can be a problem when a main verb covers two acts, both of which are supposed to be negative. In the sentence 'he concentrated more on not crashing his car on the ice than on driving it in to a tree' a second negative has been omitted, rendering the sense absurd. In such instances a recasting of the sentence is often the best route out of a construction that may end up sounding clumsy. 'He concentrated more on not crashing his car on the ice than on avoiding the tree' does the job satisfactorily.

Sometimes, negating a word will not give the direct opposite of its original sense because of the word's inherent meaning. We know what *always* means. Yet *not always* does not mean *never*: it means *occasionally* or *sometimes*. The same applies to various words with an absolute meaning; the opposite is not absolute, which means it is partial. *Not everywhere* means *somewhere* rather than *nowhere*; *not everyone* means *someone* rather than *no one*; and so on. It should be immediately apparent that there is a distinction between 'not all could see' and 'all could not see'. The positioning of the adverb *not* in such sentences requires precision. If the negation of absolutes logically creates something that is partial, one has to find another means of illustrating the opposite of the absolute: which is the simple word *no*, or its cousins *none*, *never* and the like. The opposite of one's always doing something is one's never doing it; *not* is sometimes inadequate.

Avoid DOUBLE NEGATIVES: see the entry on that subject. For warnings about beginning sentences with negatives, see the entry on NEITHER . . . NOR. See also IN-/UN- to learn how these prefixes correctly negate adjectives and adverbs.

Negation, even when done properly, can confuse readers. If a sentiment can be expressed using a positive rather than a negative, always do so. 'No one was likely to fail the examination' is not so direct as 'everyone was likely to pass'. The more complicated the potential negative, the more desirable such a solution becomes.

Negatives with auxiliary verbs See AUXILIARY VERBS.

Neither and **neither . . . nor** *Neither* is a pronoun that describes two persons or things in a negatived state – 'neither was ready to leave' or 'neither would be any use for keeping out the cold'. It is the negative of EITHER.

Neither requires *nor* in the sentence if both items are specified, and should not be used with more than two items: 'Neither John nor Susan was free to come to the meeting.' The pronouns are singular. With three people use *none* and 'or': 'None of John, Susan or George was free to come.' *Nor* may also be correctly used after other negatives, as in 'I had never seen him, nor her' or 'He was nowhere to be seen, nor heard'. Fowler highlights the danger of beginning a sentence with a negative, then forgetting that the subject of the second clause should not be negative: sentences along the lines of 'no candidate may take a calculator in to the examination, and must complete both papers', the second clause of which should correctly begin 'and all must complete'. A similar difficulty may arise in sentences beginning with *nor*: 'Nor does he accept the force of his opponents' case, and argues that' must become 'and he argues that'. As with so much written English, difficulties and ambiguities will be more easily avoided if the writer keeps sentences short and stops clauses proliferating. Otherwise, the logic of what is being communicated may fail, in this case most often because of the unwitting insertion of the double negative.

The importance of careful word order when using negatives is dealt with in the section on NEGATION AND NEGATIVES: but it must be emphasised what difficulties a misplaced *neither* can cause with word order. It is illogical to write: 'I neither saw the accident nor how the driver ended up in the ditch'; it should be 'I saw neither the accident nor how the driver ended up in the ditch'. *Neither* would only precede the verb if there were a different verb in the next clause, such as 'I neither saw the accident nor heard how the driver ended up in the ditch'. See also BOTH.

Nemesis is a term that is greatly overused and therefore has had its original sense diluted. In classical mythology she was the goddess of retribution, and ensured that someone had what was coming to him. It is best to reserve its use today for a severe act of vengeance – 'The Red Army proved to be the Wehrmacht's nemesis' – rather than for something trivial: 'Brown proved to be Aston Villa's nemesis when he scored a hat-trick against them.'

Neologism is the minting of new words: all words were *neologistic* once. However, some new words are more necessary than others, and care must be taken to ensure that a perfectly acceptable word does not already exist before imposing a new one on the English language. New words enter the language all the time because of technological changes, or changes in the experience of those to whom the language belongs: centuries of imperial endeavour brought all sorts of words, from *kiosk* to *curry* and from *wigwam* to *boomerang*, into standard English. New things, processes or ideas have to be described by new words. Usually, those words will come about by a logical means, often by reference to a classical antecedent: it is why an era of invention gave us *telephone*, *television*, *refrigerator* and *video*. Until the late 1990s nobody would have thought that the English language needed a verb *to text*. Then the *text message* was invented, possibly also inventing an adjective in the process (or, at the very least, a new compound noun). One may send a *text message*, or one may *text* someone. The new verb, made from the noun, has the advantages of clarity and concision: it is a new, logically derived, usage to describe a new phenomenon. As with *fax* about twenty years earlier, there can be no feasible objection to it. Some coinages, such as words ending in *-athon* and *-gate*, are to be avoided by writers who wish to be taken seriously, being of tired humour and instantly clichéd. Nor is it clear why words such as *learnings* needs to enter the vocabulary to describe lessons, or *podiuming* to describe being one of the first three in a sporting competition. See also VOGUE WORDS.

Never is an adverb that precedes the verbal construction – 'he never saw her'. The opposite of *never* is not *sometimes*; it is *always*. See also NEGATION AND NEGATIVES.

Nevertheless and **nonetheless** Both these words are adverbs, and have become largely interchangeable: so much so that the dictionary uses one to define the other. They are now each most commonly written as one rather than three words. There is a literal meaning for *none the less* (as three words) in phrases such as 'He was none the less stable after his ordeal than before it', where the phrase is used as a comparison. The phrases *nonetheless* and *nevertheless* have come to mean something akin to *despite that*: 'The tenor's voice was strained, but it was nevertheless a good performance.'

New words See NEOLOGISMS.

No one should not be hyphenated.

Nom de guerre and **nom de plume** The former is how the French themselves refer to a pseudonym. The latter is what the English think the French would call a pseudonym. Use of the latter marks out a writer as, at best, half-educated. See also FOREIGN WORDS AND PHRASES.

Nominative case In grammar, this is the form of a noun when it is the subject of the sentence, as in 'the dog' in the sentence: 'The dog sat by the fire.'

None is a pronoun. One of the most common mistakes in writing or in speech is a variant of 'none of us are free tonight'. One of a legion of contemporary examples appeared in the *Guardian* on 3 May 2012, in a piece by Michael Rosen: 'My view is that none of them are more correct than the others.' *None* is singular. It derives from the Old English negation of *one* and means 'not one'. Therefore one writes 'none of us is free tonight', 'none of us was there', 'none of us has done that', and so on. The dictionary now says that the use in the plural is common. That does not mean it is correct. Partridge, writing in the 1940s, also sanctioned this usage in certain instances, but in quoting a usage by Dryden reflects the dictionary's view that the usage in the plural was common from the seventeenth to the nineteenth centuries, though has since been rectified. Partridge quotes a correspondent who dismisses the singular *none* as a 'superstition', claims *no* is a contraction of it, and argues therefore that the plural usage is acceptable. The dictionary declares the etymology of *no* to be a variant of *none*. That does not settle the point about its usage, however. There was enough precedent before the seventeenth century, never mind at the time of the creation of the alleged 'superstition', of *none*'s being singular. So it should stay.

None is also an adverb whose usage is not subject to this error – as in 'he is none the worse for his ordeal' or 'they were none the wiser having read his book'.

The opposite of *none* is not *some* but *all*.

Nonetheless See NEVERTHELESS AND NONETHELESS.

Nor is a coordinating conjunction, as in: 'He had nothing to contribute to the discussion, nor did he wish to do so.' See NEITHER AND NEITHER . . . NOR.

Normalcy is an Americanism for *normality*.

Not See NEGATION AND NEGATIVES.

Notwithstanding is a conjunction that introduces a concessive clause, as in 'the man was acquitted, notwithstanding the damning evidence of the last witness'. It can also stand last in the sentence, though this is now increasingly archaic: 'the damning evidence of the last witness notwithstanding'.

Nought See NAUGHT AND NOUGHT.

Noun clauses are introduced by subordinating conjunctions, as in 'she hopes *that he will come*', 'I never dreamt *that she would do that*', 'they wished *that it had stopped raining*', and so on.

Nouns A noun is the name of something – a dog, shoebrush, desk, tree, banana, school, map and so on. It may be the subject or the object of a sentence. In 'John made the tea', the noun *John* (part of the class of nouns known as PROPER NAMES) is the subject (the agent of the verb) and the noun *tea* is the object (the target of the verb). There may be multiple subjects or objects in any sentence. Sentences may also contain nouns that are direct and indirect objects of a verb. See OBJECTS, DIRECT AND INDIRECT.

Nouns, as verbs The most promiscuous mutation of words today is of nouns into verbs. This has always happened, as the dictionary confirms: the *OED* gives the first use of the noun *battle* as a verb in 1330, though suggests *fight* is now more usual. However, in recent times such change seems to have become an especially American habit that, like so many of them, has caught on here. Gowers reflected on it decades ago in *The Complete Plain Words*, citing nouns that had become verbs that few of us now would blink at – 'feature, glimpse, position, sense' – but he also adds 'signature' which, if it was prevalent in the 1950s and 1960s, has died a welcome death by now. Therefore, we read of books being *authored* instead of *written*; money being *gifted* rather than *donated*; objects being *loaned* rather than *lent*; something being *impacted upon* rather than *suffering the impact of* or, more simply, *being hit*; a person's being *partnered* by someone else instead of *accompanied* by him; and so on. The strong contemporary American influence causing this mutation is clear from even a cursory encounter with one of that country's television programmes – a common example these days is when one hears someone has been *tasked* to do something. The first use in British English of the verb *partner*, however, is given as 2000. Many will embrace this renewed enthusiasm for turning nouns into verbs as enriching the language; pedants will argue that perfectly good words already exist for the actions described. Rather than causing the language to expand, such terms will only shunt perfectly serviceable ones out of the way and into desuetude.

Do not make nouns into verbs – 'he authored the book', 'she sources her ingredients from organic farmers' – when there is a perfectly serviceable verb available to you. The dictionary cites the first use of *source* as a verb in 1972, in America. It is perhaps of more interest that it finds a lone use of *authored* in Chapman's *Homer* in 1596, after which it becomes obsolete until resurrected in America in the mid-twentieth century (the dictionary still does not believe it is used over here, but that, I fear, will have to change). We on this side of the Atlantic must therefore decide whether we wish to engage in this American habit, or not. Since there appear to be perfectly good existing verbs for the new ones invented by our American cousins (what is wrong, in the two instances I have given, with *written* and *obtained*?), I feel we can continue to resist.

Nouns, compound This construction positions two nouns together with one taking the role of an adjective, as in 'champagne socialist'. For a detailed example, see MURDER AND MYSTERY.

Nouns, metaphorical These should always be allied with an appropriate verb so as not to mix the metaphor. For a specific example, see MORASS.

Nouns of multitude With what Fowler so charmingly calls 'nouns of multitude' (also known as 'collective nouns'), think carefully before choosing a pronoun. The idiom about whether certain nouns of multitude are singular or plural is not always settled; I also prefer the singular unless (as with the England cricket team) there is a prevailing idiom of plurality. So when one reads in a newspaper a story about a crime and about 'the Victim Support Unit, who have been in touch', it jars. Should the personal pronoun *who* be applied to an impersonal body like the Victim Support Unit? I think not. The moment one changes the pronoun to the impersonal *which* in the example above, one sees that the idiom demands a change of number too; so one has 'the Victim Support Unit, which has been in touch', which is idiomatically far happier. The same is true of all such impersonal bodies: it should be 'the Government, which has advised', or 'the county council, which has offered', or 'the governing bodies of the three schools, which have agreed to work together on the question', and so on. See also GROUPS AND VERBS, LESS AND FEWER, NUMBER(S) and PLURALS.

Nouns, verbal See GERUNDS.

Nowhere The opposite of *nowhere* is *everywhere*, not *somewhere*. Take care when using this negative term that elsewhere in the sentence you do not unwittingly perpetrate a double negative. See also EVERYWHERE AND NOWHERE.

Number(s) The noun *number*, and related words such as MAJORITY and MINORITY, are always plural. However the *Sunday Times*, on 18 March 2012, wrote that 'there is any number of Tory associations that would be delighted to have him as their MP'. See under NOUNS OF MULTITUDE for potential complications with these: consistency is the key.

The entries on EACH AND ALL; EVERY; EITHER AND EITHER . . . OR; NONE and NEITHER AND NEITHER . . . NOR highlight a common mistake when using these pronouns, in deploying them with plural verbs. There is also scope for a fault of logic when two nouns – one singular, the other plural – appear in a sentence: let us call this the Red Herring error. It occurs in sentences such as these, all found in the press towards the end of 2009: 'the potential for conflicts of interest are immense', 'if the rise of new economic powers mean our capacity', 'wide open spaces – indoors – is what we craved'. As can be seen, it happens when the writer imagines the subject of the sentence he is writing has become the noun nearest the verb. It is a facile mistake and easily avoided, but remains promiscuous. 'The wages of sin are death' is correct, as is 'the nastiest vegetable of all is Brussels sprouts'. The verb takes the number of the subject governing it. Were these two examples inverted they would have to be written 'death is the wages of sin' and 'Brussels sprouts are the nastiest vegetable'.

There is also the habit of using a singular verb with more than one noun, perhaps because in the writer's mind the individual nouns comprise one concept. For example, *The Times* on 22 August 2012 said: 'The insouciance, indifference and prejudice with which allegations of rape are being treated by Julian Assange's supporters is a stain on public life.' An Oxford don, David Priestland, made a similar error in confusing a plural subject for a singular one, when he wrote that 'my thirty years at this unusual university has . . .'

Other confusions of number include resistance to the correct 'one in five is' and the like, because one now routinely reads 'one in five are'. It is easy to see how this mistake comes about: the writer or speaker knows that there are a number of groups of five, resulting in a multiplicity of ones that form a plural. That is not the point. It remains 'one in five is'; the noun *one* is always and forever singular. If that is unbearable to some minds, then their owners should feel free to say instead that '20 per cent are'.

Where one is describing one of a group that has a common characteristic, any verb must refer to the group and not to the individual item. See GROUPS, AND VERBS.

Numbers, style of writing When writing numbers, a useful style to adopt is to write the number from nought to nine as words, and from 10 and above as figures. Newspapers follow this rule.

Numinous means sublime or awe-inspiring, and can be applied to anything that evokes the sense of a divinity. It should not be confused with *luminous*, which means light, or radiating light.

O

Objects, direct and **indirect** In 'John made the tea', the noun *John* is the subject (the agent of the verb) and the noun *tea* is the object (the target of the verb). There may be multiple subjects or objects in any sentence and, indeed, multiple verbs, as in: 'John, Mary and their parents locked the house, the garage and the garden gate before catching the train for their holiday.' Sentences may also contain nouns that are direct and indirect objects of a verb. An example of this is 'John gave the ice-cream to Mary', in which *John* is the subject, the *ice-cream* is the object of the verb *gave*, and *Mary*, as the person to whom the ice-cream was given, is the indirect object of the sentence. The object is in the accusative case. Although proper names and nouns do not inflect in English, pronouns serving as direct or indirect objects do – as in **I AND ME, HE AND HIM, SHE AND HER, WE AND US** and **THESE, THOSE, THEY AND THEM**.

Obliged and **obligated** Despite the long pedigree of the word *obliged*, which the *OED* first records as being used in 1325, we now have the term *obligated*, as in 'he felt obligated to improve his English'. It is frequently, but not always exclusively, an Americanism, a back-formation from *obligation*, and unnecessary in British English.

Obliviousness Why write *obliviousness* when you could, more easily and more correctly, write *oblivion*?

Obscene and **obscenity** Two related words that are used carelessly, rather than in a new sense for which there was a legitimate need, are *obscene* and *obscenity*. The dictionary is straightforward: *obscene* means 'offensively or grossly indecent; lewd'. It is 'grossly indecent' and 'lewd' that reflect the true meaning of this word. Many things are offensive, but not all of them in a way that has a sexual ramification, or pertains to the propriety of sexual behaviour. During the 2000s one often heard that it was *obscene* for the West to go to war in Iraq, or that poverty was an *obscenity* in the modern world. There may well have been strong objections to either, but to use *obscene* as an adjective or *obscenity* as a noun to describe them was simply wrong. The dictionary acknowledges the mutation of *obscene*, however, going back to Shakespeare in 1597, and defines it as being fit to describe anything 'offending against moral principles, repugnant; repulsive, foul, loathsome'. It notes especially its use to describe a very large amount of money being demanded in return for something. For all its four centuries' heritage, and the estimable provenance of the misuse, it still smells of carelessness and seems to betray an ignorance of the real, and valuable, meaning of the word; as does the misuse of *obscenity*. A thesaurus will supply plenty of words to describe a shockingly large amount of money, or an unjust war, or the appalling nature of poverty, without having to take one that still means something quite different, and quite specific.

Obsolescence and **obsoleteness** *Obsolescence* is the process of becoming obsolete or outdated. *Obsoleteness* is the condition of being obsolete.

Obviously is too often used today as a FILLER, especially when introducing a sentence, and has acquired the status of a CLICHÉ. The word is usually meaningless, and the only excuse for using it is as a weapon of irony – as in 'he obviously hadn't foresworn alcohol'. A sentence such as 'they obviously could not agree' can just as well do without the word.

Of course A pleonastic phrase that too often invites itself into the middle of sentences is *of course*. This is rarely necessary, because if something is *of course* one hardly needs to say so. Get straight to the point: most readers do not need an introduction to allow them time to collect their thoughts, even if the writer appears to.

Official language As explained in the entry on INQUIRY AND ENQUIRY, the ubiquity of the State in our lives, and the interference in them by bureaucrats, means that the JARGON used by these people sometimes intrudes into normal writing and conversation. It tends to be pompous, stilted, convoluted and arcane, and is therefore to be avoided if one wishes to communicate effectively. The private languages employed not just by bureaucrats, but by academics and various other professions, should not be imitated. The ideal style is one comprehensible to any intelligent person. If you make a conscious decision to communicate with a select (or self-selecting) group, so be it: but in trying to appeal to a large audience, or even a small one that you wish to be sure will understand your meaning, writing in jargon or officialese will not do. This sort of writing used to be kept from the general public thanks to the need to find someone to publish it. The advent of the Internet means that one is no longer so shielded from its pernicious effects as one used to be; and such accessibility and ubiquity threaten to have a pervasive effect on the soundness of the language and its susceptibility to corruption. It is estimated that 80 per cent of pages on the Worldwide Web are in a language purporting to be English, so the threat is severe. The first paragraph of the background chapter of the Northumberland County Council Housing Strategy 2013–18 illustrates the problem:

> The Housing Strategy is a strategic document stating our aspirations and priorities for meeting housing need across our population. It sets an over-arching framework within which more specific plans, policies and strategies will be developed setting out targets and financial details. The Housing Strategy has been designed to complement the emerging Core Strategy, which sets out the Council's strategic land use policies, and the Sustainable Communities Strategy, which outlines the overarching vision and strategic direction for Northumberland.

There is one jargon phrase piled upon another, and sentences could be shorter. Also, if one is going to overarch quite so frequently, one might at least make the hyphenation consistent.

On account of A phrase routinely used to attribute cause is *on account of* – either with a GERUND ('he had to buy a new tie on account of his other's being ruined') or suffixed by the phrase *the fact that*: 'he had to buy a new tie on account of the fact that his other one was damaged'). The sheer prolixity of this construction, which has its roots in the worst sort of bureaucratic language, should itself indicate its lack of suitability for crisp, tight prose. *Because* does the job quite well. See also CAUSE.

On to and **onto** *Onto* is a preposition invented by people familiar with its legitimate cousin *into*. *Onto* does not, however, exist. One steps *on to* a bus, or a dance floor. See also IN TO AND INTO.

One See NUMBER(S).

One (the impersonal pronoun) This useful pronoun has an elitist image. It is used in any caricature of what is deemed to be upper-class speech and is found in the most formal speech and writing. It has therefore attracted something of a stigma among anti-elitists. Some consider its use pompous, hence its value to those who wish to caricature those perceived to be grand or stuck-up. In certain circumstances and contexts it very much can appear to be pompous. I have used it throughout this book to describe the activities of an indeterminate third person, much as the French do not hesitate to do with the impersonal pronoun *on*. This little pronoun has a use that is both the same as our *one* but also rather wider in its idiomatic usages; yet the ground it covers is theoretically the same as that covered by *one*, which is why it is worth considering how exactly it is deployed. When a Frenchman says '*on dit qu'elle est folle*' he is saying 'they say she's mad', without having to specify that 'they' are any specific people other than the general run of his acquaintances. If he says '*ici, on boit du vin avec ses repas*', he is saying 'here, we drink wine with our meals'. If he says '*on ne veut pas le faire*' he is saying 'you don't want to do that'. This breadth of usage, still common in France (and enormously useful to the Francophone) is steadily being lost in English.

The pompous usage of *one* is most perceptible when it is used as a substitute for *I*. It is hard these days to excuse statements such as 'one spent the weekend in the country with one's friends' unless one is being satirical, or sending oneself up. Its use for other persons, as in the examples given in French above, is however much to be commended. If enunciating a general principle to someone else, either in speech or in writing, it is far better to say or write 'one shouldn't run off with other men's wives' than 'you shouldn't', in case the listener or reader thinks he specifically is being addressed and aspersions are being cast about his moral character. Using *one* for the first person plural risks pomposity, as it does for the first person singular, even though *on* as a substitute for *nous* is perhaps its most frequent usage in French. It is perhaps idiomatically most acceptable when outlining general principles rather than describing what the speaker and others have done: no one ought to find fault with 'one votes at general elections in order to ensure one has a say in the running of the country' as a preferable way of saying 'we vote . . . we have'. As with the *you* usage, to say *we* implies that that is why the speaker or writer and others associated with him take a specific course of action; rather than the intended meaning, which is to say why the generality of people do such a thing.

Certain people will also use the *one* construction in order to avoid talking directly about themselves, for it was not long ago considered the height of bad manners to use the first person singular except when absolutely essential. So such people would say 'one always used to go to the Riviera in July to meet one's friends', which sounds less swanky and proprietorial than 'I always used to go to the Riviera in July to meet my friends'. This usage does, these days, risk sounding pompous, and it is better to restrict usage of the pronoun *one* to circumstances where a generality is being expressed, for the avoidance of doubt or ambiguity. There should be no complaint about *one* when it is used to obviate self-advertisement, though. Understatement used to be a prominent feature of our speech and writing, but this has fallen into disuse in recent times. It remains a feature of the best writing style, even if the surrender has been signed when it comes to the spoken word.

Nevertheless, it is useful because it avoids AMBIGUITY when one is stating a general principle. To say something such as 'you don't want to go outside without a coat on' leaves the listener unsure whether it is indeed a general principle that is being enunciated, or a specific piece of advice to that person. Should one rephrase it as 'one doesn't want to go outside without one's coat on' it is quite clear that one is expressing a general rule.

One also has a role as a pronoun that creates distance between the speaker and the people whose activities he is describing. If, for example, referring to a shocking crime, a speaker were to say 'I don't know why one does that sort of thing' it is quite clear that *one* is a third person usage, meaning a person or persons unknown; it does, however, risk the rejoinder 'but one doesn't do that sort of thing'. I repeat, though: however one uses *one*, one must be sure to use it consistently.

One another See EACH OTHER AND ONE ANOTHER.

One of those In a phrase such as 'he was one of those who likes Wagner' the verb is correctly in the singular, referring back to *one* and not to *those*. To write 'he was one of those who like Wagner' would be incorrect. See also NOUNS OF MULTITUDE.

Ongoing is a tiresome and greatly overused word – not just in the context satirised for decades by *Private Eye* in 'ongoing situations', but in so much else – 'the war is ongoing', 'your education is ongoing'. Or 'my illness is ongoing'. In each example 'is continuing' would work as well, or, even better, 'continues'.

Only One of the most important questions of word order arises when the word *only* comes into play. *Only* should be positioned as close as possible to the word it qualifies, otherwise it will qualify a word the writer does not intend it to. See ADVERBS, POSITIONING OF.

Only also has a life as a COORDINATING CONJUNCTION, as in 'they would have arrived sooner, only their car broke down'.

Onomatopoeia A word with this quality imitates the sound it describes – such as *ping*, *bang*, *crash*, *woof*, *buzz*, *bell*. Overuse is to be avoided unless a comic effect is desired.

Onto See ON TO AND ONTO.

Opposite See APPOSITE AND OPPOSITE.

Or is a COORDINATING CONJUNCTION, linking two coordinate clauses, as in 'she would either have a swim, or another cocktail'. It must never follow *neither*, the correct form being 'neither John nor his brother came to tea'.

Oral See AURAL AND ORAL.

Oriented and **orientated** A person is *oriented*, not *orientated*. The action of being *oriented* is *orientation*, and a verb *orientate* is a back-formation from that.

Orphan Many believe that for a person to be an *orphan* he must have neither parent alive. This is not so. An orphan is someone who has lost either parent; those who have lost both are double orphans. It is therefore quite correct to describe a child who has lost his mother or his father as an orphan. This was well understood in the past when charities ran widows' and orphans' funds: many of the orphans were in the care of their mothers, who were widows. It is also an adjective ('the orphan child' is correct: it does not need to be 'the orphaned child'), and in explaining this the dictionary is guilty of an inconsistency. It says the adjective applies to a child or person who is fatherless or motherless or both, but in defining the noun it claims that that usage is usually applied to someone 'both of whose parents are dead', citing the correct usage as something 'rarely' found these days. That may be so, but if the dictionary is prepared to surrender on the noun then surely it must do so also on the adjective. Pedants will feel it should do so on neither.

Orthography means the correct spelling.

Orwell's rules See RULES OF GOOD WRITING.

Other is a PRONOUN, and a singular one, as in 'of the two girls, I preferred Jane but he preferred the other' and 'no other was available'.

Ought is useful in reported speech, when otherwise there could be an AMBIGUITY with the use of *should* as the past tense of *shall*. To say that 'I said I ought to go to visit Mother' leaves no doubt about a requirement to do so, whereas 'I said I should go to visit Mother' may just be the report of a simple future. 'I didn't ought to have drunk that' or 'she shouldn't ought to have said that to me' are SOLECISMS. *Ought* never requires an auxiliary verb. The correct forms would be 'I ought not to have' and 'she ought not to have'.

-our and **-or** One of the ways in which Britain and America are separated by a common language is in the difference in spelling words that in Britain end in -our, such as *savour* and *savor.* See AMERICAN SPELLING for discussion of this point. Such British nouns do lose the *u* in some adjectives derived from them, such as *humorous*, *amorous*, *vigorous* and *rigorous*. However, one would write *flavoursome*, *humoured* or *savoured*.

Ouster This is an Americanism, and one that at the time of writing has only just begun to permeate the British consciousness. If an American holding an elected or unelected post is defeated or sacked it is an *ouster*. In Britain one may be *ousted*, but *defeated* or *sacked* is more like it.

Outage This is an Americanism, used in the phrase *power outage*, where in British English we would say *power cut*.

Overall See PLEONASM.

Owing to See CAUSE.

Own The adjective *own*, indicating exclusive possession, needs to be used with care. This is especially true when emphasis is required, as in 'she went her own way', to indicate she took a course separate from those of all others, or 'it was all his own work', to indicate that he and he alone did it. However, in a sentence such as 'he drove his own car to the station', the adjective is necessary only if there has been discussion of another car that he might have driven. If there has not been, then cut out 'own'; and apply a similar test whenever tempted to use the word.

Oxymoron Two juxtaposed words that seem to contradict each other. They may both be adjectives (*bitter-sweet* is perhaps the most famous oxymoron of all), though more usually are an adjective and noun (*darkness visible*) or an adverb and an adjective (*supremely poor*). The oxymoron is a useful device for presenting an original and sharply focused thought with great economy, and if the words are chosen carefully they have the capacity to surprise and cause a deep effect.

P

Pair See COUPLE AND PAIR.

Palate, **palette** and **pallet** These are three spellings of a homophonous word that have markedly different meanings. One only has to read (as one too frequently does) of a painter mixing colours on a *palate* to see the problem: painters do not usually mix colours on the roof of their mouth. *Palate* is how one spells that part of the anatomy, as well as the figurative usage to suggest a taste for food or drink. The mixing of paint happens on a *palette*. A *pallet* is a straw bed, something goods are stacked on or a piece of armour covering the head; in that third usage it is sometimes spelt *pallette*.

Panacea A *panacea* cures everything, and is often used metaphorically – 'a panacea for the nation's ills'. As can be seen from the definition, a 'universal panacea' is a TAUTOLOGY.

Panini This is a plural frequently used as a singular. One bread roll is a *panino*. For similar abuses, see PLURALS.

Paradigm means a model, a pattern or an example. It has also become a much overworked word, being wheeled out whenever anyone wishes to convince readers or an audience that one is clever, as in 'the business created a paradigm for all its franchisees'. It is well worth avoiding as it risks becoming meaningless.

Paradox describes a statement that has an apparently contradictory conclusion, but which turns out to be true. 'He swam every day; went for a run before dinner; ate only organic foods; neither smoked nor drank; but died before he was fifty' is paradoxical.

Paragraphs Sentences may be constrained by the tenets of strict grammar, but *paragraphs* are a matter of taste. The dictionary defines a paragraph as 'a distinct passage or section of a text, usually composed of several sentences, dealing with a particular point, a short episode in a narrative, a single piece of direct speech, etc.'. It will be indicated by a line break at the end of a preceding sentence, and in print by the first line of the next paragraph being indented. The definition in the writer's mind of the particular point, or thought, will vary from person to person. Therefore what constitutes a paragraph will vary too.

An especially complex thought may prompt one writer to break it down into constituent parts of the structure and present them as separate paragraphs, even though the point is only made using a number of them. Another writer will wish to contain one point in one paragraph, however long that paragraph may have to be. Journalism, even at the quality end of the spectrum, does not favour lengthy paragraphs. They look unappealing on the printed page and may deter readers. They can be better concealed in books.

The fashion today – and it is one that I endorse – is for short paragraphs. It is not merely that they do not put the reader off: it is that, once read, they make for easier comprehension. They help support and sustain the logic of an argument. They are harder to become lost in. Few points are really so complex that they cannot be broken down. The slightest change of tack – or the need to bring in new evidence, or to open up a subsidiary line of argument – provides the perfect excuse to end one paragraph and to start another. The passing of the Victorian habit of writing paragraphs that drifted over several pages is correctly unlamented.

Some teachers argue that there is an ideal paragraph structure: however, I feel this depends on the nature of the piece of prose that contains the paragraph. A glance at an article in the tabloid press will show that its paragraphs rarely contain more than two sentences. The ideal structure favoured by some teachers contains four sentences. First, there is the 'topic sentence', which contains the theme of the paragraph. Second, there is a sentence in which the topic is explained or expanded upon. Third, there is a sentence that gives corroborative evidence for any contention the writer has advanced in the second sentence. Fourth, there is a closing sentence that refers back to the idea in the topic sentence. One can see that this prescription has its merits, not least in ordering the thoughts of those unused to such an exercise. Yet one can also see that it is artificial, restrictive and bereft of any sophistication. Those with more experience of using the language will instinctively see when the thought contained in a paragraph has reached the limits of its expression, and when the time has come to move boldly on to a new one – and, with it, a new paragraph. Variations in paragraphing are also an essential component of an attractive style.

Parataxis Clauses may be fashioned to create a literary technique. One such technique is the use of *paratactic clauses* in a passage of prose. These stand side by side with each other without any coordinating or subordinating conjunctions. Caesar's remark 'I came, I saw, I conquered' is probably history's most famous parataxis. Ernest Hemingway was a notably paratactic writer, as the following passage exemplifies: 'There were no rooms at the inn. We drove farther until we found a hotel. It was raining heavily and we got soaked on our way to the door. Our socks stank of mildew.'

Parentheses Within a sentence, *parentheses* of a more emphatic sort than allowed by pairs of commas may be introduced to give some important explanatory information. These may take the form of brackets (such as surround this clause) or – in a somewhat more interrupting fashion – dashes. The Victorian habit of putting colons or commas before dashes should be considered barbarous. It is to be avoided. A parenthesis in brackets is almost incidental to the meaning of the sentence around it. One in dashes makes an important point relevant to the surrounding sentence, and which is included in it for rhetorical reasons. It is often deployed when compiling an argument, and so has an element of aggression to it. Ordinary brackets tend to be more helpful, and to supply information, almost by way of a commentary. Consider these two examples:

> 'It had become a rite, a sacrament (that was how John Beavis described it to himself): a sacrament of communion.'

> 'But the smell of poverty when the twenty children were assembled in the dining-room was so insidiously disgusting – like Lollingdon church, only much worse – that he had to slip out two or three times.'

Both examples come from Aldous Huxley's novel *Eyeless in Gaza*. In the first the matter in brackets simply provides further illumination to the reader about Beavis's state of mind; in the second a contention is made, and the matter within the dashes seeks to support it by way of comparison. See also the entry on DASHES.

If a full sentence is quoted in brackets, put the stop inside the final bracket. If only part of the section is included within the punctuation marks, then the stop comes beyond the final mark. See the entry on COMMAS for their use as parentheses. Only when making a parenthesis (which we may define as matter which, if removed, would not alter the meaning of the sentence) should two dashes appear in the same sentence. A sentence that flouts this rule is stylistically difficult because it offends logic. For example: 'neither of the men was prepared to admit the problem – that they had run out of money – entirely' is a mess. Remove what the reader initially takes to be the parenthetical matter and what is left is gibberish. Such a sentence always has to be recast, in this case as 'the men had entirely run out of money, but neither was prepared to admit the problem'. For correct punctuation of parentheses, see QUOTATIONS AND PARENTHESES, PUNCTUATION OF.

Square brackets are used to indicate matter that was not part of a direct or indirect quotation but has been added to clarify it. For example: 'John said 'She [John's sister] will arrive later.'

Parking lot is an Americanism for *car park*.

Parody is the humorous imitation of another work, usually for satirical purposes. In *Ulysses*, for example, Joyce *parodies* the language of advertising in one of the episodes, and elsewhere parodies a range of things from high drama to logical discourse.

Parsing To *parse* a sentence is to identify each of its component parts. Those who have studied the grammar of any language at school may have done the exercise of parsing a sentence, or defining each term within it and identifying its role there. It is a remarkably useful exercise, for if we were in the habit of parsing every sentence we wrote we should make far fewer grammatical mistakes. Some grammarians and linguistics experts take parsing to an extreme level, but that need not be the case for those who simply wish to write or speak English correctly. Parsing may have a theoretical and intellectual value, but it can also be of practical use to those who make slips with their grammar. For example: working out that in the sentence 'she gave the picture to John and me' the second personal pronoun is the indirect object of *gave* prevents the horrible, but all too frequent, error of saying or writing 'she gave the picture to John and I'. Similarly, in the more complex sentence 'having taken my bath, I found myself on the terrace with her', by correctly identifying the personal pronoun *I* as the subject of both clauses, one avoids a mistake such as 'having taken my bath, she found herself on the terrace with me', in which it would appear that the woman has taken the other person's bath.

Should you have persistent difficulty with grammar, get into the habit of looking at sentences – whether they be your own or someone else's – and parse them to identify subjects, objects and verbs. Learn to separate clauses into main, coordinate and subordinate ones; to categorise words as nouns, pronouns, verbs, adjectives, adverbs, conjunctions and prepositions; and to be sure that these words stand in the correct relation to each other, in the proper cases, and making the right sense of every clause in the sentence. With practice this becomes not so much second nature as utterly subliminal. Once one has a command of the roles of the different parts of speech such as comes with the ability to parse accurately, one has one of the fundamental skills needed to become a good writer and speaker of English.

Partake If one *partakes* of something one consumes or experiences it: 'he partakes of tea every morning at eight', or 'she partakes of the sea air'. It does not mean to *take part*, or to *participate*: when one hears someone say that he will not 'partake in the negotiations' one must steel oneself not to mock the afflicted. The dictionary does claim that the verb has this meaning, but its only modern British English citation is about the young people of a nation 'partaking of its culture and traditions', which seems to me clearly to be an example of the correct meaning, not of the incorrect one.

Partially and **partly** To do something *partially* is to do it by favouring one party in the matter over another; in other words, to do it with *partiality*. To do something *partly* is to do it incompletely.

Participles Every verb has *participles*. They can be used as adjectives with both active and passive verbs. The most frequently encountered is the present active – *eating*, *seeing*, *reading*, *watching*. There is also the past participle, which requires an auxiliary verb – *having eaten*, *having seen* and so on. The future participle also requires one – *being about to eat*, *being about to see*. There are comparable tenses in the passive voice, though with more subtle shading. There is both a present tense (*seen*) and a continuous present (*being seen*); and a past participle (*having been seen*) and a future (*about to be seen*).

There is alarming scope for participles to go wrong. Onions gave a simple example in his grammar: 'After fighting the flames for several hours the ship was abandoned.' The ship did not fight the flames; but that is the logical sense of this construction. Participle clauses beginning with *after* are notorious for causing this difficulty, because the subject of the second clause is often not the subject of the participle in the first. One should note how the problem comes about: it is through the use of the **PASSIVE VOICE** in the second clause. Using the passive removes the people who were fighting the flames. Had the sentence been left in the **ACTIVE VOICE** and read 'after fighting the flames for several hours the men abandoned ship' the sense would have been clear and logical. If one way of avoiding problems with participles is to shorten sentences, another is to avoid eliminating the natural subjects of a participle by keeping the sentence in the active voice. As we shall see below, however, there are some rare circumstances where the passive improves sense rather than destroys it.

In the century since Onions drew attention to this trap many thousands of writers have chosen, nonetheless, to fall into it. The following examples were culled from the press over a few days in the winter of 2009–10. First, 'the day before he died, David Cameron and his wife played with their son'. It was not Mr Cameron who died, but his unfortunate son. Simple inversion of the clauses solves the problem. The writer, who clearly had not thought of this, had also not thought of what the subject of his sentence was. Second, this reporter was too busy reminiscing about his career to see that he had attributed it to somebody else: 'as a young reporter, Mrs Smith told me that . . .' Alteration of the word order to 'Mrs Smith told me, as a young reporter, that . . .' or, better still, 'when I was a young reporter, Mrs Smith told me that . . .' is required. Insertion of the correct subject – in this case *I* – must always rectify the problem.

Third, 'several Japanese tourists filmed the couple for 20 minutes before being arrested'. The tourists were not arrested; the couple were. In a sentence such as this perhaps the passive is the answer: 'for 20 minutes before the couple were arrested they were filmed by Japanese tourists' leaves no one in any doubt who ended up in the cells. And fourth, 'stricken with grief by the tragedy, her father attempted to console her'. That does not even have the excuse of confusion with the passive; it is simply the wrong subject, the writer's mind being confused by the presence of the 'attempted to' construction in the second clause. In a case like this, the sentence has to be recast. 'Stricken with grief by the tragedy, she was attempted to be consoled by her father' is hideous. It would be better to turn the whole idea around and to write: 'her father attempted to console her, stricken with grief by the tragedy as she was'. Better still would be: 'she was stricken with grief by the tragedy, but her father attempted to console her'.

Politicians do appear to be especially vulnerable to participle abuse. Edward McMillan-Scott, an MEP, published a press release on 14 January 2010 in which he wrote: 'As a Conservative Party member for 42 years, an MEP for 25, leader of the MEPs for four and a Conservative Board member for three years, this is no longer the party I knew.' It is hard to know where to start with this jumble, other than to note that the party was not a member of itself, an MEP, the MEPs' leader or a board member. Mr McMillan-Scott could say only what he intended to say by having two sentences. 'I have been a Conservative Party member for 42 years [and so on]. This is no longer the party I knew.'

This sort of abuse is variously known as the *hanging participle*, the *suspended participle* or the *misrelated participle*. Sometimes participles are left dangling because of the thoughtless shift in a sentence from the active to the passive voice, in which confusion the logic of the sentence is lost. 'Though refusing to concede that he had a point, it must be said that I started to see the force of his argument.' The use of the passive and the arrival of *it* as the subject of the second clause destroys the sense of the sentence: it was not *it* that refused to concede the point, but *I*.

The rule for avoiding them is deceptively simple. If you are going to use a participle construction, make sure the subject of it is the subject you intend. This must always be the actor of the verb and not somebody or something else. When one writes 'Going into the garden', one needs to have a clear idea of who is doing the going. If it is *I* there is no sense in following that clause with the statement 'she greeted me while she was pruning the roses'. It has to be 'I saw her pruning the roses, and she greeted me'. As Onions says, 'the participle must always have a proper subject of reference'. If it does not have one the result will be an illogicality; so give it one.

The shorter a sentence is, the less likelihood there will be of misusing participles. The problem arises when over two or three clauses the main subject ceases to govern the ensuing participles. Here is an extreme example: 'The children went into the barn and, being dark, they could see nothing.' The participle *being* can only correctly refer back to the children, not the barn: but we sense it is intended to refer to the barn. The subject of the third clause – *they* – seems to refer to the children's being dark again, but even if they were that would be no reason for them to see nothing. 'The children went into the barn. Because it was dark inside, they could see nothing' would obviate the problem. The iron rule about participles is that each must be closely connected with a subject; including when, as GERUNDS, they may be subjects themselves.

Passive voice Verbs have two voices, the ACTIVE and the *passive*. The passive voice of a transitive verb is used to create the form that no longer has someone doing something, but has that something being done by a person. It is the difference between 'I drank the beer' and 'the beer was drunk by me'. In good style, writers should avoid passives wherever possible. As is clear from this example, they are verbose. They are also indirect. They have political implications: they can be used to create distance and to de-personalise an action. There is a difference between 'I have decided to sack you' and 'it has been decided that you should be sacked' that ought to be too obvious to require further comment. There are more sinister applications, of the sort that turned writers and thinkers such as Orwell against them. The passive voice is part of the language of evasion. One of Orwell's rules was 'Never use the passive where you can use the active', and that was the reason why. That was also why he made the point about the political roots of verbosity, and the desire to dress up unpleasant concepts by avoiding a direct statement of them. Orwell argued that thinking more clearly is the key to political regeneration. It is certainly the key to not being taken in by the rubbish often written by others. It will warn writers against use of the passive voice – which, as Orwell hinted, people use to distance themselves from their acts. A government finds it easier to say 'restrictions will be placed upon the movement of people and upon their liberties' than 'the government will place restrictions' because the apportionment of responsibility for so unpleasant an act is so much more blatant, and therefore damaging, in the second example.

Another reason to avoid it is the complex mess of tenses that it tends to attract, rather like flies: from the mildly tiresome 'the girl was being pursued' to the exceptionally irritating 'the girl had been being pursued'. This voice also becomes extremely unattractive when compounded. Many verbs require another verb to complete their meaning. This is straightforward in the active voice – 'he hoped to see her again' – but it may lead to an abomination – 'it was hoped that she would be seen again' – in the passive. If an active sentence must be turned into the passive, only the main verb need change – 'it was hoped to see her again'. Similarly, 'they attempted to climb the hill' just needs to be 'it was attempted by them to climb the hill', and 'we intended to cut the grass' would be 'it was intended by us to cut the grass'. However, why anyone should want to turn an active into a passive is beyond me.

For all the political considerations of the passive, there remain fundamental problems of style. In her memoir of her late husband Harold Pinter, Lady Antonia Fraser writes that 'technically, since my father was an earl and my mother a countess, I could be argued to be an aristocrat'. Such an abomination is strange from so good and experienced a writer, and the tortuousness of the phrase indicates some moral difficulty that lies behind her admission. Her use of the passive leads us to question how it is that a person – even one so elevated and aristocratic as Lady Antonia – can ever be argued. A point of view can be argued; so too can a contention or a policy. But can a person? Lady Antonia could have avoided this jumble had she used the active voice – 'some will argue that I am an aristocrat' – or, had she felt the need to retain the passive for purposes of distance, had she written 'it could be argued that I am an aristocrat'.

On a pedantic note, the passive voice of the verb *to work* is, correctly, *wrought* when the object that has been worked is some sort of material or substance. Wrought iron is iron that has been worked – wrought – by a farrier.

Peal and **peel** A *peal* is a call or summons made by ringing a bell. Its homophone *peel* describes the outer covering of a fruit or vegetable.

Pecker is American slang for *penis*. It is therefore unwise for a Briton to advise an American to keep his pecker up.

Pedal and **peddle** To *pedal* is to propel using one's legs: 'They pedalled the tandem up the hill.' The latter is to sell, or, metaphorically, to propagate: 'She peddled her gossip all over town.'

Peers and their families, writing to or addressing In this age of relaxed formality, addressing a peer or his wife in conversation as 'my lord' or 'my lady' is confined to their and other people's domestic staff. Others should say 'Lord Smith' or 'Lady Smith' just as they would, if not friends or old acquaintances, say 'Mr Smith' or 'Mrs Smith'. It is perfectly correct to address a duke as 'duke'. The daughter of a duke, marquess or earl has the courtesy title of 'Lady' with her Christian name, so may be addressed as 'Lady Jane'. The heirs of dukes, marquesses and earls usually carry by courtesy a subsidiary title of their father. The younger sons of dukes and marquesses carry the title 'Lord' before their first names, as in 'Lord John Smith'. When writing, use the full title on the envelope: 'The Duke of Dorset', 'The Marquess of Monmouthshire', 'The Earl of Lowestoft' and so on. In the salutation, write 'Dear Duke', but 'Dear Lord Monmouthshire' and 'Dear Lord Lowestoft'. All children of barons and viscounts, and all sons of earls except the heir – who will usually have a peerage by courtesy – should be addressed on the envelope as 'The Hon. John Smith' or 'The Hon. Jane Smith', and then as 'Dear Mr Smith' or 'Dear Miss Smith'. When Jane Smith marries, she becomes the Hon. Mrs Brown.

Peninsula and **peninsular** *Peninsula* is the noun. *Peninsular* is the adjective, but occasionally misused for the noun. 'The Peninsular War was fought on the Iberian peninsula' is correct.

Per cent and **percent** The former is the British usage and the latter the American, though the American appears to be penetrating British English too. Britons would correctly write that 'mortgage rates rose by one per cent'.

Peremptory and **perfunctory** A *peremptory* act is one that brooks no discussion. A *perfunctory* one is discharged as a matter of routine and without any enthusiasm.

Perfect tense In English, this uses the auxiliary verb *have* and refers to an action in the recent past that may be continuing or is just completed – as distinct from the IMPERFECT, used when the action is definitively finished. Examples include 'I have eaten all my greens', as a child says when still at the table with his plate in front of him; or 'I have come here to see you', when the action of coming is still culminating; or 'I have never seen anything so shocking', to convey the notion that the object of the shock is still literally or metaphorically before the speaker's eyes. 'He had finished his dinner' suggests it had just happened whereas 'he finished his dinner' suggests the recording of an event in the past.

Peroratio is the penultimate episode of a classical argument, the rousing finish before the APOPHTHEGM that seals the argument.

Perpetrate and **perpetuate** If a man *perpetrates* something, he carries it out or performs it: 'He had perpetrated some terrible crimes during his career.' If he *perpetuates* something, he causes it to continue, though not necessarily perpetually or forever, but for the foreseeable future: 'She wished to perpetuate the arrangement.' When an American prosecutor announced, in May 2013, after the exposure of an exceptionally appalling case of sexual assault, that an offender had 'perpetuated rapes' against women, he illustrated the problem with confusing these two terms.

Personal pronouns *I*, *you* (singular and plural), *he*, *she*, *it*, *we*, *they* and the impersonal pronoun *one* all take that nominative form as the subject of a sentence, in other words when they are the agent of action. The pronoun with the verb *to be*, therefore, as in Latin, is always in the nominative case. This correct usage has all but disappeared in speech – 'it's me', 'that's him', and so on – but it persists in looking right when followed by a clause in writing: 'it was he who killed the cat', for example, or 'it might be they who called'. When the action is happening to a person or persons, all except *you*, *it* and *one* require a distinct accusative form: *me*, *him*, *her*, *us*, *them*. So one would say 'he hit him over the head' or 'she gave them some cakes'. These forms are also used after any preposition, such as in 'we thought she would get on with them' or 'I wanted to introduce you to her'. Again, confusion is avoided when the pronoun is not too far removed from the noun or proper name to which it relates: we must assume that in those last two examples a preceding sentence has identified clearly who *them* and *her* are. Perhaps the greatest source of pronominal difficulty in our language is the accusative of the relative personal pronoun, WHOM, for which see the separate entry.

Persuade See CONVINCE AND PERSUADE.

Peterhouse The Cambridge college Peterhouse is never 'Peterhouse College'; its name means *St Peter's College*, because *house* is a synonym for *college*.

Phenomena is the plural of *phenomenon*, and must never be used as the singular.

Phrases, adjectival When a long phrase is used adjectivally, it should be hyphenated: as in 'state-of-the-art technology' or 'a came-over-with-the-conqueror mentality'. See HYPHENS.

Phrases, adverbial See ADVERBS.

Picky is an Americanism. See CHOOSY.

Piteous and **pitiful** were once words with distinct meanings. The former meant to be full of pity or compassion: the latter to be worthy of receiving pity or, in a more abstract sense, to be so inadequate or inferior as to merit being pitied. *Piteous* has, according to the dictionary, been used in contexts where *pitiful* would be more appropriate since the fourteenth century in the literal sense, and since the seventeenth century in the more abstract one. It is, therefore, probably too late to seek to distinguish the two adjectives now.

Place names In the age before universal literacy many place names were not pronounced as they read. Once people could read they pronounced them as they looked: so, for example, Daventry was no longer pronounced *Daintry*, Romford was no longer *Rumford* and Covent Garden no longer *Cuvvent Garden*. (The last two are examples of pronunciations surviving beyond the great vowel shift of the late Middle Ages, as still do the 'uh' sound in *Monday*, *honey*, *none* and – though this seems to be changing – *constable*.) Norfolk is full of places that locals still do not pronounce as they seem, such as *Hunston* for Hunstanton, *Cly* for Cley, *Tackleston* for Talconeston, *Haysborough* for Happisburgh, *Wibbun* for Weybourne, *Windham* for Wymondham, and so on. In Yorkshire, Rievaulx Abbey was pronounced *Rivaz*: transmuted not just by our ability to read English, but by the ability of some to read French. See also PRONUNCIATION.

There are English conventions for the spelling of foreign words, but that is the problem: there is usually more than one convention. When writing geographical names it used to be the case that one simply took an authoritative atlas, such as *The Times*'s, and copied its spelling. However, some today would question even that. There still are many accepted English spellings for European cities that the locals call something completely different: no English writer would dream of writing *Firenze* for Florence or *Wien* for Vienna. However, the spelling of some French towns has become gallicised in recent years – we now write Lyon and Marseille whereas it used to be *Lyons* and *Marseilles*. This must be attributable to greater familiarity with that culture, both through travel and language; I start to hear Italophiles talk of *Torino*, but I doubt Turin will be displaced just yet.

There are also political considerations when it comes to using names. Where a place name has changed by general consent it becomes absurd or even offensive to use the old style: hardly anyone would call Zimbabwe *Rhodesia* now, or Sri Lanka *Ceylon*. However, where the name change has not occurred by consent a political point may just as easily be made by sticking to the old style: many people still say *Burma* and not Myanmar to signal their disapproval of the regime there. Indian place names are a particular problem: the politically correct world likes to say Mumbai, which is found patronising by tens of millions of Indians who are quite happy still calling it *Bombay*; Bollywood has yet to become Mullywood. Such usages must for the moment be matters of taste, but preferably of informed taste.

Pleonasm is one of the enemies of good writing that this book seeks to defeat. It is the use of more words in an expression than are needed to convey its meaning. Beware, especially, of the pleonastic introductory phrase. How often does one read *it is obvious that*, *by and large*, *for the most part* or *as a matter of fact*, or some other piece of padding before a phrase such as 'the economy is not getting any better', when the sentence could just as easily start with that phrase itself. Another such phrase that also invites itself into the middle of sentences is *of course*. This is rarely necessary, because if something is *of course* one hardly needs to say so. Get straight to the point: most readers do not need an introduction to allow them time to collect their thoughts, even if the writer appears to.

Some words seem to exist purely to provide a breathing space for both writer and reader. When, for example, you next read the word *overall*, note how you may almost always remove it from its sentence without affecting the meaning: such as in 'he was in overall charge' (a TAUTOLOGY as well as a pleonasm), 'overall, it made no difference', 'there was an overall view that it shouldn't happen', 'the overall case was made for keeping the rule' and so on. *Overall* has a legitimate function when describing something that really is over all: such as in politics, when to use the phrase *overall majority* conveys concisely and accurately the fact that in a legislature one party has more seats than all other parties combined, rather than just more than any individual party. It takes little time to weigh every word; and the need to weigh every word makes an important point about reading what one has written before letting anyone else see it. See also FILLERS.

Plunge was a verb that used to be restricted to describing an activity of divers or swimmers, or to what is done with dishes when they are washed up. Water was inevitably involved. It is now used to describe anything that takes a precipitate fall, such as the prices of stocks and shares, and is therefore becoming a CLICHÉ.

Pluperfect tense This is the past of the PERFECT TENSE, and is often used in reported speech to convey that a statement was originally made in the perfect tense, or to specify an individual act in the past. 'He had finished his dinner' is the way of reporting someone who said 'I have finished my dinner'. But the pluperfect is also a means of describing action in the past that precedes a more recent action in the past, for which the IMPERFECT TENSE would be used: 'He had finished his dinner when his mother came into the room and told him someone was on the telephone for him.'

Plurals With certain nouns there is a debate about whether they are, or are not, plural; and therefore how the constructions in which they appear should remain grammatical by ensuring that all the words within them stay in the correct relation to each other.

Are institutions, teams, public bodies and so on plural? Does one write 'the cabinet was divided last night on the question of the economy' or 'the cabinet were divided'? In many cases there are established idiomatic usages for what Fowler calls 'nouns of multitude'. However, in many other cases there are not. Nor, as may be expected, is usage common throughout the English-speaking world. As cricket lovers will know, England *are* either batting or bowling when the commentator is English, but when they [sic] tour Australia a local commentator will say that England *is* batting or bowling.

Fowler's point about the importance of remaining consistent is perhaps the most significant. If one is writing about a body and starts by saying 'the committee were agreed that Mr Smith be elected chairman', the committee must remain plural. If, later in the piece, it becomes singular, and possibly even reverts to the plural later on, the reader can only be confused and annoyed by the mess and inconsistency of the writing. One needs to make one's own rules, to some extent. Mine is that institutions are singular except where the overwhelming force of **IDIOM** says the opposite – such as with the England cricket team. So I would write 'the Government is', 'the Labour party is', 'the Brigade of Guards has', 'the Royal Family was' and so on. This is a matter of taste, my own taste being shaped by what I regard to be the logic of the matter: but one must, having made up one's mind, stick to it. See also **NOUNS OF MULTITUDE**.

Certain words, usually of foreign origin, are not always recognised by people as being plural. *Data* and *media* are the plurals of anglicised Latin neuter nouns and should take verbs as such: 'the data were wrong' or 'the media are scum'. A popular fast food in recent years has been the *panino*, as it is not called: the singular as used by cafés and stallholders is always the plural, *panini*: 'a cheese panini is £2'. A *panino* is a bread roll in Italian. They are *panini* only when in a multitude. One often reads of how a celebrity was 'chased by a paparazzi', which is the *panino* problem again. This useful word, which describes a particularly ruthless and unprincipled brand of press photographer, is in the singular *paparazzo*. See also **GRAFFITI**.

The plurals of most foreign words are now anglicised, since the singular words themselves are, though *media* and *data* prove that this is a question of idiom. It is quite correct to write *referendums*, *forums* and *dictums*; although *referenda* is still in common use and is not incorrect, *fora* and *dicta* passed out of idiomatic usage long ago. Nor would *formulae*, *tabulae rasae* or *copulae* be considered current. Some Greek words observe strict etymology in the plurals: for example, *criterion* becomes *criteria* and *phenomenon* becomes *phenomena*; no one has yet tried arguing that *clitorises* should be *clitorides*, however, so there are limits. *Omnibuses* have always been *omnibuses*, despite occasional Victorian jokes about *omnibi*.

When using the plurals of words from classical languages that have been anglicised, always observe conventions about gender too. One common mistake is in use of the increasingly popular noun *alumnus*, to mean a graduate of a university. The plural is *alumni*; but a female graduate is an *alumna*, and more than one are *alumnae*.

With words from modern languages the idiom may be less certain: one is as likely to hear someone from the musical world talk of *concerti* as of *concertos* (though sometimes it seems as though *concerti* is reserved for Baroque works), but one never hears anything except *sopranos*, *altos* and *impresarios*. If one heard *inamorata* in the plural it would doubtless be *inamoratas* rather than *inamorate*; a beloved man, should one wish to make his status Italianate too, would be an *inamorato*, and more than one would be either *inamorati* or *inamoratos*, the last sounding somewhat fruity, and comical.

Certain **COMPOUND NOUNS** have unusual plurals. A court martial becomes *courts martial* because in English we do not decline adjectives. Similarly we have *queens mother*, *lords lieutenant*, *lords privy seal*, *attorneys general*, *solicitors general* and *directors general*. *The Times*, in its edition of 25 July 2012, failed to grasp this point in writing about governor-generals rather than governors-general. Where the adjective precedes the noun there is less scope for confusion, which is why we know the plurals are *field marshals*, *major-generals*, *lieutenant-colonels*, *rear admirals* and *air marshals*.

It used to be the case that almost all English nouns ending in *-f* changed to *-ves* in the plural. Some still do: *loaves*, *halves*, *hooves*, *knives*, *dwarves*, *calves*, *leaves* and even *sheaves* are normal. However, *rooves*, *handkerchieves* and *beeves* are all now of varying degrees of antiquity, and *wharves* is probably on its way with them. There probably never were *chieves* or *oaves*. This is a question of usage now, and of judgement: as with any English usage, using something that is obsolete or self-consciously archaic will detract from the message in the writing by drawing attention to itself.

Some common English nouns have irregular plurals with which we are all familiar: *mouse* and *mice*, for example, or *louse* and *lice*. It never fails to surprise some literate people how many of their peers think that *dice* is a singular. It is a plural. The singular is *die*. *Spice*, it may be worth adding, is not the plural of *spouse*.

Otto Jespersen points out that some singular nouns either inevitably do change their meaning, or may change their meaning, when they become plural. It is our *custom* to shake hands, and shaking hands is one of our *customs*; but *customs* are also the formalities by which one enters or leaves a country. The plural of *colour* can also mean the flags and banners carried by soldiers on parades or hung in regimental chapels. Other examples are *spirit* and *spirits*, *honour* and *honours*, *order* and *orders*, *writing* and *writings*, *quarter* and *quarters*.

Although it irritated Eric Partridge, who becomes quite cross about it (he headlines his article on the subject in *Usage and Abusage* 'plurals, snob'), it is also the case that idiom in Britain has for centuries spoken of plural quantities of game in the singular. This remains current among those who engage in field sports or who have businesses connected with them, such as game dealers and sporting agencies. So one shoots a *brace* of *pheasant*, *grouse* or *woodcock* and not a pair; one sees a *covey* of *partridge*, a *flock* of *geese*, a *flight* of *duck* and a *leash* of *hare*; and one sees a *herd* of *deer* when out stalking. It applies to big game too: those who went pigsticking in India would talk of 'plenty of pig in these parts', and might on their sporting travels around the world have seen a *herd* of *elephant*, *buffalo*, *giraffe* or *rhinoceros*. Perhaps Partridge had pacific scruples that caused him to be angry with people who pursued such quarry; but the fact is that if one wishes to describe such beasts in the plural, that is how to do it. It is not about being a snob, it is about being idiomatically correct. Using singulars as plurals also applies to fish, something almost everyone does idiomatically and without a second thought. One would not dream of talking about *salmons*, *trouts*, *cods* or *skates*, and people who have nothing to be snobbish about quite happily talk of *haddock* when referring to a multitude. The word *fish* itself serves as a plural, except in specialist scientific or ichthyological contexts where it would be acceptable to talk of different *fishes*, or in the theological context of 'loaves and fishes'.

As well as odd plurals, let me conclude this section with a note about odd singulars. *Physics*, *ethics*, *econometrics* and other studies or sciences ending in *-ics* are singular. Also, the singular of the plural noun *troops* does not mean a single soldier. A troop is a small group of soldiers. Troops are large numbers of them. It is nonsense to use the singular as a synonym for *soldier*.

An APOSTROPHE always signifies possession when before an *s*, never a plural: *apple's* is the notorious grocer's apostrophe.

Poems, titles of It is a matter of taste whether to italicise the names of poems or give them within single quotation marks: my prejudice is to italicise poems known by a specific title and put ones generally known by their first lines in single marks: so *Fern Hill* or *In Memoriam*, but 'Shall I compare thee to a summer's day?' or 'Say not the struggle naught availeth'.

Polemic is a controversial argument couched in strong terms, often taking the form of a verbal attack on a person, an institution or a doctrine.

Policy used to be a specific word in politics but is now used in such an abstract fashion as to have become meaningless. It is one thing to have an *economic policy*, or an *immigration policy*, which sets out certain practical rules for the conduct of such business. But a phrase such as 'this party has a policy of fairness' indicates nothing specific but much nebulousness, and is part of that umbrella of vagueness under which politicians love to shelter.

Political correctness The phenomenon now called *political correctness* may well have had its roots in the habit of a certain section of society to use language as directly as possible, and the determination of those distressed on behalf of the victims of their tactlessness to do something about it (see EUPHEMISM). However, it is mainly the product of the sensibilities of privileged and educated liberals who wished to remove disadvantage or even the dispassionate perception of disadvantage, wherever possible, from those less fortunate than or different from themselves. Given the potency of language as a labelling device, it is inevitable that this political mass movement should affect the way words are used, and indeed the choice of which words are used. Language has always changed because of fashion; and because fashion has changed language, it has often changed it needlessly.

Good manners dictate that one does not insult people gratuitously or use language that they would find upsetting. Political correctness is usually an arbitrary set of rules espoused by one group on behalf of another, and often without having consulted those whom the rulemakers claim to protect. Good manners existed long before political correctness: it has never been especially polite to use terms of abuse towards minorities, even if some black people choose to call themselves *niggers*, or some homosexual men and women are happy to refer to themselves as *queers*. However, we should not forget that until quite recently it was acceptable to use terms that shock today. One example of the speed with which sensibilities change can be gauged by Partridge's entry on *nigger*. What he had to say was thought acceptable not merely when *Usage and Abusage* was published in 1947, but in the 1973 revised edition. This term, he said, 'belongs only, and then only in contempt or fun, to the dark-skinned African races and their descendants in America and the West Indies. Its application to the native peoples of India is ignorant and offensive.' Perhaps in 1947 a black man would have found it rib-tickling to be addressed in such terms by a jester, though I doubt it; I doubt it even more about 1973. It is clear it is now a term of gross offensiveness: but I doubt very much that a polite person would have attempted to make a joke of the term even in 1947.

Terms to describe sufferers from certain illnesses or handicaps are now deemed to be callous, and have changed. They are thought callous, perhaps, because what were once considered neutral terms to describe a condition – such as *spastic* or *cripple* or *idiot* or *lunatic* – have become pejorative because of their adoption by unfeeling people as terms of abuse for others. Those with Down's syndrome are no longer described as *mongols*, mainly because of the irrelevant unpleasantness of so labelling those with the Asiatic features typical of this affliction; and also because of racist overtones. These sensitivities appear humane and natural, and reflect the fact that we live in times when these afflictions are better understood and seen to have no stigma attached to them. However, there is always someone seeking to ratchet up the mechanism of sensitivity, or looking for offence where it is often very hard to find it.

Political correctness goes beyond the pursuit of good manners, tact and sensitivity when it seeks to manufacture reasons for offence, something certain politicians like to do in order to try to show that they are more alert to minorities than others may be. No handicapped person was aware, until recently, that he was supposed to be offended by his group of disabled people being termed *the blind*, *the deaf* or *the disabled* (*the dumb*, for reasons outlined above – that term having become one of abuse – had every reason not to be happy with that word being applied to them). Yet many groups working with the public are now informed, by those who make it their business to set the standard for such things, that the references have to be to 'blind people', 'deaf people' or 'disabled people'. There are euphemisms for each of these too, though they are so clunking they have hardly caught on: 'sight impaired', 'hard of hearing', 'people of restricted mobility'. Any suggestion that not to use these terms implies heartlessness or lack of sympathy for those so afflicted drives a pointless change in the language. As with all elements of usage the application of logic is valuable. It is one thing to stop using words that have been made offensive, and that are generally accepted as being so. It is quite another to invent a whole new vocabulary to replace words that serve their purpose effectively, clearly and well, and offend only those who (often not being afflicted themselves) seek to define the offence.

Much of what has been done to the language by political correctness is, however, absurd. Gender is a particular problem. It is right that writers should be aware that for the most part they are addressing an audience comprising women as well as men. The old rule that the male is to be taken to include the female at all times, and which, as I have already remarked, I have adopted in writing this book, may begin to grate. What, however, is the alternative? Writing a sentence such as 'anyone may swim if he or she has a costume' is long-winded, but is probably the best option if those hearing or reading such a thing are likely to be offended. 'Anyone may swim if they have a costume' is simply illiterate, and 'anyone may swim if he has a costume' seems to suggest that women may swim under no circumstances at all. In popular usage the non-gender-specific *they* is greatly favoured, but that is no reason to use it. Rules in language are made by logic, not by a democratic vote. In the sentence just quoted, the best option would be to recast the sentence as 'anyone wearing a costume may swim'. My own reasons for taking the course I have, in the absence of third person pronouns common to both genders, have worked very well for generations. That course may have to serve a little longer in circumstances where the highest standards of grammatical accuracy are required.

The apostles of political correctness have gone to lengths to try to ensure that gender discrimination is eliminated from the English tongue. It is up to the educated user of the language to decide whether he (or she) wishes to award them an easy victory, or to stand and fight. The most egregious example of the absurdities brought by such a victory is that a word used for centuries to describe a piece of furniture – *chair* – is now routinely used, except in some reactionary institutions like the Conservative party, to describe the person who leads a board, committee or some similar body or institution. This word has been arrived at because of the impossibility (in the eyes of the politically correct or, rather, politically correct people) of the perpetuation of the word *chairman*, an understandable dislike of the word *chairwoman* and the sheer preposterousness of the term *chairperson*. Yet it has never been satisfactorily explained why, given the nature of the label (and label is all it is), a woman cannot be a chairman.

The dictionary is helpful on this vexatious point. Its first definition of the noun *man* is 'a human being, irrespective of sex or age'. As a gloss for our politically correct times, it adds a note saying that 'Man was considered until the 20th century to include women by implication, though referring primarily to males. It is now frequently understood to exclude women, and is therefore avoided by many people.' Just as beauty is in the eye of the beholder, perhaps it is so that understanding is in the mind of the understander. The word is thought to have Sanskrit origins, preceding its Germanic ones, that are to do with the roots of our word *mind*, 'on the basis that thought is a distinctive characteristic of human beings'. Ironically, the male is now increasingly used to include the female, despite this being the age of equality. It is now the fashion (and this started in America, the home of political correctness) to refer to actresses as *actors*, a word no less masculine than *chairman*. Like most prescriptive grammarians of the past, I would argue that in all these circumstances, common sense should apply. Unfortunately, there is precious little of that in the cult of political correctness, where the main concern appears to be peer pressure, grandstanding and a different sort of prejudice from the ones that are occasionally being countered. America (which gave the world 'affirmative action' and other EUPHEMISMS that become more generally offensive and patronising the more they are contemplated) continues to make the most significant contribution to the English lexicon of political correctness. A correspondent in *The New Yorker* (4 January 2010), writing about disabled athletes, used the phrase 'a challenged runner'. It appears that *disabled* itself is now considered offensive. How long will it be before *challenged* is too?

A word that has become one of the foremost weapons of the movement is *appropriate*. Its antonym, *inappropriate*, is if anything used with even more severity. Political correctness is about PRESCRIPTION AND PROSCRIPTION, and its puritanical considerations are regularly applied with the threat that an act or a form of words is *inappropriate*, or a deviation from *appropriate* behaviour. This usage is part VOGUE WORD, part sinister EUPHEMISM. It euphemises not so much the act under criticism as the action of the critic. A man who steals a kiss from a female colleague at the office Christmas party will find himself condemned for *inappropriate* conduct. It is deemed not to be *appropriate* for a public figure to make irate remarks about the Welsh, for example. We are seldom given a standard, however, against which ideals of appropriateness can be measured.

It is deemed impolite now to use the phrase 'Christian name', even when it is apparent that the person to whom it applies is of that faith. I have used it in this book in such contexts. The politically correct term is *forename* or *given name.*

Political language is designed to be vague about outcomes and about responsibility. It favours the PASSIVE rather than the ACTIVE voice, because the passive can avoid identifying an agent – 'you will be shot' is a different matter from 'I will shoot you' – and abstracts over concretes. To say 'my party wants more flexibility in Europe' is different from saying 'my party wants Europe not to impose a specific tax on the City of London even if it imposes it on other countries'. These are the enemies of good English, as is AMBIGUITY, something politicians also prize. 'I have no intention of seeking the leadership' is a statement that lacks only the phrase 'at the moment' to rob it of ambiguity. This manipulation of language occurs elsewhere, too. If, for example, one hears a broadcasting outlet engage in an act of self-reference in describing itself as *impartial* or *unbiased*, one should be aware that this may depend on a quite radical definition of either partiality or bias. *Fact* is often used when the writer or speaker means *assertion*. Almost any adjective contained in advertisements by estate agents, used-car salesmen or political parties should be treated as specious.

As well as employing these traits of language, the political class and its imitators in big corporations invents its own private language of **JARGON** to help foster the necessary air of obscurity and vagueness about its intentions. In Britain in the last decade or so we have heard time and again of 'the target culture', 'best practice', 'prioritisation', 'vibrant communities', programmes that are 'rolled out' for the benefits of 'stakeholders', among other terms used by the propaganda arm of government. These terms are designed to convey an impression of action, purpose and (to use two other popular nouns) 'inclusiveness' and 'diversity'; but they soon wear out and intelligent people come to regard them with boredom or contempt. In response to the official propaganda the tribunes of the people in the press produce their own **VOGUE** terms: 'feral children', 'hug-a-hoodie', 'the client state' and so on. It has also become popular for writers and officials alike to stop speaking of doing things in the future, and instead to plan to do them 'going forward'. They are also agreed that any institution or service that has to be held to account or up for scrutiny must be shown whether or not it is 'fit for purpose'. Almost everything a politician has to do is a 'challenge' and it is 'critical' that he or she should be able to 'deliver' on it. No wonder people have such a poor estimate of politicians.

Polysyndeton is the use of many conjunctions, or perhaps the same conjunction many times, to create an effect: 'And Adam gave names to all cattle, and to the fowl of the air, and to every beast of the field . . .'

Populace and **populous** These two homophones are respectively a noun and an adjective and must not be confused. The *populace* is the masses or ordinary people in a society, as opposed to the ruling elite. It is also a singular noun. Somewhere that is *populous* is full of inhabitants or densely populated.

Position See ABSTRACT LANGUAGE.

Possessive pronouns These – *my*, *your*, *his*, *her*, *its*, *our*, *their* and the impersonal possessive *one's* – as the name suggests, describe ownership of a thing or of an action. They are essentially adjectival, describing the relation of one person or thing to another: *my* mother, *his* aunt, *her* dress. As with their cousins above, the use of these should be second nature to any native speaker of English: 'Mrs Smith left her umbrella on the bus', 'we took our holidays in France' or 'it is impossible to make time for all one's hobbies'. See also APOSTROPHES.

Possessives It is when we use the possessive that we are perhaps most alert to distinctions of case. There is scope for difficulty with compound possessives – phrases such as 'my wife's sister's boyfriend' or, to note a different form, 'the driver of the car's behaviour'. In instances such as the former, remember to ensure that all the necessary possessives are included. In instances such as the latter, make a stylistic judgement: it may be better to say 'the behaviour of the car's driver'. A phrase like 'we saw the woman who lives in the house on the corner's dog' is so obviously clumsy that one needs little urging to recast it as 'the dog of the woman'. There is often debate about what to do with the possessive when the singular word requiring it ends with an *s*. Does one write *Paris's* or *Paris'*? It is my unequivocal view that one writes the former. One pronounces the *s* twice, so one writes it twice. One uses the device of a lone apostrophe after an *s* only when the word is plural, for one pronounces the *s* only once: therefore, one writes 'the dogs' home', or 'the porters' lodge'. See also APOSTROPHES.

Postpositions These are related to PREPOSITIONS, but come after a verb: 'he threw it *away*', 'he went there years *ago*', and so on.

Practicable and **practical** and their antonyms IMPRACTICABLE, IMPRACTICAL AND UNPRACTICAL are not always used literately. The dictionary says that something that is *practical* is something that occurs in practice or in action, as opposed to its being speculative or theoretical. An important secondary usage of the adjective is to describe something as suited to a particular purpose, or functional. *Practicable* is a near-synonym, but has the additional shade of meaning 'able to be done or put into practice successfully; feasible'. A practical solution is one that entails action; a practicable one can be executed without difficulty. Greater difficulty comes when trying to negate these terms. *Impractical* (which the dictionary cites as first having been used in 1865) is frowned on by pedants as a Johnny-come-lately, catch-all substitute for the much older terms *unpractical* (first cited in 1637) and *impracticable* (1677), and thus as lacking the precision of either. Those wishing to be precise should first judge whether they wish to use either *practical* or *practicable* and, if negating it, to do so by *unpractical* or *impracticable*; and leave *impractical* to the Americans, in whose land it seems to have found a happy home.

Practice and **practise** The former is the noun and the latter the verb; although in AMERICAN ENGLISH the verb is *practice*.

Pre- This prefix needs to be treated with extreme caution. Some firms now offer services to their customers on a 'pre-booked' basis. How else is one supposed to book? If one books at the time of use, or afterwards, one is not booking at all. This is an entirely illogical usage. Its cousins are 'pre-used' and 'pre-owned' and even 'pre-loved', silly euphemisms for second-hand. Something that is used or already owned can only have been done so beforehand. Indeed, it is a rule increasingly observed in life that almost anything with the prefix *pre-* can do without it. Can anything that is arranged be other than pre-arranged? Can a condition that is set in advance of some compact or agreement be anything other than a pre-condition? A 'pre-prepared statement', similarly, is a tautology. There are many other such shockers.

Predicates A *predicate* is what is said about the subject of a sentence. 'My wife cooked them dinner' has 'my wife' as the subject and 'cooked them dinner' as the predicate. Subject and predicate are essential components of a sentence.

Pregnant A phrase much beloved of the tabloid press is 'falling pregnant'. Consider, for a moment, the politics of this phrase. It is intended as a parallel to 'falling ill' rather than to 'falling from grace'. It is not intended to signal any moral failing or impropriety, as it is often applied to perfectly respectable married women who have been impregnated by their husbands. When one falls ill the event has seldom been within one's control. A germ or an infection has been in the air and one has become the unwitting, and unwilling, victim of it. One does not need to have a degree in biology to understand that becoming pregnant is not accomplished in quite the same way. Yet to say that one has 'fallen pregnant' is almost a Pontius Pilate moment. It is as if the condition has been achieved without any conscious act on the part of the mother. It is nothing to do with her and she can – pending further developments – wash her hands of it. This sort of absurdity should not be indulged by this phrase's being used by intelligent people.

In a phrase such as 'she is six months pregnant' *months* is part of a compound adjective and does not require an apostrophe.

Prejudices and **values** Politicians go on about *values* when they really mean *prejudices*.

Premise, premises and **premiss** *Premise* is a term from logic from which a conclusion is drawn: 'My premise is that all small boys are hungry, and therefore you will want some chocolate.' *Premises* are either the plural of that word, or a word used to describe a residential or commercial building: 'The burglar was believed to have been on the premises in the early hours of the morning.' *Premiss* is an alternative, but increasingly antique, spelling of *premise*, and the latter is the more frequently found today.

Prepared to There was a time when grammarians were united in their ridicule for the construction *prepared to* as in 'I am prepared to vouch for the fact that . . .' The verbal construction is unnecessary and verbose: the test for this is that if the construction *to be prepared to* is removed and replaced by *will* or *shall*, the sense of the sentence remains unchanged. This, indeed, is the test for all writing; if a word or phrase can be removed from a clause or sentence without altering its meaning or rendering it more obscure, remove it.

Prepositions A *preposition* establishes a relationship between one word and another: often between a verb and a noun or pronoun. So one goes *to* church, one walks *from* the house, one sits *on* the lavatory, one loiters *by* a stream, one stands *for* parliament, one swims *with* the tide, one is tired *of* life, one lies *in* the sun, one is good *at* games. These are the most frequently used prepositions. There are many others: *between*, *around*, *about*, *through*, *over*, *below*, *until*, *into*, *beneath*, *inside*, *outside*, *notwithstanding* and so on. Some prepositions have become adjectives in modern usage – an *outside* table, an *inside* story. In some languages, such as Latin, Greek or German, different prepositions take different cases. English having lost most of its inflections, one only notices the different cases taken by prepositions with certain pronouns. All prepositions take *me*, or *him*, or *her*, or *us*, or *them*. *You* does not inflect. They also take *whom*, an accusative that requires preservation. Few would be so barbaric that they would write or say 'I gave it to *she*' or 'the bird flew over *they*', but many are barbaric enough to write 'the man to *who* I gave it' when *whom* is required. Indeed, it is in usages such as this that those (and they exist) who argue for the redundancy of *whom* are at their weakest.

The main difficulty with prepositions is that some writers choose the wrong one. However, it is the perception of many writers that there is a bigger prepositional problem still: whether a preposition may legitimately end a sentence. Most grammarians dismiss this as a fetish, and the Fowlers dismissed it as 'a modern superstition'. I am with them. The very notion gave rise to one of Churchill's most renowned *bons mots*, 'this is the sort of English up with which I will not put'. Churchill, with his instinctive feel for the rhythms of language, identified the main obstacle to this rule, fetish or superstition, which is the problem it causes with compound verbs such as *put up with.*

There is no rule, but there is a matter of taste. Good writers usually avoid putting a preposition at the end of a sentence, for reasons that are a mixture of logic and of style, except when the preposition concerned is part of a compound verb. Then, for Churchillian reasons, they put the preposition last, as to do otherwise sounds contrived and clumsy. Therefore, I would write 'the man to whom I was writing' rather than 'the man I was writing to'. I think it sounds and reads better than the alternative (and the musical effect of our words on the page is something to which I fear we pay too little attention), and I like the logic of 'the man to whom' running together. Yet I would sooner write 'it is an event we are greatly looking forward to' than 'it is an event to which we are greatly looking forward' because I feel the former is less of a distraction to the reader in its lack of awkwardness, and will communicate my meaning more effectively. Always strive to be idiomatic, and you will usually write what makes most sense.

Here are some of the most common mistakes with the choice of prepositions: they are often made when a demotic usage seeps into the consciousness of supposedly educated people. A person is absorbed *in* a task, not by it; but liquid may be absorbed *by* a sponge. One acquiesces *in* something, not with it, and one connives *at* something, not in it. One aims *at* something, not for it. One becomes angry *with* someone, not at him. One is ashamed *of* bad behaviour, not by it. A decision is *between* one thing *and* another, not one thing or another. One is bored *by* or *with* something, never of it. Something is different *from* something else, not to it or, even more abominable, than it. One is disgusted *with* something, not by it. One becomes fed up *with* things, not of them. Something is identical *to* something else, not with it. One inculcates something *on* somebody, one does not inculcate somebody with something; and one instils something *into* somebody. There is an interaction *of* two people or things, not between them. Two things merge *with* each other, not into each other. One is oblivious *of* something, not to it. One prefers something *to* something else, not than something else. One is prohibited *from* doing something, not prohibited to do it (a confusion, one supposes, with *forbidden*). One thing is replaced *by* another, not with it. One has a reputation *for* something, not of it. One is sensible *of* something, but sensitive *to* it. One is sparing *of* something, not with it. One substitutes one thing *for* another, not another thing with the first. One suffers *from* something, not with it. See also **INFORMED ABOUT AND INFORMED BY.**

Another problem with the contagion of **SLANG** and vulgar usage is that some verbs acquire pointless prepositions. Here are some examples: be inside *of*, be outside *of*, infringe *upon*, comprise *of*, meet *with* and get off *of*. Also, some vulgar usages have prepositions put to uses for which they were not intended. *Unless* does not mean *except*, so do not write 'I shall not go there unless on Wednesdays' when you mean 'I shall not go there except on Wednesdays'.

Although the English verb *compare* is partly formed by the Latin preposition meaning *with*, the dictionary has from its earliest days drawn a distinction between contexts in which one writes *compared with* and those in which one writes *compared to*. If one is using *compare* in the sense of to liken something to something else, then one uses *to*: the most famous example in our literature is 'Shall I compare thee to a summer's day?' If one is simply establishing a comparison – 'You can't compare chalk with cheese' – one uses *with*.

A common mistake is the use of the wrong pronoun after *than* in a comparative clause. There is a sense of certainty that 'she was so much taller than I' is correct. It is not. As Onions points out: 'than, when introducing a contracted comparative clause has (at least from early Modern English times) been treated as a preposition and has been followed by the accusative'. So it would be correct to write 'she was so much taller *than I am*', which is not a contracted clause, but if the verb is absent it must be 'she is so much taller *than me*'. To reinforce the point, *than* in these circumstances must take an accusative pronoun – 'a woman *than whom* I was much shorter', or 'she is taller *than him*'. However, in using a construction with nouns and pronouns it appears to be second nature to forget that the pronoun must be in the accusative, especially if it comes second after the noun. So we are always reading, or hearing, 'between you and I', 'she invited John and I', 'it was a present to my husband and I', 'I sent it to John and she' and so on.

In a sentence such as 'he likes cherries more than me' the only legitimate meaning can be 'he likes cherries more than he likes me'. If the meaning that is sought is 'he likes cherries more than I like cherries', then one should say or write 'he likes cherries more than I do', or the elliptical 'than I', which is permissible here. There is a distinction between the first person pronoun being the object of the sentence – as in 'she is taller than me' – and its being a subject, with an ellipsis – 'he likes cherries more than I [do]'. Partridge seems to have misunderstood Onions on this point, and argues that the accusative is needed only with relative pronouns such as *whom*: but this is expressly not what Onions says.

Partridge's assertion that the use of other accusatives is 'colloquial, not Standard English' is contradicted by Onions's point that *than* has been 'prepositional' for half a millennium, and his conclusion that any other use is 'pedantic'. The same applies to *as*: either 'she is not as [or *so*] tall *as I am*' or 'she is not as [or *so*] tall *as me*'. Lest this be thought a radical departure into demotic English, I should stress that Onions, one of the foremost academic grammarians of his day, took no issue with this usage as far back as 100 years ago.

Be sure that where verbs routinely need a preposition to complete their sense, those prepositions are supplied: they can go missing in long sentences, especially when the writer is overcome with the desire to avoid ending a sentence with a preposition. The quite obviously deficient 'he was not drawn to what all her friends were attracted' is the type of sentence that omits an essential *to* at the end of it. This error happens when there is a common object, often pronominal (in this case *what*), of two verbs, each of which is prepositional. Using *to* once is not enough. In some rare instances, a prepositional usage dies out. It is common to read in British novels of the

1920s or 1930s – Evelyn Waugh, Graham Greene or Aldous Huxley – that one character has *telephoned to* another. By the end of the Second World War they are simply telephoning them. Since the verb itself was relatively new – the *OED* cites its first use as 1877 – there were not centuries of custom and practice to cite as authority; and the use of *to* seems to have been a precious and somewhat exclusive affectation in any case. See also IN TO AND INTO and ON TO AND ONTO.

Prepositions, missing This often happens because of the imitation of American usage. In America, the aggrieved are always 'protesting the decision'. Here, we require a preposition (and they usually come at no extra cost) so that we may protest *against* the decision. There is a similar problem with the verb *appeal*. When someone has been sentenced to ninety-nine years in jail in an American drama, his attorney will spring up and announce that he is going to 'appeal the verdict'. A British barrister would appeal *against* it. See also AMERICAN ENGLISH AND MISSING PREPOSITIONS.

Prescription and **proscription** A *prescription* is an instruction to do something. A *proscription* is an instruction not to do it. So one says 'His prescription was to drink a glass of wine again', but 'there was a proscription against trespassing'. The related verbs *prescribe*, to instruct to do something, and *proscribe*, to instruct not to do it, must be treated with the same care. 'A daily walk was prescribed' means the person should have some exercise. 'Alcohol was proscribed' means he must not drink.

Present tense This is the most common and straightforward of all the tenses, and describes action taking place in the present. *I see*, *you read*, *he runs*, *we like*, *they sit* are all examples. For greater precision there is a CONTINUOUS PRESENT, as in *I am running*, *you are standing*, *he is thinking* and so on, which conveys the notion of an action that is under way and not yet completed.

Presently See MOMENTARILY AND PRESENTLY.

Prestigious One of the more overworked adjectives of our time is *prestigious*, used to describe anything of even the most humble eminence. It has become an almost meaningless word, not least because of the contexts in which it is applied: 'this prestigious commemorative plate appears in a limited edition', etc. This is perhaps as well, because it is inevitably used wrongly. Its etymology, from the Latin *prestigiosus*, meaning deceitful or full of tricks, tells us exactly what it should mean. The French noun *prestidigitateur*, a conjuror, comes from the same root. The dictionary speculates that the word came to have its present, vulgar meaning (first cited in 1901) because of the 'dazzling' or 'magical' nature of objects with *prestige*. It is an adjective to be avoided on account of its emptiness and its misleading quality.

Presume See ASSUME AND PRESUME.

Preterite in English grammar is another term for the IMPERFECT TENSE of verbs.

Prevalent does not mean *widespread*; something that is *prevalent* has prevailed, it is predominant or pervasive.

Prevaricate and **procrastinate** *Prevaricate* comes from the Latin verb *praevaricare*, to plough crookedly or (referring to lawyers) to collude. It means, as one would expect given that provenance, to deviate from straightforwardness, or to speak or act in an evasive way. The latest edition of the *Oxford English Dictionary*, however, has run up the white flag on its meaning. Despite citing a usage in 2005 of the word in its strictly correct sense, it says that the usual sense now is to delay action: which it admits is because of the influence of *procrastinate*. It is an interesting policy for lexicographers to accept a word into the language with a new meaning purely because people confuse it with a word that begins with the same letter, has the same number of syllables, ends with the same suffix and generally sounds similar. It might be easier, more logical and more accurate to say that the frequent use of the word to mean *delay* is simply wrong. It is odd, given the promiscuous misuse of this word, that more newspapers are not sued by completely honest politicians, who find themselves accused of shiftiness when in fact all they are guilty of is the inability to take a decision.

Previous Some SLANG creeps into polite speech because it sounds almost formal. Partridge (the acknowledged expert on slang in English) dismisses the usage of 'you have been much too previous' to mean someone has acted hastily or pre-emptively. He is right to do so. One suspects that *previous* has attained this level of usage because by being polysyllabic it does not sound as though it might be slang. Also, it is an adjective associated in the mind with legal procedure, as in 'previous convictions'. None of this is any excuse for using it in this coarse way, but these may be some of the reasons that explain it. Like much slang, its origin might also have been in humour. However, such jokes quickly wear thin, and never bear repeating in serious writing.

Principal and **principle** *Principle* and *principal* have such a straightforward distinction from each other that it is remarkable anyone should confuse them. One has *principles*, or agrees to something *in principle*. If something is the most prominent feature of a large number of them, it is the *principal* feature; and if two people draw up a contract between themselves, they are the *principals* in that contract. Even in the best regulated publications the confusion is sometimes made. The *New Statesman*, 2 April 2012, included the following sentence: 'I don't object in principal to the idea of yet another drama about the *Titanic*.'

Prior to is a pompous and prolix way of saying *before*. 'Prior to my meeting my wife I was a bachelor' sounds far better as 'Before I met my wife, I was a bachelor'.

Pristine does not mean bright, shiny and new. It means original.

Private soldiers See MILITARY RANKS.

Privy Council Its members are Privy *Counsellors*, not *Councillors*, and they are entitled to the title Right Honourable, shortened usually to Rt Hon.

Profession and **trade** A *profession* is not synonymous with a *trade*. In an age of aspiration and self-improvement, it has become common for people in white-collar trades – such as journalism, for example – to speak of their *profession*. This is a solecism. By convention in Great Britain, professions require a specific learned qualification. Medicine, the law, the Church and the officer class in the Army and Royal Navy constituted the original professions. The higher ranks of the civil service and the diplomatic corps, teaching, banking, stockbroking and accountancy all came to qualify as such because of the process of examination that was needed to enter any of them. Members of Parliament have also always, by courtesy, been regarded as professional men and women, irrespective of any evidence to the contrary. All other callings, even those of supposedly learned people such as writers or musicians, are *trades*. The dictionary noted as early as 1908 the tendency of anyone who regarded his occupation as 'socially superior to a trade or handicraft' to call it a profession, but dismissed this as 'vulgar' and 'humorous'. The movement towards blanket professionalism has continued in the last 100 years or so. Pedants or the legalistic may regard it still as vulgar, but this pursuit of *amour propre* is anything but humorous to those who undertake it. So-called professional sportsmen and -women are termed such simply to distinguish them from amateurs. A *professional* footballer earns his living from the sport; an *amateur* does not.

Program and **programme** A *program* is something a computer runs and the American spelling of *programme*. A *programme* is something one watches on television, or buys at the opera or the theatre, or that provides the outline and inspiration for a piece of music, or constitutes an agenda for an event.

Prolixity is the enemy of good writing. One of the best ways to avoid it is to read back whatever one writes, and cut out all superfluous words.

Pronouns Languages have a convenient system by which, in speaking or writing about a creature, object or person, a short word may be used as a substitute for the noun to avoid ugly repetition of it. These are called *pronouns*, and there are several types of them. The fundamental point about using a pronoun is that it has to be accompanied by the noun for which it is working, and nearby. For example: 'Mr Smith sat by the fire. *He* felt warm' is a straightforward use of the personal pronoun. *He* in the second sentence clearly refers to the proper name in the first. There are also POSSESSIVE PRONOUNS. Were the next sentence to be 'his dog came and sat by him' it would be clear that the dog belongs to Mr Smith, and the *him* next to whom the dog is sitting is also Mr Smith. This leads us towards the dangers of ambiguity. Were Mr Smith with several other men, and they had been named, it might not be clear whose dog it was, and next to whom it sat. In those circumstances it is hard to avoid simply repeating the proper name.

Some other words we commonly use in speech and in writing are also pronouns: *the same* ('I had a beer and he had the same'); *some* ('he saw me eating a plate of beef and said he would like some); *each* ('each was spoken to'); *other* ('of the two girls, I preferred Jane but he preferred the other'); *certain* ('most people present supported him, but certain of them threatened to change their minds'); *any* ('I offered him some nuts, but he didn't want any'); *either* and *both* ('they both wanted money, but I chose not to give any to either'); *all* ('there is plenty for all'); *none* ('none has owned up to doing it'); and *neither* ('neither was ready').

Jespersen stops the traffic in his *Essentials of English Grammar* when writing about pronouns with his example 'if the baby does not thrive on raw milk, boil it'. The great Dane contends that 'there is really little danger of misunderstanding *it*', and he is right. There is, though, a danger of misunderstanding the British sense of humour. Knowing very well to what *it* refers, the average

Briton will still chortle at the ambiguity, which means that the writer – who was seeking to make a serious point – will instead have created a distraction. There is a place for jokes in writing, but they are best when they are intentional.

The most common difficulties with pronouns occur when they lack the correct antecedent, or when (as in Jespersen's example) it becomes unclear what the antecedent is. Take this example: 'The woman bought a lottery ticket and proceeded to win it.' We all know what the writer is trying to say, but through lack of thought he has ended up saying something quite different. *It* can refer only to the lottery ticket, not to the lottery itself. Sometimes, confusion of thought causes writers to use a verb and then refer to it using a pronoun as though it were a noun, as in: 'John decided to propose to Mary, but she turned it down.' She could have turned *him* down, but since a proposal is not mentioned there is nothing for *it* to refer back to, other than something understood by the verb. Simply paying attention to what one has written, and thinking of the logic with which one uses a pronoun, will normally prevent such confusions as these. Idiomatically, there is one regular usage in English of a pronoun that requires no antecedent. This is when *they* is used to describe a generality of opinion or people as in 'they would, in those days, open a door for a lady' or 'they say she is going to marry him'. This usage would not normally be found in formal writing.

There is also a danger of ambiguity when more than one subject has been introduced early in a sentence, or in a previous sentence, and it becomes unclear exactly to what the pronoun is referring. 'Smith and Brown both pleased their teacher with their answers, and he rewarded them with excellent marks' gives no one any difficulties. Although there are three masculine subjects it is quite clear that the *he* can only be the teacher. However, a sentence such as 'Smith met Brown and he gave him a drink' is properly ambiguous, unless it has been made clear to the reader already who has control of a drinks cabinet. Logic may seem to dictate that the *he* automatically refers back to the subject of the sentence (Smith) but there is no reason why that should be so. There would be nothing ungrammatical or illogical about 'Smith met Mrs Brown and she gave him a drink', after all. In a sentence such as this another formula has to be used: either the use of 'the former . . . the latter', which is rather stiff, or simply the repetition of one of the proper names in the second clause in order to remove doubt. I would favour 'and he gave Brown a drink'. Jespersen presents the example 'John told Robert's son that he must help him', which he points out 'is capable of six different meanings'. Only one extra meaning should be sufficient evidence for a writer to know he has to find the means of eliminating the ambiguity.

Beware, in long sentences, of estranging the pronoun too far from its antecedent, as this too may give rise to doubts. As with much that can go wrong in writing, this fault may be rectified by the short sentence. This is true too of statements such as 'Jane had eaten up everything on her plate, but her dislike of the salad dressing caused her mother to leave the lettuce on hers'. Until we get to the words 'her mother' we think the possessive pronoun in 'her dislike' refers to Jane. It is always better if the pronoun does not precede its antecedent.

Some accidents with pronouns are the result of carelessness or illiteracy. The most notorious is a version of the greengrocer's apostrophe, where *it's* is used for *its* as in 'the business has had *it's* worst year for decades'. Variations of this horror include 'mind *you're* language' or its equally objectionable converse 'let me know when *your* here'. The third person pronoun *their*, because of an abundance of homonyms, is a minefield. In correct usage one writes 'they could not believe *their* luck'; yet one from time to time sees 'they could not believe *there* luck' or even 'they could not believe *they're* luck'. As with 'your', there may be abuses in the opposite direction: 'she could not see why *their* should be a problem', and so on. Few people are sufficiently stupid to make such mistakes; many more, however, are sufficiently careless.

The final pronominal difficulty is one created by linguistic history and evolution: there are no relative pronouns meaning *he-or-she*, *his-or-her* or *him-or-her*. Almost daily, one reads or hears utterances such as 'the teacher told each member of his class that they were to stand up' or 'neither John nor Mary had remembered their books' or 'every boy and girl had a present given to them'. The problem is at once apparent: the prolixity, in the first example, of 'told each member of his class that he or she was to stand up'; in the second of 'neither John nor Mary had remembered his or her book'; and in the third of 'every boy and girl had a present given to him or her'. Being a pedant, I regard these usages of *they*, *their* and *them* as unacceptable. However, the alternative forms verge on the absurd. Often, in cases like this, it is easy to recast the sentence to obviate the problem. In the first example one would avoid the need for a singular by writing 'the teacher told all his class that they were to stand up'. In the second, one would write 'both John and Mary had forgotten their books', which also removes the need for a singular. In the third, one would recast it as 'a present was given to every boy and girl' – a rare benefit of the passive voice. Perhaps the next development in our grammar will be to rectify this deficiency; though progressives would argue that it has already happened, and we pedants should overcome our resistance to *they*, *their* and *them*. No doubt in another century we shall have done. It is interesting to note that when a plural pronoun is required in French to cover both genders, *ils* has always been deemed to suffice; but then the French have always had a distinction between the masculine *they* (*ils*) and the feminine *they* (*elles*), which we have lacked. We seem a little way behind.

For a discussion of further possible pitfalls with pronouns, see HE AND HIM, SHE AND HER, WHOM, NOUNS OF MULTITUDE, PREPOSITIONS. There are other varieties of pronouns. See also DEMONSTRATIVE PRONOUNS, ONE (THE IMPERSONAL PRONOUN), POSSESSIVE PRONOUNS, REFLEXIVE PRONOUNS and RELATIVE PRONOUNS.

Pronunciation is outside the scope of this book. It will vary wherever English is spoken, even, in England, from one village to another. However, for the sake of clarity it is worth noting that before universal literacy there were traditional pronunciations of words that changed once people could read; for many words, notably proper names, were not pronounced as they were written. I mention this because sometimes it leads a person into the reverse error, that of spelling. *Forehead* was pronounced *forrid*; *waistcoat* was *weskit*. The days of the week were *Mundy*, *Tuesdy*, *Wensdy*, *Thursdy* and so on. Words with the vowel *o* were spoken as if they contained the vowel *u* instead: *cunstable*, *Cuvvent Garden*, *Cuvventry*, *Denis Cumpton*. In similar fashion, *Montgomery* was *Muntgummery*, *Honiton* was *Huniton* and *Romford* was *Rumford*. The word *some* and its compounds (*something*, *someone*, *somewhere*, *somebody*) behave in this way still, and *Somerset*, *Somerton* and *Somers Town* with them, as well as *son*, *done*, *none*, *monger*, *honey*, *money*, *love*, *wonder* and numerous other such words. (This is nothing to do with the 'great vowel shift', a phenomenon so named by Jespersen to describe the mutation in sound of long vowels and diphthongs.) Perhaps in another century we shall pronounce *some* like *Somme*, *done* will rhyme with *gone* and *wonder* will sound like *wander*. See also PLACE NAMES.

Proper names If there is doubt about a proper name, the *Oxford English Dictionary* or its *Concise* version often has a ruling, and I tend to follow those. The alternative is to look on Google and see which spelling of a particular word has the greater currency: one may then draw one's own conclusions.

Prophecy and **prophesy** The former is the noun – 'I will make a prophecy' – the latter a verb – 'I will prophesy'.

Propositio, in classical rhetoric, was the main contention of an argument.

Proscription See PRESCRIPTION AND PROSCRIPTION.

Prospect is a word abused by journalism. Its literal meaning is quite clear: it means a view, as in the celebrated pub the Prospect of Whitby or in Gray's ode *On a distant prospect of Eton College*. In that sense it is always a prospect *of* something.

When used metaphorically it should be the prospect *that*, as in 'the Smiths were distressed by the prospect that their holiday would be cancelled' or 'there is no prospect that he will be promoted'. *Prospects*, in the plural, refer to a general rather than a specific future, and idiomatically would take *of* rather than *that*, as in 'he has good prospects' or 'the prospects of his making a success of the venture were not good'. Journalism abuses the word, using it lazily to describe anything that may happen in the future, rather than use *likelihood*, *possibility* or any other synonym.

Prostate and **prostrate** are frequently confused. The former is the name of a gland at the neck of the bladder in male mammals and is used as a noun on its own – 'the prostate'– or as an adjective – 'the prostate gland'. The latter is an adjective, meaning lying face down – 'he was prostrate on the bed' – and is also a verb – 'he prostrated himself before the altar'. The dictionary lists a confusion between the two words – the 'prostrate gland' – dating back to the late seventeenth century.

Proved and **proven** *Proved* is part of the verb to prove, *proven* is the adjective derived from it. So one writes 'the prosecution proved that Smith was in the building at the time' but 'Smith was a proven liar'.

Provided See IF AND PROVIDED.

Psychiatrist and **psychologist** A *psychiatrist* is medically qualified; a *psychologist* is not.

Punctuation exists not merely for ease of reading, but also for ease of comprehension and the avoidance of ambiguity. If used correctly, it shows the reader how clauses in a sentence relate to each other; how sentences are delineated; and how an argument or exposition is broken up into PARAGRAPHS. As well as the technical aspects of punctuation that I shall outline here, it also has a vital stylistic dimension, which in the purest prose stems from punctuation being used precisely. Further details and discussion may be found under individual entries for punctuation marks. See also PUNCTUATION, AVOIDING COMMON MISTAKES IN.

A sentence begins with a capital letter and ends with a FULL STOP. In between those two points may come one, or several, CLAUSES. Clauses are often, but not always, separated from each other by commas. One important point about commas is both technical and stylistic: there are tendencies, according to the writer, to use these either excessively or insufficiently. It is the mark of the skilful writer that he uses them just when they are needed.

A comma helps define clauses that, if not so defined, could struggle to convey their accurate meaning. They also, as in this sentence and in the one preceding it, separate parenthetical matter from the main thrust of a sentence. See the entry for COMMA for a more detailed discussion.

More profound breaks in meaning than enabled by commas may be introduced by the SEMICOLON, which is often used to suggest a nuance between the meaning of two clauses. See the entry on that subject, and the one on COLONS, which make a more profound break still and have several specific uses.

Within a sentence, parentheses of a more emphatic sort than allowed by pairs of commas may be introduced to give some important explanatory information. These may take the form of brackets (such as surround this clause) or – to create a more staccato effect – dashes. See the entry on PARENTHESES and DASHES for more detail.

Questions, literal or rhetorical, must be terminated with a QUESTION MARK, and exclamations should be terminated with an EXCLAMATION MARK. See the entries on these subjects, and also APOSTROPHES, CONTRACTIONS and HYPHENS.

Accurate use of punctuation may, as much as careful word order, help avoid ambiguity in a sentence. However, in some cases of ELLIPSIS in sentences – the leaving out of words that, if included, might remove any hint of ambiguity, but which are left out for imagined reasons of elegance or felicity – punctuation is not enough. In a sentence such as 'the boy ate the beefburger with relish' are we to suppose he ate it enthusiastically, or with the complement of some sauce? The ellipsis is 'the boy ate the beefburger [that was covered] with relish'. A comma after *beefburger* would lead most readers to suppose the former, but even that is not certain. Sentences such as that, where phrases may be either adjectival or adverbial, are better recast: 'the boy ate the beefburger and relish' may mean only one thing; as may 'with relish, the boy ate the beefburger'.

Punctuation is important in all contexts, but especially with PARTICIPLES. The sentence 'the man having refused to open the door, the woman did it herself' is correctly punctuated. Inserting a comma after 'man' would make an absurdity of the sense. Sentences with participle constructions tend to be long; there should, therefore, always be proper regard to the use of punctuation.

Punctuation, avoiding common mistakes in If writers stick to the rules of punctuation as set out above they will come to no harm. Sometimes, as with all sets of rules, the exercise of judgement may be needed to avoid ambiguity or confusion. One of the prejudices of this book is against HYPHENS, whose use is defined in a separate entry. They have a place in compound adjectives, but rarely in compound nouns. No one would hyphenate *test match*; but should one not, on the same principle, leave the hyphen out of *cross-examination*? I should say it is necessary. The word *cross* is susceptible of too many interpretations. A *cross examination* could be an exhibition of bad temper in examining somebody or something. At all times in such circumstances, apply common sense before proceeding.

The greengrocer's apostrophe is the term given to the illiteracy of inserting an apostrophe before the plural of a noun – such as in *apple's*, *carrot's* or *potatoe's*. A variant of this is to take a word ending in *s* and make it plural by adding another *s* after an apostrophe – for example, *a brass*, *some brass's*. See APOSTROPHE for a detailed account of the potential pitfalls.

Avoiding ambiguity is one of the great purposes of the comma. Fowler gives two examples – 'he stopped, laughing' and 'he stopped laughing' – to demonstrate how its inclusion or omission can change the meaning of sentence. See COMMA for a full discussion of the ways in which this punctuation mark is misused. See also QUOTATIONS AND PARENTHESES, PUNCTUATION OF.

Purport means to appear to be something, as in: 'He purported to be a former SAS officer, because he had detailed knowledge of their training techniques.' It does not mean to *claim*.

Purse and **handbag** In Britain, a *purse* is used to contain coins and notes. In America, it is what the British call a *handbag*.

Puzzle and **riddle** A *riddle* is not a *puzzle*. The dictionary defines a riddle as 'a question or statement intentionally worded in a dark or puzzling manner, and propounded in order that it may be guessed or answered . . . an enigma, a dark saying'. There is nothing so sinister about a puzzle, a term that may be applied to the most harmless toy for children, or a pastime for older people.

Pyrrhic victory A *Pyrrhic victory* is not a pointless one. It is one won at so high a cost as to be questionable in its value to the victor.

Q

Qualitative and **quantitative** are written thus. The omission of the penultimate syllable is an illiteracy.

Quality The use of this noun, meaning the specification or condition of something – 'it was of low quality' – as an adjective is illogical. When someone says 'it was a quality garment' they imply it was of high quality, but it could just as easily be of low quality. If the garment is fine or of high quality, say so.

Quantity One has a *quantity* of a single commodity but a *number* of disparate commodities: 'a substantial quantity of coal was found in a number of collieries', but not 'a large quantity of people worked there'.

Queen Mother See ROYALTY.

Queen's Counsel, writing to or addressing This is a mark of seniority and distinction conferred upon certain barristers, who may then use the letters 'QC' after their names and who in being formally addressed in writing or being referred to formally should be accorded that suffix. Judges of the Crown Court and Recorders who are Queen's Counsel also retain the suffix – 'Judge Smith QC' – but judges of the High Court and above do not.

Queer is usually deemed to be an insulting term to use about a homosexual person but, as with the use by some black people of the even more offensive *nigger*, it is frequently used by those who are homosexual to describe their orientation and that of others like them. Those who are not should avoid the term in this context unless deliberately seeking to offend.

Query Used as a verb, it is a pompous and prolix way of saying or writing *ask*.

Question marks Any question in writing – whether it be literal, such as 'Have you put the kettle on?', or rhetorical – that is, a question that expects and requires no answer, such as 'Why shouldn't I have another glass?' – should terminate with a question mark. Just because a sentence contains an element of questioning does not mean it should take a question mark. 'He thought he should ask her what he should do?' is wrong because a direct question is not posed.

Queue The Americanism for the noun is *line*, for the verb is *stand in line*, and neither should be used in British English.

Quiet and **quieten** A battle the Fowlers prosecuted a century ago in *The King's English* about the verb *quiet* may have been lost, but there is no harm in mentioning it here. They deplored the verb *quieten* since it was a longer, and ignorant, version of the verb *quiet*. One would now write without a second thought (or even a first one) 'she quietened the child and he fell asleep'. It would be more correct to write 'she quieted the child', and be prepared to invite the quizzicality of one's readers.

Quintessentially See METAPHORS AND METAPHORICAL USAGE.

Quit, as the past tense of the verb, is an Americanism. Whereas an American would say 'I quit my job', a Briton would say 'I quitted', though he would be more likely to say 'I gave up'.

Quite The same strictures apply to this intensifier as to the use of RATHER. Therefore, one says or writes that 'it was quite a smell' and would insert an adjective thus – 'it was quite a bad smell'. 'It was a quite bad smell' is a SOLECISM, for if the adjective were removed, leaving the phrase 'it was a quite smell', the sentence would make no sense. *Quite* can either mean 'a lot' of something, or 'a little'. 'Quite a swell' means an excessive swell; 'it was quite good' means it was just a little better than ordinary.

Quotation marks If some prose (or, indeed, verse) includes dialogue, there will have to be quotation marks. These distinguish the voice of characters from the voice of the narrator. They will also have to be used if the writer is using a direct quotation from a source, to distinguish his own remarks from those of some other writer or speaker. If a quotation stretches over more than one sentence, do not insert the closing quotation marks until after the last sentence of the quotation has finished. If a quotation runs into a new paragraph, do not put the marks at the end of the paragraph break; but do open the first sentence of the new paragraph in the quotation with new marks, thus:

> 'I told him that he was a fool. He seemed unable to grasp the point. I tried again, but to my frustration there was no recognition of the fact.
>
> 'I hoped it would sink in eventually.'

If writing the name of a book, or a ship, italicise it: *The Canterbury Tales* or the HMS *Pinafore*. It is a matter of taste whether to italicise the names of poems or give them within single quotation marks: my prejudice is to italicise poems known by a specific title and put ones generally known by their first lines in single marks: so *Epithalamion* or *Idylls of the King*, but 'One day I wrote her name upon the strand' or 'Say not, the struggle naught availeth'.

Quotation marks are often used, notably in journalism, to question the veracity or accuracy of something by drawing attention to it in a snide fashion, sometimes with the preceding adjective 'so-called', rather than actually quoting something that has been said. This needs to be done with great care if one is to avoid a LIBEL writ. A remark such as 'we have all heard about Brown's "honest" way of life' could land the writer in serious trouble if Brown's dishonesty cannot be proved. Note how if a quotation is used within a quotation, different quotation marks must be used – doubles within singles, or vice versa.

Quotations If one is going to quote a phrase, be sure to quote it accurately. Also be sure it is relevant to your argument, and not just prompted by a desire to show off. Showing off *and* misquoting is a combination fatal to a writer's credibility. Milton did not, for example, write in *Lycidas* about 'fresh fields and pastures new', nor Shakespeare that 'all that glistens is not gold': though many subsequently have. See also ALLUSIONS, USE OF.

Quotations and parentheses, punctuation of The positioning of punctuation marks relative to PARENTHESES and QUOTATION MARKS is often a source of confusion. It is entirely logical, however, and should not give any difficulty. When a complete sentence is given in quotation marks, the full stop must come inside them, thus:

'I shall have none of that nonsense in here.'

However, this is the correct punctuation for a sentence that includes both matter within quotation marks and matter without them:

Mr Smith said 'I shall have none of that nonsense in here'.

If you are quoting matter that itself includes a quotation, the positioning of the full stop is again logical:

'Mr Smith said "I shall have none of that nonsense in here".'

Note the full stop comes after the internal quotation mark but before the quotation mark that comes after the end of the complete quoted sentence. Similarly, had the writer said

Jones remarked: 'Mr Smith said "I shall have none of that nonsense in here".'

that punctuation would be correct, as the full stop completes the sentence in direct speech and therefore must come between the single and the double quotation marks. In the following example, however, there is a problematic juxtaposition of single and double marks at the end of the sentence before the full stop:

Mr Smith said 'my favourite poem is "I wandered lonely as a cloud"'.

Professional typesetters usually introduce a small space between the single and double marks in order to distinguish them. Note the punctuation required in a sentence that contains an insertion that is outside quotation marks, such as:

'I think we shall have breakfast now', said Mrs Smith, 'and then go for a swim.'

There is also a typesetting convention for dialogue. Take, for example:

'I think we shall have breakfast now,' said Mrs Smith.

Although the sentence on its own would have had a full stop, according to convention one puts a comma in its place before 'Mrs Smith said' and keeps it inside the quotation mark.

Mrs Smith's statement would not have required a comma between *now* and *and*, but the insertion requires a parenthesis to be distinguished, and the commas therefore come outside the quotation marks. The Fowlers were against such use of commas, claiming that quotation marks were stops enough. Subsequent practice and logic disagree with them.

In like manner, should a sentence include a statement in parentheses it should have any final punctuation outside the closing bracket, as in this example:

He saw no reason to go to France for his holidays (and, in any case, he had plenty to do at work).

This could also be written as follows, with a subtle difference in punctuation:

He saw no reason to go to France for his holidays. (In any case, he had plenty to do at work.)

Since the second sentence is contained completely within the brackets, the full stop comes before rather than after the second parenthesis. A good stylist would observe that, in the second example, the parentheses are not really needed at all.

When quoting from other books, the writer should ensure that the placement of the final quotation mark takes into account the position of any punctuation in the original text. If a whole sentence in its own right is quoted in the middle of another sentence it may lose its initial capital letter and its full stop and simply be absorbed into the punctuation scheme of the greater sentence it helps create – for example one might write: 'The notion that, as Churchill said, "never in the field of human conflict was so much owed by so many to so few" was absolutely correct.'

Quote and **quotation** *Quote* is the verb: *quotation* is the noun, often shortened to 'quote', especially in popular journalism. The word 'quotes' is sometimes similarly used as an abbreviation for quotation marks – 'the sentence was written in quotes' – but that is SLANG and should be avoided in formal writing.

R

Race and **racial** As with the distinction between COASTAL and COASTAL, the Fowlers argued that *race* should be an adjective, not *racial*, as race was not a word of Latin origin. The battle is still on: we speak of 'race riots' but usually of 'racial prejudice'. The matter appears to have become idiomatic rather than etymological, and only the most extreme pedant would consider *racial* incorrect. So little regard is given to strict etymology now that no one would be likely to complain at the formation of an adjective from an Anglo-Saxon noun in this fashion – except on the grounds of instant redundancy, there already being a suitable alternative in the dictionary. *Racialist*, common a generation ago, has now been usurped by the ubiquitous *racist*.

Racked and **wracked** The former usually describes being tortured on the rack, and has acquired a metaphorical sense of describing emotional or psychological distress. The latter describes having undergone wreck, usually shipwreck, and to be utterly destroyed and ruined.

Radiographer and **radiologist** A *radiographer* is a technician trained to operate radiographical equipment; a *radiologist* is a qualified physician who specialises in radiology, the branch of medicine that deals with the diagnosis of disease by use of X-rays.

Raft A raft is a rudimentary floating object most familiar for aiding the escape from drowning of those who are shipwrecked. It has since the nineteenth century been used metaphorically in American English to describe a multiplicity or collection of people or things, presumably from the idea of a raft containing many people. This usage has now become so clichéd as to be meaningless, especially in political contexts – 'The Chancellor announced a raft of tax cuts', or 'the Prime Minister said a raft of new policies would help the country', and so on. The term is to be avoided.

Railroad is an Americanism for *railway*.

Raise and **rise** The word *raise*, as a noun and as a verb with a new meaning, has crept into British English from American. Britons have, or ask for, a *pay rise* rather than a *raise*; and their children are *brought up* rather than *raised*. Milton demonstrated the legitimate usage of the verb – to elevate something – in his exordium to *Paradise Lost*: 'What in me is dark, illumine; what is low, raise and support.'

Rare and **scarce** There are some adjectives that offer gradations of description, but which we tend to misuse. To take one example: *scarce* and *rare* do not mean the same thing. A *rare* stamp is one that was printed in small quantities and (pending the discovery of a cache of thousands of them) that will always be in short supply. A *scarce* stamp is one that has not always been in short supply, but which at this particular point is hard to find because the market lacks sellers of them. *Rare* objects are usually valuable; the price of *scarce* ones rises with their scarcity, but falls when they become more plentiful. The terms are not synonymous or interchangeable.

Rather There are several pitfalls associated with this apparently innocuous word. As with *somewhat*, it may be used to qualify certain adjectives, and indeed some adverbs; and when it qualifies incomparable adjectives the usage commits an offence against logic, which is to be avoided. Something cannot be 'rather unique' or 'rather dead'. Something can, however, be 'rather large' or 'rather ugly', as these are adjectives that admit of degree. If the adjective you are about to qualify with such an adverb is an ABSOLUTE then do not qualify it. If the sense of what you wish to say seems to demand it, then it may be a sign that you should choose a different, non-absolute adjective. If you find yourself about to write, for example, 'rather innocuous', write instead 'rather mild', *mild* being an adjective susceptible to degree.

Also, one does not prefer to do something *than* to do something else; one prefers to do something *rather than* to do something else. So 'I prefer to swim than to ride' is wrong; 'I prefer to swim rather than to ride' is correct but prolix. It is better, if possible, to use nouns: 'I prefer swimming to riding'. Finally, when using the construction *rather a* do not be tempted to invert it when an adjective comes along. There is nothing wrong with 'she was rather a harridan' and a good writer would add an adjective as follows: 'she was rather an ugly harridan'. The construction 'she was a rather ugly harridan' is to be avoided; if the adjective is removed the construction 'a rather harridan' makes no sense, whereas 'rather a harridan' would. The same stricture applies to QUITE.

Re This Latin word, a shortening of *in re*, which means *in the matter of* and therefore *about* or *concerning,* was a staple of mid-twentieth-century bureaucratic communication, as in 'Re: your tax return'. It should be avoided.

Reactionary and **reactive** are not to be confused. The former is an adjective used to describe a policy or a person that is resistant to social or political progress, and wishes to revert to an earlier state of affairs. It may also be used as a noun to describe one who holds such views. *Reactive* is an adjective used to describe a person, object or process that reacts or responds to something after the event – the opposite of *proactive*.

Really is one of the most ubiquitous FILLERS in spoken English, along with *actually* and *in fact.* A sentence such as 'I thought I'd really have to go to sleep' displays how pointless the word is. Some people may not think quickly enough to eliminate it in speech. It should be much easier to do so in writing.

Realtor is an American term for what the British call an *estate agent*. Although *real estate* as a term for property has slowly crept into British English usage, the word to describe someone who facilitates deals in it has not.

Reason In a sentence such as 'the reason I did not go was because I was ill', omit either *because* or *the reason . . . was* to avoid a tautology.

Rebut See REFUTE, REBUT AND REJECT.

Recycling Sometimes even a participle becomes a noun. One of the VOGUE preoccupations of this era is environmentalism, and it has had an effect on language. What we used to call 'material for recycling' – which is what some of us still call it – has simply become *recycling*; however, the word is not a noun, it is a participle.

Redundant words Some writers seem unaware of their use of redundant words. Why should someone say 'the painting we bought was the best one in the gallery', when the *one* is redundant? Another example of this pointlessness is 'the restaurant we ate in was one known around the world'. There was a time when grammarians were united in their ridicule for the construction *prepared to* as in 'I am prepared to vouch for the fact that . . .' The verbal construction is unnecessary and verbose: the test for this is that if the construction *am prepared to* is removed and replaced by *will* or *shall*, the sense of the sentence remains unchanged. This, indeed, is the test for all writing; if a word or phrase can be removed from a clause or sentence without altering its meaning or rendering it more obscure, remove it. Our language, written and spoken, is littered with pointless words that are verbal tics or FILLERS: words and phrases such as *actually*, *really*, *in fact* or, perhaps most vacuous of all, *in actual fact*. Some people appear incapable of eliminating these in speech; it ought to be far easier to do so in writing.

Even apparently sharp writing may contain redundancies.

One can often express things more concisely by using a verb instead of a noun. Why write 'both examples are illustrations of the depravity of politicians' when you can write 'both examples illustrate the depravity'? Depending upon the context, one might not even need the word *examples*. One cannot always do entirely without abstract nouns: but the less abstract language, the better. Another such is 'these things are reminders of . . .' when one could without impairing the sense write 'these remind us'; *things* is also all too often a word with no point to it. Nouns (notably, again, abstract ones) in verbose constructions also sometimes take the place of simple adjectives. The teacher who says 'there is too much noise in this class' would better say 'this class is too noisy'.

As the entry on ADJECTIVES makes clear, many of these are superfluous and clutter up prose and its meaning. Some adjectives are instantly redundant. Consider the sentence: 'He had eaten three different Mars bars.' The Mars bars were *different* from what? *Different* is unnecessary; the sentence conveys just as much information without it. For pointless prepositions, see under PREPOSITIONS.

Referendum The plural *referendums* is quite correct, though the more classically minded will prefer *referenda*. The Latin plural is not necessary, however, because the singular noun is now sufficiently anglicised. The same is true of *forums* and *dictums*, among others. See FOREIGN WORDS AND PHRASES and PLURALS.

Reflexive pronouns The reflexive pronouns *myself*, *yourself*, *himself*, *herself*, *itself*, *oneself*, *ourselves*, *yourselves* and *themselves* are horribly misused today. Perhaps it has something to do with the increasing self-obsession of modern life. It should have purely an emphatic use, as in 'I did it myself' or 'he attended to the matter himself', which suggests a point of contrast – he did it himself as opposed to someone else doing it for him – or it should serve as the object of a reflexive verb, as in 'you should be ashamed of yourselves' or 'she promised to take care of herself'. What it emphatically is not is a synonym for the

PERSONAL PRONOUN in any of its cases. Phrases such as 'he gave it to myself' or 'I saw yourself there' are sheer abominations.

Reflexive verbs are ones with which one does the action to oneself – in French they are preceded in the infinitive by the reflexive pronoun *se*, as in *se pencher* (to lean), *se laver* (to wash oneself), *s'asseoir* (to sit down) or *se tromper* (to be mistaken).

Refutatio is the part of a classical argument in which the writer or speaker seeks to refute or dismiss, by recourse to evidence and logic, the arguments of his opponents.

Refute, rebut and **reject** *Refute* is a verb often used by people who simply mean CONTRADICT (discussed in a separate entry) or *deny*. *Contradiction* and *denial* are forms of assertion; they rely on the force of will of the gainsayer to press home his point, rather than upon any evidence contrary to whatever it is he is contradicting. *Refutation* requires proof. You may say that a painting is beautiful, I that it is ugly. Since it is a subjective exercise, neither of us can prove his point. We are merely contradicting each other, or each is denying the truth of the statement made by the other. I may say the train for London is scheduled to leave at 11.30. You may say it goes at 11.45. By recourse to the timetable, I can *refute* your claim. To *rebut* a contention is to offer an argument against it, but not necessarily to prove it is wrong. To *reject* is simply to throw a claim out, without necessarily proof or argument of any description.

Regrettably and **regretfully** If something is described as having been done *regrettably*, then it is to be deplored by all right-thinking people and made a cause for regret, as in 'regrettably, the child died before its third birthday'. If something is done *regretfully*, then the person doing it is full of regret for his actions, as in 'Regretfully, we must dispense with your services.'

Rein and **reign** The former is a harness used to drive horses or teams of dogs, usually used in the plural; the latter describes the period on the throne of a monarch, or the period in office of a pope, and it may be used figuratively to describe any other period of power – 'Mrs Thatcher's reign at Number 10'. To write that 'he held the reigns of power' would be illiterate.

Reject See REFUTE, REBUT AND REJECT.

Relative clauses A relative clause will be introduced by a relative pronoun, as in 'she drank the cocktail, *which her friend had ordered for her*' or 'he introduced his wife to the doctor, *whom he had met on holiday*'. See CLAUSES.

Relative pronouns The relative pronouns are *as*, *such as*, *that*, *what*, *which* and *who*. The first two most people would not recognise as pronouns at all, but the first is (though it sometimes pretends to be adverbial) and the second truly is.

Perhaps the most common mistake of all with pronominal usages is the misuse of *which* and *that* as relative pronouns. It is probably not an exaggeration to say that almost everyone believes they are in most contexts interchangeable. They are not. The two sentences 'the dog that was run over belonged to Mrs Smith' and 'the dog, which was run over, belonged to Mrs Smith' say different things in two quite different ways. The first suggests there were a number of dogs, and the one that happened to be run over belonged to Mrs Smith. The second supposes there was only one dog. It happened also to be run over, which (unfortunate though that may be) is not the point of the story. The point is that it belonged to Mrs Smith. *That* defines; *which* is parenthetic, or non-defining. If one is having a conversation with another about the merits of various cars, and one wishes to make the point that a car one used to own broke down, one would say 'the car that I used to own broke down', implying that cars one did not own did not break down. If one says 'the car, which I used to own, broke down' one suggests that the main point one is making is that the car broke down and, incidentally, one used to own it. The reverse also applies. If one says 'the coin that I found in the garden is valuable' one implies that one has found coins all over the place, but it is only the one found in the garden that is worth anything. If that is the only coin one has found, and one wishes to stress its value but provide the incidental information that one found it in the garden, then one must say 'the coin, which I found in the garden, is valuable'.

A book review in a magazine early in 2010 exemplified in two successive sentences the incorrect, and then the correct, usages of *which*. 'It was not surprising that they rejected the UN partition resolution which gave them only half of their country', read the first. Perhaps it was a stylistic consciousness that prevented the writer from using a second *that* after the conjunction earlier in the sentence; yet it led him to use a parenthetic *which* when he should have used a defining *that*. To avoid repetition he could have omitted the conjunction without any danger of creating an ambiguity; or he could have inserted a comma before *which*, making it into a parenthesis without disturbing the sense of what he was writing. The next sentence – 'There followed a war between the Palestinians and the Jews, which saw 200,000–300,000 Palestinians driven, one way or another, from their homes' – uses the pronoun correctly.

In talking about people rather than things or abstracts there appears to be no such distinction; there is only the relative pronoun *who* or *whom*. (*Who* should be used only with reference to persons; I write more about this below.) So one would have to distinguish the two meanings by use of punctuation. 'The girl whom I saw was wearing a pink dress' is a statement that suggests that a number of people have seen girls, but the one that this person saw was (unlike the others) wearing a pink dress. 'The girl, whom I saw, was wearing a pink dress' conveys the information that we know there was one girl, that the important point is that the speaker saw her, and he can disclose she was wearing a pink dress. However, there is another way to make the distinction. It was quite common, and accepted, usage until the early part of the last century to use *that* for *who* or *whom* just as in clauses featuring objects or abstracts: so one would have said 'the woman that had a hat on broke her arm' to indicate that she was one of a number of women being considered but the only one who had a hat on; but 'the woman, who had a hat on, broke her arm' would be used to indicate that the woman has already been specified, that she broke her arm, and that (by the way) she was wearing a hat. Of the two types of usage, I prefer the first. The second, using *that*, is not incorrect, but it now seems archaic; and if one punctuates correctly there is no risk of ambiguity.

Lest these sorts of distinctions seem pedantic in the extreme, Onions gives an example that shows their value. It is 'all the members of the council, who were also members of the Education Board, were to assemble in the board room'. The meaning to be conveyed is that only those members of the council who were members of the Education Board as well were to meet in the board room; and Onions argues this would be clear only if the punctuation were to be removed and the relative pronoun *who* were replaced by *that*. That may have been true at the time he wrote a century ago, according to the prevailing idiom; and, as I have said, his point shows the importance of the distinction. However today the idiom requires simply that the two commas in the sentence be removed, dispensing with the parenthesis, and then the meaning is clear.

What is always wrong, it must be stressed, is to use the pronoun *which* to refer to people, and the pronoun *who* to refer to objects. Less heinous is the use of the possessive pronoun *whose* when not applied to people. Its usage in a phrase such as 'John asked Mary whose book she had borrowed' is straightforward and understood; but during the last century usages such as 'he despised a government whose policies could have brought about such a thing' or 'she collected her car, whose damaged windscreen had been repaired' have become accepted, to avoid the apparent clumsiness or pomposity of the strictly correct alternative. That would be 'a government of which the policies' and 'her car, of which the damaged windscreen'. Pedants may legitimately stick to such usages, which are not yet universally regarded as outmoded, and which I would argue are still more acceptable than the alternative in the most formal writing. We are lucky we have a word such as *whose* at all; there is no equivalent in French, for example, where a construction using the pronoun *dont* – meaning 'of which' – has to be used instead.

That, when used as a relative pronoun, may in certain idiomatic usages be omitted, even now in quite formal writing. 'The car that I bought had an interior that I thought was very tasteful' overdoes the *that*s, and one of them may without difficulty be omitted – preferably the first. Some grammarians have sought to lay down rules for when the relative pronoun, and indeed *that* when used as a conjunction, may successfully be omitted: but to my mind each case has to be judged on its merits. If there is a danger of ambiguity or confusion, leave it in. If there is not, take it out, on the principle that any superfluous word should always be removed from a piece of writing. So one ought to leave the conjunction in a phrase such as 'he saw that the dog, being run over, would have to be put down', as removing it would give the hasty reader the impression that the man had seen the dog being run over, which he had not necessarily done. The verb is susceptible of two meanings, which makes the conjunction especially valuable in removing a possible ambiguity. However, in a sentence such as 'she wore the dress that she had ironed', where *that* is a pronoun, removing it creates no ambiguity; 'she wore the dress she had ironed' can mean only one thing. However, were the sentence to read 'she wore the dress she had bought in London' one might be led to think that London was the place where she wore the dress, not where she bought it. Were it to read instead 'she wore the dress that she had bought in London' the meaning would become a little clearer: she has many dresses, and may have bought them in various places, but she wore the one that she had bought in London. We are not sure what to make of the dress if the pronoun is removed. It should be obvious that the pronoun *which*, if used correctly in its non-defining and parenthetical sense, may never be removed. A correctly framed sentence, such as 'she wore the dress, which she had bought in London, to the party that evening' must change its meaning if the *which* is removed. The punctuation has to be removed too, and the sentence then ceases describing a specific dress and describes instead one of many dresses she has – one she happens to have bought in London. The entire emphasis is altered.

Something that is always ugly is the construction *that which*: 'I chose to wear a dress different from *that which* I had worn the previous day', or 'he would not order a claret other than *that which* he chose every time he ate in the restaurant'. If one must write such a sentence, the correct usage in both cases is the only slightly less inelegant, and much more confusing, *that that*. No doubt it is its propensity to confuse that causes it to be replaced by *that which*. The elegant writer would recast both sentences: 'I chose to wear a dress different from the one I had worn the previous day' and 'he would not order any claret other than the one he chose every time he ate in the restaurant'. See also CONJUNCTIONS.

Relevant has become political jargon, as in phrases such as 'It's a socially relevant issue'. One should assume that most of what is advanced by politicians is pertinent to society, otherwise they would not bother to advance it, so such expressions are pleonastic and redundant.

Reluctant and **reticent** To be *reluctant* is to be unwilling to do something. Sometimes the adjective *reticent* is used by mistake – 'he was reticent to agree'. The *reluctance* of one who is *reticent* is solely in his willingness to speak. However, the dictionary cites a wrong usage of this as far back as 1875.

Repairable and **reparable** The dictionary gives the first use of *repairable* as dating from 1489, of *reparable* from years later: both seem to be current, though pedants prefer the idiomatic usage of the latter, citing its Latin antecedents (via the French) as the justification.

Repeat The logic of this word should be borne in mind. When something is repeated for the *second* time it is its *third* occurrence: and so on.

Repetition of words is a vice that indicates bad writing. An essential of good style is a large vocabulary. This does not merely enable the writer to choose the word that exactly suits his purpose, it also gives him the discrimination to reject those that do not. There is a further use of a large vocabulary, and that is to help avoid repetition. A piece of writing that includes the same words or phrases over and over again is tedious to the reader. Words have a musical quality, even when not read aloud, and too many of the same note will jar. Repetition retards the process of communicating meaning and causes the reader to doubt the clarity of thought, and therefore intelligence, of the writer. In some writing it is impossible to avoid repeating certain words or phrases. A report may well require the frequent mention of a person's name. If that person has a job title, then his post may be varied with his name – 'Mr Smith' or 'the minister', for example. Personal pronouns may also be used, but this may lead to vagueness or confusion if the report is about more than one person of the same gender.

There is no excuse, however, for repeating nouns, adjectives, verbs or adverbs that have synonyms. It is also wise to be sparing with conjunctions. A phrase such as 'he argued that it was important that politicians should remember that their policies had a widespread effect that was not always obvious' is just shocking and thoughtless. The sentence should be recast, perhaps as follows: 'he argued the importance of politicians' remembering that their policies had a widespread, and not always obvious, effect'. The surviving *that* is important for the avoidance of ambiguity. It is not their policies that the politicians should remember, but the effect they have.

There will be some instances in any piece of writing in which it is legitimate to repeat a phrase not merely for emphasis, but for clarity. Such a device is common in speech-making: remember Churchill's 'we shall go on to the end, we shall fight in France, we shall fight on the seas and oceans, we shall fight with growing confidence and growing strength in the air, we shall defend our Island, whatever the cost may be, we shall fight on the beaches, we shall fight on the landing grounds, we shall fight in the fields and in the streets, we shall fight in the hills; we shall never surrender'. However, it also has its uses in normal prose-writing. Without repeating more than one word – the preposition *in* – Ruskin in this extract from *The Poetry of Architecture* repeats the form of a phrase but builds up a clear picture of an aspect of design that offends him: 'and the whole system becomes utterly and absolutely absurd, ugly in outline, worse than useless in application, unmeaning in design, and incongruous in association'.

The most common form of repetition is of a substantive word, repeated for emphasis: 'The satires are savage – perhaps satires should be; but Pope's satires are sometimes what satires should never be – shrill.' This only just works, and one imagines that *satires* is repeated, and not replaced by a pronoun in a couple of instances, not for the avoidance of ambiguity, but to impress upon the reader that Pope's works under that name are not what the writer nor the reader understands by the term. Sometimes, humour is advanced by repeating whole phrases, as in this extract from *Martin Chuzzlewit* by Dickens: 'These injuries having been comforted externally, with patches of pickled brown paper, and Mr Pecksniff having been comforted internally, with some stiff brandy-and-water, the eldest Miss Pecksniff sat down to make the tea . . .' As with any form of joke, joke by repetition can wear thin, so be sparing. The main stylistic argument against repetition is that it may be distracting to the reader. So too, however, may be the use of increasingly florid synonyms, so be thoughtful when using them.

Nor is it just the repetition of words that is tiresome in writing or in speech. Any attempt to be concise or interesting must be thwarted if the same idea is repeated. And to repeat the same thought using different words – as in 'stupid idiot' is a tautology and another sign of unclear thinking. See also ANAPHORA.

Repetitious and **repetitive** are almost synonymous. The shade of difference between the two in British English usage is that the former has a strain of the pejorative about it, emphasising the tediousness and futility of the repeat; the latter is a neutral statement of fact. In American English the two words appear to have become interchangeable, with *repetitious* the more popular of the two.

Reported speech A report of actions that have taken place and are completed requires the past tense. In some journalism writers use the present tense even when reporting past events in order to convey a sense of immediacy. This may have its place in writing, for example, an account of an interview, but it has no place in news reporting, where it simply conveys a tone of cheapness and sensationalism. In more formal writing, in which a writer may be giving an account of events, it is simply wrong. So if a writer wishes to report or record that the Prime Minister said 'I have told the French president that we can accept no more imports of French beef until the French authorities have re-established proper quality control', he has to put everything one tense back – the present becomes the imperfect and the perfect becomes the pluperfect. Therefore, this sentence would be written: 'The Prime Minister said he had told the French president that Britain could accept no more imports of French beef until the French authorities had re-established proper quality control.' Note too that the pronoun *we* has to change – since 'he' or even 'they' would be unclear, the word 'Britain' – which is what the Prime Minister meant – must be substituted for it. For stylistic reasons, in reporting long passages of speech break them up to help the reader, but avoid undue repetition of 'he said'. There are other options – 'he claimed', 'he asserted', 'he continued' and so on.

A further point about reported speech: in its purest form it contains no question marks, because no direct question is asked; and no exclamation marks either, for there are no exclamations. Both question and exclamation are neutralised by the report. Were one reporting 'Will you come to dinner with me?' one would write 'he asked whether she would go to dinner with him'. Note also the change of verb, to make it impersonal in the report. 'I don't believe it!' is reported as 'he said he did not believe it'. When writing in reported speech about events destined for the future, use the form 'the captain said that after his successful debut, Smith would go on to open the batting for England' rather than 'Smith was to go on to open the batting'. See also SEQUENCE OF TENSES and SHALL AND WILL.

Respect is a much-misused word today. See **TABLOID PRESS**.

Respective(ly) This adjective and its associated adverb needs to be deployed with care. A correct usage is 'Smith and Jones were fined £50 and £100 respectively'. The adverb indicates that the two men were fined the two sums in the order in which they are listed – £50 for Smith and £100 for Jones However, in a phrase such as 'Smith and Jones paid their respective fines' the adjective is superfluous, since no differentiation is made between the fines. And in the statement 'Smith, Jones and Walker were respectively fined and imprisoned' the use of the adverb makes no sense at all, since two actions are attributed to three names. Were there just two names it would make perfect sense.

Responsible Only sentient beings can be *responsible*. To say that 'the rain was responsible for the road accident' is nonsense. The rain can aggravate conditions that caused the accident, or can help lead to the accident occurring, but an accident implies human error, so it is a person who is responsible.

Rest room In America, this is not a place where one goes to sit or lie down: it is the *lavatory*.

Reticent See **RELUCTANT AND RETICENT**.

Revealed See **DISCLOSED AND REVEALED**.

Reverend, use of In America, it is normal usage to address or refer to an ordained minister as 'Reverend Jackson'. It is a solecism in British English. See **CLERGY, WRITING TO OR ADDRESSING**.

Revert This in itself means to restore, return or go back to a previous condition or habit or custom, with specialist legal meanings connected with the restoration of property. Therefore 'revert back' is a solecism and a tautology: *back* is the only direction in which a thing or a person can *revert*. See **ADVERBS, USED POINTLESSLY**.

Riddle See PUZZLE AND RIDDLE.

Ringer and **wringer** The former is either a bell or bell pull, or one who rings a bell, or it is slang for someone passing himself off as someone else. A *wringer* is a mangle, a device for squeezing the excess water out of washed clothes.

Rob See BURGLE AND ROB.

Roll out This is a peculiarly silly contemporary cliché, an egregious part of management-speak in which five-year plans, new products, or even websites are 'rolled out', that is to say, put before the public, initiated, launched or begun. It is hard to take anyone who uses this phrase so seriously as he would wish.

Round See AROUND AND ROUND.

Round robin A *round robin* is not a communication that is sent to many people: it is one that is signed by a number of people, originally in a circular pattern to disguise the order in which they had signed. However, the incorrect usage dates back to the 1870s, and is now the more common.

Royalty, correctly styling The Sovereign is always His or Her Majesty. The Queen Consort of a King is also Her Majesty. The husband of a Queen Regnant is usually a Prince and is styled His Royal Highness. The children of the Sovereign, his or her grandchildren through the male line and the grandchildren of the Prince of Wales are also styled His or Her Royal Highness, as are the wives of male royal highnesses.

Care needs to be taken with the title *Queen Mother*, accorded to a Queen dowager who is the mother of the reigning sovereign, which expires with the holder. The last person to be so called, Queen Elizabeth, is still referred to as 'the Queen Mother' as if the title was hers alone. In the twentieth century both Queen Alexandra and Queen Mary were also Queens Mother (note the plural: the use of 'mother' is adjectival, and so does not become plural). If Queen Elizabeth must be referred to in another way, it is as 'the late Queen Mother', distinguishing her from her predecessors. The best usage for all former Queens Mother, as with Queens Dowager (those, like Queen Adelaide, without a child who ascends the throne), is simply to take the regnal name – so the last Queen Mother is now, correctly, simply Queen Elizabeth.

Royalty, writing to or addressing To start with the Sovereign: she should be addressed simply as 'Madam' at the start of any letter, which should conclude with the equally simple 'Yours faithfully'. Her sons should be addressed as 'Sir' and her daughter as 'Madam'; this rule holds good for all those bearing the style and title of Royal Highness. In speech, address the Sovereign, her daughter and other female Royal Highnesses as 'ma'am' and all male Royal Highnesses as 'sir'.

Rubbish Nouns do transmute into adjectives, and one especially depressing example of this in recent years has been *rubbish* becoming an adjective – 'a *rubbish* football team', 'a *rubbish* film', 'a *rubbish* pop group'. It is depressing because it is not as though the English language lacks terms to describe low quality or inadequacy. I should not have to stress that these absurdities have no place in serious writing, but I shall.

Rules of good writing As literacy became more widespread after the expansion of the middle classes from the time of the English Civil War onwards, and especially after the 1870 Education Act in Great Britain brought reading and writing to the children of the working classes, so a language whose form had been agreed by educated people began to mutate in a fashion that lay outside that agreement. Two types of offence provoked hostility – or snobbery, depending upon one's point of view – to this mutation. The first was the sheer misuse of words, and the abuse of grammar. The second, related to the first, was the difficulty in communicating effectively that these CATACHRESES and SOLECISMS caused. Some people were now being educated to a point where they learned not only how to use words that would once have been above their station, but to use them with something approaching grammatical propriety. However, they were often nonetheless verbose, particularly if they worked in any sort of petty officialdom. It was the sight of these offences that caused various learned men (and, at that point, they were almost exclusively men) to begin to write manuals telling the newly literate and the insufficiently educated that, if they wished to use these precision tools of language, they had better use them according to the rules that those more experienced in them had always adopted.

The brothers Fowler, in 1906, opened their magisterial work *The King's English* with five rules about a writer's choice of words. To generations of users of English these became a holy writ of literary fundamentalism. We should therefore note them here:

Prefer the familiar word to the far-fetched.

Prefer the concrete word to the abstract.

Prefer the single word to the circumlocution.

Prefer the short word to the long.

Prefer the Saxon word to the Romance.

The Fowlers added that 'these rules are given roughly in order of merit', which one assumes is how *circumlocution* came to survive beyond the proof stage. The rules are the codification of the book's first sentence, codified, it seems, for the benefit of the hard of understanding: 'Any one who wishes to become a good writer should endeavour, before he allows himself to be tempted by the more showy qualities, to be direct, simple, brief, vigorous and lucid.' *Endeavour* is a synonym for *try*.

The Fowlers' book is still in print more than 100 years after its first appearance and has sold hundreds of thousands of copies. Yet the message remained, and still remains, slow to sink in. That was why George Orwell, in his 1946 essay *Politics and the English Language*, also set some rules for the struggling communicator:

i. Never use a metaphor, simile or other figure of speech which you are used to seeing in print.

ii. Never use a long word where a short one will do.

iii. If it is possible to cut a word out, always cut it out.

iv. Never use the passive where you can use the active.

v. Never use a foreign phrase, a scientific word or a jargon word if you can think of an everyday English equivalent.

vi. Break any of these rules sooner than say anything outright barbarous.

Another way of making the last of those points is Winston Churchill's celebrated line about 'this is the sort of English up with which I will not put'.

Everyone who writes a book about English usage will have his own rules, and presume to inflict them on his readers. I am no different. The Fowler/Orwell rules seem serviceable to me, given the importance of a writer's being understood and communicating a message or idea. Rather than outline rules, perhaps I may be allowed to outline the bones of a philosophy with which I approach English as a professional writer.

First, I see no reason for orthography to be varied, since we have had a completed standard dictionary for nearly ninety years. Second, I see no reason for grammar to be varied, since there has been general agreement among educated people about how it should work for even longer than we have had a dictionary. That agreement has been based on sound logical and historical principles. The grammar agreed upon is one that allows such a high degree of precision that it eliminates almost all ambiguities and is easily comprehensible. Perhaps the last important development in our grammar (as opposed to a change's being caused by deliberate neglect or abuse, as with the very useful SUBJUNCTIVE MOOD) was that of the passive voice, as we now recognise it, in the early nineteenth century. Jane Austen wrote that 'the house was building'. Within a few decades this had become 'the house was being built'. This change in grammar seems to me defensible in that it imposed greater precision and removed scope for AMBIGUITY. These must be the aims of any system of grammar.

Third, given that we have (according to the latest edition of the *Oxford English Dictionary*) over 171,000 words in our language, plus another 47,500 classed as obsolete and 9,500 derived from existing words, I see no reason for a word to be used in other than its etymologically correct sense. This is not to be construed as an objection to new words' entering the language: only a fool would take such a view, since new concepts, objects and experiences occur all the time and a new word may be required to describe them accurately. Usually, those words will come about by a logical means, often by reference to a classical antecedent: it is why an era of invention gave us *telephone*, *television*, *refrigerator* and *video*. However, wilful misuse of a word to describe something for which plenty of other words already exist seems to me to be unpardonable, even if in some instances the dictionary has capitulated and admitted to a new meaning. It can also be confusing to those readers who have a careful appreciation of the meaning of words. I would refer readers who still harbour doubts about this to the entries on PREVARICATE AND PROCRASTINATE and FLAUNT AND FLOUT, for example. There is a difference between a word that subtly changes its meaning over a long period of time – such as *naughty*, for example, where the logic of the change can be traced – and one that changes its meaning because of the ignorance of people who use it in mistake for another similar word. We live in a harsh world, and one of its harshnesses is that we are sometimes judged by the way we use our language. One who uses a word wrongly may go undetected among his peers only to be snared at a crucial moment by someone he is trying to impress. It is better, if one seeks to be taken seriously, not to run the risk of such humiliation.

My fourth and final prejudice, now that I have expressed my strictness about grammar, spelling and vocabulary, is about concision in expression. There is little point in spelling correctly, having immaculate grammar and using each word in its correct sense if one is verbose. Most of us, when we read verbose writing, think of it as flannel. We lose respect for the writer and discount his opinions. One should strive not to have that effect on one's readers. Therefore, use the minimum number of words to say whatever you have to say.

Run American politicians *run* for office: in Britain they *stand*.

S

Same, the This is a PRONOUN, as in 'I had a beer and he had the same'.

Sanitarium and **sanatorium** both mean a hospital or a nursing home, or a place where the sick are restored to health. The second usage is far more common.

Sarcasm See IRONY AND SARCASM.

Sat and **sitting** One often sees the solecism 'people were sat'. This is grammatically impossible. What a writer who abuses the verb in this way means is 'people were sitting', or 'people were seated'. Best of all – since we should always prefer the active voice to the passive – he would have written 'people sat'. See also STOOD AND STANDING.

Satire is the process of holding up people, institutions, customs, follies or vices to ridicule, often by use of some of the other rhetorical devices – notably PARODY, HYPERBOLE, MEIOSIS, CATACHRESIS and PARADOX.

Scarce See RARE AND SCARCE.

Sceptic is the British spelling; the American spelling is *skeptic*.

Science, the It has become fashionable to put a definite article in front of the noun *science* when a speaker or writer is referring to a particular branch of it, such as that examining global warming. From the tone of voice used by those who do so, it seems they feel that to speak of *the science* adds extra authority to their pronouncements. Instead of saying 'the science supports our view' they should say 'scientific analysis' or 'the results of scientific research'. *The science* sounds pompous and silly to that large portion of mankind who are not scientists. There is also, perhaps, something faintly sinister about the way the use of the definite article seems to make an abstract noun into a concrete one, with all the ramifications of reducing debate on it.

Scotch, **Scots** and **Scottish** *Scotch* is the adjective for whisky and is used in certain other phrases: 'Scotch eggs', 'mist', 'ale' and 'broth', for example. The people and everything else – except the tree, *Scots pine* – have the adjective *Scottish*. As for nouns, there are Scotsmen and Scotswomen, or simply *Scots*.

Searing Its metaphorical use has become an overworked cliché, as in 'it was a searing experience for both of them'. Unless writing about cooking meat at a high temperature, or cauterising a wound, avoid. See METAPHOR.

Seasonable and **seasonal** *Seasonable* applies to something that is suitable for a certain time of year – it is seasonable to have snow in January, or hot sunshine in July, or to have gales around the equinoxes, or to wear an overcoat in winter. *Seasonal* describes something that occurs at a particular time of year – strawberries in June, raspberries in July, apples in August, walnuts in September.

Second and **secondly** See FIRST AND FIRSTLY.

See The verb *to see* has been distorted to allow inanimate objects or even concepts to 'see' in a way of which they were previously thought incapable, as in 'today sees the arrival of the new teacher', 'the revised plan sees the demolition of the old buildings', 'the road sees a new development in traffic calming' and so on. As with other overused verbs, this usage betokens a reluctance to think more energetically and specifically, and a failure to think logically about the feasibility of a verb taken out of its literal context. See also DO.

Seeing This has become an all-purpose conjunction, developing from its original status as a participle, as in 'it was a surprise that he ate anything, seeing he was so ill'. Along with *considering*, *bearing in mind* and *given that*, it has usurped the place once held by *because* and *since*.

-self/-selves See REFLEXIVE PRONOUNS.

Semicolons These introduce into writing a break more significant than the comma, but less so than the colon or the full stop. One frequent use for the semicolon is in introducing a nuance, or a contrast between clauses. One such example is this description of Walter Hammond's batting: 'He did not walk to the wicket; he strode.' The semicolon also separates what Onions and the Fowlers would have called 'independent sentences' – or what I would call clauses – each of which has a subject and a predicate. For example: 'He sat down at the table; his wife sat next to him.' A semicolon never introduces a list – that is the job of the colon – but it may punctuate one. For example: 'The following are the duties of a housemaid: sweep out the grates; lay the fires; dust the furniture; sweep the floors.' See also PUNCTUATION.

Sensual and **sensuous** The first adjective is applied to someone abnormally predisposed to pursue gratification of the senses, as in 'she was a highly sensual woman'. In contemporary usage it is usually connected with carnal pleasures. The second adjective is applied to something gratifying to the senses, as in 'the sensuous pleasure of listening to Beethoven or eating foie gras'.

Sentences Look at a page of prose – such as this – and you will notice that most obviously it consists of paragraphs. Within each paragraph are sentences. There are three sorts of sentence: the *simple sentence*, the *complex sentence* and the *compound sentence*. They all begin with capital letters. The dictionary defines a sentence as 'a series of words in connected speech or writing, forming the grammatically complete expression of a single thought; in popular use often such a portion of a composition or utterance as extends from one full stop to another'. Within the sentence, groups of words will be arranged – it is to be hoped with grammatical accuracy – within CLAUSES. In defining the sentence the dictionary goes on to make a more technical definition peculiar to grammar, which we must take note of: 'the verbal expression of a proposition, question, command, or request, containing normally a subject and a predicate (though either of these may be omitted by ellipsis)'. We had better define some of these terms. A PREDICATE is what is said about the SUBJECT. 'The boy hit the ball' has 'the boy' as the subject and 'hit the ball' as the predicate. A simple sentence is as just defined and exemplified – one that has a subject and a predicate. A complex sentence has a SUBORDINATE CLAUSE. 'The boy hit the ball, which flew over the hedge' would be an example of that. A compound sentence has more than one subject or predicate. 'The boy hit the ball, which flew over the hedge, but which the dog retrieved' is a compound sentence.

In this book, I have followed the dictionary's 'popular' definition of the sentence as being the matter between full stops. Not all grammarians choose to do this, and they are quite justified in doing differently. What I call a clause they call a sentence, provided it satisfies the rule above of having subject and predicate. Onions, for example, whose usage differs from my own, would call the first clause of each of the examples of a complex and compound sentence given above sentences in their own right, because 'the boy hit the ball' satisfies the requirement for a sentence as codified in his grammar. The Fowlers took the same view. I do not dispute that they are right, but in the century since they wrote, even most educated people's definition of what constitutes a sentence has become what the dictionary now says it is: the matter between full stops.

Not all sentences contain the traditional subject, object and verb: some contain fewer components, many have more. A sentence may consist of only one word. 'Yes!' 'No!' 'Hello?' are all sentences – Jespersen calls them 'amorphous sentences'. Onions said there were four sorts of sentences: statements, commands (or expressions of wishes), questions and exclamations. A one-word sentence has an ellipsis, or series of missing words that are understood, that if undone would provide the missing matter: 'Yes (you may)!' for example. A detailed knowledge of such things is not necessary to speak or write English correctly: many people manage to do so without a degree in linguistics. It is, however, valuable to understand a little about the structure of language, to ensure that any sentence one writes in formal English contains the components required to make it grammatical.

Where Onions and the Fowlers remain unchallenged is on the notion that this matter must, in order to constitute a grammatical sentence, have a subject and predicate. One of the great and pervasive offences against good grammar, to be seen almost every day in a newspaper or magazine, is the 'sentence' without a main verb and, more to the point, without a coherent ellipsis. Such an example is: 'I saw the dog. Ugly brute.' The omission of the verb *to be* in the second sentence is not coherent because it is not idiomatic in the way that sentences such as 'Yes!', 'No'! or 'Hello?' undeniably are.

In terms of style, short sentences are preferable. They are clear and aid comprehension. See also PARSING.

Sequence of tenses This is another of those rules that come so easily to those who have learned Latin or Greek but can seem a struggle for those who speak English. It is the matter of ensuring that, in REPORTED SPEECH or in accounts of past events, everything remains logical by observing the need to put everything into the past. Onions defines it as 'the principle in accordance with which the tense in a subordinate clause "follows" or is adjusted to that of the main clause'. This means that when the main clause has a present, perfect or future verb any subordinate clause is in the present; and if the main clause has a past or pluperfect, then a subordinate clause is in the past. 'I have laid the table so that we can eat dinner' and 'she will buy the tickets so that we may take the train' are examples of the first; 'they went to the shop and bought some ham' and 'we had some champagne and it made us drunk' exemplify the second. Onions specifies an exception to this rule, which is where something is 'universally' true or true at the time of speaking. I do not entirely agree with him. His first example is an arguable point – 'he had no idea what economy means' – and one can see how it may apply to other such concepts – 'he did not believe that the earth is round'. Yet in reported speech it would now, I think, be idiomatic to write 'he had no idea what economy meant' or 'he did not believe that the earth was round' without conveying any sense that economy now meant something different, or that the earth had changed shape.

So we should stick to the rule that once the verb in the main clause goes into the past tense, so must every other verb. Logic demands this, however strange the outcome may seem to untutored eyes and ears. Suppose a man says at this moment: 'When I look into the bathroom mirror I see that I am bald.' If he chooses to record this statement in writing tomorrow, or in a year's time, he must say: 'I said that when I looked into the bathroom mirror I saw that I was bald.' Were he to put what he said in quotation marks, quoting directly what he had said, then he would not have needed to alter the tense. However, since he has decided to use an indirect quotation, he must put everything into the past tense. In some minds confusion will arise because the man, who presumably is still bald, is saying that he *was* bald, as if that condition has passed. However, to say 'when I looked into the bathroom mirror I saw that I am bald' is simply wrong and illogical. It is not only with practice that one learns how to master the sequence of tenses; it is also with practice that one comes to understand that it is logical and makes sense.

The sentence 'the leader of the party said he had ordered a review, and Mr Smith will repay the money immediately' is wrong. It should be 'Mr Smith would repay the money'. If the main clause is in the past tense, so must everything else be, even if one of the subsequent clauses refers to action in the future. 'I said that I shall go there' is also wrong: it should be 'I said that I should go there'. Perhaps in instances such as this there is a problem with the ambiguity of *should*, which as well as being the past tense of *shall* may also be interpreted as *ought*. The problem needs to be resisted. Precise writers will use the correct past tense of *shall* in reported speech. Should they wish to convey a sense of duty or obligation in the action they would write 'I said I ought to go there', which removes any ambiguity.

The basic rule of not switching tenses in order to preserve the logical sequence is straightforward. In reported speech, everything, even the future, is in the past ('he said he would be going there the following day'). However, there are other considerations of the sequence of tenses that the usage of verbs throws up. Sometimes one reads sentences such as 'the Government has not and will not pretend to have all the answers', which is grammatical nonsense; it must be 'has not pretended to have all the answers, and will not'. If one chooses to mix up tenses in a clause and use different auxiliaries, it is important that the verb works for both or all of them; and, if not, to adjust it accordingly. A report of actions that have taken place and are completed requires the past tense. In some journalism writers use the present tense even when reporting past events in order to convey a sense of immediacy. This may have its place in writing, for example, an account of an interview, but it has no place in news reporting, where it simply conveys a tone of cheapness and sensationalism. In more formal writing, in which a writer may be giving an account of events, it is simply wrong.

Sewage and **sewerage** Since the mid-nineteenth century, that great era of improved drainage, these two words have been used as if interchangeable to mean the effluent carried away by a drainage system. Correctly, however, *sewage* is the effluent, and *sewerage* describes the network of drains used to carry it away: 'Sewage is removed using a sewerage system.'

Shall and **will** One fundamental problem with verbs in all moods, voices and tenses is the failure to observe the correct rules when using *shall* and *will* as auxiliary verbs, and therefore the imperfects *should* and *would*, the perfect tenses *should have* and *would have*, the future perfects *shall have* and *will have* and the continuous futures *I shall be going* and *I will be going. Shall* derives from an Old English verb expressing simple futurity, *will* from an Old English verb expressing desire or will. The Fowlers dedicate enormous amounts of space to the question of the distinctions between these two auxiliary verbs and, I fear, complicate it unnecessarily. Onions is more amusing on the subject: 'The traditional idiomatic use of shall and will is one of the points that are regarded as infallible tests of the true English speaker; it offers peculiar difficulties to Scots, Irishmen, and Americans, the main difference being that these use will in many places where the Englishman uses shall.'

It may be helpful if we seek to distinguish between two sorts of unconditional futures: let us call them the *simple future*, in which the writer makes simple statements of fact about future events, and the *future of resolve* (I should have written 'the future of will', but it is probably best to avoid that ambiguity in this context), in which he expresses determination or compulsion. In the simple future, the auxiliary verbs are as follows: in the singular, *I shall*, *you will*, *he*, *she or it will*; in the plural, *we shall*, *you will*, *they will*. So we write that 'I shall go to town tomorrow' or 'they will have jam for tea tonight'. However, when the action in the future is a question of resolve – whether a person being determined to do something himself, or to ensure that another does it – the use of auxiliaries is reversed: in the singular, *I will*, *you shall*, *he*, *she or it shall*; in the plural, *we will*, *you shall*, *they shall*. Therefore we write 'I will never smoke again', 'he shall be punished' or 'you shall go to the ball'. The Victorian schoolmaster had a way of impressing this distinction upon his charges, with the story of the boy who drowned: for he had cried out 'I will drown, and no one shall save me'; by confusing his auxiliaries, the boy expressed his resolve to be drowned, and not to be saved. This applies also in the past and other tenses; and *should* and *would* also have subjunctive and conditional usages that I deal with below.

As Onions also illustrates, *shall* and *will* retain an existence as independent verbs that dates back to Old English. He defines it, in a passage leading up to the one I have quoted above, as follows: 'The fundamental meaning of shall is "to be under a necessity", "to be obliged" . . . the fundamental meaning of will is "resolve, intend".' Fowler writes of the sense of 'intention, volition or choice' that must be conveyed by the statement 'I will' or 'we will', and how therefore it is nonsense to say it in a context such as 'I will get up in the morning' (my example, not Fowler's). So when the commandment says 'thou shalt not commit adultery' it is seeking to place you under an obligation not to do so, just as the drowning boy, his grammar askew, was putting any potential rescuers under an obligation not to save him. 'Thou wilt not commit adultery', by contrast, has the status of a straightforward prediction. There is logic, once one understands this, in the use of *shall* and *will* to provide the future tense. I can predict that you *will*, or they *will*, do something. Since I know my own obligations, I know I *shall* do it. If I have an extreme determination or resolve to do it, then I *will* do it. If I am seeking to compel others, then they *shall* do it. These rules today are widely flouted, and not just by Scotsmen, Irishmen and Americans, and this dereliction has caused our language to lose precision.

'Shall I go to London tomorrow?' is a straightforward question. 'Shall they go to London tomorrow?' has the force of 'Must they?' or 'Is it inevitable that they will?' 'Will they go?' is the simple question for the third person plural. Partridge contends that it is idiomatic to answer a question with the same auxiliary used in asking it, so writers of dialogue should be alert to this if they agree with him: I am not sure that I do. By his rule, if one asks 'Will you go away?' the answer should be 'I will'. I cannot see what is wrong with answering 'I shall', particularly if (as Fowler would observe) whether I went or not was not a matter of 'intention, volition or choice', but merely a straightforward confirmation of what was going to happen anyway. *Should*, as the past tense of *shall*, denotes all the feelings that *shall* does; as does *would* for *will*. Some of these usages now seem archaic, such as the simple expression 'I would not' for 'I didn't want to', or Rupert Brooke's 'would I were' for 'I wish I were'.

When these auxiliaries appear in dependent clauses that

relate to a main verb in the past tense, they must be in the past too. 'She realised that if she sat in the bar a moment longer, she would be late' is one example. 'We understood that if we failed to pay the bill on time, we should be taken to court' is another. In the latter, the impulse today is to use the solecistic 'we would be taken to court'.

The conditional usages of *should* and *would* in main clauses follow the same rules that I have just outlined. 'I should like to do that' is correct for simple conditional futures. 'I would like to do it' carries with it an additional expression of resolve, and would be justifiable only in response to an assertion such as 'you don't want to do that'. Fowler was unhappy with what he regarded as the tautological use of the phrase *would like*, since the notion of *like* was contained in *would* in this sense, conveying a meaning of desire or intention. He attributed this to confusion between the idiomatically correct 'I should like' and the archaic 'I would', and I am sure he was right. It remains correct to say 'I should like to thank all those present for their understanding'; in reported speech, this would become 'he said he would like', to reflect the exact meaning of what he actually said. See also CONDITIONALS.

Partridge attacks the usage 'I shall go; he doesn't want to', as being unacceptable in formal writing. So do the Fowlers. They prefer the repetition of the verb. Today, usage accepts that it is more elegant to avoid the repetition, and that to do so does nothing to impair meaning or accentuate ambiguity. One can avoid repetition by writing 'he doesn't want to do so', but that does not seem necessary either, and also risks the overuse and debasement of *do*. I fear that what was once branded as 'colloquial' is now standard, but it is hard to see how the language has suffered because of it.

Shame is an overworked and hyperbolic tabloid term. See the entry on the TABLOID PRESS.

She and **her** *She* is the feminine pronoun in the nominative. The accusative and possessive are *her.* It is considered pedantic to say 'it is she', but it is still entirely proper to write such a thing in formal prose. As with *he* and *him*, in demotic usage one would normally say (but not write) 'it's her' instead of 'it is she'. See also PERSONAL PRONOUNS.

Ship and **boat** A *ship* of the Royal Navy is never a *boat*; and its sailors are *in* it, not *on* it.

Ships, names of Ships are like books. If writing their names, italicise them: so write RMS *Queen Elizabeth* or HMS *Trinidad*.

Shocking See UNDERSTATEMENT.

Shot and **shoot** *Shot* is the past participle of the verb *to shoot*. It is also the name of the lead pellets contained in a shotgun cartridge that are discharged when a shotgun is fired, and is used to describe the discharge of the gun – 'we heard three shots'. It may be used in certain contexts to describe one who does the shooting, as in 'he was an exceptionally good shot'. These just describe the uses of the word in the context of firearms. Shot is also used to describe the taking of pictures – 'the photographer took a dozen shots of the scene'; and, under American influence, to refer to measures of alcoholic spirits or other beverages – 'he ordered a shot of vodka' – or a vaccination – 'I had to have a tetanus shot after cutting myself'. A *shoot* is an organised event for those who participate in the sport of shooting – whether the American turkey shoot or the English game shoot. It is also used to describe a photographic session.

Should and **would** The rules for SHALL AND WILL apply to these words as conditionals and as past tenses in reported speech (though see also OUGHT). For a full explanation of their use, see CONDITIONALS.

Show, showed and **shown** *Show* is the present tense of the verb, *showed* the past and *shown* the past participle, correctly used in the following examples: 'I show people how to write', 'he showed Jack the door' and 'he has shown us all what he can do'.

Sick and **ill** One who is *sick* is vomiting. One who is *ill* is laid up or unwell. See U AND NON-U.

Sidewalk is the American term for *pavement*.

Sight See CITE, SIGHT AND SITE.

Silicone and **silicon** *Silicone* used to be the term given to a compound of *silicon*, and was used as a noun and as an adjective. It is now an obsolete term, and the word *silicon*, indicating a non-metallic compound, should be spelt thus.

Simile is the comparison of one thing with another for the purposes of description or illumination: 'All the world's a stage, and all the men and women merely players.' The main danger with them is that they become overused, clichéd and worn out. Examples of clichéd similes are 'like a knife through butter' and 'eat like a horse'. A failed simile – one that conveys entirely the wrong idea – would be something along the lines of 'Their passion was like a December morning in Murmansk'. See METAPHORS.

Since See AS, USED AS A CONJUNCTION.

Sing, sang and **sung** The imperfect tense and past participle of this simple little verb can give problems. The imperfect is *sang* – 'they sang *Happy Birthday* to him before the party ended'. The past participle is *sung* – 'you have sung for your supper' – and so is the passive voice – 'a solemn mass was sung in his memory'. On 6 July 2012 the normally alert *Sun* newspaper confused its tenses: 'Pop star Suggs had to be hauled away by security guards after drunkenly invading a stage as Sting sung at a black tie event.'

Single-handed is not, contrary to the assertion of the late Sir Kingsley Amis, an adverb. It is an adjective, as the dictionary confirms. The adverb is *single-handedly*.

Singulars, irregular Physics, ethics, econometrics and other studies or sciences ending in *-ics* are singular. Also, the singular of the plural noun *troops* does not mean a single soldier. A troop is a small group of soldiers.

Sit For the abuse of the passive voice of this verb, see SAT AND SITTING. When one poses for a portrait painter, one *sits to* him.

Site See CITE, SIGHT AND SITE.

Situation See ABSTRACT LANGUAGE.

Skeptic See SCEPTIC.

Slang What we understand to be *slang* has shifted over the centuries. The dictionary begins by defining it as 'the special vocabulary used by any set of persons of a low or disreputable character; language of a low and vulgar type'. However, it says this has now 'merged' into a later definition (the first citation given of the first usage is 1756; the first of the second 1818), which is 'language of a highly colloquial type, considered as below the level of standard educated speech, and consisting either of new words or of current words employed in some special sense'. This makes it clear that slang is no longer the exclusive province of the submerged tenth, that it has a blurred border with what we used to call COLLOQUIALISM, and that it covers, for example, the vogue for public schoolboys to describe something of which they approve as 'well wicked'. Slang tends to distinguish itself from colloquialism by being the argot of a distinct group, except when it tips over into obscenity. Colloquial speech is more widespread and less exclusive. The difficulty with slang in written English is that readers who are not part of the group may not understand it. Colloquialism often fails in formal writing because it seems out of place, and alters the desired tone: it may only, in such writing, be used self-consciously, notably for comic effect.

Good non-fiction writing will sometimes feature slang, but this will usually be for comic or satirical purposes. In these contexts it is usually obvious, and clear to the reader that the writer knows it is slang and is using it for effect. (The question of how tiresome that effect may be, and how it detracts sometimes from good style, is a different matter, but worth considering.) Do not draw attention to it by the arch device of putting it in quotation marks. If one is going to use it, one should use it out in the open. This is not least because the act of trying to do so may be all the deterrent one needs from the crime itself. Should one be writing fiction, however, it is likely to be impossible to portray a remotely realistic character without recourse to slang in any dialogue.

Slang or colloquialism – as the boundaries are blurred these days it is hard to tell which is which – has particularly potent force in describing physical or mental characteristics of our fellow man. Think of someone who has *got the hump*, or is *potty*, or even *randy* or *saucy* or *fly* or *bent* or *tasty* (an adjective susceptible of more than one slang usage), or has been *poleaxed* or *flattened* or *shafted*, and one begins to realise how widespread such usages are.

Various trades have their own slang; so too does mainstream slang have its descriptions of those trades. A carpenter may be known as a *chippy*, an electrician as a *sparks*. A *chippy* is also a popular haunt of the British, for it is where their fish and chips, a form of *grub*, come from; just as their beer, or *booze*, comes from a *pub*, a *boozer* or even an *offie*. Much slang concerns bodily functions and sexual activity, and perhaps better comes under the heading of vulgarity: though what I class as vulgar usage is more defined by its grammatical accuracy than necessarily by its vocabulary. It is possible to talk in slang almost entirely while remaining grammatically correct.

Other slang comes from regional dialects into the mainstream of colloquial English. One such word that has become ubiquitous in recent years, especially among inadequately educated writers and speakers, is the adjective *picky* to describe the state of mind of someone who in formal writing would be described as *discriminating* or *fastidious*. This is an odd development, for our slang already had a word to fulfil this function, *choosy*. *Choosy* now takes on an air of formality, promoted to that rank by the invasion of *picky*. *Picky* is heard frequently in American usage, a survival no doubt from the dialects of those from the English provinces who migrated there centuries ago. It may have pushed its way into mainstream English slang from American television and films, and not necessarily from the influence of English dialect. **COCKNEY RHYMING SLANG** is a peculiar form of dialect and has passed into mainstream slang too, in some cases.

One of the problems of slang is that it often removes the freedom from ambiguity that correct language has. Take the vogue – now just about passed – for young people to describe as 'wicked' something that they thought was 'good', as in 'that new song is well wicked'. Slang also has the habit of taking a word that is accurate in certain contexts and making it inaccurate in others. Partridge offers a good example of this with the word *gang*. It is correct to use it of workmen or criminals; to use it about 'a set, a clique, a fortuitous assemblage of idle or harmless persons is to fall into slang'. There are numerous other examples, few of which any but the most thoughtless would be tempted to use in formal writing or speech. It is one thing to describe a male person of a certain age as an 'old man'; quite another to use the term to signify a woman's husband or someone's father. On the subject of family members, see **KIDS**.

Some slang has invaded and corrupted correct usage. For example: *fine* is an adjective and not an adverb. It should not therefore be used as one. The verb *to be*, which is a law unto itself, takes an adjective, so one may say 'I am fine' or 'she is fine' just as one may say 'he is ugly', 'they are slow' or 'we are tiresome'. Verbs such as *look* (in its meaning of *seem*), *seem* itself, *smell*, *taste*, *sound* and all other verbs that link with an adjective or a noun – 'it looks fine', 'tastes fine', 'sounds fine', 'seems fine' and so on – are other exceptions. However, one should not use *fine* with any other verb in this way. To say 'it went fine' or 'she's doing fine' are slang usages with no place in formal speech.

Slang is essentially local in its origins and usages and there will be different conceptions of it wherever English is spoken. For example, in British English *bash* is a slang term for hit, but in Australia it is standard English. See also **COLLOQUIALISMS**; **IDIOMS AND IDIOMATIC USAGE**.

Snicker and **snigger** have been synonyms for over 300 years, meaning to laugh in an underhand way; though the former is now regarded as an American usage. It is not incorrect in English, however, though *snigger* is to be preferred.

So Eric Partridge objected to the use of *so* as an intensifier, calling it slovenly: he preferred 'it was very kind of you' to 'it was so kind of you'. That distinction appears now to have been lost, and the use of *so* in this context must now be considered a matter of taste. It has become idiomatic to intensify an adjective with *so*, as in 'he was so wet you could shoot snipe off him' or 'she was so ugly all the mirrors broke'; but in this case it has come to mean *of such intensity* rather than *very*, and its usage seems defensible enough. One is on safer ground objecting to the use of *so* to mean *therefore*, rather as *as* has usurped the role of *because*. This makes sense because of the danger of ambiguity: 'the man had walked miles in the hot sun, was parched, tired and so desperate for water' could mean he was *very* desperate for water, or, *therefore*, was desperate for water. A writer who does not misuse *so* in either way will be in no danger of misleading his readers.

So is also to be regarded as a colloquialism in a phrase such as 'I went to the bar so I could see her', when *so* means *in order that* or *in order to*. As with *as*, it runs the occasional risk of redundancy: 'He had left the parcel behind, but not deliberately so.' A phrase such as 'I put on a hat so as not to catch cold' is heading out of colloquialism and into vulgarism. One would do better to say 'I put on a hat in order not to catch cold', or better still, if subjunctively minded, to say 'I put on a hat that I might not catch cold'; though the latter may court accusations of **ARCHAISM**. In a construction such as 'he worked so hard as to fall asleep', idiomatic usage prefers 'he worked so hard that he fell asleep'. One construction in which *so* is preferred by grammarians is 'so admirable a child as she was', which is reckoned better than 'such an admirable child'. Also, use *so* as a comparator: 'it is not so bad' is preferable to 'it is not that bad'. See also AS, USED AS A CONJUNCTION for the distinction between *as far as* and *so far as*. *So long as* is to be preferred to *as long as* in a sentence such as 'I shall stay in England so long as I live', where it indicates time.

Soar as a metaphor has become a cliché, as in 'share prices soared yesterday'. Unless writing about a heaven-bound rocket or a bird of high, swift flight, avoid it.

Solecism is an enemy that this book sets out to defeat: it is a violation of the rules of grammar or syntax. 'He gave the present to my wife and I' is not the worst imaginable example. It would be a CATACHRESIS to confuse it with *solipsism*, the belief that the self is the only reference point of true knowledge.

Some is a pronoun: 'He saw me eating a plate of beef and said he would like some.'

Sometime, some time and **sometimes** *Sometime* is an adverb that refers to an indeterminate point in the future, as in the phrase 'let's see each other sometime'. It can also be an adjective – 'he is a sometime fellow of his college' means he held that appointment but does so no longer. *Some time* may refer to the past or the future and refers to a point when something has happened or will happen: 'At some time between 1987 and 1994 the two of them met, or 'he promised to deliver the package at some time the following week'. *Sometimes* means occasionally, and refers to an event that may be repeated – 'sometimes when we are bored we play cards', or 'we sometimes look at the book you gave us'.

Somewhat has to be used with care before certain adjectives. It will not make sense before incomparable ones – adjectives that cannot have comparatives or superlatives. One can be *somewhat ugly* or *somewhat stupid* but something cannot be *somewhat full* or *somewhat empty*. See ABSOLUTES.

Sorted and **sorted out** *Sorted* appears to have come into vogue after a rash of violent British gangster films in the 1990s. When something is *sorted*, in the current usage, it is *sorted out* in the language of civilised people. The term, used in those gangster films with an undercurrent of menace or smug satisfaction that asserts the moral (and quite often physical) superiority of the sorter, is used now by those who wish to impress upon others that a serious difficulty has been overcome; and that it has been reflects some credit on the person who did so.

In fact, something can only be *sorted* if it is a multiplicity. It is a verb used to indicate that order has been imposed on a confusion of objects. Mail is sorted; buttons in a box are sorted; so are seeds for planting. Adding the word *out* requires little effort, but by doing so the speaker loses the allegedly witty imitation of a cinematic hard man.

Source is a noun and not a verb. We now regularly hear of cooks *sourcing* their ingredients, but the verb in fact dates back no longer than to 1972, and to an American usage. Why *get*, or the slightly more pompous *obtain*, cannot be used instead is unclear. There is no need to mint new verbs where perfectly useful ones exist.

Speciality and **specialty** The latter is the Americanism for the former, though the medical profession in Britain uses the jargon word *specialty* to describe a doctor's particular field of practice.

Specially See ESPECIALLY AND SPECIALLY.

Spelling Underpinning my approach to giving advice on good English is the assumption that my readers can spell. I realise this is a bold assumption: it is possible to obtain a first-class degree in English from our best universities without being able to spell, as I have noticed when reading applications for jobs in journalism from those with such qualifications. Spelling has been standardised in this country effectively since the completion of the *Oxford English Dictionary* in 1928: I see no reason for orthography to be varied, since we have had a completed standard dictionary for nearly ninety years.

There is a small group of words in frequent use that many people have trouble spelling correctly. This does not pretend to be an exhaustive list, but it is one that contains the most troublesome of the words that cause difficulty in this respect:

Accommodation
All right
Bellwether
Cemetery
Committee
Consensus
Definite
(Just) Deserts
Desiccate
Diarrhoea
Drunkenness
Dumbbell
Embarrassment
Fulfil
Gauge
Harass
Harassment
Humorous
Independent
Jewellery
Liaison
Lightning
Linchpin
Manoeuvre
Mantelpiece
Memento
Millennium
Minuscule
Misspelt
Possession
Privilege
Publicly
Quandary
Questionnaire
Receive
Recommendation
Restaurateur
Rhythm
Separate
Skilful
Stratagem
Succeeded
Supersede
Tyranny
Weird
Withhold

There are also words (many of which are discussed in separate entries) whose spellings are similar and are even homophones, but that mean very different things, such as ascent/assent, bare/bear, brake/break, cession/session, complement/compliment, currant/current, cygnet/signet, discreet/discrete, faint/feint, gage/gauge, gamble/gambol, gorilla/guerrilla, grisly/grizzly, humerus/humorous, idle/idol, leak/leek, lesser/lessor, literal/littoral, meat/meet/mete, metal/mettle, muscle/mussel, naval/navel, pedal/peddle, populace/populous, key/quay, reign/rein, sloe/slow, stationary/stationery, straighten/straiten, their/there/they're, waiver/waver, ringer/wringer, your/you're.

There is genuine dispute concerning the correct orthography of certain words. In most cases these disputes were raging before the dictionary was completed and no consensus had been reached on the spellings among the educated. The dictionary failed, in these instances, to settle them. As a matter of taste I would include the *e* after the *g* in words such as *judgement*, *acknowledgement* and *abridgement* as it seems necessary for correct pronunciation. As I note elsewhere, forms such as *connexion*, though still favoured by the dictionary, have long been regarded by most of us as archaic. Their alternatives were current and popular long before the dictionary was completed, which makes its rejection of the alternatives the more peculiar. The second edition of the dictionary continued to discount them. The third, now in preparation, will be interesting in this respect.

Splice and **split** are sometimes confused, perhaps because *splice* reminds some writers and speakers of *slice*, and therefore they think it conveys the idea of cutting something. To *splice* two things is to join them: it has nautical origins, in splicing or joining two pieces of rope or cord: but is also used in carpentry, to join two pieces of wood, and in cinematography, to join two separate parts of a reel of film. *Split* has quite the opposite meaning.

Split infinitive The *split infinitive* is a great obsession among grammarians, whether they be for or against it. This began with Latinists, notably Bishop Lowth in the eighteenth century, arguing that since the INFINITIVE was intact in that language, it had better be as intact as possible in our own too. There is no reason in that sense why this should apply in English. However, the division of *to* from its verb was seized on by the Fowlers, correctly in my view, as inelegant. This rational observation carries more weight than a dubious precept such as Lowth's. It is hard to see why the phrase *to boldly go* is any less direct or forceful than *to go boldly* or *boldly to go*. The meaning is as clear in any of the three forms as in another; but for the sake of logic and clarity *to* and the verb whose infinitive it forms are always best placed next to each other rather than interrupted by an adverb. In nearly thirty years as a professional writer I have yet to find a context in which the splitting of an infinitive is necessary in order to avoid ambiguity or some other obstruction to proper sense. Some writers may feel that complications arise where auxiliary verbs are brought into the phrase: 'she used frequently to visit her mother at weekends', or even 'she frequently used to visit her mother at weekends', will always seem to some writers more problematical and unnatural than 'she used to frequently visit'. However, the principle is the same as with the present tense, and a correct usage with an auxiliary is just as easy to grasp as one without one. When dealing with the passive infinitive, such as in the sentence 'she knew what it was like to be overlooked', the infinitive would be split by the entirely unidiomatic 'she knew what it was like to repeatedly be overlooked'. There is nothing wrong with 'to be repeatedly overlooked' – or, for that matter, 'to be overlooked repeatedly'. What is stylistically important is that the elements *to be* are not separated.

Spoilt and **spoiled** In the matter of irregular past participles, *spoilt* is a special case. A dish kept in the oven too long may be *spoilt*, but somewhere that is pillaged has been *spoiled* (a contraction of *despoiled*). See also LEARNED AND LEARNT.

Spoonerism This is a mistake in speech, either accidental or deliberate, named after the Revd William Spooner (1844–1930), the warden of New College, Oxford, who had a propensity to do this in speech. It is the exchange of initial letters, opening syllables or morphemes of consecutive or near-adjacent words. Thus we would have his masterpiece, 'kinquering congs their titles take', when he mispronounced the name of a hymn, or the apparently apocryphal 'three cheers for the queer old dean'. They are consciously used for humour, such as the description of someone as a 'shining wit'.

Sport, language of Sport creates its own argot and usages that almost never have a place in respectable writing. It has manufactured verbs for those lucky enough to win prizes – we hear of them 'podiuming' or 'medalling'. Another abomination that is moving outside sport and into the rest of life is when a person has to *commit* to something. This always requires the reflexive pronoun and almost never has it: correctly, a player *commits himself* to the team. There are also gruesome sports clichés that often have an application wider than the game itself, such as 'over the moon', 'it's a game of two halves', 'game, set and match', 'the going is good' and 'going through hoops'. See also **TABLOID PRESS** and **JARGON**.

Spring, sprang and **sprung** The latter two are sometimes confused. *Sprang* is the past tense of the verb *spring* – 'he sprang to attention'. *Sprung* is the past participle, for use with the perfect and pluperfect tenses – 'he has sprung to life' and 'she had sprung up from behind a hedge'. The usage is parallel with the imperfect tense and past participles of **SING**.

Stammer and **stutter** *Stutter* is an Americanism for the speech impediment the British call a *stammer*, though *stutter* is widely used and understood in British English, and has in everyday use nearly supplanted the native usage. It is more correctly used in British English to describe the misfiring of an engine, or more particularly the interrupted, irregular noise made by an engine that is *stuttering*.

Stand, take the This is an Americanism, which grates when used in British English. In American courts of law, a witness will *take the stand*. In British ones, he will *enter the witness box*. The term has insinuated itself into British English because of the ubiquity of American courtroom and police dramas on British television.

Standard English Whether the linguistics experts like it or not, there remains an idea of 'standard English' as it is spoken in Britain; there are different but related standards in other countries where English is the principal or a principal language, notably in America, but also in Australia, India and the Far East. These standards are set by an educated class within those communities: and those who wish to be included, or to consider themselves included, in that class must subscribe to the rules. In Britain, most serious newspapers and editors who work for book publishers continue to conform to the national, educated standard. So, at least in its serious programming, does the BBC, the state broadcaster; and other networks in their news and documentary output make an attempt to do so. Conformity with the local standard is usual in other anglophone countries in their publications and in mainstream broadcasting. In some cases this standard is quite unlike British English: in an Australian newspaper one will often read, in a report of an assault, that the victim has been 'bashed'; a slang word in British English, but normal usage in Australian. The reverse is seen in educated speech in India: the standard of writing on a newspaper such as *The Times of India* is of a strictness and formality hardly seen in the British quality press since the 1950s or 1960s, and is intensely refreshing in its conservatism and purity.

Standard English (however, sometimes, inexactly understood) is also a measure that certain of us impose upon others – those applying for a job, for example, or seeking other favours. It is a fact that people are judged by how they speak and write, however offensive or unfair that may seem to some. This is partly the legacy of a popular grammatical movement in the late nineteenth and early twentieth centuries whose textbooks remain on the shelves of many professional writers to this day. It is also because of the British trait of looking down upon people whom we consider less educated than we are: for a grammatically precise command of English and an ability to choose words correctly have long been considered by many to be the mark of an educated person. Millions of English speakers believe there is such a thing as good English, and aspire to write it and speak it. Few Britons in recent decades will have learned the standard in schools. As a result, they cannot use the precision tool of our language to its full capabilities. One of the aims of this book is to help develop, or refresh, the skills required to write and speak grammatically correct English and to make the right choice of words when doing so.

Standing See STOOD AND STANDING.

Standout is an Americanism, an adjective meaning what in British English would be represented by *outstanding*. An American would say: 'it was the movie's standout scene'; a Briton would say 'it was the outstanding scene of the film'.

Start again and **start over** The former usage is standard English; the latter American.

Stationary and **stationery** *Stationary* is an adjective describing something that is not in motion; *stationery* is what one writes letters on.

Stood and **standing** A common fault when using the past tense of this verb is to say 'he was stood'. 'He was standing' is correct or, better, 'he stood'. An inanimate object that lacks the ability to move itself but that has to be positioned can be *stood* somewhere – it would be correct to say 'the clothes horse was stood in front of the fire' – but beings with the power of locomotion do not require another to place them in this way. The verb *stand* is also used in British English when a politician seeks office – 'he stood for election'. The Americans say that he would *run*. See also SAT AND SITTING.

Straight(ened) and **strait(ened)** A *straight* is a part of a race-course that has no bend on it; a *strait* is a passage that is narrow.

Straightened means made straight; *straitened* means confined or constrained. The two adjectives are often confused, usually the former conveying the meaning of the latter. Similarly, *strait-laced* and *straitjacket* are spelt thus.

Strike See STRONG VERBS.

Strive The past tense is *strove*, something of which *The Times* newspaper was unaware on 26 October 2013 when it wrote that 'Michael O'Leary, the brash chief executive, strived to squeeze every last penny out of passengers'. See also STRONG VERBS.

Strong verbs We learn when very small that if we wish to put a verb into the past tense we simply add *-ed* to it. We also learn very quickly thereafter that in many cases, especially with the most simple English verbs, we would be wrong. That is because the English verbs that are the most essential to our life, because they describe some of the most essential actions of our lives, are of Germanic roots. As with many equivalent verbs in German even today, they change their whole form in the imperfect tense and have, quite often, another form altogether in the perfect and pluperfect. We call them *strong verbs*. So when a child says 'I *drinked* my lemonade' we have to tell him that he *drank* his lemonade. Should he become more sophisticated yet and say that he *has drinked* his lemonade, or even *has drank* it, we have to tell him he *has drunk* it. There may be similar problems in learning how to use verbs such as *eat*, *see*, *sleep*, *run*, *ride*, *steal* and *tread*: but these are everyday verbs that we soon master and that give no trouble to anybody.

There are difficulties with verbs that we use infrequently, however. A resurgence in popularity towards the end of the last century for P. G. Wodehouse, in which an aunt or two always 'hove into view', persuaded some people who chose to adopt this cliché as their own that there was a verb *to hove*; so one reads horrors such as 'she hoves into view'. *Hove* is the past tense of the verb *to heave*, just as *wove* is for *weave*. Should one wish to write the past tense of the phrase *stave in*, it is *stove in*. We know the past participle of *strike* is *struck*; but there is also the metaphorical usage, used these days almost exclusively to describe an emotional blow, which is *stricken*. It is not the case that *struck* is used only in a literal sense: one who is *struck dumb* has probably suffered no physical blow at all. A verb that seems similar, *strive*, has *strove* in the imperfect and *striven* as its past participle in all senses, though that does not prevent the occasional sighting of the illiteracy *strived* in either the imperfect tense or the perfect and pluperfect tenses.

Style It should be obvious that a good writing style facilitates reading and comprehension, and may even cause pleasure on the part of the reader. This book aims at helping its readers to perfect such a style. Its key structural points are the careful choice of words; use of correct grammar; brevity; accurate punctuation; short sentences; and logical paragraphs. Wit and insight will also help inform style and create ease of reading, but teaching those is beyond the scope of this work. A good style is not one that shows off the vocabulary or the extensive reading of the writer. It is one that combines clarity of expression with ease of reading while conveying the maximum information, with every word essential to the task and used in the correct grammatical framework. It may also display wit, and the best style will convey information in an interesting way whose originality and freshness – whether in insight or metaphor, or both – causes the words to lodge in the reader's mind with ease. Good style also includes words that are used in their accurate sense. The expansion of the literate class from the mid-nineteenth to the mid-twentieth centuries resulted in many more people who knew how to read and write, but not necessarily how to write well. Achieving stylistic excellence was a matter for the individual's further study and application. Few could be bothered to do this, but many had jobs in which they had to communicate with the public – perhaps as minor functionaries in central or local government, or in other parts of the bureaucracy, or in clerical roles for great corporations. The ready availability of bad English in wide circulation that was the result helped provoke Orwell's statement that a 'mixture of vagueness and sheer incompetence is the most marked characteristic of modern English prose'. For some fundamental rules of good style, see RULES OF GOOD WRITING.

Subject The *subject* (of a sentence) is the agent of a verb. In the sentence 'the cat sat on the mat' the cat is the subject and the mat the object. Subjects do not have to be animate. In the sentence 'the desk stood by the window', the desk is the subject.

Subjunctive mood As well as being the mood of verbs used for certain sorts of conditional expressions, it is (or was) most frequently used in dependent clauses of sentences expressing will, desire, necessity, possibility or hope. 'I command that he *be* executed' uses in the dependent clause the present tense of the subjunctive mood of the verb *to be*; 'she wishes that he *were* here', 'it is essential that he *be* brought here' and 'he would be happy if he *were* here' are all examples of the subjunctive. In certain forms it is markedly different from the most common mood, the INDICATIVE; in others it is indistinguishable. Over the last century-and-a-half or so it has come to be regarded by most British English speakers as an unnecessary facet of language. Few will have heard of it unless they have been taught Latin or French to a reasonable level. Since some archaic usages of it survive in everyday speech, everybody will have used it without realising he was doing so. This will have been not merely in the conditionals already described, but in phrases such as 'God save the Queen', 'lest we forget', 'so be it', 'far be it from me to say that', 'may he rest in peace' and 'be that as it may'.

The hostility towards the subjunctive is to be deplored. Its correct use adds precision to meaning. It distinguishes a certain family of verbs, and the meanings and sentiments they convey, from certain others. Onions argues that one reason the subjunctive fell out of favour in English was because we lost so many of our inflections as the language evolved. However, the subjunctive has decayed visibly in the era since most of the inflections went. This, I fear, is for another reason offered by Onions: 'the loss or decay of precision in expressing thought-distinctions; hence the substitution of indicatives for subjunctives'. We no longer, unlike the French (or the Germans, for that matter: credit where it is due), summon up the clarity of thought that tells us there is a distinction of mood between those verbs that express will, hope or desire, and those that do everything else. The French especially remain particular about the subjunctive. Anyone who cannot deploy it when required (which is in circumstances similar to those in English, and others besides) is regarded as an inadequate speaker of that language. In English usage, it is one area where the Americans (with, as I have already noted, their peculiar combination of conservatism and gratuitous innovation) put us to shame. It should be understood that in outlining the scope and correct usage of the subjunctive here I am making a case not merely for its retention, but for its renewed usage.

Let us jump in at the deep end and imbibe a pure subjunctive of the sort that our American cousins drink every day, but which we would find not to our taste, or unpleasantly intoxicating: something such as 'I order that he be brought here'. The third person present subjunctive of the verb *to be* is 'he be'. It naturally, in this mood, follows the verb of will. It is easy to memorise the present subjunctive of the verb *to be*, for in all persons it is *be*. Let us drink deep of these, for example:

'If I be wrong, I shall be defeated.'

'Though you be old, you are handsome.'

'Unless she be reasonable, I shall not continue.'

'He commanded that we be silent.'

'He desires that you be comfortable.'

'It is necessary that they be strong.'

No educated American would blink at any of these. For our part, the current idiomatic usage has us reaching either for an auxiliary verb, which is tolerable, or for an indicative, which is demotic and downright wrong. A careful person may write 'if I should be wrong', which is a subjunctive (albeit a diluted one); most would use the indicative and write 'if I am wrong'. The same applies to the other examples. Even in instances where the subjunctive is used by more than just pedants, it is in increasing disuse. 'I wish it were that simple' is increasingly rendered as 'I wish it was'.

If we make up our minds that we wish to use the subjunctive, where, and how, do we do so? We have already seen its use in certain conditional clauses, which are principally how it survives today. The more specialist use of it is in dependent clauses. 'It is the committee's decision that he be admitted to the fellowship' is an example of a dependent clause expressing desire or will. 'It is desirable that a gentleman hold open the door for a lady' is another, and one that demonstrates how the subjunctive of ordinary verbs in the present tense does not add the *s* in the third person. Another example is 'her father demanded that she tell him where she had been'. This also demonstrates how the present tense of the subjunctive is used in reported speech after verbs of will and desire. Today, except in America, these usages would usually include the auxiliary *should* before the verb. The point is that they do not need to do so. In addition to its use in subordinate clauses after verbs of will and desire, the subjunctive also has a role after what we may term verbs of exhortation and suggestion: 'she urged that he be included', or 'I propose that she come'. What will be seen to link all these verbal usages is that the outcome of the exercise – whether it be *hoping, suggesting, willing, urging*, or even *ordering* or *commanding* – is not certain: it relies on the actions of others. The subjunctive is a mood that is used to convey an underlying ambivalence or uncertainty, hence my use of it after 'whether' in the preceding sentence.

Clauses beginning with *if* often need a subjunctive, as do some sentences where the if-clause is an ellipsis, and so imagined. We say 'I should like to have some champagne' because there is an imaginary clause that says 'if it is [or *be*] permitted' or 'if there is [or *be*] enough left'. Similarly, 'What would you call your dog?' imagines 'if you had one'; and 'she might have telephoned' imagines 'if she had been considerate', or something of that sort. All those verbs are subjunctives. More obvious is the usage after *if* itself, as in: 'If he were to join us, would you mind?' Clauses with *as if* or *as though* also take a subjunctive: 'it was as if she were up in the clouds' or 'I felt as though I were drowning'. *Though* itself takes one too: 'though I be prejudiced, I feel my wife is beautiful', as do clauses with *whether* that raise a doubt about outcome, such as 'whether or not he be qualified, he intends to drive the car' or 'we tried to discover whether he were the culprit'.

Both *until* and *unless* can take a subjunctive. The sentence of the law once was 'that you be hanged by the neck until you be dead'. Less finally, it would be correct to write that 'he has decided to bide his time until his father come'; or 'she said she would not enter the house unless the rat were dead'. Students reading English at Cambridge University were once asked to say where the verb was in Donne's line 'Till Age snow white hairs on thee'. Once one realises that *till* takes a subjunctive, and that that subjunctive is the verb *snow*, all is clear. *Lest*, too, takes this mood, and it remains a very useful but underused word: 'he refused to drink any whisky lest he have to drive' or 'I took an umbrella with me lest it rain' are examples. *Lest* never takes a subjunctive auxiliary such as *should*, *would* or *might*.

Words like *however*, *whatever* and *whoever* may take a subjunctive in relative clauses expressing doubt or uncertainty: 'however it be depicted, what he did was still wrong'; 'whatever be your excuse, you had no right to do it'; and 'whoever it be who told you, he was lying' are all examples, though they sound archaic today. There is also a past tense of the subjunctive that may be used in reported speech: 'She said that whoever it were who told him, he was lying.' Again, such a usage may be hard to defend against archaism. It is a question of idiom, but it seems to be that a subjunctive usage after verbs of will or desire sounds the least anachronistic when used today. Whether even that can survive another generation or two ignorant of classical and other modern languages is a matter for conjecture. See also CONDITIONAL CLAUSES.

Subordinating conjunction This conjunction – usually 'that' - introduces either noun clauses or adverbial clauses. An example of the former is where the clause says that something *is*, *was*, *had*, *would be* or *will be*: as in 'I imagined *that he would be late*' or 'he saw *that she was better*'. An adverbial clause is one such as: 'I slept *after drinking the brandy*'. The clause in italics is adverbial because it modifies the verb.

Substantive is a synonym for NOUN.

Substitute has been a verb in English since the fifteenth century, meaning to install someone in a role previously undertaken by another. It correctly takes the preposition *for* – so one would write 'Smith was substituted for Jones in the eighty-fifth minute' – in other words, Smith replaced Jones on the field. The same applies to the noun – 'she was a substitute for Mary'.

Such and **such as** The sentence 'he resented the fact that he had no power to refuse the summons, *as* his colleagues had', is wrong. It is also ambiguous: do his colleagues have the power to refuse, or have they already refused? If the second clause began '*such as* his colleagues had' it would be correct: the *such* can refer only to *power*. *As* can be used as a pronoun when it refers to a verbal idea (or ideas) rather than to a noun: for example, when one writes 'they go to the opera and dine afterwards, *as* one does', that is correct.

Superlatives One often hears reference to 'the eldest son' when there are only two sons available; or 'the youngest child' when there are only two children. For a *superlative* – normally an adjective with the suffix *-est* – to be used there have to be more than two things or people being compared. If there are just two then the COMPARATIVE – normally ending in *-er* – must be used. Therefore, in the two examples just given it would be 'elder son' and 'younger child'. Adjectives that are **ABSOLUTES** cannot have superlatives.

Surplice and **surplus** The former, which according to the dictionary describes 'a loose vestment of white linen . . . worn . . . by clerics, choristers and others taking part in church services', derives from the latter, which means 'an amount remaining in excess', a word from old French that went into medieval Latin. The *surplice* was worn over normal clothing and thus *surplus* to it. The two spellings should not be confused. It is notable that *surplice* appears in English at the end of the thirteenth century, over eighty years before *surplus* – so its derivation is not from the English word, but from the French or Latin.

Suspended participles See **PARTICIPLES**.

Suspicious and **suspect** *Suspicious* is an adjective meaning either to create suspicions or to harbour them. Examples are 'His behaviour was suspicious' or 'I was suspicious of his motives'. To be *suspicious of* something or someone is to *suspect* it or him, and *suspect* is also a noun – the person *suspected* of having done something, usually a crime. It is slang to describe someone as a *suspect* character: he is a suspicious one. Another usage that is now common is 'a suspect package', a package suspected of being a bomb: that appears to have gained currency and it is too late to undo it.

Syllepsis is the use of a verb to govern both a concrete and an abstract object, as in 'he found a £10 note, and God'. It may be used in an attempt at humour. See also **ZEUGMA**.

Sympathy See **EMPATHY AND SYMPATHY**.

Synecdoche is the representation of a whole by a part, or a part by a whole: 'all hands on deck', or 'the guns will number from the right'. Do not confuse it with **METONYM**, which is the use of a word such as a place or an institution to represent something else.

Synonym A *synonym* is a word that has a similar meaning to another word: *vast* and *big*, for example, or *little* and *small*. When choosing a synonym take care that it truly is one, and not a word that exaggerates or diminishes the meaning of the word you seek to replace. Synonyms are useful for the stylistic purpose of avoiding the REPETITION of words in a piece of writing.

T

Tabloid press Much tabloid journalism is, in style, immaculately clear – short sentences, short paragraphs, short words and short articles make not just for easy comprehension but also for a lively page of a newspaper. One of the substantial effects of the popular press has, however, been to invent clichés and misuse words. The tabloid style has also introduced new moral concepts, such as 'falling pregnant' (see PREGNANT). These matters are not a problem in the context of such publications, but become one when imitated in formal writing.

At its worst, tabloid style is the fuel that feeds the vice of exaggeration that inevitably strikes the wrong tone. There are certain words and phrases that are staples of tabloid journalism, an honourable trade whose customers require its products to be not merely direct and comprehensible – so should all journalism be – but to speak their language. Those of us not employed by the tabloid press, and who do not have to abide by the formulas that cause it to be profitable, have a choice in this matter. We can use its language, and have our thoughts interpreted as being rooted in the same clichéd and apparently superficial ground from which tabloid style grows, or we can choose to avoid the formulaic and the sensational in our own speech and writing and seek to convey a more measured and original voice. Someone who writes, or speaks, in the manner of a tabloid newspaper risks becoming a parody of one.

The language of tabloid exaggeration is apparent on every page of what the trade calls the 'red-top' newspapers. Prices 'soar', and then they 'crash'. In politics, 'rows' about 'issues' are always 'erupting', and they are inevitably 'furious'. The 'key' participants in them 'clash', and they evince 'rage'. The consequence of an 'outrage' is that there will be a 'probe', leading up to a 'damning report'. Its 'shock findings' will be followed by a 'clampdown' (or a 'crackdown'). The opponents of the transgressors will 'slam' their behaviour and seek to 'topple' them.

Any death, especially of a 'teen', is a 'tragedy', and if more than one person dies it is a 'catastrophe'. It leaves grieving 'loved ones gutted'. Should the victim be a young girl, she was 'bubbly', especially if blonde. Young men, unless proven criminals, had in their lives had 'huge respect' from their 'mates'.

On the sports pages, managers of soccer teams 'vow' that their sides will do better, knowing they risk being 'axed' if they do not. Should a team suddenly become 'brilliant' it will be because a 'star' player has shown he is a 'hero', and can expect a 'hike' in his wages. He may then 'launch' a new career as a fashion 'icon'. Should the team 'crash' to defeat in a cup final, all its 'fans' would be 'devastated'.

'Celebs' will usually have 'amazing lifestyles' that are 'revealed' by the tabloid press as a series of 'stunning events'. These will often be 'fuelled' by champagne and sometimes by drugs. They entail living in a million-pound 'home', but also possibly sharing a 'love nest' with a 'stunner' and, as the paper will 'reveal', a 'love child' as a result of extensive 'cheating' on a spouse. The wronged woman (for it usually is a woman) will be 'brave' during her 'ordeal': until it 'emerges' that she has had a 'toyboy' too, with whom there have been nights of 'nookie'. This tale may well also be a 'nightmare' for those concerned in which they endure a 'frenzy' and possibly even a media 'hell'. Women in such stories never wear dresses during their 'glamorous' nights out, only 'gowns'. And 'gowns', like 'mansions' or 'homes', come with an obligatory adjectival price-tag, usually the product of guesswork rather than of research, and often therefore 'a £1,000 gown'. Anyone in public life who is in trouble – a judge, an MP or an Army officer – is usually 'top' (or, in more thoughtful articles, 'senior') and his predicament is one of 'shame' that leaves him 'disgraced'.

Anyone who has been educated at a public school is a 'toff'. He lives in a 'mansion' – as may some grammar-school or comprehensive-school types who have become 'fat cats', particularly if they also own a 'Roller' and the women of the family go 'horse riding'. Such pursuits are 'posh', and none is 'posher' than a 'blood sport'. Sometimes such people have made their 'dosh' thanks to a 'scam'. They are also often members of 'exclusive' clubs.

Some of the words in quotation marks are pure slang and have no place in respectable writing – 'celebs', 'nookie', 'posh', 'dosh' and 'scam', for example. Others come under the heading of coy or vulgar euphemism – 'toyboy', 'love child', 'love nest', 'cheating' and 'stunner' are what might more directly be called *gigolo, illegitimate child, flat, committing adultery* and *mistress*. Some are simply failures of terminology: those who ride horses go *riding*, not 'horse riding'; and those who shoot or hunt practise *field sports*. 'Blood sports' is a politically loaded term used by those opposed to field sports, which is frequently used unwittingly by those who do not object to them.

The main objection to most of the tabloid language highlighted above is that it devalues the currency. If somebody is *devastated* because his football team has lost a match, how does he feel when he gets home and finds his wife and children have been killed in a fire? If a woman is *brave* because of her reaction to the way in which her philandering husband embarrasses her publicly, how are we to describe her if she endures with courage and fortitude a horrible and potentially fatal illness? How can the ordeal of one experience compare with that of the other? If one death, however sad for those concerned, is a *tragedy*, how does one describe the moral effect of a plane crash in which many people are killed? If a man who scores a goal is a *hero*, what term do we reserve to describe one who wins the Victoria Cross? If an MP suffers *shame* because he claims for a food-mixer improperly on his expenses, what does he suffer if he is convicted of a criminal offence? If he is *disgraced* for being found in bed with someone else's wife, what adjective do we use of him if he is found to have perpetrated a systematic fraud, or is convicted of paedophilia? Above all, if unexceptional facts (often supplied to the newspaper by a celebrity's public-relations adviser) are described as having been *revealed* when, in fact, all they have been is *disclosed*, what verb is to be used for something that is a genuine revelation?

Other words have become clichés and are therefore meaningless. Little weight is carried now by the metaphorical use of verbs such as *soar*, *crash*, *launch*, *emerge*, *fuel* and *clash*. Nouns such as *toff*, *fat cat*, *clampdown* and *icon* are just lazy labels for people or for abstract activities; so too are phrases such as *damning report* and *shock finding*. *Respect* (huge or otherwise) in this context is an absurdity. It has become a word used in urban argot to describe not a feeling of reverence by one for another, but what a self-regarding person who has watched too many gangster films imagines is the estimation in which he should be held by others.

Brilliant is an adjective that should now only be used to describe a bright light: some newspapers apply it to so many columnists, series, special offers or free gifts that it is remarkable that their readers have not been blinded. I have given warning throughout this book of the dangers of promiscuity with adjectives. Their usage reaches its nadir in tabloidism, as *top*, *senior*, *furious* and *amazing* all show. People who buy the sort of newspapers in which this language is routine do so with certain expectations. People who read publications with a reputation for being more measured have expectations too, but they are likely to be different. Such readers are bemused, or may even feel insulted or patronised, when the writing they read is laced with sensationalism. It is a cheap effect easily obtained by what for a tabloid writer is likely to be a deliberate choice of language, but which for any other writer may be like a disease picked up by an unfortunate chance. It is therefore well to take precautions.

It is not only words that become clichéd in journalistic overuse; it is also formulas and constructions when they are overused in writing. One of these is the habit – reviled by Fowler in the early twentieth century but still current today – of a writer's attempting to be interesting by giving much information about a subject before disclosing who the subject is. A news story in a tabloid newspaper in January 2010 began: 'Eyes bulging with fury, cheeks purple and moustache bristling, the sergeant major draws himself to his full height . . .' In formal writing it is better to declare whom or what one is writing about before engaging in a detailed description of the subject. The sensation it creates is cheap and can mislead the reader. It is akin to the effect, itself rarely welcome, of using a pronoun in a sentence before its technical antecedent. Unless one is performing in the more routine parts of the tabloid press, or self-consciously writing parody, this sort of thing is to be avoided.

Talk to A phrase such as 'I think Jeff will talk to that point' is another example of office jargon, and illiterate. Jeff will talk *about* that point, or discuss it.

Talking of Fowler defines a usage called the 'converted participle' in which a participle, by idiom, stands alone: his first example is: 'Talking of test matches, who won the last?' and the subject of the second clause deliberately has no relation to the participle in the first. This he relates to the GERUND, saying it is a shortened version of the archaic *a-talking*. In the last century the idiom has taken root and no longer seems worthy of comment. The participle does not need a noun because it is, as a gerund, a noun in itself; that is why it is not wrong to adopt this usage.

Target The noun *target* has in recent years become a verb; the dictionary finds various usages of this sort for the word since the 1970s. (There was a medieval verb *to target*, meaning to protect oneself with a targe or shield, which the dictionary describes as obsolete, with which the new usage should not be confused.) One can see how and why people have been tempted to adopt this new usage. The first step was the metaphorical use of the noun. For centuries a target was something at which an archer, or a sniper, could aim. Then businesses had targets, abstract ideas of goals that had to be reached in each financial year. Then governments and bureaucracies had them too. Once one has metaphorical targets, one no longer aims at them; one *targets* them. Now all sorts of things are *targeted*. The very promiscuity of a popular metaphor warns intelligent writers or speakers to avoid it for risk of being considered boring. That aside, is *target* a legitimate verb? No doubt in years' time it will be, and our descendants will wonder what all the fuss was about: just as we look in the pages of books such as *The King's English* and wonder why its authors became so exercised about the new usages of old words with which we no longer have any quarrel. For the moment, some of us cannot understand why spending cuts need be *targeted* on a specific department of state when they can just as well be *aimed* or *directed* there.

Taught and **taut** *Taught* is the past participle of the verb to teach – 'he taught Latin'. *Taut* is an adjective that means 'tightly drawn, stiff, tense, not slack': it also has a naval usage – a *taut* ship – to describe a vessel that is strictly run. The two words should not be confused, though they were by *The Times* on 9 October 2012: 'The affected joint is red and swollen, and the surrounding skin often taught and shiny.'

Tautology is a stylistic (and logical) fault that causes the same idea to be repeated within a single statement: 'It was the only unique example in the world.' An idea is repeated unintentionally and immediately, usually because of a failure to think about what the individual words in the statement mean. So one will read that someone was 'frequently in the habit' or 'often had a routine of' doing something. One hears reporters on television say that people 'continue to remain' in a certain condition. Many verbs that begin with *re-* invite a tautology if they are accompanied by *again* – such as 'resume again', 'repeat again' or 'replenish again'. 'Revert back' is a tautology, as is 'recoil back'. Partridge has a long list of such offences, of which a few specimens may suffice here: 'collaborate together', 'descend down', 'mingle together' and 'refer back' all make the point that a meaning already contained in the verb does not need to be expressed immediately in a complement. There are similar examples of nouns needing adjectives even less than is usually the case: 'ugly monster', 'savage brute' and 'stupid fool' are some of the more obvious;

there are many others. This affliction may also affect verbs in the form of needless adverbs: it is hard to see the point of 'she drank thirstily' or 'he ate hungrily', because people normally do, just as they also 'yell loudly', 'rage angrily' and 'stop completely'. *Fully* can be a particular problem: when used with certain verbs it is meaningless, because the verbs themselves are absolute, and therefore *fully* is inevitably tautological. Verbs such as *abandon, convince, cede, close* and *stop* are but five examples: there are countless others. For example, a window may be *wide open* or *a little open*, but in either case it is *open*: once it is open even a little way it is *fully open* in that it is not closed. So to express its being open to its greatest extent, it is better to say *wide open*.

Even without highly descriptive nouns, adjectives may be pointless because they are tautological. There is no point in saying an 'established convention' or an 'earlier precedent', because all conventions are established and all precedents are earlier. Similarly, one need not talk of a 'convicted criminal' – the libel laws of our country make it clear that to describe someone as a criminal without his having been convicted as such is to invite a demand for substantial damages – or of a 'pair of twins', since twins always are. 'Global pandemic' is another example, and a newspaper article recently talked of 'live vivisection'. Nor is tautology confined to adjectives and nouns. The solecism 'revert back' is a tautology because *back* is the only way one can revert. There are other examples, not least 'advance forward', 'dive down' and 'mount up'. And many everyday phrases, uttered almost as fillers, are tautological: for example, 'added bonus', 'basic essentials', 'close proximity', 'completely exhausted', 'exactly the same', 'end result', 'free gift', 'personal opinion', 'prior experience', 'blue in colour', 'small in size', 'summarise briefly', 'surrounded on all sides', 'true facts', 'usual custom' and 'very widespread'.

Tear up is an Americanism meaning to cry, become lachrymose or to have one's eyes fill with tears. It is not to be confused with *tear up*, which in British English at least is used to mean destroy something, literally or metaphorically, by ripping it into shreds. In this American usage *tear* rhymes with *beer*; in Britain it rhymes with *hair*.

Tenses of verbs See under PRESENT, IMPERFECT, FUTURE, PERFECT, FUTURE PERFECT and CONDITIONAL.

Terror and **terrorism** *Terror* is what one feels when one is terrorised; *terrorism* is the practice of inflicting it, usually for political reasons. A senior Scotland Yard anti-terrorist officer who finds himself described as a 'terror chief' – as one occasionally reads in the newspapers – is manifestly nothing of the kind.

Testify While this is a perfectly good English verb, it is another importation from American crime programmes when used instead of *give evidence*, which is the more usual British English usage.

Text Until the late 1990s nobody would have thought that the English language needed a verb *to text*. Then the text message was invented, possibly also inventing an adjective in the process (or, at the very least, a new compound noun). One may send a *text message*, or one may *text* someone. The new verb, coined from the noun, has the advantages of clarity and concision: it is a new, logically derived, usage to describe a new phenomenon. There can be no feasible objection to it, or indeed to other such words and usages created by the advance of technology for which no previous word or usage existed.

Than *Than* is often to be found not far from *as* or *so*, and often being used wrongly. The most notorious is 'twice as many visitors came to Britain than last year'; 'as last year' is correct. *Than* has very limited legitimate usage: it is correct in a comparison (and in comparison-equivalents, such as *rather than* or *sooner than*), or in constructions with *other* ('other than Smith, they could not think of anyone to ask') and *otherwise* ('it was safer to do it that way than otherwise'). *Different than* is an abomination, and one does not prefer to do something *than* to do something else; one prefers to do something *rather than* to do something else (see RATHER). See also PREPOSITIONS.

Thankfully A phrase such as 'thankfully, no one was injured' shows a misuse of this adverb akin to that of HOPEFULLY. Being injured thankfully is a peculiar concept, unless one is a masochist. It would be correct to say 'it was fortunate that' or 'we should be grateful that'.

That (conjunction) Sometimes the conjunction *that* is lost in an ELLIPSIS, which is considered now to be acceptable if there is no ambiguity as a result: 'they wished [that] it had stopped raining' causes no confusion whereas 'he believed she didn't' may well. The use of conjunctions in certain contexts has become a question of idiom. The Fowlers in 1906 saw it was happening, and the contagion has spread far since then. 'Quite legitimate, but often unpleasant' was how they characterised it. The examples they gave were 'I presume you know' and 'I assume you know', in both of which they would have liked to see a *that* before *you*. However, as I have observed elsewhere, a cluttering of *that*s may become tiresome and verbose. Conjunctions only really need be used where there is scope for ambiguity and confusion if they are not. 'He drove the car he had hired earlier' makes perfect sense and requires no conjunction after *car*. 'I knew he saw she understood' needs a conjunction somewhere to break up the staccato verbs and avoid any confusion: best after *saw*.

That (relative pronoun) For the correct usage, and for the distinction between *that* and *which*, and *that* and *who*, see RELATIVE PRONOUNS.

The The definite article is *the*, as in '*the* dog', '*the* cat' or '*the* definite article'. Onions reminds us that it was originally considered 'the demonstrative adjective'. *The* is relaxingly consistent: 'the dog', 'the dogs'. *The* also has an emphatic usage, in which it is deployed to convey authenticity or uniqueness – 'his was one of the largest houses in the area – perhaps the largest' or 'you say you are John Smith – not the John Smith?' This usage is more acceptable in speech than in formal writing. There are idiomatic usages where nouns seem to survive without articles. Some of these are in everyday use – we go to bed, we eat lunch, we drink beer, we visit grandmother and we do all these things without the need for an article. The article would only be used if we needed to create a sense of the specific – 'the bed in the spare room is uncomfortable' or 'the beer in that pub is disgusting'. Certain other specialist idioms exist where the article is dispensed with: see CARNIVAL, CONFERENCE, LAST POST and MAGNA CARTA.

Their, there and **they're** The third person possessive pronoun *their*, because of an abundance of homonyms, is a minefield. In correct usage one writes 'they could not believe *their* luck'; yet one from time to time sees 'they could not believe *there* luck' or even 'they could not believe *they're* luck'. As with *your*, there may be abuses in the opposite direction: 'she could not see why *their* should be a problem,' and so on. Few people are sufficiently stupid to make such mistakes; many more, however, are sufficiently careless.

Theoretically Like ACTUALLY and ARGUABLY, this adverbial sentence-starter often has nothing to do with a theory, but has become a verbal tic or a filler.

These, those, they and **them** For a distinction between *them, these* and *those*, see DEMONSTRATIVE PRONOUNS. *They* is the third person plural nominative pronoun and *them* is its accusative.

They, used for he or she See PRONOUNS.

Third and **thirdly** See FIRST AND FIRSTLY.

Though should take a SUBJUNCTIVE, although these days only the most precise writer or speaker would do so: 'though it be expensive, that make of car is more reliable'. The word is almost always interchangeable with *although*, except at the end of a sentence where it operates as a synonym for *however* – 'She was late for her meeting, though.' See ALTHOUGH.

Threaten When using this verb, choose the subsequent preposition carefully. When the threat is from someone, use *by*: 'she was threatened by her boyfriend' or 'John feels threatened by him'. When the threat is of something, use *with*: 'he was threatened with the loss of his job if he spoke his mind', or 'she was threatened with the loss of her licence if she broke the speed limit again'. The distinction can be seen neatly in the sentence 'he was threatened with punishment by his teacher', though an elegant writer would avoid the passive voice.

Tie It is usually sufficient to tie something to something else. To tie it *up* to something else employs a superfluous adverb that adds nothing to the sense or the meaning of the phrase.

Till and **until** are interchangeable, and technically should take a SUBJUNCTIVE – the sentence of the law was once 'you shall be hanged by the neck until you be dead' – but, as with THOUGH, only the most precise writer or speaker would do so today.

Titillate and **titivate** To *titillate* is to excite the senses, and is used these days predominantly to indicate sexual excitement – 'he felt it would titillate her to read his letters'. To *titivate* is to spruce oneself up by improving one's dress or appearance – 'the women retired to titivate themselves before the dinner'.

Titles of literary works See ITALICS, USE OF.

Titles (of rank) See separate entries under BARONESSES, BARONETS, COUNTESSES, DUKES AND DUCHESSES, EARLS, KNIGHTS, MARQUESSES, PEERS AND THEIR FAMILIES, ROYAL FAMILY, VISCOUNTS for how to address or refer to such people. See also ACADEMICS, CLERGY, HONOURABLE, JUDICIARY and MILITARY RANKS.

Tmesis is the separation of parts of a word, or compound word, by another word or words. In British English it is often found in slang, in usages such as *abso-bloody-lutely*, and rarely in formal writing.

To be The verb *to be* is the fundamental verb. It is intransitive and has no object, in that it does nothing to anyone or anything else. It describes a subject of a sentence: 'I am tired'; 'you are angry'; 'he, she or it is lost'; and so on. Having no object, it must take a nominative pronoun, which in speech (and not just demotic speech) it hardly ever does. It is second nature for us to say 'that's her', 'it's him' or 'it's me', and in speaking or writing dialogue it would now sound pompous or unreal to say anything else. See I AND ME, HE AND HIM, SHE AND HER.

To die for is a cliché used now only by people who do not wish, or cannot hope, to be taken seriously. See VOGUE WORDS.

Tortuous and **torturous** Something *tortuous* is either literally twisted or metaphorically devious: or, when applied to prose, it is twisted to the point of incomprehensibility. Something *torturous* is either literally or metaphorically excruciating or painful.

Toward and **towards** See -WARD/-WARDS.

Tractable and **treatable** Although *treatable* pre-dates *tractable* by nearly 200 years, pedants prefer the latter to the former since both come from the Latin *tractabilis*; the former came into the language from upstart medieval French, though the word *traitable* survives in that tongue to this day. The best guide for using, or choosing not to use, any changing word today is whether or not a perfectly good alternative exists. Such a rule, sternly applied, would have done for *tractable* in the early sixteenth century. Idiomatically, *intractable* seems to remain the favoured negation.

Trade See PROFESSION AND TRADE.

Trade union The plural is usually *trades unions*, unless one trade has more than one union representing it (as is sometimes the case, though less often now than it used to be). Sometimes it is *trade unions*, which is also correct. The plural of *trade unionist* may either be *trade unionists*, if they are members of the same trade, or *trades unionists*, if the term refers to members of different ones.

Tragedy See TABLOID PRESS.

Train station is an Americanism for *railway station*.

Trainee See -EE ENDINGS.

Transitive verbs A *transitive verb* is one that causes a subject to do something to a direct object – 'the dog ate the bone' or 'the woman threw the ball'. For an INTRANSITIVE verb misused as a transitive, see GROW.

Transpire is a verb that went from the literal to the metaphorical more than 250 years ago but has now taken a further step towards incoherence of meaning. In its literal sense it means to emit through the skin in the form of a vapour. The metaphorical meaning followed closely from this, meaning to become apparent or, as the dictionary puts it, 'to pass from secrecy to notice'. Yet it now seems to mean *happen* or *occur*, which is just silly – 'it transpired on a Saturday afternoon'. If you must use this in a metaphorical sense (and it is perhaps overdue for a rest), be sure to use it accurately. See METAPHOR.

Treachery and **treason** *Treason* is a particular act of treachery by a subject against the state towards which he owes allegiance. It breaks a law and carries with it severe penalties. *Treachery* may be used to describe treason, but may also be used (however histrionically) to describe the betrayal of one person by another in a private relationship. *Treason* cannot be so used.

Treatable See TRACTABLE AND TREATABLE.

Tribunal and **tribune** are not the same thing. The former takes its name from the raised platform in the Roman basilica where the magistrates were seated, and means a court of justice, or a place of judgement or decision. A *tribune* is a person, originally a member of the Roman tribunal, and someone who would see justice done. The usage of the word has been extended to mean a popular leader, spokesman or demagogue.

Triumphal and **triumphant** *Triumphal* is an adjective meaning pertaining to or of the nature of a triumph: so one speaks of a 'triumphal arch', or a 'triumphal parade'. *Triumphant* has a less oblique meaning, signifying the sense of victoriousness and the rejoicing in it: 'he made a triumphant speech' or 'it was a triumphant moment'.

Troop is not the singular of troops. That is *soldier.* A *troop* of men still means a plurality of soldiers.

U

'U' and 'Non-U' In 1956 Nancy Mitford made waves with an essay, in a collection called *Noblesse Oblige*, that described the usages of her class (she was the daughter of a peer) and compared them with terms used to describe the same items or abstracts by people in lower social classes. It is hard to determine whether this was an exercise in rampant snobbery or in sociology. Whatever its intention, it has stuck. She did not invent the terms *U* and *Non-U* to describe these two forms of usage – that had been done two years earlier by Alan Ross, a linguistics professor. However, once Ross had had the idea, Mitford went off with it. There is no need for an exhaustive list, not least because some of the usages were archaic even then, and have disappeared almost entirely now: even duchesses today say *mirror* and *ice cream* rather than *looking-glass* and *ice*. Some have stuck and continue to be indicators of the class of the speaker or writer. If the writer and his audience do not mind being looked down upon by pedantic aristocrats and members of the *haute bourgeoisie*, then none of this really matters. If one does mind, then one had better take care. Partridge gives a superb example of the problem in *Usage and Abusage*, and the entry on the word *lady*. He says it 'should not be used as a synonym for *woman*, any more than *gentleman* should be used as a synonym for *man*'. He then strikes the killer blow: 'Only those men who are not gentlemen speak of their women friends as *lady friends*, and only those women who are not ladies speak of themselves as *charladies* and their men friends as *gentlemen friends*.' His point, perhaps less visible in what we are told is a classless society, was about the ghastliness, not to say ludicrousness, of mock gentility. One suspects that was part of Mitford's intention too.

Writing is about communication, and if the writer and his readers know exactly what a *cycle* is, then there is no need to affect the U term *bicycle*. However, all writers need to know their audience, especially if they are writing commercially, because they wish to retain that audience for the future: and writing in a language that is common to the audience, even if it means the writer himself inching up the social scale a notch or two, is at times useful.

For that reason I used to advise colleagues on a quality newspaper to bear in mind the sensitivities of the readers, because it was hoped they would continue to buy the newspaper and not feel alienated by its diction. The readers communicate with each other on *writing paper*, not *notepaper*. They eat their turkey or roast beef for *Christmas lunch*, not *Christmas dinner*, unless the meal is specified as taking place in the evening. If it does, the men might wear a *dinner jacket*, not a *dress suit*. (*Evening dress* is white tie, a white waistcoat and a tailcoat.) Their lunches or dinners include a *pudding*, not a *sweet*; a *dessert* may be taken after the pudding and the cheese may consist of nuts, fruit and fortified wines. They use *napkins* and not *serviettes*. They go to the *lavatory*, never the *toilet*, though they use *toilet paper* because the stuff is part of their toilet. In their *houses* (never *homes*) they have a *drawing room* or a *sitting room*, never a *lounge*. In those rooms there are *sofas*, not *settees*. If they are *sick* they are vomiting; if they are *ill* they are laid up. I must stress that there is nothing inherently wrong with the non-U alternatives to these usages. However, I repeat, we are an old country with a class system, and in our society what we say inevitably stands as a badge of who we are. Our reaction to what we read says it just as clearly to ourselves, which is why writers with a certain audience that they wish to propitiate need to speak the same language as their readers.

un- and **in-** See NEGATION.

Understatement One important aspect of tone in writing is the presence, or more often the absence, of *understatement*.

It used to be one of the facets of the British national character that the strongest adjective of disapproval was *shocking*, and that for someone to say he was *unhappy* was a sign of perilous unease. See also LITOTES, MEIOSIS and VERY.

Underway and **under way** There is no such word as *underway*. Therefore, a project or mission does not get *underway*, it gets *under way*.

Uninterested See DISINTERESTED AND UNINTERESTED.

Union Flag and **Union Jack** The *Union Flag* is correctly described as the *Union Jack* only when on the jackstaff of a British warship at anchor or alongside the jetty.

Unique *Unique* is one of the more frequently misused adjectives. The point about its meaning manifestly needs to be laboured. Something that is *unique* exists alone of its type. Each human being is unique. The *Mona Lisa* is unique. Table Mountain is unique, as is Sydney Harbour Bridge or the Empire State Building. Therefore, to argue that something is 'more unique', or that it is 'the most unique in the world' is literally meaningless. Scarcely less vacuous are phrases like 'almost unique' or 'nearly unique'. Something is either unique or it is not. See ABSOLUTES.

United Kingdom See BRITAIN AND BRITISH ISLES.

Unknown Warrior The tomb in Westminster Abbey commemorating all the fallen of the Great War who have no known resting place is the tomb of the *Unknown Warrior*, not of the *Unknown Soldier*.

Unless is a conjunction introducing a conditional clause. It should properly take a SUBJUNCTIVE – 'she said she would not enter the house unless the rat were dead' – but that would now be considered an example of pedantry. *Unless* does not mean *except*, so do not write 'I shall not go there unless on

Wednesdays' when you mean 'I shall not go there except on Wednesdays'.

Unlike requires a direct comparison but often does not have one. 'Unlike John, Mary applies herself to her work' is correct. 'Unlike John, her clothes were clean' is not. It implies John was unclean whereas the reference is presumably to his clothes. Similarly 'unlike in France, property is expensive' is wrong: it should be 'unlike in France, in Britain property is expensive'.

Unpractical is a venerable and entirely correct way of negating *practical*, and purists will prefer it to *impractical*, which is a corruption of *impracticable*. See IMPRACTICABLE, IMPRACTICAL AND UNPRACTICAL; also PRACTICABLE AND PRACTICAL.

Unresponsible See IRRESPONSIBLE.

Unscathed Logic in language is often damaged by negation. I have spotted in a newspaper the phrase 'least unscathed' when of course the writer meant 'least scathed' or 'most unscathed'. The last of those would have been an absurdity, since if one is unscathed one cannot be more or less unscathed than any other unscathed person. This rule applies to all adjectives negated in this way. See DOUBLE NEGATIVES.

Unsocial and **unsociable** have almost, but not quite, the same meaning. The first describes someone who is not fitted for society; the second, one who may be fitted for it but has no desire to participate in it. Someone who is *antisocial* acts to the detriment of society.

Until See TILL AND UNTIL.

Use and **utilise** The latter is a verbose and pompous extension of the former, though popular with Americans and bureaucrats.

Used to A form of the past tense that suggests a certain activity was once carried out habitually but is now discontinued – 'I used to catch the bus to school' or 'she used to have her hair cut once a month'. The construction 'I didn't used to do that' is an inelegant and clumsy way of saying 'I used not to do that', which implies that one now does it routinely.

V

Values See PREJUDICES AND VALUES.

Venal and **venial** Someone who is *venal* has a price. He is corrupt and can be influenced by money. A venal person will take a bribe and either have no principles to start with, or for a mercenary consideration will overlook them. This is not a *venial* fault; a venial offence is one that is trivial and easily pardonable.

Vendetta A *vendetta* is a blood-feud, usually between families, originating in Corsica and Sicily. In English it used to describe an extreme form of grudge, held to the point of destroying someone, or his career or reputation. The correct verb is to *conduct*, or *prosecute*, a vendetta.

Verbal adjectives See GERUNDIVES.

Verbal nouns See GERUNDS.

Verbless sentences Since to be properly formed a sentence requires a subject, an object and a verb (though there are rare idiomatic exceptions – see SENTENCES), *verbless sentences* are solecisms. Often, what comes out as a verbless sentence could have been perfectly grammatical had it remained as a clause following a colon or semicolon. An example comes from Jonathan Steinberg's superb biography of Bismarck: 'Another example of Burke's principle of unintended consequences.' Had the author not wanted this to stand in its own subordinate clause, he could simply have inserted the verb *to be* in the form of 'it was' at the start of the sentence, and all would have been well.

Verbosity is an arch-enemy of good writing. The best writing uses the fewest words. See also FILLERS, PROLIXITY and REDUNDANT WORDS.

Verbs, as many of us were told in primary school, are 'doing words'. They describe action, and the interaction of subject and object. In the sentence 'the man read the book' the interaction of man and book – subject and object – is described by the verb *read*. They are qualified by ADVERBS, as in 'I read slowly'. Given the tenses, voices, moods and other properties of verbs (are they transitive, intransitive, or both?) there is plenty of scope to mangle their usage. When one adds auxiliaries into the mix the prospect can become even more daunting. However, if one keeps a clear head and cool demeanour, all will be well. One should not pretend, though, that mastering the use of verbs can be achieved without also mastering a lot of detail, because it cannot: and this reflects the significance of verbs in our language. As 'doing' words, they communicate what is happening, has happened, will happen, might happen or should happen; and they have to do so precisely.

For the basic state of verbs, see INFINITIVES. For what not to do with infinitives, see SPLIT INFINITIVES. For the way in which verbs describe action in the past, present and future, see IMPERFECT, PERFECT TENSE, PRESENT TENSE, FUTURE TENSE and FUTURE PERFECT TENSE. For the way in which verbs describe possibility, see CONDITIONALS. For why certain verbs do or do not take a direct OBJECT, see TRANSITIVE VERBS and INTRANSITIVE VERBS. For the different voices of verbs, see the ACTIVE VOICE and the PASSIVE VOICE. For the different moods of verbs, see the IMPERATIVE MOOD, the INDICATIVE MOOD and the SUBJUNCTIVE MOOD. For verbs that behave in odd ways, see STRONG VERBS and IRREGULAR VERBS. For adjectival and other uses, see

PARTICIPLES. For using verbs correctly in reported speech, see SEQUENCE OF TENSES. For verbs that complement other verbs to create past tenses and the conditional, see AUXILIARY VERBS.

Very In modern times, thanks partly to the sensationalism of some of the mass media and to the histrionics of both indigenous and imported television dramas, no point is considered adequately made unless it has been beaten home with adjectives, adverbs and prolixity. The overuse of *very* is another one of these sins, though one that applies more widely than just in expressions of obloquy, and helps writers and speakers surrender a sense of proportion in handling all manner of subjects. Such a tone is not the mark of a good communicator, who will convey disdain or disapproval with understatement and subtlety rather than by shouting and screaming.

Viable The dictionary defines *viable* as 'capable of living', and is therefore a term that should correctly be applied to beings, organisms and plants capable of life. However, it also cites a number of uses of the word in which it is used figuratively 'of immaterial things and concepts' (there are two from the nineteenth century too, but these seem to be consciously rather than unconsciously metaphorical, and it is clear that the writers understood very well the literal meaning of the word). So we hear today that, following an injection of cash, a business will be *viable*; or that a committee has looked at a plan, and it is *viable*. While the metaphorical meaning reflects the literal – the business will continue to 'live', the plan will have 'life' – one wonders whether those who apply the term in this way understand what its literal meaning is. Widespread metaphorical usages such as this also diminish the force of the literal usage, if that survives (as, no doubt, *viable* will). It is true that, without the development of metaphorical usages, our language would be far less rich than it is now. However, there are plenty of other, more precise and more accurate words that could be used in the contexts above. There is nothing wrong with the adjectives *feasible*, *workable*, *reasonable* or even *possible*, all of which are easily understood by a reader, and none of which makes the sense any less precise. One of the features of precise writers and speakers is that they seek to preserve the force that words have, something that metaphorical use may dilute.

Viscounts and **viscountesses, writing to or addressing** A viscountcy (sometimes called a viscounty in archaic usage) is the second rank in the peerage, above a barony but below an earldom. In written address the holder of this rank is addressed or referred to in the first instance as 'Viscount Dorchester' and subsequently as 'Lord Dorchester'; his wife as 'Viscountess Dorchester' and subsequently as 'Lady Dorchester'. In the peerages of the United Kingdom Scottish viscountcies were created with 'of' somewhere, unlike those in England or Ireland. Today only two viscountcies use this form – the Viscount of Arbuthnott and the Viscount of Oxfuird; so if you know Lord Dorchester is a Viscount, do not write to him or about him as 'the Viscount of Dorchester', because he wouldn't be. In conversation, unless you are on familiar terms, address him or his wife as 'Lord Dorchester' or 'Lady Dorchester'. His children, irrespective of gender, have 'the Hon.' before their Christian names and family surnames, but this is used only on envelopes, visiting cards and in the Court Circular.

Vision If a politician has *vision* it merely means that he has managed to devise an idea of what to do that is different from that of his opponents.

Vocative See CASES.

Vogue words If one reads any of the twentieth-century works on good usage one always finds a section on *vogue words*: references to words that, at the time of writing, were much in fashion and being overused; or words whose legitimate meaning or usage was being abused at the time. The overused words of this age tend to have short lives, though some become distressingly persistent: an example is the use of the verb *to address*, which used to be restricted to the action of writing a destination on an envelope or talking to a public meeting, and is now used to describe someone giving his attention to almost anything. Such words tend to be imported to the minds of their users by the mass media. Since the mass media pursue novelty, the next wave of vogue words usually comes along before the old one has reached the shore. Nor is it only the media's exploitation of popular culture that brings these words into fashion. All-day news channels (or, to use the vogue term, 'rolling news') latch on to popular terms and exhaust them.

In Britain in the last decade or so we have heard time and again of 'the target culture', 'best practice', 'prioritisation', 'vibrant communities', 'programmes' that are 'rolled out' for the benefits of 'stakeholders', among other terms used by the propaganda arm of government. These terms are designed to convey an impression of action, purpose and (to use two other popular nouns) 'inclusiveness' and 'diversity'; but they soon wear out and intelligent people come to regard them with boredom or contempt.

Not all such terms pass their sell-by date quickly. Richard Nixon was brought down in the Watergate scandal in 1974. Ever since, any scandal of almost any description seems to be denominated by having the suffix *-gate* applied to it. In 2010 a dispute over the use of scientific data in the global warming debate was called 'climategate', and the falsification of an injury in professional rugby became 'bloodgate'. The ultimate absurdity, at the time of this book's composition, was when the Government Chief Whip was allegedly rude to a policeman manning the gates of Downing Street and the ensuing furore became known as 'Gategate'. It subsequently became 'Plebgate', and shortly afterwards the habit of certain food suppliers of passing off horse as beef led to 'horsegate'. This usage ceased to be funny, let alone interesting, not long after it was first coined. Nor is this the only suffix to be so abused. The vogue for contests of endurance has led to an epidemic of nouns ending in **-ATHON,** while the **-AHOLIC** ending has spawned its own set of ridiculous neologisms, such as 'shopaholic'. The rule is simple: if you spot a new coinage of any other sort, regard the joke as already over, and move on.

It is not only words, but also phrases, that offer themselves up for exhaustion. A popular film called *To Die For*, released in 1995, caused the phrase to become the (almost immediately tiresome) term of superlative approbation among a certain sort of people for some years. Many of us have been told that a friend has eaten a lobster cocktail 'to die for', or seen a set of watercolours of similarly lethal effect, and had to clench parts of our anatomy. It is a matter of taste whether the term 'achingly' as in 'achingly modern' or 'achingly chic' is even more sickening.

These popular phrases vie with one another for the prize in idiocy. Only marginally less offensive is a phrase weather forecasters use to impart some sense of homeliness and affection to their work when they have to describe some unpleasant aspect of the climate: that we are going to have 'a wet old day', 'a strong old wind', 'a cold old night' or a 'foggy old morning'. The absurdity of this term requires no amplification beyond its very expression.

It is easy for the intelligent, thoughtful writer to avoid such lapses. Yet one needs when writing to weigh every word, so that the less obvious, but still irritating, words and clichés are omitted too. See also POLITICAL LANGUAGE.

W

Wait See AWAIT, WAIT AND WAIT FOR.

Waiver and **waver** A *waiver* is an exemption – 'he signed the waiver form to obviate the need for a visa'. To *waver* is to engage in irresolution or indecision – 'she wavered over whether or not to marry him'.

Wake up See AWAKE, AWAKEN AND WAKE UP.

-ward/-wards One may make a rule about the adverbial (and indeed adjectival) use of words ending in *-ward* or *-wards*. It seems that in most idiomatic usages the adverbial type ends in *-wards*: 'they went forwards', 'she fell backwards', 'the boy came towards me', 'carry on downwards', 'the road goes upwards', 'proceed inwards' and so on. By contrast, the adjectival usages drop the last *s*. Stevenson wrote 'I have trod the upward and the downward slope', a soldier takes a 'forward position', there are 'backward children' (or there were before political correctness), 'outward-bound courses' and 'inward-looking people'.

Warn *Warn* has not developed into an intransitive verb, despite an enormous effort by semi-literates over the centuries to make it do so. One can *warn* somebody, and one can *warn against* something; but one cannot simply *warn*. If for some reason one cannot use an object, use the phrase *give warning*: 'He *gave warning* that the weather would be terrible.'

We and **us** *We* is the nominative form of the first person plural personal pronoun. The accusative is *us*. See also I AND ME, HE AND HIM, SHE AND HER.

Wedding See MARRIAGE AND WEDDING.

Weekend In Britain, people do things *at the weekend*. Only in America do they do them *on the weekend*.

Weights and measures The use of the terminology of weights and measures is often wrong in vulgar speech, and should not be translated into the written word. A man may be described as being 'six foot tall' and weighing 'twelve stone'. In both cases in formal writing the plurals should be used. Liquid measurements seem to be immune to this sort of solecism: no one would ask for 'three pint of beer'. Adjectival uses do not need to be plural: a 'ten-gallon hat', a 'five-pint jug' and a 'three-foot rule' are all correct.

Well We seem to be reaching the end of the period in our history in which the adjective *well* has been widely used as an attempted witticism by educated people to mean *very*: the rash of films about cockney gangsters has left this as another legacy. Individual gangsters were 'well hard', and if they carried a firearm (or 'shooter') they were considered 'well tasty'. The vogue for sounding like an East End thug transmuted into sounding like a black musician, and the highest term of approbation became 'well wicked'.

Wet and **whet** A newspaper in October 2013 talked about someone 'wetting an axe'. This would, if taken literally, indicate that the axe was being dipped in water. What was meant was 'whetting an axe', meaning it was being sharpened.

What A popular vulgarism is found in a sentence such as: 'she had twice as many as what I did' or, still worse, 'she had twice as many than what I did'. The *what* in each case is superfluous; the *than* in the second example is simply wrong.

Whatever Those who write correctly would argue that a clause introduced by *whatever* must take a subjunctive, as in 'whatever be your excuse, you had no need to do it'. They would be right, but this usage now seems archaic. The use of *whatever* as an expression of indifference is an example of contemporary slang.

Whether A now-archaic SUBJUNCTIVE concerns clauses with *whether* that raise a doubt about outcome, such as 'whether or not he be qualified, he intends to drive the car' or 'we tried to discover whether he were the culprit'. For the use of *whether* to introduce the idea of something that may not happen, see IF AND WHETHER and DOUBT THAT AND DOUBT WHETHER.

Which For the distinction between *which* and *that*, and between *which* and *who*, see RELATIVE PRONOUNS.

While and **whilst** *While* is the contemporary, *whilst* the archaic, but relatively harmless, spelling.

Whisky is the Scottish drink. The Irish, and the Americans, make *whiskey*.

Who For a discussion of this word, and its distinction from *that* and *which*, see RELATIVE PRONOUNS.

Whoever, like WHATEVER, traditionally took a subjunctive – 'whoever be right, I am wrong' – but, as with *whatever*, this is now considered archaic.

Whom *Whom*, the accusative of the pronoun *who*, is now in such disuse that many who hear or read it regard it as an affectation. This is ridiculous. Since prepositions require an accusative, it is essential in formal writing, and even in intelligent speech, to write or say *to whom*, *from whom*, *by whom* and so on. *Whom*, and not *who*, should be the object of verbs: 'the man whom I saw', 'the girl whom I met' and so on.

However, as bad as not using *whom* at all is the art of using it wrongly. In the winter of 2009–10 this appeared in a newspaper: 'The task of cutting is likely to fall to George Osborne, whom we hope will embrace the bold ideas . . .' Take out the 'we hope' and it clear that the *whom* has no place there. Mr Osborne, or rather his pronoun, is the subject of the clause and not its object. It is more often that one encounters the problem in reverse, as in 'Mr Osborne, who we used to see in the House of Commons', which cries out for a *whom*. It is sometimes possible, and always if possible desirable, to obviate such difficulties by splitting sentences into shorter ones. In colloquial speech *whom* has almost entirely disappeared; it should not do so in formal writing. As noted in the section on VERBS, the pronoun with the verb *to be* always takes the nominative case in formal writing; 'it's me' is colloquial and acceptable in informal speech.

Whose For the use of this possessive, which can be deployed as legitimately with inanimate objects and abstracts as with people, see RELATIVE PRONOUNS. Do not confuse with the contraction *who's*, as in 'we know who's been here', as distinct from 'whose dog is this?'.

Will See SHALL AND WILL.

With is a preposition used to describe the comparison or accompaniment of one thing *with* or *by* another – 'if you compare like with like' or 'I went to the shops with my mother'. It has however developed as a vague, all-purpose conjunction with a variety of meanings, all of them imprecise, and whose usage dilutes the precision of the language. Instead of 'Essex won the championship, with Yorkshire coming second', say 'and Yorkshire came second'. 'With the weather being so cold, pipes froze' is better expressed as 'the pipes froze because the weather was so cold'; 'with the war over, rebuilding could begin' should be 'when the war was over' or, if the present tense is preferred, 'now the war is over'.

Word order In Latin prose, word order can be helpful because of its use in providing emphasis in a language without punctuation as we understand it. However, it has less significance because one can always tell by looking at the nouns which is the subject, and which the object. Take, for example,

Sir Christopher Wren's celebrated epitaph in St Paul's Cathedral, *Lector, si monumentum requiris, circumspice*. It translates as 'Reader, if you seek his monument, look about you'. Put those words into any other order and they mean the same thing. *Lector* will always be vocative and will be the person to whom the imperative *circumspice* is addressed; *monumentum* will always be accusative and must be the object of the second person singular verb *requiris*; *si* will always, as a conditional conjunction, govern that main verb. It doesn't work in English: 'Monument, if you look about his reader, seek you' is gibberish.

The loss of inflections in English is one reason why word order has such significance. Once nouns lost an inflection in the accusative it was important that they were placed after the verb that had them as its direct object: as in 'the cat sat on the mat'. There is no problem of comprehension with 'sat on the mat the cat', though in most types of prose today it would be considered rather arch and breaking out of the idiom, as well as bad grammar. 'On the mat sat the cat' has the same problem. 'On the mat the cat sat' and 'the cat on the mat sat' convey the correct meaning but completely defy idiom. 'The mat the cat sat on' is a different matter altogether, being comprehensible only in answer to a question about a number of mats. All other combinations are nonsense or change the meaning completely.

In English, poetry is a rule unto itself, though the best poetry adjusts conventional word order only when there is no danger of ambiguity from the absence of inflection. At the opening of Book II of *Paradise Lost*, Milton, though he puts the main verb near the very end of a long sentence, creates no doubt about the meaning of his verse:

> High on a throne of royal state, which far
> Outshone the wealth of Ormus and of Ind,
> Or where the gorgeous East with richest hand
> Showers on her kings barbaric pearl and gold,
> Satan exalted sat, by merit raised
> To that bad eminence.

Milton was an exemplary Latinist, and his word order could have been borrowed from Virgil. We may linger for a moment in doubt over whether the kings were barbaric, or whether the pearl and gold were, though we are helped by the metre to a correct understanding of the sense; but the delay in meeting the main subject and the main verb, even after clauses in which the word order is itself inverted, does not harm our comprehension of the passage. Contemporary prose demands a more logical order, not least because it contains no metrical devices to steer us towards an understanding of the sense of a passage. Subject, verb, object is a good rule for the foundation of the clearest writing. In some prose, notably fiction or descriptive writing, there is plenty of scope to alter that order. However, inversions may be used by writers even in the most formal prose, or in reporting; but these days a departure from the normal word order draws attention to form at the expense of content. In reporting dialogue, 'said Mr Smith' is no more exceptional than 'Mr Smith said'. However, such usage has the status of being formulaic now. Sometimes a distinctive effect is desired; and an unorthodox word order, by drawing attention to itself, may create that effect. The Authorised Version of the Bible has countless examples: 'In that night was Belshazzar the King of the Chaldeans slain'; 'and when they came that were hired about the eleventh hour, they received every man a penny'; and 'then drew near unto him all the publicans and sinners for to hear him'. The Bible was written 400 years ago in this translation and its prose is consciously poetic; which makes a point about the effect of departing from the normal word order.

Two other points should be stressed here: that **SPLIT INFINITIVES** are to be avoided, but the fetish of not putting a **PREPOSITION** at the end of a sentence need not be respected unless the idiom demands it. Sentences that begin with *and* or *but* are not wrong but unhappy, for they suggest incompleteness, and refer to sentences preceding that have, presumably, been inadequately completed. *Yet*, *however* and *furthermore* are less troublesome in this respect. See the section on **ADVERBS, POSITIONING OF** for a discussion of how to convey the correct meaning when using that part of speech. Meaning can also be altered by words such as *even* or *at least*. The difference between 'even she could not believe it' and 'she could not even believe it' should be obvious; as should 'he hoped he would at least be invited in' and 'he at least hoped he would be invited in'.

The importance of using the right word order can be seen in this example, from a contemporary newspaper article: 'A shop assistant was stabbed to death eleven times at a store in Thurmaston, Leics.' In this case, even altering the order of that sentence will not redeem it. It has to be rewritten as 'a shop assistant at a store in Thurmaston, Leics, has died as a result of being stabbed eleven times'. It was also announced that 'wisps of hair from Charles Darwin's beard are to go on public display years after he was born in a Natural History Museum exhibition'. In that case, simply altering the order of words or punctuating better would have resolved a doubt about the great evolutionist's place of birth. It was also reported that a farmer had been out 'shooting dead rabbits'. This seems a pointless exercise, until one realises that he had in fact been shooting rabbits dead.

Variations of word order are used to emphasise certain ideas in response to specific questions or assertions. The difference between 'they drive on the right in France' and 'in France they drive on the right' is the difference between two possible preceding statements. The one preceding the first is 'everyone drives on the left', and the main point that someone wishing to contradict this assertion must make is that some people drive on the right; and France is an example of where this is so. The one preceding the second is somebody saying that in France specifically they drive on the left; the main point about the response is that in France they do nothing of the sort. Word order will depend, as in these examples, on what has to be emphasised. 'Yet again he has made this mistake' suggests the most important thing about the statement is that the mistake has been made for the umpteenth time; 'he has made the mistake yet again' is more about recognising culpability.

I have already noted the problem with beginning a sentence using *and* or *but*; but beginning sentences with other conjunctions is a matter of individual taste. In journalism I have never worried about it – *however* is fine, as are *but* and *and*. However, I am not sure I would introduce a sentence with these conjunctions in writing more formal than journalism, though *however* (as the alert reader will have noticed) provides me with no difficulties at all. Writers of fiction, for rhetorical effect, have licence in these matters, notably when reaching a climax: whether in Hardy's antepenultimate sentence of *Tess of the d'Urbervilles* – 'And the d'Urberville knights and dames slept on in their tombs unknowing' – or in John Cowper Powys's sublimely bathetic conclusion to *Wolf Solent* – 'And then he thought. "Well, I shall have a cup of tea."' See also **AMBIGUITY**, for the importance of placing words in order to convey a precise meaning; and **QUITE** and **RATHER**.

Word order also has an effect on style. It is essential to put the words of any sentence into a logical order, not just to avoid ambiguity but also to escape any charge of pretentiousness in diction: Shakespeare might have been able to get away with 'When to the sessions of sweet silent thought/ I summon up remembrance of things past' but those writing prose should not attempt such a word order unless they wish to become objects of curiosity. There is an archaic, or pretentious, ring these days to sentences with inverted word order. Conventionally, a sentence proceeds as follows: subject, verb, object. So we say 'the boy ate the pie' and not 'eating the pie was the boy' or 'the boy the pie ate'.

As can be seen from the last example, in our uninflected language there is scope for ambiguity when the word order is inverted. It could be that the pie ate the boy, but that is unlikely. In an inflected language such as Latin or Greek it would be obvious who was doing the eating, and what was eaten, because of different endings for nouns that are nominative and those that are accusative. English does not have that luxury except when certain pronouns are used. Some inversions of word order are more acceptable than others, and these are where the inversion helps provide an emphasis deemed necessary by the writer: such as 'in my class at school were Smith, Jones and Brown' rather than 'Smith, Jones and Brown were in my class at school'. In that example, the writer has chosen to emphasise the common educational experience that he had with the three other men, rather than making the three other men the most important feature of his statement.

The Fowlers also illustrate the different principles of inversion in paratactic and syntactic clauses. A paratactic clause is one that follows another without any connecting word that indicates the relation of the two clauses, or whether the second is coordinate with or subordinate to its predecessor. An example of **PARATAXIS** is found in 'his crimes were terrible: chief among them was the murder of Smith', compared with 'his crimes were terrible, chief among which was the murder of Smith', the second part of the latter being a relative clause. The inverted word order of the paratactic clause is unnecessary: it could as easily read 'the murder of Smith was chief among them'. However, where there clearly is a subordinate clause, the relative pronoun needs to precede the subject for the sentence to make sense.

It is also common to invert word order in sentences featuring negation. For the sake of emphasis one might write 'never had I been so insulted' rather than 'I had never been so insulted'. In some statements inversion is essential if they are to make sense: 'by no measure can he be said to be the best batsman in their team' must be right, since 'he can be said to be the best batsman in their team by no measure' sounds bizarre. The most frequent form of inversion is seen when asking questions: 'Would you help me?' is used as opposed to 'you would help me'.

The placement of adverbs in phrases with auxiliary verbs used to cause grammarians great debate and worry. Some held that one should no more split an auxiliary from its verb than one would split an infinitive. So one would always write 'never had I seen such a sight' rather than 'I had never seen such a sight' or 'I never had seen such a sight'. At this stage in the development of our language, the only remotely sane advice must be to do what appears most idiomatic, and what best serves the purpose of the writer. It may be that in certain contexts to write 'he had especially wanted a blue car' would be inadequately emphatic; and that the sense the writer wishes to convey would be better represented by 'especially, he had wanted a blue car'. This would make sense had this sentence been preceded by one or several that listed this man's desires. The only rule in this matter is comprehensibility.

The importance of careful word order when using negatives is dealt with in the section on NEGATION AND NEGATIVES. See also COMMAS.

Words, meaning of The *Oxford English Dictionary* is a magnificent, if occasionally flawed, work. The online second edition is a valuable resource, and available to almost everyone with a library ticket and an internet connection. If one visits the website of one's local public library, there is usually a reference section. It will state whether the *OED* is available, and, by typing in the number on one's library ticket, one can access the work.

I dare to say the work is flawed because the *OED* and I have one serious difference of opinion. It can be best summarised as follows: I take the view that once the meaning of a word was settled with the publication of the dictionary, it had no great need to change unless technological advances or other developments caused it to be varied. If a group of people insisted on using the word in an incorrect way, and were at odds with the dictionary's definition, then they and their usage were wrong. The *OED* has never dealt in arbitrary definitions. An etymology is always supplied, giving legitimacy to the defined meaning of any given word. However, on some words the *OED* has surrendered to usage: if people insist on using a word incorrectly, and that incorrect usage becomes popular, then the *OED* will record the fact and, to all intents and purposes, sanction it. I take a more conservative view. The incorrect use of a word happens because people confuse its meaning with that of another (such as people saying *flaunt* when they mean *flout*). Since this purports to be a book on correct English, I cannot see the logic or the value in proposing to the reader that he should use the language wrongly. Words do change their meaning, and have done over the centuries (see NAUGHTY). But once the language is codified by a standard dictionary, the justification for their doing so is less obvious, and is usually attributable to influence rather than any great social or technological changes.

Worthwhile is a single word. *Worth while* is a solecism. One writes 'her charity work was very worthwhile'. The only context in which one may split the word is to say 'was worth her while', or something similar.

Would See CONDITIONALS and SHALL AND WILL.

Would have must never be substituted by the abominable *would of*. 'I would of told him' is a shocking vulgarism.

Wracked See RACKED AND WRACKED.

Wrought The passive voice of the verb *to work* is, correctly, *wrought* when the object that has been worked is some sort of material or substance. Wrought iron is iron that has been worked – wrought – by a farrier.

Y

Year-old The use of this expression requires care with HYPHENS. Used as a noun – 'the seventeen year-old was rather beautiful' – it must be hyphenated, and is one of the relatively few compound nouns to be so. Used as an adjective it requires two hyphens, thus: 'A seventeen-year-old youth was charged with the offence.'

Years If describing an interval of time one could say either 'from 1914 to 1918' or 'between 1914 and 1918', not 'from 1914–18' or 'between 1914–18'.

Yet is a coordinating CONJUNCTION.

Your is the second person singular possessive pronoun. Do not confuse with the contraction *you're*. One writes 'I shall give you your pocket money' and 'you're lucky I didn't leave'. There is no such word as *your's* to indicate possession. One writes: 'This is my chair, and that one is yours.'

Yourself See REFLEXIVE PRONOUNS.

Youth As a noun referring to an individual, it can only refer to a male – 'he was a pimply youth' or 'a number of youths were arrested', the second statement indicating that all those rounded up were young males. 'The youth of today', however, can be taken to include males and females. Either sex can have a misspent youth.

Z

Zeugma A construction in which, typically, one verb has two objects without its being repeated; it sometimes is deployed with humorous effect, the verb being used in one instance abstractly and in the other concretely. 'He lost his nerve, and then his money' or 'she packed a change of clothes and a hell of a punch' exemplify this. In strict rhetorical terms, however, the use of the verb to govern in one sense a concrete and in another an abstract object is called SYLLEPSIS.

31901057016604